WITH UNITED STRENGTH

H.H. Shaikh Zayid Bin Sultan Al Nahyan
The Leader and the Nation

Dedication

TO MY FATHER HIS HIGHNESS

SHAIKH ZAYID BIN SULTAN AL NAHYAN

PRESIDENT OF THE UNITED ARAB EMIRATES

IN RECOGNITION

OF HIS UNPARALLELED ACHIEVEMENTS

IN THE INTERESTS OF HIS PEOPLE

AND HIS NATION.

Muhammad Bin Zayid Al Nahyan

WITH UNITED STRENGTH

H.H. Shaikh Zayid Bin Sultan Al Nahyan
The Leader and the Nation

**THE EMIRATES CENTER FOR STRATEGIC
STUDIES AND RESEARCH**

Published in 2004 by
The Emirates Center for Strategic Studies and Research
PO Box 4567, Abu Dhabi, United Arab Emirates
E-mail: pubdis@ecssr.ac.ae
pubdis@ecssr.com
Website: http://www.ecssr.ac.ae
http://www.ecssr.com

A catalogue record for this book is available from the British Library

ISBN 9948-00-400-0 standard hardback edition
ISBN 9948-00-401-9 super deluxe edition

CONTENTS

In the interests of clarity and consistency, the transliteration applied in this book has been kept to a minimum:

- Common names such as Mecca, Koran or Nasser have been reproduced in their familiar English spelling.

- In terms of vocalization for all other location, tribal or personal names, the *a*, *i* and *u* have been used and not the *e* or *o*, as there exists no parallel vowel for the latter in the Arabic language. Thus, it is 'Shaikh' and not 'Sheikh,' and 'Zayid' instead of the more common 'Zayed.'

- Where applicable, the Arabic *ayn* is represented by ['] while the *hamza* is indicated by the symbol [’].

- The word *Al* in conjunction with tribal names has been capitalized while *al* as the definite article has been left in small letters. No hyphenation is applied in either case.

ABBREVIATIONS AND ACRONYMS

ADDF	Abu Dhabi Defence Force
AmConsul	American Consul
ARAMCO	Arabian-American Oil Company
DSS	Distinguished Student Scholarships
ERWDA	Environmental Research and Wildlife Development Agency
FAO	(United Nations) Food and Agriculture Organization
FO	Foreign Office, United Kingdom
GCC	Gulf Cooperation Council
GDP	Gross Domestic Product
MERC	Marine Environmental Research Center
NARA	National Archives and Records Administration, United States
OIC	Organization of the Islamic Conference
OPEC	Organization of Petroleum Exporting Countries
PDTC	Petroleum Development Trucial Coast
TSDO	Trucial States Development Office
UAA	United Arab Amirates
UAE	United Arab Emirates
UDF	Union Defence Force
UK	United Kingdom
UN	United Nations
US	United States

FOREWORD

When the Emirates Center for Strategic Studies and Research (ECSSR) first sought my approval for the idea of publishing a biography of His Highness Shaikh Zayid Bin Sultan Al Nahyan (May Allah Protect Him), the President of the United Arab Emirates (UAE) and the Supreme Commander of the UAE Armed Forces, I immediately accepted the proposal with great enthusiasm. Certainly, there existed a number of good reasons for such a decision. In the first instance, the Center's intention was to produce a serious academic study, an approach that would distinguish this book from other more popular styles of biography. Standards of objective scholarship would be applied and scientific methodology employed in order to prepare an authoritative account of the life and achievements of the nation's leader, whose own life history has blended so harmoniously with that of his country. Indeed, it is to him that the credit should be given for transforming the essential character of our country into a new reality, which is cherished by all its citizens.

I also recognized that the proposed book offered a good opportunity to shed light on an important era in contemporary history, which requires deeper insight and warrants serious analysis. Although the history of the UAE is still very new, it is important to place events in their proper context and provide a framework in which the relevance of specific developments can be understood. The work presented here should be seen as a contribution to such an endeavor. Its focus upon the issue of unity, which has undoubtedly been a constant concern of His Highness Shaikh Zayid, is especially significant. This book illustrates clearly the subtlety and clarity of his political thinking, revealed not only in his own words, but also in those of his contemporaries whose private judgments have been locked in archives for many years.

In this context, I view it as a great honor to write the foreword of this book, which seeks to offer an analysis of the different factors that have had a bearing on the character and personality of His Highness Shaikh Zayid, endowing him with unique skills and capability to assume the roles of leader, Ruler, President and Father of the Nation. The many obstacles he encountered served only to strengthen his determination to fulfill the mission that was his from his early days—to protect and promote his homeland and his people. This, he chose to accomplish through selfless cooperation with his fellow Rulers, seeking to share strength and resources to the ultimate benefit of all.

This book seeks to illuminate the rich historical background to the life of His Highness Shaikh Zayid Bin Sultan Al Nahyan and examine the sources of his leadership, which guided the UAE towards attaining goals that seemed at the time unreachable. From his early years onwards, His Highness Shaikh Zayid set out with a firm commitment to undertake the formidable task of creating a better life and future for the citizens of his country. His ultimate aim was to build the modern state of the United Arab Emirates. The achievement of this goal required the formulation of a clear national strategy, setting the necessary objectives and incorporating them into properly prioritized plans—a process that facilitated the smooth realization of his vision. He ensured that the strategy for change was in harmony with the provision of the necessary resources. Above all, he was absolutely determined that the immense wealth and economic capacity of the nation should be used to develop the country and to improve the quality of life for its entire populace. The combination of the determined leadership of His Highness Shaikh Zayid and the diligent effort of the country's citizens helped to accomplish this transformation of our society. We are all blessed with the honor of being a part of the United Arab Emirates.

I am pleased to express my deep gratitude to the pioneering figures who stood by His Highness Shaikh Zayid with great determination and strong will to bring about the establishment of the UAE Federation, most importantly the late His Highness Shaikh Rashid Bin Sa'id Al Maktum, UAE Vice President and Ruler of Dubai, and Their Highnesses the Rulers of the emirates and Members of the Supreme Council who witnessed the birth of the Federation. This also includes all UAE citizens, living and deceased, who worked hard to overcome the difficulties and obstacles in the path of the Federation and who joined hands with experts, Arabs and others, to build our homeland.

My special thanks are due to His Highness Shaikh Diyab Bin Zayid Al Nahyan, the Director General of the Diwan of His Highness the President of the United Arab Emirates, who supported the idea from the outset and provided valuable assistance in making it a reality. I should also like to express my appreciation for the effective and tangible cooperation extended by the relevant ministries, government departments and institutions in the United Arab Emirates, as well as to many individuals from the UAE, who contributed valuable information from their own personal experiences to this project.

The task of completing the work and publishing this unique manuscript was undertaken by the Emirates Center for Strategic Studies and Research. The concerted effort and spirit of the project team was instrumental in successfully bringing this work to fruition. It is only through their collective perseverance and commitment that the many different aspects of this book could be integrated into a coherent form. My overall thanks go to the Director General of the ECSSR, Dr. Jamal S. Al Suwaidi, for his energy and dedication in leading and supervising the whole project. His initiative has produced a uniquely valuable study. I remain indebted to the principal author of the book, Andrew Wheatcroft of the University of Stirling in Scotland, and greatly appreciate his efforts. His extensive archival studies have produced important results. Other team members whom I would like to thank include Aida Abdullah Al Azdi, Dr. Mamdouh Anis Fathy and Dr. Christian Koch, who through their meticulous efforts were able to produce the final Arabic and English manuscripts suitable for publication, as well as the staff and team members of the Department of Publications, Translation and Distribution of the ECSSR, who were instrumental in handling the day-to-day tasks of completing the

Arabic and English versions of the book on schedule and in the best possible way.

My profound thanks are also due to many other personalities who were contemporaries with His Highness Shaikh Zayid Bin Sultan Al Nahyan and who assisted with their time and offered personal insight on his life and achievements. This includes former senior British officials who served in the Gulf region and witnessed that eventful period. I should also like to acknowledge the cooperation of many officials and researchers from different countries who contributed valuable comments and suggestions to this project.

I sincerely hope that this pioneering book will prove to be a significant addition to the existing literature on His Highness Shaikh Zayid Bin Sultan Al Nahyan, in which the reader is presented with a vivid picture of the creative aspects of His Highness Shaikh Zayid as reflected in his innumerable achievements over the years. I also expect that this work will pave the way for more detailed and original scholarly research on His Highness Shaikh Zayid, who has set a powerful example for all to follow.

Muhammad Bin Zayid Al Nahyan

INTRODUCTION

Leaders with exceptional qualities have defined human history. They have possessed a strong will, profound insight and a deep-rooted belief in the inherent value of their mission. Imbued with these characteristics, they have guided mankind through the tumultuous events of history. More importantly, they have provided their people with the link in the ever-changing world between the secure and familiar past and the uncertain yet inescapable future. From time immemorial, and certainly in the annals of recorded history, such personalities have been few and far between. One might argue that they are even more of a rarity in the modern world.

By any objective standard, His Highness Shaikh Zayid Bin Sultan Al Nahyan, the President of the United Arab Emirates, has to be considered one of those truly unique personalities. He is a widely respected leader and a pioneer of modernization, who has guided his desert land and people from the desperately harsh conditions of the not-so-distant past into an era of unprecedented progress and prosperity. Where, in the past, opposing tribal interests too often resulted in open warfare and endless hostilities, today there stands one cohesive nation-state existing in peace and harmony and providing a model for others to emulate. The founding of the United Arab Emirates in 1971 can thus be seen as the crowning achievement of Shaikh Zayid's life and career.

More remarkable still is that the rapid transition of the past 40 years, which has encompassed a wide spectrum of social change, has been achieved in almost complete harmony and without serious dislocation. In most other instances where societies have absorbed such tumultuous change in a short period of time, civil strife has often been the result. History provides numerous examples. However, in Abu Dhabi and later within the United Arab Emirates, this danger was averted, mostly due to the efforts and vision of Shaikh Zayid. He possesses an exceptional ability to reconcile the seemingly irreconcilable—the conflicting demands of tribe and state, emirate and federation, heritage and modernity. It is equally significant that he has deliberately chosen a painstaking route to building national unity through economic development and a growing social interdependence, a quest that culminated in the establishment of the UAE Federation in 1971.

For present and future generations to gain a proper understanding of Shaikh Zayid's achievement, his work needs to be viewed from both a global and a regional perspective, setting it in the context of other attempts at nation-building, both successful and unsuccessful. What is remarkable about the modern history of the United Arab Emirates is that it represents the only thriving federation throughout the Middle East, that the process was achieved without violence, and also that the Federation has attained a level of popular legitimacy unmatched by most other governments. The personal charisma of Shaikh Zayid, his insistence on maintaining traditional values in government and society, and his deep commitment to effect improvements in the quality of life have formed the bedrock of this success.

While much has already been written about the life of H.H. Shaikh Zayid Bin Sultan Al Nahyan, this book offers an entirely new perspective. Previously published works have depended to a large degree upon a very restricted range of sources. Often, they have represented a single researcher's point of view, while others have lacked a thorough academic basis.[1] The systematic approach adopted in this book, however, distinguishes it from those works. The objective from the outset has been to present a study that fully documents both the character and the political achievements of Shaikh Zayid, and to do so in a manner that compares well with other studies of contemporary world leaders. This book is not intended as a narrative presenting a day-to-day account of historical events and facts. Instead, through careful use of documentary evidence and a thorough reassessment of events, it aims to present a true appreciation of his pivotal role by reflecting on his decisions, philosophy and approaches.

This project represents an attempt to examine the multi-faceted life and career of Shaikh Zayid by using a historiographical method. It recognizes that the principal subject is an Arab Muslim and, therefore, the product of economic and social circumstances very different from those that prevail elsewhere. The approach selected has led to techniques of gathering and assessing evidence which made possible an analysis of the factors behind the remarkable success of Shaikh Zayid. Indeed, there is no dearth of chronicles detailing his life and work. Systematic efforts have been made within the United Arab Emirates to establish reliable chronologies and to record his many speeches and public statements on world, regional and local matters. While all these reveal what Shaikh Zayid has done, and often when he did it, few explain his extraordinary political acumen in guiding his nation on the road to modernization, and often fail to indicate the circumstances and motives that propelled him in a particular direction.

The book also offers a fresh analysis of those aspects of the history of the region that have a bearing on the character of Shaikh Zayid. As a scholarly project, it follows a long tradition of historiography that examines the impact of a ruler's character and actions upon the fate of a nation, an approach first developed by medieval Arab and Muslim historians such as Al Tabari, Ibn Kathir and Ibn Khaldun. Yet, the formulation and practice of history have varied widely over time and place. Historical writing has steadily broadened its scope from merely recording all the facets of the past to interpreting these events for present and future generations. It is in this context and from such a perspective that this book has developed.

This project grew from a shared belief among all concerned that the creation and development of the United Arab Emirates was an event of major significance, especially in the history of the Gulf region. Cynics might say that the UAE's success is merely due to the fact that it is an oil-rich nation, but such an assessment is simplistic given the scale of its political, social and economic achievements. Furthermore, any review of the history of nations will show that conflict and war between ethnic and cultural groups can easily impede the creation of effective unity. Certainly, in terms of the region's history and the factors existing at the time of the withdrawal of the British protective umbrella from the area, the establishment of a federation was far from a foregone conclusion. Inspired leadership was the catalyst required for the dream of unity to materialize.

What was gradually revealed as the writing of the book progressed was the degree to which Shaikh Zayid has followed a principled and consistent line of policy throughout the history and development, first of Abu Dhabi and thereafter through the birth and progress of the United Arab Emirates. It would therefore be implausible as well as a historical distortion to detach the development of both Abu Dhabi and the UAE from any perspective on the career and political ideals of Shaikh Zayid. His principled approach was articulated through his constant preoccupation with social welfare, a clear concept for the advancement of political unity, and a genuine concern for the environment and natural resources. Moreover, all three elements of Shaikh Zayid's policy have grown systematically and coherently over time. Thus, although this work contains many personal details relating to Shaikh Zayid, it is not intended to be a biography as much as an analytical study of his political methodology. It documents Shaikh Zayid's unique capacities of leadership, intuitive political skill and resolute determination in sustaining his principles of unity and peaceful development. His achievements merit prominence among those of historical leaders who have succeeded in building a nation.

It may be argued that to attempt an assessment of a man who, at the time of writing, is still an active leader full of ideas and plans is premature, to say the least. Yet, just as it is customary for great artists to be honored with a retrospective exhibition of their achievements, even though they may still be producing new work at a rapid rate, so the same honor may be extended to Shaikh Zayid. A retrospective reviews the body of work at a defined point in time and analyzes and assesses it in historical terms. In many instances, his work of development, built in most cases 'from the ground up,' is still in the growing phase. In other areas, much has been accomplished already and has now reached fruition. Frequently, as in his pioneering environmental activity, ideas continually evolve. The book highlights this process and shows how his creative thinking is based on a lifetime of experience. This line of continuity explains why it may be illuminating to see the context in which his plans have developed, sometimes over more than five decades.

A number of over-arching themes run through the book. The first is Shaikh Zayid's preoccupation with peace, conciliation and security. This theme relates to the background from which he has emerged. The Bani Yas, of which his family were by common consent the traditional and hereditary leaders, often displayed great skill in 'governing the ungovernable,' that is, the independent-minded Bedouin tribes. Shaikh Zayid's grandfather, known as Shaikh Zayid the Great (Ruler of Abu Dhabi from 1855 to 1909), stands out among those Bani Yas leaders who are credited with successfully forging unity within this unwieldy tribe with its disparate, fissiparous tendencies. However, when the political system failed, as it did in the years after the death of Shaikh Zayid the Great, Bani Yas politics degenerated into chaos and mayhem. To avoid such a recurrence, when Shaikh Zayid Bin Sultan became involved in the political sphere, he developed an effective political strategy based on the understanding and management of sectional interests, with peace, conciliation and security as his prime aims. These elements of Shaikh Zayid's political orientation emanate from his early days, and to comprehend his later career one thus needs to delve into the events of his youth.

The second theme is modernity and progress. In Shaikh Zayid's predecessor, His Highness Shaikh Shakhbut (Ruler of Abu Dhabi from 1928 to 1966), the emirate of Abu Dhabi possessed a Ruler who brought many benefits to his people. He maintained the peace for more than three decades, establishing a new tradition far removed from the situation in which he himself acceded as Ruler. Yet, to him the idea of modernity and progress, which began to encompass not only Abu Dhabi but the entire Arabian Gulf region from the 1950s onwards, was deeply unwelcome. Here, Shaikh Zayid, the younger brother, displayed a level of sagacity about the changing environment, viewing it not as a threat to the traditional way of life but as an opportunity to enhance the well-being of an entire people. Whereas Shaikh Shakhbut's approach to progress was conservative, Shaikh Zayid understood the new currents in society, recognizing that the winds of change could not be resisted. This perception ultimately allowed him to reap the benefits of a unique period in the history of the region.

The third theme of integration, solidarity and cooperation figures prominently within the narrative of this book. Shaikh Zayid always looked beyond the borders of a single nation, and beyond the forces that used collaboration merely as a slogan, to an older and more embracing tradition. He advocated integration and Arab solidarity as a basis for development and progress in the Gulf and other Arab states, embodying thereby the common destiny of the whole Arab nation. He used the notions of unity and federation as a means to bind the disparate Trucial States into a single nation, the United Arab Emirates. He employed the economic leverage at his disposal to sustain the legitimate demands of the Arab world in 1973, and he saw Muslim cooperation as a reflection of the universal concepts of brotherhood advocated by Islam. There can be few leaders in the Arab and Islamic communities, and even beyond, who have not been subjected to his gentle persuasion in furthering the cause of Arab solidarity as a means of securing a more equitable and stable world order. This book examines his steady, consistent political practice in this arena, with a history now extending back over several decades.

Each element in Shaikh Zayid's political praxis forms part of a seamless whole. The words that embody the idea of a single entity – *unity, unification, working together* – are a constant refrain in his discourse. Unity, thus, is the fourth theme, both in the political and ethical sense. Shaikh Zayid seems to make no essential distinction between these two. Unity is both a politically effective and an expedient form of behavior, just as much as it constitutes a morally correct course of action. These twin aspects of his concept of unity are of crucial importance. While Shaikh Zayid has exerted all his political skills over more than three decades to advance the cause of unity, he was well aware that at times events needed to follow their own course and timetable. His political acumen is also clearly reflected in the special nature of development as it has taken place, first in Abu Dhabi and subsequently in the United Arab Emirates.

What has clearly emerged from this study is that the success of Shaikh Zayid has been founded on the close contact that he has maintained since his early career not just with the leaders of society, but also the population at large. The degree to which he has retained personal knowledge of the concerns and underlying motives of ordinary people has emerged consistently throughout the process of research. Societies in the Arabian Gulf have their own distinctive history and structure, based on a traditional and tribal character. Although the population of the Gulf states has grown substantially since the 1960s, it is still small enough for face-to-face politics. The biography of Shaikh Zayid shows how and why he mastered the skills of individual negotiation and diplomacy with his people. The record also reveals the consummate skill with which he achieved his long-term goals by employing all the resources at his disposal. A close relationship with his people has provided the most reliable foundation for this continuing success. Yet, he has proved equally adept at dealing with his fellow Rulers and with the international community. The efficacy and subtlety of his negotiations, which led to the formation of the United Arab Emirates, confounded those who believed, first, that unity was impossible and, second, that even if it were achieved, it would prove short-lived.

To contextualize and cover these momentous years, the book is divided into three major sections comprising ten chapters. Part I, entitled *The Heritage*, covers the history and background of the region from the emergence of the Bani Yas and the establishment of Abu Dhabi through Shaikh Zayid's birth until his accession as Ruler of Abu Dhabi in 1966. Part II, *The Transformation*, details the economic dynamism of the region, beginning with the oil exports in the 1960s and covering the ensuing process of modernization both in economic and social terms. Part III, entitled *The Union*, covers the political restructuring brought about by Shaikh Zayid from the 1970s to the present, forging the former Trucial States into the United Arab Emirates.

From the start of this project, broad parameters were set for the collection of materials on the subject. Nothing, however insubstantial it might have appeared at the time, was excluded. In addition to the primary archival and published secondary materials, such as monographic studies, general and popular books, and academic articles, a variety of oral and visual materials were also assembled and evaluated. Primary material is invaluable in a work such as this. Nevertheless, all these sources have been subjected to the same evidential test, and each statement and position has been confirmed from various independent sources. Strenuous efforts were made to obtain archival and documentary material, particularly when the information from other sources proved inadequate or of poor evidential value. This systematic process has revealed the degree to which many of the existing secondary texts simply echo each other, without reverting to the original sources.

By amassing, sifting and collating data gleaned from different points of origin, a fresh and authoritative perspective has developed. The result is a work of reference amply documented with archival evidence. It is based on objective analysis and applies rigorous historiographical standards of accuracy that are appropriate in a study dealing with such a major topic. The writing of this book also proves that to document the achievements of H.H. Shaikh Zayid Bin Sultan Al Nahyan and to chart the development of the United Arab Emirates under his guidance is a worthy task and an undertaking of lasting importance.

This book is not a hagiography. It does not suggest that Shaikh Zayid is the epitome of wisdom or perception. He, himself, has always resolutely rejected any such notion. What is asserted here is his undeniable sagacity and political skill. There were many occasions when he was urged to take actions that differed from the course he ultimately decided to follow. On every issue, he listened to a variety of opinions, but he never hesitated to take a different path if his perspective and sense of right led him in that direction. In retrospect, his judgment has usually proved correct. Conversely, there were occasions when his initial course of action led to misgivings. In these instances, he never hesitated to make the necessary adjustments or to change direction. Every decision was the product of patient reflection, keeping in mind a broad vision of future consequences. Like most great statesmen, he was always aware of this wider scenario. His people and his community have always been his primary interest. And, since this book focuses on his life and career, it naturally follows the contours of his own priorities and concerns, particularly social causes.

No book can be classed as 'definitive' and, as additional information becomes available, the detailed narrative of events may undergo some alteration. Nevertheless, it is anticipated that the overall analysis of Shaikh Zayid's significant role and his impact on the region's history as presented in this book will stand the test of time.

PART
I

THE

HERITAGE

CHAPTER
1

The Arabian Tribe

In November 1968, the United States Consul General in Dhahran, Saudi Arabia, wrote in confidence to Washington of his first meeting with the young, new Ruler of Abu Dhabi, Shaikh Zayid Bin Sultan Al Nahyan. Lee Dinsmore was immensely impressed with the Shaikh's acuity, his animated and dramatic way of speaking and his obvious political sagacity. The Consul observed, "…he is seen…objectively as a power to be reckoned with because of his intelligence, his money, his willingness to use it to gain support." He hinted that he found it hard to be objective, being easily swayed by the Ruler's magnetic appeal. "Sheikh Zayed of Abu Dhabi is animated, a spinner of yarns, gesticulating and changing facial expressions, using earthy parables to make a point." But in what was a short telegram, he made one point with some emphasis. At the start of his report, Dinsmore stated that this was a man who "has also lived simply the life of a desert Sheikh," and he stressed that others whose judgment he trusted had told him that "Zayed is a capable, strong and straightforward desert Arab."[1]

For Dinsmore and his superiors in the Department of State, being a "desert Arab," a Shaikh who had lived as Zayid did, among his people in the harsh and rigorous conditions of the Arabian desert, meant acquiring over time a certain kind of character, making him an honorable man to be reckoned with. The term was used as a kind of shorthand. This chapter explores what is meant by a "desert Arab," and the influences that the environment and tribal society had on the formation of Zayid's character, which the Consul General found so impressive.

The People and the Place

In 1863, just over a century prior to Dinsmore's report, a British envoy had recorded his impressions of a visit to the Arabian Gulf. Lieutenant Colonel Lewis Pelly was no romantic, but there was something about the peoples of the Gulf that struck him as remarkable:

> Meeting these Arabs you readily comprehend how they once stormed across the world; and you could leave them, persuaded that they still possess qualities which may again render them renowned, should outward circumstances favour…I left the Arabs, impressed that their vices and their virtues, their customs, their manners, and their government, have been in a great degree formed by physical and accidental circumstances. A man who finds himself doomed to live in the Bedouin desert, cannot render himself similar to that of a man born of the same original stock who finds himself among the natural bounties of Arabia Felix.[2]

He concluded, rather as Dinsmore did a century after him, with an observation about the qualities of the desert life, "…and as soil is, so the mind of man."[3]

Pelly apologized to his audience for this "seeming digression," since the task he had set himself was to discuss the trade in the Gulf. He realized, however, that the issues of the environment and the character of the people were crucial. He had also observed first hand a factor that later generations have tended to overlook. For him, there was the sense that to talk of 'Arabs' as a generality, as some kind of composite character, was a delusion. First, Pelly argued that while there were common characteristics in Arab societies, there were also those generated by a response to a particular environment. Second, he saw in the Arabs whom he met a capacity for greatness, with qualities implicit in the society that shaped their culture. What links Pelly and Dinsmore is that they both looked beyond the stereotypes of 'the Arab' to the strength and potential that lay beneath. This aspect relates directly to any understanding of Shaikh Zayid Bin Sultan. It would be extremely simplistic to characterize him as merely embodying his culture and environment, for great men everywhere exceed the average model. Nevertheless, to have any sense of the elements at work in his character demands an analysis of his physical environment and social background in the manner initially outlined by Pelly.

All the Arab peoples can trace their origins to harsh desert regions, and the impact of that environment has conditioned almost every aspect of their culture. It gave them the hardiness and self-reliance that would enable them to conquer the lands from the shores of the Arabian Sea all the way to the Atlantic Ocean. During the seventh century CE, many Arabs converted to Islam—a faith that was revealed in the Arabian desert, with the Word of God expressed in Arabic through the Holy Koran. From this point onward, the Arab peoples, their faith, their language and their society, were in harmony, each element complementing the other. The energy radiated by these desert peoples was remarkable, not just in terms of their rapid territorial advance both westward and eastward but also in their achievements. This nomadic race built great cities like Baghdad, Cairo, Seville and Cordoba, and many willingly converted to Islam. Over the course of a century, the Arabs increasingly turned into a settled people, yet the bonds of tribe and common heritage never weakened.[4]

The culture into which Shaikh Zayid was born was rooted in tribal traditions. To understand the meaning of the tribe in eastern Arabia requires non-Arabs to jettison their preconceptions. For Westerners in particular, tribes and tribalism continue to be considered a primitive stage on the journey towards the formation of the modern nation-state. Many British officials who came to the Arabian Gulf brought those perceptions with them to the region, seeing the Arab tribes not for what they were, but as a way of life frozen into the patterns of the past.[5] However, in Arabia, tribalism was a positive force, providing strength and social cohesion. Indeed, what made Shaikh Zayid "capable," in Dinsmore's words, were precisely those values embedded in the tribe, qualities that would enable him to lead a new nation at an accelerated pace into a world of technology and innovation. In Shaikh Zayid's hands, the culture of the tribe would prove sturdy, adaptable, and resilient enough to cope with unparalleled change. Instead of being a barrier to modernization, it was precisely the culture of the tribe that empowered the peoples of the Gulf to accept unprecedented development in the span of a single generation.

The conditions of life for desert nomads linked every aspect of their society to survival in a manner without direct parallel. The fact that they managed to sustain life for themselves and their livestock in a region that seemed to the outsider to be without water or food was in itself remarkable.[6] They did so through an intimate knowledge of the environment—where pasture could be found and water could be located. From this basic lifestyle, those outsiders saw them as developing a 'pure' form of society, shorn of all inessentials. Although singularly poor in resources, they were uniquely attuned to their circumstances. The Arab Bedouin held rather specific virtues, related to his environment. As the renowned historian Ibn Khaldun remarked, "They go alone into the desert, guided by their fortitude, putting their trust in themselves. Fortitude has become a character quality of theirs, and courage their nature. They use it whenever they are called upon or an alarm stirs them."[7]

Despite the harsh conditions, the Bedouin tribesmen prized freedom and independence. Yet, survival also dictated that they develop the habit of cooperation. They functioned in groups when it was in their interest and accepted leadership when they respected the leader.[8] The links that joined them and held them together were intangible— no Bedouin could claim to control another. They came together freely, bound by a code of honor that underpinned every aspect of their culture. Their society was created by the interplay of three separate but interwoven elements. The first was the physical environment that determined the parameters of their world. The second was the political structure that encompassed their social life—the tribe and tribal leadership. The third was the moral structure that connected them, largely embodied in the code of honor, common in its essence to all Bedouin.

These three elements are the themes of this chapter. Each contributed to the character of the "desert Arab." They also provide the unseen substrata of Shaikh Zayid's personality.

The Geography of a Desert Land

The Arabian peninsula extends almost three million square kilometers. Since ancient times, it has often been described as a land of desert and mountains. Though this description is largely true, there are also fertile areas.[9] A chain of rocky hills runs down the peninsula's western side, rising to mountains 4,000 meters high in the present territory of Yemen. Along the coast of the Arabian Sea, the hills gradually give way to a plateau that extends deep inland.

Continuing around the coast, the land rises again to the ranges of the Jabal al Akhdar in the Sultanate of Oman and, thence, to the craggy spine of the Musandam peninsula, which borders what is arguably the world's most strategically important waterway leading into and out of the Gulf—the Strait of Hormuz. Each of these hill and mountain ranges is distinct from the other. Collectively, they support a diverse range of economies and peoples. The coast of the Arabian Gulf is low-lying, all the way up to the mouths of the Tigris and Euphrates rivers.

Similarly, the map shows a desert that extends from the coast of the Arabian Sea up to the coastal strip that borders the Mediterranean. Yet, within this vast area, there are many different forms of arid land. To the north, al Hamad, and portions of the Nafud extend all the way southward to the Asir mountains in the southwest. To the east lies the Dahna' with the desert region of al Dhafrah stretching to the coast of the Gulf. To the south of the Dahna' and inland from al Dhafrah lies the 'sand sea' of the Rub' al Khali. Al Dhafrah and the Liwa oasis comprise the territory of the Bani Yas, the tribe into which Shaikh Zayid was born.

From the nineteenth century, eyewitness reports describe this landscape and the way of life it supported. Passing through the Bani

Yas land in December 1801, David Seton, the British Resident in Muscat, noted:

> To the Southward of Bedih lies Zufra [Dhafrah], the Country of the Beni Yas which consists of about 1000 Men…their country is a desert except here and there a few Islands in the sand where they feed their flocks; off their Coast are three islands, Buzubbeh [Abu Dhabi], Surco [Zarkuh], the name of the other unknown, the first is nothing but sand, but has a well of fresh water to which the Beni Yas resort in the hot weather when their own Country is dry, it is near the Main, the other is a fine Island, and has the remains of an European Fort and Settlement on it.[10]

A more recent writer, J.B. Kelly, who knew Abu Dhabi in the early days of Shaikh Zayid's rule, has provided an additional *tour d' horizon*:

> That part of Arabia…is largely a depressing waste of sand dune, salt flat and gravel plain. It consists, broadly speaking, of a coastal tract with an off-shore chain of islands, and a desert hinterland. The islands begin off the coast of Qatar and end to the north-east of Abu Dhabi town, which itself stands on an island. The coastal tract, a succession of sand and gravel plains interspersed with *sabkhah* [original italics], or salt flat, runs from the foot of Qatar eastwards towards Abu Dhabi and then turns north-eastwards, extending to beyond Ras al-Khaima, the northernmost of the Trucial Shaikhdoms, where it is forced into the sea by the massive cliffs of the Musandam peninsula, which juts into the entrance to the…Gulf. The desert hinterland behind the coast is dominated by sand dunes, which grow more formidable in size as they approach the Rub' al-Khali. There are two fairly large oases in the region, Liwa, in the middle of the desert hinterland, and Buraimi [al Ain],[11] at its eastern edge, by the foothills of the western Hajar.[12]

The Arab peoples of the peninsula have adapted to each of these different desert areas and found ways of surviving in such extreme conditions. Springing from a common stock in ancient times, in the far southwest of the peninsula, their forefathers migrated first to the extremities of Arabia itself and then west through North Africa to the Atlantic Ocean, on into Spain and eastward as far as India. Aspects of this process of migration and adaptation continue to the present day.

In lands far beyond those in which Arab armies made their conquests, traders established connections between Arabia and the lands to the east and west.[13] Even today, Arab communities are to be found in practically every continent. The quality of adaptability that served them well in the desert landscape has proved equally important in less challenging environments.

The harshness of that original environment is hard to comprehend. The salt flats and low hills inland from the Gulf were even more barren, if less dramatic, than the huge sand ridges of *al Ramlah*—'The Sands.' The explorer Wilfred Thesiger, crossing into Abu Dhabi from the west in 1948, revealed the utter desolation of this region:

> We decided we must make a detour and cross these salt-flats near their head, otherwise the camels might become inextricably bogged, especially after the recent heavy rain. They would only have to sink in as far as their knees to be lost…The flats themselves were covered with a crust of dirty salt which threw up a glare into our faces and, even through half-closed eyes, stabbed deep into my skull. The camels broke through this crust and floundered forward through liquid black mud. It took us five unpleasant, anxious hours to get across…On the far side we camped among undulating, utterly lifeless white sands, where even the salt-bushes were dead and their stumps punctured our naked feet like needles.[14]

The key to life in any desert area is water, and in al Dhafrah water could be found in unlikely places. A geologist's perspective saw only the flow of water from the mountains to the sea:

> When there is sufficient rainfall, fluvial gravels and sands are transported down the mountain sides and across the valley floors within the mountains; today, such rainwater reaches the sea [and is therefore 'lost'] about once in every ten years in the northern Emirates, but south of Jabal Faiyah it always dissipates within the sand dunes…[15]

However, the water that "dissipates" into the dunes could be found and used. Some of this water was trapped in inland *sabkhahs*, flat areas of sand, silt or clay, overlaid with a thin crust of hardened salt. Elsewhere it was held in deeper pockets under the sand dunes. The unusual geological structure of the desert sands of Abu Dhabi retained water in a way such that it could be used by those Bedouin who knew the invisible places where water was to be found.[16] Every desert dweller had a mental map of where water was to be found in his own territory.

The quality of the water varied widely. Fresh 'sweet' water from the mountains was only to be found in al Ain; water on the island of Abu Dhabi was always brackish, while in the Liwa oasis system, the original home of the Bani Yas, there were approximately 30 small oases, each with a supply of water. But in Liwa, unlike al Ain, the availability of water depended on the annual rain, which could fail over a period of many years.[17] In the oases, the earth was fertile and capable of supporting date gardens. The gardens, some owned by the Bani Yas and others by their allies, were tended by families who lived in *barasti* huts at the base of the dunes.[18] On the coast, some members of the Bani Yas became fishermen, leaving their flocks to be cared for by other allied tribes. Such interdependence was characteristic of the Bani Yas alliance system, as was an inherent flexibility. These qualities were so marked among the people of Abu Dhabi that the latter were characterized as "the versatile tribesman."[19]

Tribal structures are often presented as fixed and unchanging. But reality does not support such stereotypes.[20] Life in such a harsh environment as the Arabian desert produced a unique culture—one that was forced to adapt to necessity. Yet, understanding this capacity to adapt is not easy. To achieve any appreciation of its true meaning, culture and philosophy, tribal culture must be approached with an open mind and a sense of intuition. It should be remembered, with Pelly's words in mind, that there is no single pattern of 'the tribe' in Arabia. Each of the desert Arab tribes adapted to the conditions that confronted them. In general, the tribes were divided into two broad categories. First, there were those that drew sustenance from the desert, depending on livestock and agriculture in the oases. Second, there were those that made a living from the sea by fishing, pearling or maritime trade. Uniquely, the Bani Yas of Abu Dhabi fell into both categories. Some of them were desert nomads, who, at particular seasons of the year, would come down to the coast and take up the lives of fishermen or pearlers.

As the fishing season ended, they would revert to their desert lives. To them, this simply seemed a natural opportunity, which they used to the fullest; to the analyst, they thereby became "versatile" because the constraints and opportunities inherent in their immediate environment imbued them with a set of special qualities.

Traditions and Values

Arabs share a common heritage, culture and ethics that has at times united them. But, increasingly, it is apparent that the practical manifestations of this shared culture have varied with time and place. The phenomenon of migration and the adoption of new occupations by tribesmen, necessitated by changed economic circumstances, have had their effect. By nature resourceful, some tribesmen responded opportunistically to the challenges of the environment. The tribesmen of the Gulf took advantage of the opportunities offered by the sea and developed a living from fishing and pearl diving. The tribesmen of the Hijaz became increasingly involved with the great pilgrimages to the holy cities, which were the greatest sources of income in the whole of Arabia. The adaptability of the Arab peoples in the desert can be seen, in retrospect, as one of their most striking and effective qualities.

Another characteristic of desert Arab society is its strong sense of history.[21] Even today, among some tribes the story of the tribe's past is recalled orally, recited to all the people so that it is not forgotten.[22] That past has a current relevance. Every Arab is formed by this deeply rooted sense of his tribal heritage.[23] Even from early times not all the peoples of Arabia have lived in or were from the desert. The urban cultures of great cities like Mecca and Medina have ancient roots, but for many Arabs, the sea has been their primary source of livelihood. This has had a formative influence on those tribes that lived by pearling, fishing and maritime trade. More specifically, the tribe provided the framework within which the character and skills of Shaikh Zayid were developed.

The tribes of the Arabian Gulf have experienced a slow movement towards change, accelerating in the twentieth century and reaching an almost breakneck speed in more recent times. One can trace the beginning of that period of transformation to the early nineteenth century, when external powers – Egypt, the Ottoman Empire and the European nations, notably Britain – began to take a much more active interest in Arabia. From that point onward, the tribes of the Arabian peninsula began the process of re-shaping themselves into what ultimately, in the twentieth century, have become nation-states. Of course, the circumstances of geography and social structure cannot determine the fate of each individual, but it is remarkable how the forces described above have also given Shaikh Zayid a social and human context within which to accomplish the creation of the United Arab Emirates.[24] Thus, in his case, the tribe has performed a double function. It has inculcated the personal qualities that have made him an effective leader, and provided a basis for collaboration on a broader scale within society that eventually paved the way for a federation.

Therefore, it becomes clear that the way of life, particularly in the Abu Dhabi region of the Lower Gulf, was not determined according to the rules and structures of a single pattern of tribal organization.[25] Within this complex local pattern, there was still great diversity, both in lifestyle and tribal settlements. Some remained more or less sedentary, while others were nomadic. The crucial point is, however, that these tribes, in alliance, created a form of social and political unity:

> …the coastal tract, with Abu Dhabi town and the islands, and the desert hinterland, with its oases of Buraimi [al Ain][26] and Līwa, together form a single economic unit, the whole depending for its viability upon each part, and each part being incomplete if severed from the other parts.[27]

Other research supports this impression. It makes the link between social forms and the environment:

> The inhabitants of the region, members almost without exception of tribes long established there, dwell in a society developed over centuries to meet the demands of their arduous environment. For generations they have followed the classic patterns of nomadic and semi-settled life in Arabia, depending for subsistence on their animals and on the dates of Buraimi [al Ain] and al-Jiwa [Liwa].

Some parts of tribes have tended to stay close to their date gardens, while others sojourn during the harvest season at their gardens and then return to the desert in the winter: no valid distinction can be drawn between 'nomadic' and 'sedentary' tribes…The movements of the tribes are not wanderings upon impulse; their well-established courses take due cognizance of the rights of others. This way of life cannot be regarded as being *per se* [original italics] either better or worse than other ways to be found elsewhere; it merely represents, in the absence of modern techniques making practicable new types of activity, the best human use possible of such lands as these.[28]

This natural tendency to include rather than to exclude, to add to one's family circle, to form alliances, to build larger and more powerful groups, is deeply rooted in the character and practice of all the desert Arabs. The reasons are obvious and expedient. A larger group was stronger than a smaller one, and in the harsh conditions of the desert, it made sense to reduce as far as possible the number of one's adversaries, both real and potential. Thus, the tribal connection by descent came first, building upon a constellation of smaller clans and sub-units. To that conglomeration would be joined a larger galaxy of allies and friends. An excellent example of this natural bonding was the Bani Yas alliance.[29]

In parallel, therefore, to the common characteristics among Arab tribes, are the elements of differentiation. On the one hand, there is uniformity among the tribes, stemming from their common origin and heritage. On the other, there are the adaptations made by particular tribes to the circumstances both of the physical and the political environment.[30] In part, this has taken place because each of the tribes has become segmented[31] over the centuries into many sections and sub-units.[32] The fact that two individuals shared a common ancestor 20 generations ago does not determine their current relationship, unless both parties wish it to do so. Nevertheless, linkages and common ancestral connections can be affirmed as a means of asserting brotherhood and family ties.[33]

Thus, there are two elements within the genealogical connection —'antecedents' (descent) and 'kin.' Although both terms have technical meanings for anthropologists, their usage here is more general.

Antecedents are a chosen narrative of identity: no one has a personal memory of his forebears extending back more than a few generations. Beyond that, it is a matter of myth, reconstructed memory, ascribed values and carefully chosen symbols of desired – often heroic – characteristics.[34] Antecedents are, in part, a matter of individual ascription and choice.

In the matter of kindred, there is much less choice and more immediate constraints. Kin are those whom individuals make part of their family and/or tribal connection. There need be no specific antecedent link.[35] Kinship, in this sense, is a very potent concept, bound deeply to notions of family ties. At a deeper level, the capacity of the Arab family to bind within it those from the outside is ultimately allied closely to the desert customs of honor including hospitality,[36] generosity, sanctity of the guest, chivalry[37] and courage.[38]

The Role of Honor in Arab Tribal Society

The concepts and categories of honor embody the codes mentioned above and provide the underlying structure of Arab society. For the individual tribesman, as has been suggested above, loss of honor is a form of 'social death,' and much of this code still determines the way in which an Arab behaves towards strangers and to those outside his immediate kin. It was said more than a hundred years ago that the tribes of Arabia "look upon hospitality not merely as a duty imposed by divine ordinance, but as the primary instinct of a well-constituted mind."[39] Once a guest has sought and been granted hospitality or sanctuary, he comes under the protection of his host. One leading authority suggests that no other nation in the world regards the "covenant of protection" as highly as the Arabs.[40]

From a historical perspective, these suggestions prompt several further questions. What did the code of honor allow the rulers to do? To what degree did honorable conduct demand support from an ally and at what cost? When could a ruler honorably end a quarrel for the sake of the general peace? In practice, while the idea of honor is at the heart of the Arab social code, its precise application varied from place to place:

> The notion of honor is probably important in almost all Arab societies, but accounts that are both detailed and reliable are surprisingly few…The vocabulary of honor is much the same everywhere in the Arab world, but though words such as *'ird*, *sharaf* 'honor', *'ār* 'dishonor' and *'ayb* 'a shame, a disgrace' are very widely distributed, the meaning that is attached to them varies greatly from place to place.[41]

The concept of concern here is *sharaf*, often described as the idea of collective or group honor. Just as the physical environment provided the basis upon which one's social relationships were grounded, so the connections between individuals were structured as a set of mutual dependencies or oppositions based on the notion of honor. The operational dimension of the concepts, moreover, was both personal and communal. Special emphasis has always been placed on the latter, as each individual, each family, each sub-section of a tribe formed a segment of the whole.[42] So too, the individual in this system necessarily formed a part of the larger group: "People may alter their place in the set of categories, but they cannot be without a place."[43]

Within such a framework, every person is mindful not only of his own desires and wishes, but of the network of mutual connections and responsibilities to which he belongs. However, far from being static, the network encapsulates a subtle and adaptive social system, one based less on conflict than on discussion and debate. Discussion between and among tribesmen could be forthright, while never stepping beyond the bounds of what was considered legitimate within the tribe's code of honor. Furthermore, it was possible in a raiding culture to capture another tribe's camels after a battle as the spoils of war and not have this action thought of as being dishonorable. Yet, to take goods covertly by stealth was theft, and was regarded as dishonorable. A man's honor was impugned if you accused him of acting surreptitiously behind the victim's back rather than openly. To say that someone had abandoned a companion in a fight was unquestionably dishonorable, although honor might not oblige one to enter a quarrel in the first place.[44] However, to

accuse an individual, for example, of failing to stand by his word –
his guarantee – is to cast shame on his name and is an offense against
his honor.

Within these limits and within the proper forum – the *majlis* –
discussion was free. The crucial dimension in social and political conduct
was argument and persuasion:

> …when one examines the ethnographic record to determine what
> it is that Middle Eastern tribesmen are doing in political acts, one
> finds that they are talking to each other probably more than they
> are fighting…the basis of power is *persuasion* [original italics]
> rather than the exercise of force.[45]

Thus, the most powerful man is not necessarily the one who commands
the greatest military power, but the one who is held in the greatest esteem
as a man of honor. Of course, armed strength was never discounted,
but "by learning how to be persuasive, one becomes a man of honor in
tribal societies, and persuasion is more central to the workings of tribal
society than the use of force."[46]

One of Shaikh Zayid's most valuable attributes was his understanding of the complex codes and categories of honor, and how these
dominated the relationships between the tribes. While the tribes might
organize themselves in many different ways, the sense of what was
honorable and what was not remained part of their common Arab
identity. At one time, these issues of honor forced tribes to war. It was
the political genius of Shaikh Zayid Bin Sultan to see that those same
codes could be used to unite them. Part of this understanding grew
from the way in which his grandfather and namesake, Shaikh Zayid the
Great, had succeeded in bringing former enemies to sit and talk with
each other. In their political practice, both Shaikh Zayid Bin Sultan
and Shaikh Zayid the Great built upon the essence of their family
tradition, bringing former enemies together, listening to the arguments,
using persuasion and not force to build an agreement. That was the
Bedouin way.

The Bani Yas

All Arab tribesmen needed to be resourceful to survive in the desert but, in the area that now forms Abu Dhabi, a distinctive form of tribal structure emerged that transformed those inherent capacities to adapt and to survive into a more politically significant form. Within the various types of Arab tribal structures, the 'system' of the Bani Yas possessed unique and valuable characteristics.[47] Few serious studies have been made of the structure and character of the Bani Yas, although they merit considerable interest stemming from the special qualities that have promoted their long-term success.[48] But even the terminology used to describe the structure of the tribe is sometimes convoluted. At times termed an 'alliance,' at others a 'confederation,' more recently simply a 'tribe,' the essential characteristic of the Bani Yas was its responsiveness to change.[49] A core of family groupings, bonded together by mutual interests that had been developed and sustained over more than two centuries, it attracted allies and supporters who did not form part of the core. Yet, that galaxy of allies also proved long lasting, enduring for many generations.

The question of whether the Bani Yas have a single common ancestry or comprise an alliance of both blood-related and non-consanguineous groups is largely of academic interest. The key fact is that they have been the strongest tribal organization in southeast Arabia and have been led throughout by the Al Nahyan of the Al Bu Falah. However, the reasons for their success are partially due to their 'open' tribal structure. If a tight, consanguineous, agnatically determined tribal system might be perceived as closed and incapable of adaptation, the Bani Yas structure was both stable and open to change.[50] New allies and supporters could be bonded into the system by mutual interest and blood links through marriage, but the essence of the connection was mutual interest and dependence. Moreover, within the Bani Yas polity, there was a universal accord that the leadership of the group should be drawn from among the members of the Al Nahyan family. This accord was sanctioned only by undisputed consensus since the eighteenth century, when the system first came into being. According to tradition,

Al Falah, the leader of the Bani Yas, was succeeded towards the end of the seventeenth century by his son Nahyan, whose three brothers Sa'dun, Muhammad and Sultan all supported Nahyan in governing the tribesmen. Thus, they and their avatars became the Al Bu Falah, the descendents of Falah. Thereafter, Nahyan's descendents were traditionally looked upon as providers of the Shaikh of the Bani Yas.[51] However, the Al Nahyan were not so designated because of any specially sanctified descent or social superiority; they were looked upon as competent, and they were also regarded as men of honor.

The first fully researched modern overview of the role and nature of the tribes in Abu Dhabi was written in 1955; this was supplemented and extended by a major study completed in 1997.[52] They suggest that the dominant force in the region was the Bani Yas, and their principal allies the Manasir, 'Awamir and Dhawahir.[53] While these tribes are loosely organized into sections and sub-sections, this is a tribal pattern different from that which existed in other parts of Arabia.[54] In many parts of the great deserts to the north and south, each tribe has its exclusive *dar* or homeland, in which it is usually to be found and where the wells are the property of a particular tribe. This was not the case in Abu Dhabi, where members of all tribes in alliance shared the available resources and protected each others' assets. Thus, when Bani Yas tribesmen journeyed from the Liwa or al Ain oases to the coast for fishing, their livestock and date palms would be left in the care of their allies and associated tribes.

The Bani Yas system was shaped by certain special factors related to the environment and political conditions of the terrain occupied by the tribe. One of the distinguishing marks of the Bani Yas alliance of Abu Dhabi was that they were people inhabiting both the coast and the sea as well as the land bordering the boundless 'inland ocean,' the great desert of southern Arabia. Some had settled in the oases of the region rather than wander as nomads from place to place. On the coast, they were involved in fishing and pearling. Edward Henderson, who knew the region before the transformation produced by oil, described the Bani Yas as "…an Arab tribe, some settled, some seamen, some bedouin."[55]

The impetus for survival forced some of the Bani Yas who initially lived as nomads in the desert at Liwa to exploit the resources of the sea from the second half of the eighteenth century. This dual way of life continued henceforth so that the system embraced both nomadic herdsmen and sedentary populations. Thus, there were members of the Bani Yas and of the Manasir tribe who followed wholly 'sedentary' occupations, such as pearling and fishing on the coast and the cultivation of dates at Liwa. Equally, there were members of both tribes who were Bedouin and semi-Bedouin—they spent part of the year in the date gardens or on the coast and part of the year grazing their camels in the deserts. Some members of the allied tribe of the Na'im settled in the al Ain oasis, while others – especially of the Al Bu Shamis section – may be described as semi-sedentary. That is to say, they did not own settlements, but they did not wander far afield like the true Bedouin, preferring instead to remain on the fringes of the deserts. Even the Dhawahir, located largely in al Ain, sometimes grazed their flocks in the surrounding deserts. Hence, the tribal structure continued to embrace both settled and nomadic peoples.

In this complex structure, a successful leader was one who could speak intuitively to all groups. The shaikhs had to strike a delicate balance between all the groups and sub-groups. It was possibly the most intricate of all the tribal structures in Arabia, with various interest groups within the different segments of the Bani Yas and the allied tribes, each making their individual demands to the tribal leader. While it required great skill to keep all the forces in balance and in harmony, it took extraordinary capacities to hold it together over the long term.

To the outsider, tribal life might appear confusing, but within the society, every tribesman knew to which group he belonged, and he needed to carry no document or passport to prove it. People could recite their genealogies back to their distant ancestors. The members of the Bani Yas were sure of their identity, of their loyalties, their allies and mutual dependencies. The system might best be considered in terms of a central core or nucleus with a surrounding periphery. At the core were the clans that comprised the Bani Yas, while the periphery included the tribes and family groups in alliance with them. Often the connections between the core and the periphery were so strong and of such long duration that, for most practical purposes, the distinction did not exist. In both cases, the groups in either category had come together by consent. Where the core ended and the periphery began was not immediately clear to the observer, yet those who participated in the system understood intuitively.

The strength of the Bani Yas connection was that it was an alliance system based upon mutual interest and hallowed by custom. It had, after all, been in existence since the early to mid-eighteenth century. It did not depend exclusively upon agnatic, blood links between its members.[56] It was inherently flexible, attracting to it a wide and diverse set of groups, some nomadic, some settled, some making a living from the sea, some from livestock and others by cultivation. The desire to seek consensus rather than a confrontation was strong within the traditions of the Bani Yas. This was of special importance given that the other major element conditioning all aspects of social life in the region – as in many other Arab groups – was the compelling power of custom and tradition. The social model that the Bani Yas structure offered to Shaikh Zayid was of an adaptive rather than a rigid system, one that he could use to his advantage. Its tradition was to seek connections of mutual interest, to look for harmony rather than conflict.

Does "the versatile tribesman" of Abu Dhabi already alluded to differ from the adaptability generally characteristic of the Arabs? The special quality of the desert people has been well understood in Arab society since the time when Ibn Khaldun wrote his great *Muqaddimah*. He saw what anthropologists have subsequently noted, that peoples living under marginal conditions of necessity possess a particular capacity for resourcefulness.[57] However, in Abu Dhabi the groups that made up the Bani Yas moved beyond 'resourcefulness.' They based their social and political structure around versatility and collaboration. As Clarence Mann remarks in his study of Abu Dhabi:

> The variety of their [Bani Yas] composition, occupations and political associations has provided the means by which their primary shaikh, the Ruler of Abu Dhabi, has been able to extend his influence throughout the wide area presently claimed.[58]

The ways in which the tribes of Abu Dhabi differed from the classic desert tradition gave them, potentially, an edge in adapting to the pressures of a vastly different new world which emerged after the discovery of oil. Although the tribal structures in Arabia generally encouraged the formation of alliances and connections, the Bani Yas had a special reason for uniting. In isolation, they lacked power, being few in number. Their power was derived from the strength of the alliance. To that might was added that of other allies, like the renowned desert warriors of the Manasir tribe, whose connection was loose, yet hallowed by enduring custom and tradition. In turn, successful leaders of the Bani Yas alliance advanced their power through an understanding of the social complexities of their 'system.'

The firm foundation of the system was evident in its capacity both to survive defections and to incorporate new elements. All Arab tribal structures were essentially fissiparous, dividing into smaller groups or segments as pressure grew on resources. In the traditional anthropological segmentary model, where these groups would be linked by blood, there remained some indissoluble bond. In the Bani Yas system, where mutual interest rather than kinship held the structure together, different elements might detach themselves or later return. The Al Bu Falasah – to whom the Al Maktum of Dubai belong – for example, split and settled in Dubai in 1833. The Al Qubaisat departed and returned on more than one occasion. They sought to establish an independent power base of their own in Khur al 'Udaid during the reign of Shaikh Khalifa Bin Shakhbut until 1837, under Shaikh Zayid the Great until 1878, and again under Shaikh Shakhbut Bin Sultan up to 1966. But after each of these episodes of secession, the Al Qubaisat were reconciled and rejoined the Bani Yas system when they realized that it was in their interests to do so.[59]

From childhood, Shaikh Zayid Bin Sultan was immersed in the history of the Bani Yas. The stories of successful and less successful rulers, conspiracy and sedition, the formation of great alliances, and the extensions of tribal power provided political lessons and examples. This history taught him two cardinal principles. The first was that a successful ruler had to keep the loyalty and trust of his whole tribe and its allies. The second was that to achieve success, a ruler had to act with courage and conviction, inspire his people, and unify differing interest groups. In the long history of the Bani Yas only his grandfather provided an effective example of a leader who truly unified his people.

The Shaikh as a Unifying Symbol

Among the Bani Yas, as in all Arab tribes, the role of the Shaikh was crucial. The success and very survival of his people depended upon him. Therefore, his socio-political role within this society was of primary importance. A successful shaikh, like Zayid the Great, was not merely a bold warrior and leader in battle. In this context 'successful' has a much broader meaning than a leader who simply excelled on the battlefield. The qualities that tribesmen shrewdly esteemed as leading to long-term success related more to an active mind than to a strong arm. A leader was gifted with insight, forethought and wisdom. In the oral history of a tribe:

> A chief who is commonly spoken of as a *ṣāḥeb al-marǧala* stands in high esteem ... Such a one has a brave strong heart, *ḳalbeh ḳawi*; knows how to wrestle with the greatest danger, *maʿeh fetel*; has a broad outlook, *maʿeh ʿerf*; thinks of the future, *šôfteh baʿide*; and never acts hastily, *leh ṣabr*. He who is merely a daring fighter ... is not fit to be either a chief or a leader in time of war.[60]

Leaders of this quality existed as an ideal rather than the norm. However, tribal society recognized the supreme importance of these higher qualities. When such a leader emerged, the tribal system allowed squabbles and conflicts to be set aside and the tribal units to come together. Within the context of the Trucial States, this hidden capacity to coalesce and to act in concert was to prove a key factor, first in the career of Shaikh Zayid the Great and, more recently, in that of his namesake, Shaikh Zayid Bin Sultan.

This concept of the 'successful shaikh' was rooted in a common social understanding among Arab tribes. All tribesmen were deeply imbued with the concept of honor and such phrases came easily to their lips. The pursuit of honor and the fear of losing honor lay at the root of most tribal conflicts. The social scientist Bichr Farès went so far as to say that it was these elements of honor that 'constituted' Arab society.[61] The successful shaikh could gain and sustain his authority only if his people freely and honorably gave him their respect and loyalty. He provided support for them and their families, protection over their territory and wise leadership. His authority was essentially political, based not on force but on a process of exchange. This was the matrix within which all leaders in the Gulf had to function.

Yet, beyond the social and political setting in which Arab tribes were situated and governed, geographical considerations also had a primary importance. Just as ideas of honor are central to tribal relationships, so too were issues of territory. For example, the *de facto* 'boundaries' of the tribe's territory were of great importance, as they often related directly to whether a tribe was at war or peace with its neighbors. Among those who lived in the harsh world of the desert, 'honor' and 'territory' defined the boundaries of their existence.

The role of the shaikh or tribal leader was fundamental. He ruled by consent, although there were many stories of tribesmen, who were sturdy individualists, disputing with their leader in the *majlis*.[62] As such, these relationships were complex and essentially reciprocal. Ultimately, the shaikh was loyal to his people and they to him. He was expected to be generous and act constantly on their behalf, even if it were to his detriment. In return, they gave him their allegiance, to the extent of going to war at his command and even of sacrificing their lives at his behest. But their loyalty was ultimately conditional on the shaikh fulfilling his part of the customary bargain. While the role of the shaikh was not hereditary, as in the case of the Bani Yas, often a tribe accepted that one family or sub-clan would provide their leader. In the case of the Bani Yas, this was the Al Nahyan. Yet, if a shaikh did not justify his people's support, they would replace him with another member of his kin. Thus, in choosing that leader both the chosen shaikh and his kin were always aware that the tribe's loyalty was contingent on success, and all recognized that a weak or ineffective leader could jeopardize a system of alliances built up over generations.

The Bani Yas polity was based upon a complex network of relationships based on honor rather than power gained by coercion. As no shaikh could compel his people if they refused to accept his leadership, they would simply leave him and either become independent or join another tribe. Equally, no tribesman to whom his shaikh had behaved fairly and generously could legitimately desert him in time of need. These ethics were born in the unyielding conditions of the desert, where life or death depended more on instinct and trust than on persuasion and coercion. Not, of course, that debate was alien to the desert Arab; in fact, the reverse was true. However, the place for debate was in the camp, in the *majlis*, or in poetic contests. On a journey in the desert, on a raid, or in battle, argument was stilled. Yet, at its very base, all these relationships were rooted in mutual confidence, and it was this bond of trust that secured Shaikh Zayid's authority among the people.[63]

Respected men of honor, such as Zayid the Great, frequently did not deliver formal decisions so much as observations, their judgments often sagacious rather than legalistic. Their oratory, apparently vague and general, would not seem ambiguous to their listeners. Uppermost in such judgments was the desire to preserve the honor and dignity of all those involved. Men of honor, universally respected, emerged rarely. Often generations would pass without such a personality appearing among the tribes. However, this was the model agreed by all as the best method of resolving problems, both of politics and human relationships, recognizing that there was no clear boundary between the two.

Among the most powerful components of Shaikh Zayid Bin Sultan's heritage, then, were the extreme rigors imposed by a harsh environment, a life of grinding desert poverty and a culture based on a complex structure of honor. Yet, he was equally the inheritor of the tradition of the "versatile tribesman," a culture of adaption that responded to shifts and changes in circumstance. This was the background on which his life would be inscribed. The form that this life would take was not determined, save by God. However, the formative influence of his origins and surroundings has been powerful, for in learning to use the knowledge gleaned from them, he became elevated to that cherished 'position of honor' in the Arab world.

Therefore, Shaikh Zayid Bin Sultan has been successful primarily because of his skills and talents, but these have a particular social context. He matches in every aspect the traditional qualities associated with a great leader. He is esteemed, according to the standards of the tribe, for his qualities of wisdom, patience, respect for others and putting the interests of the people before his own. The tribesmen laud his courage and bravery while appreciating his sagacity and forethought. They respect him and give him their loyalty. This fundamental relationship of mutual trust between the ruler and the ruled lies at the heart of the Arab tribal system.

Loyalty was the principle on which the whole notion of tribal honor was founded. It extended beyond Shaikh Zayid's own tribe and allies, providing a common bond with tribes other than his own. They recognized that he kept his promises and took care of his people, and they judged, correctly, that he would also behave honorably towards them. Neighboring tribes respected him as a man of power for his defense of his people's land. They recognized him as a leader willing to use his resources for the benefit of the people, a trait that characterizes the ideal chief.

However, Shaikh Zayid's greatest asset has been his refusal to be bound by the residue of the past and by defunct custom. He is perceptive in his judgment, knowing when to follow a traditional path; but he also has the intuitive sense to know when he should break new ground, thus adapting flexibly to the demands of the moment. The Arabian tribe was undoubtedly the *fons et origo* of his character, yet he also successfully transcended its limitations.

CHAPTER
2

A Turbulent Era

In late October 1914, any observer on the tip of Cape Musandam might have noticed a large flotilla of warships and naval transports entering the Strait of Hormuz, heading north into the Arabian Gulf. By October 23, the largest military presence ever deployed by a European power lay at anchor in the Lower Gulf.[1] This was not the first time that the Europeans had intervened on a massive scale in the region. Less than a century before, in November 1819, a large force had arrived in the Gulf and set out to overawe all the Rulers along the coast. From that expedition, the first treaty between Britain and the Rulers of the region emerged in January 1820, which set the political pattern for a relationship that would endure for 150 years.

The motives that impelled both expeditions were the same—economic and geopolitical. Trade in the Arabian Gulf can be traced back over five millennia, possibly longer, constituting perhaps the longest continuous record of sustained commercial links in human history.[2] Over this long period, the waterway has provided an artery for the flow of both goods and communication between East and West. As a result, the peoples who lived along its shores were always in contact with the world beyond their immediate region. This long history of economic and cultural connections antedated the start of sustained Western contact through the visits of Portuguese traders in the sixteenth century. Before that, the states in the East were already well aware of the importance of the Gulf. For example, a large Chinese naval fleet visited the area in the fifteenth century, and records of Arab traders in the great commercial centers of India and Indonesia predate this.[3]

Furthermore, contact between Arabia and the world, both eastward and westward, came by land as well as by sea. The maritime routes from the head of the Gulf to India and points beyond are well known. However, the inland routes were of considerable importance both for the local inhabitants and in terms of long-distance trade. Inland locations like al Ain emerged as centers of exchange for desert travelers, points where food and water were available and commodities could be traded. Al Ain was the crossroads that led west to Abu Dhabi, east to the Batinah coast and, skirting the desert, south towards Dhufar and the Arabian Sea. This network of overland connections was less obvious than the maritime traffic of the Indian Ocean, which comprised large trading dhows that could be found in all the major ports.[4] Nor were there the long caravans of camels that traversed central Arabia heading north towards the Mediterranean. Nonetheless, the trade links existed and goods moved back and forth across southeastern Arabia. Thus, the states that later formed the United Arab Emirates, Abu Dhabi in particular, were never completely insulated from outside influences. Since at least the sixteenth century, powerful external pressures – whether from Iran, the East, inner Arabia, or the West – have been a constant factor in the Gulf equation.[5]

For the outsider, it was never easy to comprehend the local political and social dynamics. Europeans frequently misinterpreted pragmatic political or economic decisions for something that was entirely colored by ethnic or sectarian differences. They mistook the mantle and phraseology of religion for the whole truth, failing to comprehend the underlying realities. Furthermore, part of the tradition of the region was a cautious approach to the motives and intentions of both allies and enemies, with the defense and welfare of family and tribe constituting the dominant forces. Consequently, tribal politics possessed a complexity and subtlety that often deceived outsiders, who expected something much less sophisticated. In the case of the Bani Yas, tribal politics had two underlying and sometimes contradictory tendencies—the desire of the participants to maintain independence and a parallel desire to collaborate and create alliances. The task of the tribal shaikh was to manage these tendencies while ensuring a coherent political direction.

The Role of the Bani Yas

In Chapter 1, the social and cultural characteristics of the Bani Yas were described in some detail but there was little discussion on how these attributes have played a role within the context of the region's history. A conflict within Oman, involving all the tribes from the Omani highlands to the shores of the Gulf, set the pattern of life in southeast Arabia. What began in 1718 as a struggle for power and authority in Oman led to a fundamental tribal division that still had its echoes two centuries later. In a structure where honor played such a crucial role in determining social relationships, quarrels that were political in nature could all too easily be presented as more complex struggles. The 'civil war' between the two groups later known as the Hinawi and Ghafiri – after the Bani Hina and the Bani Ghafir, the centers of the two rival constellations – acquired the characteristics of a classic feud based on concepts of honor.[6]

There have been few tribal conflicts in Arabia so destructive and long lasting in their effects.[7] This struggle galvanized Inner Oman throughout the remainder of the eighteenth and into the nineteenth century. Moreover, the tribal polities bordering the Gulf – which after 1820 was usually referred to as the Trucial Coast by the British – soon became embroiled in a quarrel not of their making. Hinawi or Ghafiri labels became attached to antagonisms that had little to do with the struggle beyond the mountains. However, the underlying patterns described above conditioned the structure of collaboration and alliances even into the twentieth century:

> Since the Civil War each tribe has been identified as being either Ghāfiri or Hināwi, and there are only a very few cases of a tribe changing sides. Until this very day every local tribesman of the UAE, too, knows which faction his tribe belongs to and usually

also knows where most of the important tribes between Ra's
Musandam and Dhufār stand. On innumerable occasions since
the middle of the 18th century the forming of alliances and the
outcome of disputes among the tribes of the Trucial States... have
been decisively influenced by the division of the land into the
Ghāfiri and Hināwi groupings.[8]

The division polarized the tribes far beyond those immediately involved
in the rivalry, and resulted in a situation in which 'my enemy's enemy is
my friend.'[9]

In broad geographical terms, most of the lands to the north of
the Dubai creek and in the mountains were dominated by the Ghafiri,
while the Hinawi were powerful in all the arid lands to the south
and west of the Hajar range.[10] It is important to note that an ethnic
dimension to the conflict existed initially, with the Hinawi largely
attracting the support of the Yamani/Qahtani tribes who had formed the
first wave of conquest from the southwest, and the Ghafiri appealing to
the Nizari/'Adnani tribes, which had entered Oman from central and
northeastern Arabia. However, the two groups did not ultimately align
themselves purely on a tribal or sectarian base. Instead, political and
economic factors proved to be the main reasons for the division. Thus, in
each group, one could find tribes of Yamani and Nizari origin in alliance
and adherents of both Sunni and Ibadi approaches to Islam.[11] Largely for
geopolitical reasons, the Bani Yas were Hinawi, as were their main tribal
allies, the Al 'Awamir, the Al Manasir and later the Al Dhawahir.[12]

The polarization implicit in the Hinawi–Ghafiri struggle
undermined the traditional self-regulating mechanism of compromise
that existed within Gulf society. However, the need for self-protection
also helped to consolidate group identity. The growth of the Bani Yas
polity occurred within the chaos and confusion generated by the
difficult circumstances and tribal wars in the region. The first marked
extension of tribal power came in 1761 with the occupation of Abu
Dhabi island, after which successive Bani Yas groups started moving
between Liwa and Abu Dhabi.[13]

There are several versions of how the town of Abu Dhabi –
literally the 'father of the gazelle'[14] – was founded. One version claims

that a shaikh or tribesman of the Al Nahyan, the leading family of the Bani Yas, noticed a gazelle drinking from a source of fresh water on one of the barren islands fringing the Gulf.[15] Another story is that an Al Nahyan hunter, chasing a gazelle, caught it and then sought a water hole to quench his thirst. He discovered one, only to find that it was dry. Eventually, both the hunter and the gazelle died of thirst.[16] Yet, there is a deeper significance attached to this legend. To those well-versed in the interpretation of myths, the stories share a common theme —the vital importance of water to a desert people. The underlying message of the first version is that water brings life while the antithetical version highlights the fact that without water there can be no life. Ultimately, the town of Abu Dhabi could only exist and flourish because of the availability of water, brackish but potable. As such, water lies at the heart of the founding myth common to the Al Nahyan. In the twentieth century, Shaikh Zayid Bin Sultan created a new version of the story by bringing fresh, clean and sweet water all the way from the mountains to Abu Dhabi. The profound symbolism, as well as the practical importance, of this act requires no interpretation.

The creation of the settlement at Abu Dhabi in 1761 gave the Al Nahyan access to the sea and to new marine resources that could be exploited by fishing and pearling. Dalma island, under the control of the Bani Yas, soon became a center for such trade. While some members of the Bani Yas were to settle permanently on Abu Dhabi island as early as the reign of Shaikh Diyab Bin 'Isa (c.1783–1793), it was not until the rule of Shaikh Shakhbut Bin Diyab (1793–1816) that the seat of government was transferred from al Mariyah in Liwa to Abu Dhabi. On the barren island of Abu Dhabi, the only substantial buildings in the early settlement were the large al Husn fort on the island, which was built in 1795, and the stone tower built in 1798 that protected the fort from the mainland at al Maqta. The fishermen and pearlers lived in *barasti* dwellings under the protection of the tower and the fort. Due to the scarcity of resources, the settlement could only support a limited number of people.

After Abu Dhabi, the Bani Yas quickly extended their dominion over many other islands and long stretches of the coastline. With their strength and wealth growing apace, the Al Nahyan soon found themselves leaders of a tribe that was vigorously expanding both inland and along the coast. This process was first initiated by Shaikh Shakhbut Bin Diyab and continued by his sons, in particular Shaikh Tahnun Bin Shakhbut (1818–1833) and Shaikh Sa'id Bin Tahnun (1845–1855). Led by the Al Nahyan, the Bani Yas expanded their hold on the Abu Dhabi coast as well as over the inland settlements of Liwa and al Ain.

Shaikh Shakhbut Bin Diyab became leader of the Bani Yas in 1793 following the death of his father, Shaikh Diyab Bin 'Isa, and consolidated Bani Yas authority both inland and on the coast.[17] The building of the fortifications at Abu Dhabi was a prudential move to deter the growing threat of raiders from the west. Approximately three decades after the Bani Yas extended their domain to Abu Dhabi island, parties of Wahhabi raiders began to infiltrate al Dhafrah. As the Wahhabi raiding parties grew in number and power, Shaikh Shakhbut found that he did not have the resources necessary to protect all the inland settlements. Instead, the Bani Yas rallied to expel the invaders.[18] In May 1848, his grandson Shaikh Sa'id Bin Tahnun summoned the Al Nahyan tribesmen and their allies to drive out the Najd raiders from the bases they had occupied around al Ain.[19] Still, the frequency of the attacks ebbed and flowed. As detailed below, it was not until 1869 that his grandson, Shaikh Zayid Bin Khalifa, finally expelled the last of the raiding parties.

By 1816, Shaikh Shakhbut Bin Diyab had led the Bani Yas for 23 difficult and challenging years. Thus, when his elder son Muhammad took over from him in that year, it seemed he had little desire left to rule. Accorded due respect by his son, he simply retired from office. Although Shaikh Shakhbut Bin Diyab continued to retain the authority and standing that stemmed from being the leader of the tribe, he left the exercise of power to his son. The long career of Shaikh Shakhbut illustrates the political sophistication of the tribal system. In a pattern repeated at intervals in the nineteenth century, a leader could withdraw from political contention and live in complete security.[20] Alternatively, he could move to another town or live under the protection of another tribe without fear of reprisals. Both tradition and self-preservation underlined the need to avoid a rift or any insult to tribal honor.

From the outset, it seems clear that Shaikh Shakhbut did not wish to interfere with the rule of his son Muhammad, although there can be no doubt about his continuing influence. He established himself at al Ain, building the al Miraijib fort and nurturing the connection with the Al Dhawahir that would eventually lead them into a long-standing alliance with the Bani Yas. However, two years after his withdrawal, in 1818, his energetic younger son Tahnun, exiled under his brother, returned to restore his father's power and to rule with him. Muhammad, in turn, went into exile, leaving Shakhbut and Tahnun to rule jointly. In a familiar pattern, Shaikh Tahnun exercised power while his father remained a figure of authority behind the scenes as an advisor and head of the ruling family.[21]

Under Shaikh Tahnun's dynamic rule, the wealth and strength of the town of Abu Dhabi grew enormously. His energy was prodigious. One report described him as "a patriotic leader, fond of war-like sports and who excels in fighting techniques. He is robust and is renowned for his bravery."[22] Throughout, Shaikh Shakhbut remained a notable influence in the background. The peace treaty of January 1820, signed with the British, was drawn up in the name of Shaikh Shakhbut as the established Ruler. This pattern of dual rule, with Shaikh Tahnun as the active leader, was to continue for 15 years.

In 1833, Shaikh Shakhbut persuaded Shaikh Tahnun to permit two of Shakhbut's younger sons, Khalifa and Sultan, whom Shaikh Tahnun had banished from Abu Dhabi to return. This decision was to have unforeseen consequences. Within a few months, they had jointly overthrown their brother, with Khalifa taking over as the head of the tribe. He led the Bani Yas from 1833 to 1845. It seems odd, in retrospect, that they could overthrow a successful ruler with such ease, and gain the support of the family in doing so. Yet, in practice, any strong ruler made enemies. Factionalism prevailed, and when one ruler replaced another, the family of the deposed ruler became a likely focus for future dissent and subversion of authority.

Meanwhile, Shaikh Shakhbut, still the doyen of the Bani Yas, entered into yet another joint arrangement with his sons. By this time, he had played a pivotal role in Abu Dhabi for more than 40 years. He regularly intervened in important matters such as settling the conflict between Abu Dhabi and the Qawasim shaikhs and recognizing Dubai's independent status in June 1834.[23] However, his influence was waning. On May 21, 1835, it was only as Personal Representative of Shaikh Khalifa – who was described as the leader of the Bani Yas – that he signed the maritime truce with the British.[24] This suggests not only that he had conceded his full authority over the Bani Yas to his son Khalifa but also that he was still active and must have died at some point after the signature of the treaty, and not in 1833, as is often suggested. While there is no record of exactly when he died, it was before 1845, when Shaikh Tahnun's son Sa'id came to power, after a coup which overthrew his uncles Khalifa and Sultan in much the same way that they had ended his father's rule.[25]

Shaikh Khalifa Bin Shakhbut was, like his brother Tahnun, a Ruler of high quality, as the account by Lieutenant H.F. Disbrowe noted:

> From that time to the present (A.D. 1833 to July 1845) he remained at the head of the tribe, and by his gallantry, firmness and prudence, raised it to be one of the most powerful of the maritime and inland communities of the…Gulf. He moreover ever showed himself disposed to cultivate a good understanding with the British government, and strove, not without success, to restrain his people and dependents from committing irregularities at sea.[26]

A strong ruler, like Shaikh Tahnun or Shaikh Khalifa, who governed with a firm hand, always aroused enmity in a system in which central control was traditionally weak or non-existent. The success and survival of Shaikh Shakhbut, who was also a strong Ruler, was indicative of the need to persuade as well as to command. The Bani Yas political system required enormously skillful management if it was to avoid twin perils—paralysis, where the ruler did nothing, or factional chaos, if he attempted too much and alienated powerful elements within the family and the tribe.

If nothing else, the events of 1845 and earlier years demonstrated the need for a strong but flexible ruler. The people of Abu Dhabi were tired of chaos and disorder and sought an extended period of stability. Such were the circumstances when the son of Shaikh Tahnun, Sa'id Bin Tahnun, accepted the role of Ruler with the support of the Al Nahyan. Shaikh Sa'id was careful not to return from exile to Abu Dhabi until he had secured this public acceptance.

> In due course, Shaikh Syud [Sa'id] arrived, and finding himself well received by the majority of the Beniyas Tribe, and also that he was supported by the Resident, who had been studiously watching the course of events, and now hastened to give all the moral aid in his power to ensure the establishment in authority of the lawful chief, he at once placed himself at the head of affairs, and was speedily recognised by the whole of the Beniyas as their true and rightful chief.[27]

For a decade, Shaikh Sa'id was a very successful Ruler, until he faced an unexpected crisis and ultimately failed in the political balancing act.

> In 1855, Shaykh Sa'īd bin Ṭaḥnūn of Abu Dhabi was confronted with a difficult decision. A tribal elder killed his own brother. Was Shaykh Sa'īd to punish him? People in Abu Dhabi urged against it…he disregarded the advice he had been offered and killed the offender. This so outraged people in Abu Dhabi that the whole population rose up against Sa'īd, who had to flee the country and was killed the next year while trying to regain control.[28]

As in 1845, the will of the people was a determining factor in the selection of the new Ruler. If a ruler lost the confidence of the people, then he could not hold on to power. Sometimes the transfer of power was by force, sometimes, as with Shaikh Shakhbut Bin Diyab, an accommodation was made that allowed power to shift by peaceful means. While British officers at the time tended to focus largely upon the violent shifts of power, it is important to recognize that the use of force actually represented a failure within the system. The desired outcome was a change of authority by non-violent means, with the new Ruler being chosen by the Al Nahyan from among their number on behalf of the Bani Yas as a whole. This process led in 1855 to the selection of the cousin of Shaikh Sa'id, Shaikh Zayid Bin Khalifa, as the next Ruler. Shaikh Zayid Bin Khalifa (1855–1909), like his predecessor, came to power from exile, which had kept him secure from the intrigues of Abu Dhabi.[29] As the son of Shaikh Khalifa Bin Shakhbut, he had many allies within the ruling family who had memories of his father's rule. Still, he refused to accept the offer until it was clear that it had the support of the family as a whole.

The Rule of Shaikh Zayid Bin Khalifa

The problems and pressures which confronted any Bani Yas leader demanded qualities of a high order. The Ruler of Abu Dhabi needed simultaneously to preserve – and even extend – his authority without alienating any of the individualistic and freedom-loving tribes of the area. In retrospect, Abu Dhabi was fortunate in having a succession of competent and authoritative Rulers for most of its history. From the late eighteenth century, two in particular, Shaikh Shakhbut Bin Diyab and Shaikh Zayid Bin Khalifa, possessed the unique combination of qualities that allowed them to survive and succeed. Both mastered the complexities of the Bani Yas political system and achieved a lasting and fruitful period of rule.[30] Since the First World War, only Shaikh Zayid Bin Sultan has demonstrated the same subtle blend of skills that are the prerequisites for true and enduring success.[31]

The Domestic and Regional Context

The selection of Shaikh Zayid Bin Khalifa in 1855 as Shaikh of the Bani Yas elevated a young man, barely in his twenties, to a position of authority at a most critical moment.[32] The young Shaikh Zayid recognized from his early days as Ruler that he needed to retain the support and allegiance not only of his immediate family, but also of his tribe and allies. He saw clearly that no tribal leader could disregard the interest of his people.[33] It was his particular political genius that allowed him to retain the loyalty of his people for over 50 years and to consolidate the position of Abu Dhabi as the most powerful and effective emirate in the region.

The central task that he faced was the threat to the territorial integrity of Abu Dhabi. Any leader was expected to protect the territory of his people and their allies. A ruler gained in stature by extending his territory and increasing the number of tribesmen who accepted his leadership. In 1855, there were challenges on both fronts. In this context, his predecessors – with the exception of Shaikh Shakhbut Bin Diyab – might be considered 'daring fighters' rather than 'prudent and successful chiefs.'[34] The records are full of their valor but, taken as a whole, they lacked the political sagacity of Shaikh Zayid. While he too was a warrior of renown, he used war as a last resort rather than a first option.[35]

Shaikh Zayid Bin Khalifa, whom history knows better as 'Zayid the Great,' also recognized a new but essential fact—that the nature of politics within the Gulf was changing. The old antagonisms had lost their meaning. The northern Qawasmi emirates now sought the support and friendship of Abu Dhabi although they had earlier opposed the Bani Yas.[36] The Saudi state in Najd had collapsed under joint pressure from the Ottomans and the Al Rashid of Ha'il.[37] In 1869, the common interest of the Imam in Oman and the Ruler of Abu Dhabi led to a joint expedition to clear the al Ain area of Wahhabi infiltrators who had entered the oasis from the west in 1853.

As Shaikh Zayid the Great's reputation grew, his connections with distant Arab rulers became more extensive. In 1880, during the Hajj, he met the Sharif of Mecca and formed a bond of mutual interest.[38] He also sent his son to Bahrain to consolidate the traditionally amicable relations between the Al Khalifa and the Al Nahyan.[39] This policy of rapprochement had a number of aspects. First, Shaikh Zayid the Great sought to reduce the unnecessary tensions among customary enemies. Traditional war was a function of the system of honor, and he was renowned as a great warrior. However, the bitterness and bloodthirstiness that had crept into the conduct of war with the Hinawi–Ghafiri struggle was steadily diminishing. Instead, he came to be seen as a peacemaker[40] within the area, and other rulers and tribal shaikhs turned to him for the maintenance of order or the settlement of disputes.[41] One direct result was that in 1888, the Sultan of Muscat entrusted Zayid the Great with the keeping of the peace in the areas under his suzerainty close to al Ain.[42] Zayid the Great's success in taking control of the hinterland is evident from the Political Resident, Major Percy Cox's report of his visit in 1905. The Resident, who visited the oasis complex for the first time in five years observed:

> …a considerable extension of Sheikh Zaeed's domination in the oasis, entirely enveloping the Dhowahir and extending now even to the Naeem, the chief Ghafiri element, whose Sheikhs are indeed of no personality and could no doubt be absorbed at once, but Sheikh Zaeed's policy is evidently one of pacific absorption, in which he has certainly had a considerable measure of success…[43]

Second, Shaikh Zayid the Great succeeded in consolidating his base among the tribes, by employing both persuasion and force. To oppose him was to risk bringing retribution upon the tribe, while to support him brought security, wealth and often direct financial subsidy.[44]

Third, he understood an essential equation in the tribal system— that political power depended to a large degree upon a ruler's wealth and his capacity to reward loyalty. Therefore, he sought to advance the economic position of the Bani Yas alliance. By the 1890s, Abu Dhabi dominated the pearl trade with more than 410 boats, and the Shaikh enjoyed increasing revenues.[45] As a result, the town itself continued to grow, with the population reaching close to 6,000 by the year 1907. The settlements at al Ain, which were a matter of particular concern to Zayid the Great, also expanded.[46]

The International Context

The international context within which Zayid the Great built up the power and influence of Abu Dhabi also changed dramatically over the course of his rule. By 1855, the political equation of the Trucial

Coast included a new element—the British. From the first treaties for maritime security in 1820, which were renewed annually until 1843 when a ten-year maritime truce was agreed, the British had begun to play an increasing role in the region. In 1823, the first local Arab Residency Agent had been appointed in Sharjah to send information to the Resident in Bushire.[47] While the British officers visiting the local Rulers stressed that Britain's sole interest was in maintaining maritime peace and freedom of trade, the Rulers perceived Britain as having wider ambitions within their territories.[48] They had reason for their suspicions. For example, the Treaty of Peace in Perpetuity, which all the Rulers accepted in 1853, included a new clause in addition to those strictly relevant to a 'perfect maritime truce.' For the first time, a treaty between Britain and the Arab states enunciated the principle that "the maintenance of the peace now concluded amongst us shall be watched over by the British government…"[49] The words "watched over" expressed a new concept, and one that lent itself to limitless extension. This enabled the British authorities to assume an active rather than a merely responsive role for themselves in the region.

This agreement, which Shaikh Zayid Bin Khalifa had inherited, led to a number of clashes with the British authorities. Over time, however, he came to realize that he could gain more from developing a good relationship with the British than by opposing them.[50] It should be stated that, from the outset, the British regarded Abu Dhabi in a favorable light. The Bani Yas had not been a target of the expedition of 1819, and they had been admitted in 1820 to the treaty system rather than forced to comply with the terms laid down by the British authorities in India.[51] As a result, there are strong indications that after a period of conflict with the British, Zayid the Great recognized the potential for managing his relationship with the British authorities in the Gulf.[52] He saw that with their aid, some of the long-standing problems relating to tribal authority and territory could be resolved. He adroitly turned this relationship to the advantage of Abu Dhabi, a fact that the British authorities grudgingly recognized but could not undermine. As Cox observed in 1906, "…it must be admitted that his [Zayid the Great's] influence among those whom he controls is on the side of law and order so long as it is compatible with his own undisputed supremacy."[53]

Zayid the Great understood the essential political principle embodied in the treaty system. The British did not want the trouble and expense of governing vast areas of Arabian desert, which could only be controlled by troops on the ground. They preferred the more effective 'gunboat diplomacy' that achieved a measure of influence at a low cost. This worked to the benefit of his people. Abu Dhabi was heavily engaged in pearling, but unlike the Qawasim tribes to the north, the Bani Yas were essentially a land power.[54] Britain remained interested primarily in preserving a free flow of maritime trade and was for the most part content to leave tribal rivalries in the hinterland to follow their own course, without intervention.[55] This strategy worked in favor of Abu Dhabi, which managed to build its economic and military capabilities without being involved in any conflict with Britain.

Thus, from the 1870s, Shaikh Zayid began to use the Trucial system to his advantage. He invoked it to resolve the recurring problem of the Al Qubaisat, who once again had left to establish themselves independently at Khur al 'Udaid, under the protection of the Ruler of Qatar.[56] He decided to place the problem firmly in the hands of the British authorities. While his pearling boats and other vessels were being harassed by the Al Qubaisat in violation of the treaty, Shaikh Zayid pointed out the contradiction that the same treaty prevented him from disciplining his dissident tribesmen. Furthermore, as their Shaikh, the Resident would hold him responsible for their actions. Shaikh Zayid argued this anomaly persuasively in letter after letter to the Resident, and the justice of his case within the logic of the Trucial system was self-evident. The Resident, who in 1869 had imposed sanctions on Abu Dhabi for taking military action against Qatar, now became a strong supporter of Shaikh Zayid's position. For the next ten years (1869–1879), the British authorities in the Gulf stood behind Shaikh Zayid over Khur al 'Udaid, even when the Foreign Office in London pressured them to withdraw their support.[57] In April 1878, Shaikh Zayid and his men, accompanied by the Resident and the warship *HMS Teazer*, sailed to Khur al 'Udaid. Finding the settlement empty, as the Al Qubaisat had fled, and rendering it uninhabitable, the party then proceeded to locate the members of the tribe. Far from being vengeful, the Shaikh invited the Al Qubaisat to return to Abu Dhabi. At this point, it seemed that they "wished to go," and that it was actually the Qatari Ruler who had been trying to prevent their departure. Shaikh Zayid immediately sent boats for them, and when all the dissident tribesmen returned to Abu Dhabi, they found that they "were welcomed and well treated by their Chief." [58]

Shaikh Zayid the Great had discovered how to manage the British to his advantage. He could enlist British support because he could thereby guarantee the maritime peace. The benefits were palpable. By patient diplomacy, supported by the authority of British officials, the breakaway factions of the Bani Yas were thus brought back into allegiance. The integrity of the tribe was restored. As on previous occasions, the defectors were not punished but welcomed instead. The Ruler of Abu Dhabi made it clear that he valued all his tribesmen and that in his view the unity of the tribe was a primary objective.

In this way, over a period of almost 40 years, Zayid the Great found a means of working collaboratively with the British officials in the Gulf, who quickly learned to respect his political skill. [59] He established relationships of mutual respect with successive Political Residents, who regarded him as a man of his word, "the doyen of the Trucial Chiefs" of the Gulf. [60] They were content that he should develop the Al Nahyan role and interest in al Ain after 1869, a move that was seen as a force for stability on an otherwise turbulent frontier. [61] The treaty relationship, based on the British preoccupation with maritime 'piracy' still prohibited any kind of warlike activity at sea. At the same time, the British were more relaxed over military activity on land, seeing it merely as a traditional exercise of desert warfare. This worked to the benefit of Zayid the Great, for his expanding emirate of Abu Dhabi was, as stated before, essentially a land power.

It was not until the latter part of Zayid the Great's rule that the nature of the relationship with the British began to undergo a qualitative transition. Beginning in the 1870s, the influence of Britain within the region, although secured by treaties with the Rulers, was being challenged by the increasing attention paid to the area by the Ottoman authorities, especially after their occupation of al Hasa in 1871. Other challenges stemmed from Russian involvement in Iran and French intrigues in Muscat.[62] Thus, the last years of the nineteenth century saw the pressure for a deeper British involvement increase sharply.[63] The 'Exclusive Treaty' of March 6, 1892 signed between the British and the Rulers of the Trucial Coast drastically curtailed the rights of the local Rulers, who signed away their right to correspond with any government other than Britain, to allow any non-local to reside in their domains without British sanction, or to "cede, sell, mortgage or otherwise give for occupation" any part of their territory save to the British government.[64]

This was not the end to new demands. In general, the British government was beginning to alter the basis of its relationship with the Rulers of the Gulf, becoming steadily more demanding and imperious.[65] Before he took up office as the new Viceroy of India in 1899, Lord Curzon had traveled in Persia and believed he had acquired an instinctive understanding for the geopolitics of the Gulf. In November 1898, he wrote, "Above all, it seems to me important that the...Gulf should not be allowed to become an arena of international rivalry."[66] What he meant by this is clear from both private and secret correspondence —the British intended to dominate the Gulf, by one means or another, keeping all other powers at bay. This meant that they would encroach increasingly on the sovereign rights and privileges of the local Rulers.

There had been a growing belief in governmental circles that Britain should exert more power in the Gulf, as there was a strong new perception of constantly increasing external threats to British power in the region. The issue was formally debated in Parliament, and as a result there was pressure from both London and the British authorities in India to show other powers – the Ottomans, Persia, Russia, Germany, France[67] – that the Gulf formed an intrinsic part of the 'Indian frontier:' "The moment we have a foreign Power acting in the...Gulf we at once make a great break in that long defensive position that, extending from the English Channel to India and the Far East...if we allow another Power to plant itself down in the...Gulf that position is broken."[68]

The first visit by a Viceroy of India to the Gulf in November and December 1903 thus marked the definitive shift in British political attitudes. Thereafter, the subtle balance in the relationship between Britain and the local Rulers began to alter irrevocably. On November 21, 1903, the Viceroy, Lord Curzon, and his flotilla of warships anchored off Sharjah and he held a formal meeting aboard the cruiser *HMS Argonaut* attended by all the Rulers of the region and their sons.[69] Curzon spoke warmly of the role played by the British and the long heritage of friendship. He only hinted at the future change in the relationship, talking of the British as the constituted guardian of the "inter-tribal peace" and the "overlords and protectors" of the Rulers of the Gulf.[70] On November 23, Curzon then laid out the new policy: "[W]e could not approve of one independent Chief attacking another Chief by land, simply because he was not permitted to do it by sea, and thus evade the spirit of his treaty obligations."[71]

In the past, the British authorities had honored the precise and limited declaration of the earlier treaties. Now, they were venturing into new and undefined territory with Curzon's new concept of the "spirit of the treaty obligations."[72] What Curzon failed to mention – or possibly recognize – was that in practice the "condition of affairs so peaceful and secure," as he put it, had resulted from allowing the intrinsic political mechanisms of the region to work without hindrance.[73] Peace had been maintained because a strong and capable Ruler was perceived as a man of power by the people of the region, and not because of any previous British policies.

The new British policy was, as Curzon knew, a strategy involving high risk, which stemmed not from any desire to improve the conditions of the people in the region but from the need to enhance the strategic position of the United Kingdom.[74] This firmer and more determined British rule was to be the main means through which social stability would be maintained and advanced. Yet, the British made no greater commitment to the area, took on no additional obligations, and added nothing to the local finances, administration or the local economy. It was conveniently assumed that the increased power came without entailing greater responsibilities. In the process, British policies began to erode the base of the local system of control that was embodied in the rule of Zayid the Great. Although there had been minor clashes from the mid-1890s, it was after Curzon's visit that the British began to assume an increasingly peremptory tone in their dealings with him.

Zayid's very success had exposed an essential ambiguity in the British structure of indirect control in the Gulf. On the one hand, they wished to spend as little as possible to support their role in the region. A later Political Resident, T.C. Fowle, characterized the system as being run "with a handful of officials … without the payment of a single rupee of subsidy, or the upkeep (on our part) of a single soldier, policeman or levy…"[75] On the other hand, the British wanted, after Curzon, to achieve a degree of control only compatible with a much greater investment of manpower and money. The peace along the Trucial Coast and inland was kept not because of any chimerical reverence for British authority but because Zayid the Great used his hard-won power to maintain it on the ground. While the British did not have to support a "single soldier, policeman or levy," he did so, as the only means to secure good order within the tribal structure. This role initially won grudging respect from the British authorities, but also became an increasing cause of antagonism towards him. The British were content to accept the benefit that his power provided, but they also regarded him as too powerful and, therefore, a potential threat.[76]

Pressure increased on Zayid the Great, as the old politics of latitude was gradually replaced by the more imperious style. In most cases, it was manifest in a series of testy incidents. For example, in 1900, he requested the Resident's permission to adopt a new flag to be flown on his vessels. In 1820, the British had laid down patterns based on the Qawasim colors, then the strongest tribe of the region. Eighty years later, this was no longer true, and Shaikh Zayid wanted a flag that reflected the status of the Bani Yas. The regulations had never been enforced, and by 1900 the original designs were virtually unknown. Still, the Resident denied the request and, after more than two generations of disuse, sought to enforce the 1820 regulations. This included sending regulations to all the Rulers, with copies of the original design, since no one was entirely sure what precise form the 'standard pattern' had taken. Where once the British had interpreted the treaty regulations flexibly, they now seemed bent on enforcing them rigidly.[77]

As a result, from the late 1890s, the good relations maintained earlier were undermined. Several other incidents marked this decline in mutual understanding. In 1895, Zayid the Great had informed the Resident and received his endorsement of an agreement with the inhabitants of the island of Zura for Zayid the Great to establish a base and depot for provisions on their island. Zura was a sandy tract in the sea between Ajman and Hamriyah. However, when in 1897, Zayid the Great's father-in-law, Sultan Bin Nasser Al Suwaidi, sought the Resident's permission to move there, the British authorities procrastinated. By 1898, Al Suwaidi, who was known as a man of peace and a rich trader in pearls, was reluctant to delay his move any longer. With the Shaikh of Ajman's agreement, he began to build his settlement on the island, under the protection of Zayid the Great. On October 8, 1900 the British authorities suddenly instructed Zayid the Great to put a stop to the building work, on the grounds that it upset the political balance in the area. The following February, he wrote to the Resident, expressing his surprise at the sudden change of attitude and saying that he had not been accustomed to such treatment from the British.[78] The dispute continued, with numerous moments of crisis and attempts at settlement until 1905, when the new Acting Political Resident Major Percy Cox, visited the island and decided that the settlement should, in effect, be permanently prohibited.[79]

Other events were to follow. In 1906, after the debacle over Zura, in another unexpected reverse from the Political Resident, Major Cox decided to intervene against Shaikh Zayid the Great and the majority of the other Rulers over an internal dispute with one of the tribes.[80] The Shaikh wrote courteously to Cox, stressing his inability to oppose the Resident's wishes, but also adding that the terms of the settlement were not those he had hoped for. Meanwhile, the Resident had pointed with some pride to the "general tranquillity" that had resulted from the policy of tacit "overlordship" practiced by the British.[81] Like Curzon, he also failed to make the connection that the absence of war was a consequence of the established power of Abu Dhabi and its Ruler. This provided the political and social mechanism within the tribal system by which peace was maintained in the region. Through the initiative of Zayid the Great, conflict was resolved by traditional systems of conciliation, customary in the region, but which in the absence of a general peace had previously fallen into disuse.

Thus, it was highly significant that in September 1905, the five Trucial Shaikhs "held a meeting at Dibai [Dubai], the venerable Zāid-bin-Khalifah in effect presiding."[82] At that meeting, they agreed to the peaceful resolution of a tribal dispute, without British involvement, which would in earlier times have led to war. Respect for Zayid the Great meant that the desert tribes did not dare to raid, while others thought twice about disturbing the peace if that would mean incurring his wrath. Following the first meeting of the Rulers, "A written agreement, dated about the end of April 1906, was also drawn up, in which the respective spheres of tribal influence…were defined."[83] The agreement stemmed from an appeal to Shaikh Zayid Bin Khalifa for protection after a group of Bani Qitab tribesmen had tried to capture the petitioners' fort. In the interests of keeping the peace, the Ruler of Abu Dhabi put pressure on the tribe, forcing them to withdraw. In this, he had the support of the Rulers of Dubai and Sharjah. The result was that "counsels of moderation prevailed."[84]

This subtle process of constraint and deterrence was more often than not invisible, but highly effective. However, the Resident, Major Cox, sought to undermine this pacific collaboration. So, before the April 1906 agreement outlined above, he addressed "a remonstrance" to Shaikh Zayid, even though this was a matter that clearly fell outside the scope of the treaty. In this, he was reflecting a changed political attitude in Britain to the affairs of the Gulf. He now had a new agenda and was already moving far beyond the formal agreements and their focus on warlike activity at sea. The process of "watching over" the affairs of the Gulf was being extended to matters on land and to complex issues between the tribes.

Despite all these irritations, Zayid the Great always maintained a positive and friendly tone in his correspondence with Cox. The Resident for his part had a high regard for Shaikh Zayid. He wrote in

1904 to the British authorities in India, "Sheikh Zaeed's influence was much stronger than that of the Sultan of Muscat…and was as far as one could judge almost invariably exercised in the interests of the general peace."[85]

The Region without Shaikh Zayid the Great

The death of Shaikh Zayid the Great in 1909 created a power vacuum within the region. The prime advocate of conciliation, who possessed the power and the tribal authority to enforce peace, was removed from the picture. The consequences of his departure would become clear in what became known as the '*Hyacinth* incident' that occurred in the year after his death. This underlined the potential for violence that still lay within the region but which had successfully been contained by Shaikh Zayid the Great's authority.

With some merchants in Dubai having long been suspected of dealing in arms, a British party of 100 armed men landed from the *HMS Hyacinth* in December 1910, without the Ruler's permission, to seize the suspected contraband. In the ensuing fighting and subsequent shelling, 37 Arabs were killed and many buildings damaged. Five British sailors were also killed. The naval commander suggested a full-scale bombardment of Dubai and occupation of the town by at least a thousand men with artillery support.[86] In the end, no further action occurred.

> [The episode, however,] figured prominently in the English and Indian newspapers and provoked an important exchange of official correspondence. To the *Times of India* the incident came as a complete surprise. They could not understand how the Trucial Coast, which had been at peace with Britain for more than half a century and which had undergone these [*sic*] sobering influence of trade, should suddenly become the scene of bitter fighting.[87]

The answer might be that the "sobering influence" had been not trade, but the dominating presence of Zayid the Great. His death in 1909 created the potential for enormous problems in the Gulf. It removed the most important actor in the 'policy process' of the region, the complex structure of pressures and counter-pressures that kept the ever-present potential for disorder in check. Other local Rulers recognized the benefits of the system. On many occasions, tribal leaders and ruling shaikhs had accepted the decision and will of Zayid the Great because they trusted and respected him, not because of any particular agreement or allegiance. In effect, he had provided the mechanism that policed and maintained the peace. Sometimes a word would be sufficient; on other occasions, he would need to gather his forces to quell wrongdoers. The result was the "peaceful and secure" situation to which Curzon alluded. However, as mentioned, the system was already under strain as a result of the new interventionist policies of the British government. All in all, without the presence of Zayid the Great, it seems questionable in retrospect whether the peace could have lasted as it had during the decades of his rule.

His death came at a time when the other main actor – the British government – was intent on aggrandizing its position. While the officials sorrowed for a great man, they also wrongly believed that the region would function better without a strong ruler, one capable of standing against them. In the years immediately after the death of Zayid the Great, British confidence and success seemed at its zenith. During those years, the British government reached an accord with the Ottomans over boundaries,[88] signed agreements with Bahrain and Kuwait[89] that gave them a veto over the signature of any agreement with regard to the lease of oil rights, and prepared to make the Trucial Shaikhs sign similar agreements.[90] Their aim was to make the Rulers of the region wholly dependent on British advice and goodwill.[91] At each revision of the treaty system, the responsibilities of the British government were enlarged and the independence of the Rulers was diminished. The result was that in most of the Gulf states by the outbreak of the First World War, all contacts with foreign companies and governments could only take place through the British authorities, who also controlled all visas and access to the Gulf states.[92] To many, it seemed that the British 'Raj' (the Government of India), which sent its officials to the Gulf, wanted to exert the same power in the Gulf that it exerted on the subcontinent.

However, British prestige and confidence was set to suffer a decline from the high-point of 1913. The arrival of the naval force and the Indian army mentioned at the start of this chapter was clear evidence to the peoples of the Gulf of the military might of the British. The flotilla duly sailed north up the Gulf, anchored close to Kuwait and landed its troops without opposition. They set out to march north, first to Basra and then on to Baghdad to expel the Ottomans from the territory of present-day Iraq, and thence to undermine the loyalty of all the Arab provinces under Turkish rule. At roughly the same time, Allied troops were to land at Gallipoli, close to Constantinople, with the same aim of delivering a mortal blow to Ottoman strength and prestige.

In both cases, the strategy proved a disaster. The Indian army failed in its objective in the south, was besieged in Kut al 'Amara and ultimately forced to surrender under ignominious circumstances. The Gallipoli incursion fared no better, having to undertake a humiliating withdrawal. News of the catastrophe spread immediately throughout the Gulf and the wider Arab world and dealt a huge blow to British prestige. As the element of trust had already been weakened by the *Hyacinth* incident in 1910, Gulf Rulers, who had once feared the might of the British navy and the power of the Resident began to wonder whether they could actually enforce their edicts.[93] For almost a century, the British had controlled the Gulf by what they liked to call 'moral power,' in effect by a complex system of bluff and threat.[94] After Kut and Gallipoli, their credibility was severely damaged. Nor was there, after the death of Zayid the Great, any local ruler with the authority to sustain a long period of stability.

The Inter-War Years: 1919–1938

In the years that followed the Allied victory in the First World War in 1918 there might have been a return to the pre-war peace. But all the elements in the equation had changed. None of the old forces for stability, be they political or moral, remained intact. Politically, the break-up of the Ottoman Empire eventually produced a number of new Arab states – Iraq, Palestine, Syria and Lebanon – but all of these were under the rule of either Britain or France, and sanctioned by the new League of Nations. The Arabs felt cheated, for they had expected their national demands to be treated with the same care as was being extended to the former subjects of Germany and Austria-Hungary. The new arrangements did not produce stability. Arabs did not accept foreign rule willingly. Egypt, under British suzerainty since 1882, experienced an upsurge of popular dissent in the revolution of 1919.[95] After much fighting and many deaths, Britain granted Egypt a form of limited independence in 1922. The Iraq mandate was steadily eroded by new treaties in 1922 and 1930, with the country gaining full independence in 1932. Palestine, saddled with the impossible burden of a new Jewish 'National Home' within its borders, experienced violent Arab resistance from the moment of its proposal. France manipulated the situation within its mandated territory more subtly, fragmenting Arab opposition, and playing on the ethnic and religious divisions within its new territories.[96]

News of all these changes quickly spread throughout the Gulf. Arab newspapers and magazines from Egypt, Palestine and Iraq circulated widely. Knowledge of the political realities undermined respect for Britain's moral authority. Moreover, there were no local rulers with adequate prestige to give support to the British, had they wished to do so, as had been possible during the rule of Shaikh Zayid the Great. In every one of the Gulf states except Dubai, the Rulers changed in the decade between 1919 and 1930, and even in Dubai the Ruler's authority was being challenged. Similarly, on the British side, instead of the long-serving Cox, who had gained a knighthood and been promoted to serve in the new government of Iraq, there was a succession of Political Residents, none of whom remained in service long enough to understand the region or to gain the respect of the Rulers.[97]

Worse still, the prestige of the Political Resident was diminished by a series of ill-considered economic measures. The costs of waging the First World War had nearly ruined the thriving British economy of 1914. Economic stringency at home led to budgetary cutbacks in all areas of government. The ship assigned to the Political Resident so that he could tour the coast and entertain the Rulers in suitable style was withdrawn, and he was forced to travel as a passenger on the regular steamer of the British India Steam Navigation Company. When he arrived in one of the coastal states, there was no longer any British sovereign territory on which he could entertain local Rulers and dignitaries. Thus, in the complex system of tribal values, he was diminished by being unable to return hospitality received.[98] A matter that doubtless seemed utterly trivial in London assumed the status of a major problem in the Gulf. When his 'yacht' was finally restored to him in 1930, the damage had already been done. Lost prestige could not easily be restored. A decade had passed in which the power and presence of the Political Resident had become little more than a memory on the coast, so much so that, in 1929, it was found that no one could even recall the names of Cox's successors.[99]

Had the British returned to the Gulf in 1918 with abundant energy and a determination to sustain the peace, the situation might have been redeemed. But they displayed indecision and inertia. Too much energy was wasted on internal governmental squabbles in London over which department should be responsible for the Gulf.[100] There was an exaggerated concern with seeking economy at a time of financial stringency, as with the removal of the yacht from the Political Resident.[101] In short, the confident hand on the rudder sought by Curzon gave way to the politics of drift.[102] This power vacuum had dire effects in Abu Dhabi, where none of the immediate successors of Zayid the Great had the capacity, under the prevailing circumstances, to manage the complexities of the Bani Yas system.

The maintenance of order on the Trucial Coast had always been a balancing act. For more than half a century, the strong personality of Zayid the Great had suppressed disorderly tendencies. Self-interest bound the elements of the Bani Yas alliance together and, as one scholar has observed, "To survive, Rulers have had to display a remarkable combination of fearlessness, fairness, honesty, intelligence and generosity, and to make sure that none of their relatives became disaffected in any way."[103] Zayid the Great's successors could, for a time, benefit from the penumbra of his presence but, at some point, the inherent centrifugal tendencies of the political system would reassert themselves. As early as 1912, the new Ruler of Abu Dhabi, Shaikh Tahnun Bin Zayid (1909–1912), was called upon to support his allies, the Al Dhawahir, against attacks by neighboring tribes at al Ain.[104] In 1919–1920, his successor, Shaikh Hamdan Bin Zayid (1912–1922), again had to intervene between the tribes, in this case between the Al Manasir and the Al 'Awamir, both of whom were allies of the Bani Yas. However, three new factors emerged which put pressure upon the structure. The first and second, the loss of Zayid the Great and the diminishing effectiveness of British authority, have already been outlined. The third factor had both political and economic roots.

In the heart of Arabia, the power and authority of Abdul Aziz, the Ruler of Najd, had been greatly enhanced by the First World War. He had already driven the Ottomans from the al Hasa province bordering the Gulf in 1913. In 1918, the British regarded him as potentially the most powerful force in the region. Where once the desert tribes had looked to Zayid the Great as the 'strong man' with resources to back him, increasingly it was Abdullah Bin Jilwi, the representative of Abdul Aziz in al Hasa, who made a play for their allegiance. He aided those tribes that attacked the Bani Yas and their allies, intending thereby to weaken the only competing source of power and stability in the region.[105] In one aspect, the move was wholly traditional, part of the to-and-fro of tribal politics, but in another it had modern economic motivations. The possible existence of oil reserves in the region was a factor even before the First World War and, from 1918, Saudi Arabia was concerned to secure as much of the potential oil as possible.

The successors of Zayid the Great had relatively few resources at their disposal to resist this pressure. The Rulers' income was in decline as a consequence of the post-war weakening of trade, at a time when the demand for subsidy and assistance from the tribes was increasing. In addition, the British government gave them little by way of positive support. The intense pressure produced a corresponding reaction at the heart of the Bani Yas. Stable authority vanished, with a succession of short-lived Rulers. In a period of 54 years, between 1855 and 1909, there had been only one Ruler in Abu Dhabi. In the 19 years from 1909 to 1928, there were four. Hamdan Bin Zayid was followed in short succession by his brothers Sultan Bin Zayid (1922–1926) and Saqr Bin Zayid (1926–1928). The cycle of instability and disorder at the heart of the family was only brought to an end in 1928 with the accession of Shaikh Shakhbut Bin Sultan.[106]

The period between 1922 and 1928 can be regarded in two ways. Either it was a return to the violent ways of tribal politics prevalent before 1855, or it was an aberration produced by a set of special circumstances. The British authorities at the time took the more negative view. However, in historical perspective, the second interpretation may prove more realistic. In almost a century and a half, the only point at which violent means were employed to change the political order was the brief interlude between 1922 and 1928; at all other times, the mechanism for transition by consensus operated effectively. However, the events in Abu Dhabi need also to be viewed in the broader context of the region and the world beyond. The consequences of the First World War were social and political destabilization on every continent. It took many forms, most of them destructive and violent. Political and economic turmoil was prevalent. Then, in 1929, just as the political structures began to recover, the world economy was plunged into the Great Depression of the 1930s. It was into these precarious times that Shaikh Zayid Bin Sultan Al Nahyan was born and raised.

The Young Zayid Bin Sultan

In the days before birth certificates and written records were maintained, details of birth dates remained a matter of memory. No one now remembers the day or even the year of the young Shaikh Zayid Bin Sultan's birth. The best estimate is some time in the last year of the First World War, in 1918. The first written mention of him is as a young child, traveling with his mother from Abu Dhabi to al Ain. In retrospect, this was a journey of sadness, because he would never see his father alive again. On July 12, 1926, perhaps sensing danger, Shaikh

Sultan had entrusted his eldest son Shakhbut with the security of the family, including his wife Shaikha Salamah Bint Butti Al Hamid and his youngest son Zayid, and sent them to the safety of al Ain. Only his third son Khalid stayed behind with him in the town of Abu Dhabi.[107] Within days, Shaikh Sultan was killed and Zayid and his brothers were fatherless. Shaikh Sultan's oldest son, Shakhbut, took charge over and cared for all his siblings, but especially for his youngest brother Zayid, for whom, as far as was possible, he took his father's place.

The young Zayid, thus, had two strongly contrasting experiences in his early youth. As a very young child, he had lived in his father's house in Abu Dhabi and later in the Ruler's residence, the al Husn palace. At a very early age, he began to learn the verses of the Holy Koran. He was not much older when he began to sit quietly in his father's *majlis*, listening and learning. Soon, he acquired the confidence to ask questions of the visitors, and he became marked out as someone wise beyond his years.[108] But with the move to al Ain in 1926, and his life among his mother's people, the Al Qubaisat section of the Bani Yas, he grew up within a purely Bedouin environment.[109] In his grandfather Butti's *majlis*, he saw at first hand the tribal issues and concerns which he had largely experienced second hand in Abu Dhabi. He heard the issues of honor and warfare debated daily, more so in the troubled conditions of the 1920s and 1930s.

Later, he began to realize that not much had changed, in the ceaseless shifts and interplay among the tribes, from the issues that had confronted his namesake, the young Zayid Bin Khalifa, a century before. In the al Ain of his youth, Zayid Bin Sultan knew and listened to men who had fought alongside Zayid the Great. This grandfather, whom he had never known in person, had embodied the virtues of the desert ruler: fearlessness, fairness, honesty, intelligence and generosity. He saw in practice, day by day, that those qualities were required to manage the tribes. He realized that tribesmen could be led but would not be driven.

These pressures formed the background to the childhood and youth of Shaikh Zayid. Most children are invisible to all, save their immediate family, but it seems that from these early years he had already begun to make his mark. The Bedouin tribes of al Ain knew him, even as a boy, as a skilled hunter and an unusually effective marksman— skills that were much admired. Strong, athletic and endowed with great patience, it was also evident that he possessed more than the mind and boldness of a simple desert warrior. While there was never any question as to his physical courage or bravery, he made it clear from an early age that conflict always represented the last resort. He strongly believed that there was little that could not be resolved by honest discussion and negotiation. Above all, he had, as both his friends and the tribesmen saw, the true quality of leadership—the capacity for patience. The young Zayid was willing to wait for as long as was necessary, until the propitious moment for decisive action. It was a trait that was to serve him well.

The Ruler's Representative
in Al Ain

The political turning point in Abu Dhabi came in 1928 with the
selection of Shakhbut Bin Sultan, a grandson of Zayid the Great,
as the new Ruler. This heralded the coming to power of a new generation,
headed by a man who had the support of his uncles and brothers as
well as wide backing within the family. There was a general weariness
resulting from the turmoil and disorder of the immediate past and a
hope that peace could be restored. This desire was evident to the Arab
Residency Agent in Sharjah who visited Shaikh Shakhbut immediately
after his accession as Ruler. He noted, "Sheikh Shakhboot and the
notables of Abu Dhabi came on board. The Captain asked them about
the state of affairs in Abu Dhabi territory. They said that there was
tranquillity and peace."[1]

The new Ruler had many positive qualities. He was amiable, soft-
spoken and had an engaging personality. Importantly, Shaikh Shakhbut
had the committed support of his three brothers, for their mother
Shaikha Salamah had made them all take an oath not to act against
each other. That fraternal solidarity gave a crucial strength to the new
leadership in Abu Dhabi, which soon became a pillar of stability in an
area under the constant stress of change.[2] It was further strengthened
by the absence of any disruptive contention within the ruling family,
and by the fact that Shaikh Shakhbut had the support of his uncle
Khalifa Bin Zayid, the senior surviving son of Zayid the Great. From
this point onwards, Shaikh Shakhbut was to rule for almost 40 years,

after which he handed over the rulership of Abu Dhabi to his younger brother Shaikh Zayid Bin Sultan.

When Shaikh Shakhbut took over as leader of the Bani Yas and Ruler of Abu Dhabi, many things had changed in the 20 years since the death of Zayid the Great. The intricate system of connections between the desert tribes and the Ruler in Abu Dhabi had disintegrated beyond a point where Shaikh Shakhbut could restore it. Nevertheless, he made valiant efforts during the 1930s to extend his authority to the hinterland and, by 1939, the British officials believed that he had strengthened Abu Dhabi's control over its core territory of Liwa and al Ain. The military report of that year noted that "the dominant position is now held by the Shaikh of Abu Dhabi."[3] However, this position was not as entrenched as originally perceived, and until Shaikh Zayid took over as the Ruler's Representative in al Ain in 1946, Shaikh Shakhbut's authority over the tribes remained tenuous.

Other problems confronted Shaikh Shakhbut. These were as much economic as political. The finances of the Ruler of Abu Dhabi were strongly linked to the pearling trade, an industry that generated revenues of about £3 million in 1925 for the whole Gulf area.[4] Given the large share of Abu Dhabi in the business, a portion of that money came as tax revenue to the Ruler. However, with the downturn in the world economy and the development by the Japanese of the cultured pearl, the industry was precipitated into a crisis. The effects were manifold. Not only were the Shaikh's revenues reduced dramatically, but many formerly wealthy families were ruined, a situation that in turn caused unemployment and discontent among the tribesmen who were involved in the pearl fisheries.

From the outset, Shaikh Shakhbut was cautious over expenditure. The Shaikh's income from pearling had never been rashly spent. Any idea that this tax revenue was used to create a luxurious lifestyle was quickly dispelled by a visit to the Ruler's fort in Abu Dhabi. The Ruler lived in Spartan simplicity. Traditionally, most of his income was redistributed in the form of subsidies to the tribes—customary payments on which the tribal shaikhs had come to depend. They, in turn, distributed the largesse to their followers. By this means, the wealth generated from the coast reached the people of the interior. However, with his tax revenues from pearling dropping rapidly, existing subsidies had to be cut or abandoned altogether. Without this money at his disposal, the new Shaikh would inevitably find it difficult to maintain the loyalty of his tribal allies. Meanwhile, Shaikh Zayid witnessed first hand how the progressive impoverishment of the tribesmen of al Ain threatened the intimate link between tribal loyalty and the Ruler's largesse.[5] This situation was further complicated by the fact that although Shaikh Shakhbut possessed many positive qualities, observers did not perceive him as an inspirational leader of tribesmen. An English visitor, Roderic Owen, who liked and admired the Ruler, as well as respecting his wit and intelligence, later remarked that "he mightn't be nearly so effective with a mass, not having that theatrical flair to which a mass responds."[6]

With the downturn in the world market for luxury goods and the invention of the cheaper Japanese cultured pearl, the Gulf felt the chill wind of the worldwide depression. In this way, the global economic downturn had a profound impact at the local level. The town of Abu Dhabi had grown in strength on the proceeds from pearling, but that was its only resource. Unlike Dubai, Abu Dhabi did not possess a natural harbor where ships could anchor. Therefore, as the pearling industry declined so did the town. By comparison, in al Ain there was more abundant water, agriculture and a steady flow of travelers who boosted trade. Even in Liwa, the original home of the Bani Yas, where water was less certain, the tribes could continue their age-old existence tending the date palms and their herds. The Bani Yas had first come to Abu Dhabi because it provided a livelihood, but with the decline of work and trade on the coast, the balance of power again shifted inland into the tribal areas over which Shaikh Shakhbut had less influence.

At first sight, this appears hard to understand. Shaikh Shakhbut Bin Sultan appeared very much a Bedouin. He shared with his youngest brother Shaikh Zayid a love of the desert and the simple life. His greatest pleasures were traditional—falconry and writing poems. However, the loyalty of the tribesmen was intensely personal and pragmatic. They tended to follow a leader whom they admired and who gave them tangible support. The tradition of the ruler giving payments to his tribesmen was well established and formed an essential part of the Bedouin economy. Shaikh Shakhbut's inability to continue this tradition caused them real hardship. In the context of the 1930s and 1940s, there was probably very little he could do to retain their loyalty. Even when the flow of money increased, whether from oil exploration or rent paid for facilities by the British government, Shaikh Shakhbut continued to exercise extreme caution over any expenditure.

The root of this financial prudence is not hard to discover. The formative first decade of Shaikh Shakhbut's rule coincided with the depths of the Great Depression. For him, it was the defining period of his rule. The catastrophe that confronted Abu Dhabi as revenues dissipated imbued the Ruler with a deep-rooted conservatism that never left him. Shaikh Shakhbut had this characteristic in common with many of his generation throughout the world who experienced these years of hardship and lived always with the fear that those dark days would return.

The Discovery of Oil and the Changing International Environment

Just as the Ruler's income was virtually obliterated by the precipitous decline in pearling revenues, two new sources of income providentially emerged. The first, money from the British government to provide facilities for the Royal Air Force, came with strings attached. It meant greater British interference in the affairs of Abu Dhabi, but nevertheless earned Shaikh Shakhbut Rs 4,800 (Indian rupees) per year.[7] However, this was insufficient to compensate for the decline in pearling tax revenues. Oil exploration rights, as the second potential source of income, was much more significant at the time, but minimal by comparison with the unimaginable wealth generated by oil exploration in later years.

In the early 1930s, the entire regional power structure would be transformed by the prospect of oil being discovered under the desert sands of Abu Dhabi. The British government was determined that British companies should be responsible for developing any oil assets in the Trucial States, especially since the American oil companies had already monopolized the oilfields of Bahrain and Saudi Arabia. Under the agreement of 1922, the British could block outside connections, but they could not force the Shaikhs to agree to oil exploration by any particular company. In 1935, a subsidiary of the British-owned Iraq Petroleum Company (IPC) created an exploration company, Petroleum Development Trucial Coast Ltd. (PDTC). In 1939, this company, under considerable pressure from the British government, signed an agreement with Shaikh Shakhbut. He bargained hard and held out for better terms than the Rulers of the other emirates with whom the British were also negotiating. As a result, he received the largest sum paid to any Ruler in the Trucial States—Rs 300,000 as a signature payment and an annual income of Rs 100,000, which would go up by regular increments.[8] This more than made up for the reduction in pearling income. Even before any oil was actually discovered, this industry provided the Ruler with greater resources than any of his predecessors had ever possessed.

However, the attitude of both the oil companies and the British government towards the Rulers of the region manifested the fundamental ambiguity in the relationship. There was no doubt that the Ruler of Abu Dhabi had full and sovereign rights over all his territories. It was as a sovereign that he and his predecessors had entered into a series of treaties with the United Kingdom. Yet, for *raisons d'état*, the British were constantly enlarging the area of their intervention while offering nothing in return. The Rulers, on the other hand, looked upon the agreements as being fixed in law and by custom. They believed, correctly in terms of international law, that they had no obligations towards Britain beyond those explicitly stated in the treaties. Moreover, the Rulers alone had responsibility for the governance of their states. Any mineral concessions and related revenues, as well as any money paid by the oil companies, was not simply largesse, but rightfully due to them. In respect of the first oil contracts in the Trucial States, the British authorities represented the interests of the British oil companies rather than the interests of the local states.[9]

Nevertheless, the oil companies began making substantial payments to the Rulers of the Coast.[10] The sums were, in effect, non-refundable fees for the privilege of exploring for oil, and they had the impact of making the Rulers, including Shaikh Shakhbut, aware of the potential power that now lay in their hands.[11] Throughout the 1930s, Shaikh Shakhbut had resisted accepting at face value the recommendations made by the British, and on many occasions his persistence paid off handsomely. He had wisely refused the first contract proposal, rightly believing that this did not represent the best offer. However, his prudent negotiation met with resentment from the British authorities. To compel Shaikh Shakhbut to sign the agreement, the Political Resident, Fowle, put extraordinary pressure upon the Ruler by falsely accusing him of malpractice, and refusing him travel papers for journeys outside Abu Dhabi. This high-handed attitude was not limited to the Political Resident. Informed of Fowle's imperious approach to the Ruler, J.P. Gibson, Principal Secretary of the Political Department, India Office, commented that he would be "delighted to see Abu Dhabi getting a good knock on the head."[12] Eventually, an agreement was concluded in 1939, just nine months before the outbreak of the Second World War. From 1939 to 1945, while all the Rulers of the Gulf gave their support to the Allied cause, Shaikh Shakhbut never forgot the way in which he had been pressurized, falsely accused and affronted in 1939. He never trusted the British government thereafter.

For the duration of the war, all disputes remained in abeyance. Yet, immediately after the war, old controversies were rekindled. On August 22, 1945, one week after the Second World War ended with the unconditional surrender of Japan, the Ruler of Abu Dhabi wrote to the Political Resident in Bahrain, "You stated [in a letter of July 10] that the British Government exercises jurisdiction over British subjects and all foreigners in my territory and that it is an old custom. If God willing I, on my part, is [sic] still maintaining this custom and approve of it."[13] The measured tone of this statement is significant. It is the Resident and not the Ruler who has said that it is "an old custom." Shaikh Shakhbut knew this was not the case, and the private correspondence of the British officials supports his stance.[14] Once again, Shaikh

Shakhbut knew that there was an attempt to deceive him. Moreover, the return to this old policy of pressure and aggrandizement by the British confounded Shaikh Shakhbut and his fellow Rulers. They could not understand why, after six years of cooperation with the Allies during the war, it was necessary, with peace in sight, for Britain to tighten its grip on their countries.[15]

For almost 20 years, Shaikh Shakhbut had sought, generally in vain, to protect his country from growing external control, which yielded no benefit to Abu Dhabi. Instead, it represented the degree to which the nation had become progressively embroiled in international political and economic issues. The Arabian Gulf had largely escaped the direct consequences of the Second World War, not being in an active war zone. The only serious action was a raid on Bahrain by the Italian air force, which caused some damage.[16] Even the social and political transformation that convulsed Iraq, Syria and Egypt, mostly as a consequence of the war, had only an indirect effect on the Gulf. However, the broader transformation that was occurring in the Arab world was inescapable.

Where the Gulf had once been a wholly British concern as the main route to India, the war with Japan had heightened the awareness of the United States government to the vital importance of the region. The discovery of oil in the eastern province of Saudi Arabia and the involvement of US companies in the other oil interests of the region slowly tilted the prevailing balance of power in the area. The turning point was the meeting of President Roosevelt and King Abdul Aziz of Saudi Arabia at the Great Bitter Lake in Egypt, in February 1945. From that point onward, it became clear that the United States intended to play a much more active role in the Arab world generally and in the Gulf in particular.

At the same time, the external powers now faced an Arab world gripped by a growing sense of its own unique identity. The foundation of the Arab League in 1945 had a profound symbolic as well as political importance. By the end of the war in Europe and Asia, all strategic analysts were aware of the enormous economic and political power latent in the Arab world. Although the flow of oil from Saudi Arabia and the Gulf was only a fraction of what it was to become in later years, the three great powers – Britain, the United States and the Soviet Union – knew that the entire economic and political geography of the world had shifted. Each of the former allies was determined to secure its own interests, and the United States in particular was resolved to play its own part in the area rather than simply leave matters to British initiatives.[17] For the Rulers of the Gulf, chafing under British tutelage and patronage, there were the renewed stirrings of their potential power.

Two years later, in April 1947, the independence of India brought about another major change in the relationship between Abu Dhabi and the British Empire. The Foreign Office in London would henceforward be the sole British policy maker in the Gulf, a role it had previously shared with the British administration in India. Although the Foreign Office would use many of the same officers and local staff, it nonetheless operated under a markedly different set of political and diplomatic objectives to those that had hitherto been enforced from India. All these shifts and alterations would have an impact on the Ruler of Abu Dhabi and on the conduct of his government. Yet, there was also a broader and more widespread perception within the country that the patterns of the past were undergoing a transformation.

Internal Transformation

Following the accession to power of Shaikh Shakhbut Bin Sultan in 1928, Abu Dhabi had settled down to a period of relative political calm, if not economic stability. The circumstances of Shaikh Shakhbut's accession demonstrated that there were subtle changes in the structures of power within the state. He was the Ruler, with his prerogatives intact, but his accession had been a collective decision by his family, in which all his brothers concurred. At the same time, it had become clear, even during the early 1930s while the young Shaikh Zayid remained more of an onlooker than an active participant, that a new formulation of the governing polity was emerging and that Shaikh Zayid was regarded as part of the inner family circle that guided Abu Dhabi.[18]

The accession of Shaikh Shakhbut marked the potential for a more collaborative era in the guidance that the Ruler exercised over Abu Dhabi. After 1928, the Ruler remained the central channel of power and authority, respected for the office that he held. Axiomatically, the Ruler was most effective when he ruled with the active consent of his immediate family and his close allies. Serious tensions would only arise when that essential harmony was disrupted.[19] This was very much in keeping with the dynamics of traditional tribal government and understood clearly by all those who operated within the system. The new formulation developed tendencies already implicit in the tribal structure.

The traditional structure of authority was for a ruler to exercise full power tempered only by the rights of his family and tribe to replace him if he failed to perform his role effectively. If it became necessary, it was the responsibility of the immediate family to perform this corrective function, on behalf of the wider social grouping. However, it was essentially a negative constraint. The transformation engendered by Shaikha Salamah when she bonded all her sons together in support of their brother was to move the immediate family towards a more active and positive political role.

This subtle shift was obvious to the small group of people close to the affairs of the state. Increasingly, the British entered into discussion and had contact not only with Shaikh Shakhbut but with other members of his immediate family, including his uncle, Shaikh Khalifa and his brothers.[20] For example, the Political Agent in Bahrain, Lieutenant Colonel Gordon Loch, visited Abu Dhabi in February 1935 to settle a pending payment for the use of air facilities. He described how Shaikh Shakhbut and his uncle Shaikh Khalifa jointly received him in a friendly and welcoming manner. Loch stressed that it was not easy to reach an agreement, but in the end they did so. He described how he settled the issue with the Shaikh, in the presence of his relations.[21] The fact that the settlement was made in the presence of Shaikh Shakhbut's relations is significant, for although the agreement was signed and sealed in the name of Shaikh Shakhbut alone, it was plainly a collective family decision to accept the terms offered.

These changes went largely unnoticed, while others were more obvious. As the Political Agent in Bahrain, who was responsible for Abu Dhabi, reported at the end of 1944, "The country is opening up and the inhabitants of the remoter parts of the interior are becoming accustomed to the sight of military vehicles, aircraft and anti-locust parties carrying on their multifarious works and duties." [22] Before the war, Britain had attempted to isolate the Gulf from commercial and political entry by outside powers, but after 1947 this was a losing battle. In the post-war years, a younger generation of British officials, which had learned its diplomatic skills in other Arab countries before coming to the Gulf, replaced the older generation which still instinctively saw the Gulf as an outpost of the Raj, Britain's Indian Empire. The new men arrived as a fresh generation of Arab leaders was emerging, and the young diplomats treated them with much greater respect and tact than their predecessors had ever done. With the older generation of Rulers like Shaikh Shakhbut, born a decade before the First World War, they still encountered many difficulties, especially since Shaikh Shakhbut's personal experience had given him no reason to trust the word of British officialdom. However, with Shaikh Zayid, a man of a younger generation, they were able to form an immediate bond.

It was in the interior and not on the Abu Dhabi coast that the process of change after the Second World War began in earnest. The oasis complex of al Ain lies far inland from the town of Abu Dhabi. [23] Edward Henderson, the representative of PDTC, described driving into the oasis from the coast in 1948:

> ...a cluster of low mud-brick houses set in large date groves, and in between the villages was open scrub. To the north was a small forest of acacia and other thorn trees; to the south were two gaunt ribs of Jebel Hafit and the main mass of the mountain which shuts in the oasis. There were several further palm groves...Each village had several [forts], varying from single watch towers, usually round and about thirty feet in height, with a crenellated top, to those in which the shaikhs lived, large buildings with a maze of one-storeyed rooms surrounded by curtain walls, with turrets at the corners and over the gate. [24]

In addition to the Bani Yas, there were a number of important tribes in the area around al Ain. The Al Dhawahir, with their villages at al Hili, al Qattarah, al Jimi and al M'utarid, raised livestock and grew fruit, dates and vegetables to support themselves. Many members of the Al Na'im tribe lived in the oasis area, with their base in Hamasah. The Al 'Awamir were settled widely in the area and had traditionally supported the Bani Yas.[25] Detached from the events of the coast, the strongest influences upon the oasis complex were from the tribes of Inner Arabia and Oman. Trade and communications flowed from the Batinah coast through the oasis, then to the coast at Abu Dhabi and back to the south. The dominant force in the region was the Abu Dhabi emirate and, to a much lesser extent, the Sultanate of Muscat.[26] Saudi Arabia exercised a more distant influence through control of a number of the desert tribes, notably the Al Murrah.[27]

Shaikh Zayid had grown up during a period of great difficulty in al Ain. His brother the Ruler's efforts to protect the undoubted rights of Abu Dhabi in the hinterland around al Ain, in Liwa and among the tribes did not have the desired effect. Shaikh Shakhbut remained aloof to reports that all was not well inland. Tribal politics is as much concerned with power as with rights, and as Shaikh Zayid grew towards manhood, he watched the power of Abu Dhabi ebbing away. He saw that the tribes like the Al Na'im were beginning to see Shaikh Shakhbut as uninterested and were looking west, towards the strong and powerful Ruler of Saudi Arabia. The government of Saudi Arabia had long sought to extend its control over some of the Abu Dhabi tribes. Over many years, the tax gatherers dispatched by the Ruler of al Hasa, Abdullah Bin Jilwi, had claimed payment of *zakat* on livestock and other resources.[28] From the early 1930s, this claim had been backed by a hidden sanction that those who did not obey the wishes of Bin Jilwi would be subject to raids by the tribes under his control. Already in the late 1920s, the British traveler Bertram Thomas, then in the service of the Sultan of Muscat, had written to the Political Resident in the Gulf that "immediately before the arrival of Ibn Saud's zakat collector, one of the Bani Yas tribes was raided by the al-Murra and lost a hundred and fifty camels. Payment of zakat…is therefore a kind of insurance against the raider."[29]

The Saudi collectors came and went—one of many factors in the interplay between the tribes at al Ain and in many parts of al Dhafrah. Since Shaikh Zayid effectively grew up in the oasis, more than any other member of the ruling family, he was identified in the 1930s as belonging to al Ain, not only by descent but also due to his tribal lifestyle. He made no secret of the fact that he was happier in the desert than on the coast, and when away, he never hid his longing to be back among his people at the foot of Jabal Hafit. Although his brother Shaikh Shakhbut visited the oasis quite frequently, and indeed would eventually spend his last years in his house in al Ain, he never achieved any great rapport with the tribes, for reasons outlined earlier. However, during his visits, he could easily see that Shaikh Zayid, his favorite younger brother, was loved and respected by the tribesmen. The relationship between Shaikh Shakhbut and Shaikh Zayid was a blend of paternal and fraternal feelings. There was mutual affection, loyalty and trust. Indeed, in later years, as Shaikh Shakhbut became more fearful and suspicious, Shaikh Zayid was the only one of his brothers whom he would allow to sleep in his residence in Abu Dhabi.[30] For his part, Shaikh Zayid always sought to protect his eldest brother from risk and danger.

The Ruler was a politically astute man. He recognized the talents of his youngest brother, and he also knew that he could trust him implicitly with a position of power. Thus, when the need arose for a man to sustain the Bani Yas in the tribal domain at al Ain, he had no hesitation in giving the task and the formal title of Ruler's Representative to Shaikh Zayid. The situation was complex and difficult. The rights of Abu Dhabi in al Ain and Liwa were disputed but never seriously questioned. Nevertheless, these rights did not exist in a vacuum. They needed to be maintained by political and ultimately by military measures.[31] Political measures meant sustaining the support and loyalty of tribes beyond the core of the Bani Yas and their allies. This had been the secret of Shaikh Zayid the Great's long and successful rule. As this predominant political support dwindled over the years, the military power of Abu Dhabi decreased concomitantly, reflecting a situation in which tribesmen comprised the fighting force. Thus, restoring the powerful position that Abu Dhabi had held among the tribes under Zayid the Great required sustained attention and great sensitivity to the nuances of tribal politics. As in the last years of the nineteenth century, the balance of local power at al Ain was in flux, to which the growing pressure from Saudi Arabia contributed.[32] From his youthful years in al Ain, Shaikh Zayid noted an important truth—when Abu Dhabi was strong, politically and militarily, its rights were never challenged. It was only in moments of weakness that it became vulnerable.

It would require a combination of energy, knowledge and patience to seize the initiative for Abu Dhabi and to rebuild the tribal alliances that had preserved the inland peace up to the time of the First World War. However, the stakes were now even higher. Already, the economy of Abu Dhabi depended upon the contract payments due from the oil companies for exploration rights. Those payments depended on the ability of the Ruler to guarantee the exploration teams access to all parts of his domain, especially tribal areas in the desert far from the town of Abu Dhabi. In this context, therefore, control of al Dhafrah, especially Liwa, and above all of Abu Dhabi's rights in al Ain, were a matter of supreme importance to Abu Dhabi. Shaikh Shakhbut had no illusions. In placing Shaikh Zayid in command at al Ain, he knew he was entrusting the future of the ruling family and the entire nation to his youngest brother.

The Ruler's Representative: Zayid's Pragmatism and Policies

The appointment of Shaikh Zayid Bin Sultan as the Ruler's Representative in al Ain in the immediate aftermath of the Second World War had been closely related to both changing local and international political circumstances. In terms of the history of Abu Dhabi, it was an event of major importance, reflecting the significance of al Ain for the history and development of the entire state. Not since the time of Shaikh Shakhbut Bin Diyab in the 1820s had so senior a member of the Al Nahyan family governed in the oasis complex.[33]

Late in 1945, Shaikh Khalifa Bin Zayid, the elderly patriarch of the Al Nahyan, died in al Ain. Despite his advanced years, in the words of Lieutenant Colonel Galloway, the Political Agent in Bahrain, "He played a prominent part in the affairs of Abu Dhabi and was Shaikh Shakhbut's chief adviser and confidant."[34] Although he had no official role in al Ain, his death left a void in the political sphere and Shaikh Shakhbut filled it quickly by appointing his younger brother Shaikh Zayid to be his official Representative. The precise timing of his appointment remains uncertain. Shaikh Zayid did not take up his post immediately, because he was accompanying his cousin, Shaikh Muhammad Bin Khalifa, on a journey to India. On January 17, 1946, he returned to Abu Dhabi, and shortly thereafter he set out for al Ain.[35] Certainly, when a visiting British oil executive, B.H. Lermitte, arrived in al Ain around February 15, 1946, Shaikh Zayid was there to greet him.[36]

The new Ruler's Representative immediately faced some pressing problems. The oasis complex was the only part of Abu Dhabi where agriculture was possible on a sustained basis, and its prosperity was consequently based on the supply of water. Over the centuries, a network of *aflaj* – subterranean channels – carried waters of the Jabal Hafit down to the villages. A group of officials, *arif*, was charged with the maintenance of the system and the distribution of the water, but in the strained conditions of the 1930s little or no money had been spent on the upkeep of the system. In some of the *aflaj* the flow of water had diminished or even ceased altogether, and in others it was restricted due to the lack of regular scouring and cleaning. Moreover, as the power of the Abu Dhabi Ruler in the oasis waned, the officials failed to fulfill their duties impartially. Water was the most precious commodity in such an arid environment, and access to it was increasingly restricted to those with powerful connections or who were prepared to pay for the privilege.

Thus, the first and most crucial economic and humanitarian task facing the young Shaikh Zayid on his appointment was the management and restoration of this most essential service. Without an assured supply of water, the whole oasis complex could eventually become uninhabitable. The Ruler gave Shaikh Zayid full authority to act on his behalf, but provided little by way of money or other resources. For more than 20 years, as the latter knew well before his appointment, a privileged few had enjoyed the first call on the water resources, while there was growing hardship for those who were deprived of a reasonable share for their crops. Yet, to change what had over a long period of time become an established practice, with considerable benefits to members of the ruling family, required great tact and diplomacy.

The new Representative's greatest asset was his strong personality and the fact that he was already well known and trusted by the people of the oasis complex. In his official residence, Shaikh Zayid received a constant flow of tribesmen, who came with their grievances or requests, or simply to talk to 'their' Zayid. Such gatherings allowed him to enlist the active support of the inhabitants in his initiatives for development, even though he could offer very little material reward. Of course, he also enjoyed the confidence of his brother, the Ruler. There seemed at this point to be little hint of the strained relations that emerged in later years. It could not have been otherwise, for a Ruler as politically sensitive as Shaikh Shakhbut would not have handed one of the prime assets of his state to someone whom he perceived as a rival. No doubt, he also calculated that if Shaikh Zayid were able to strengthen Abu Dhabi's authority in al Ain, it would be immeasurably to his own benefit and that of the ruling family.

The effect of Shaikh Zayid's appointment was immediate. Armed with his new powers, he issued instructions for the comprehensive overhaul of the *aflaj* system. This system tapped the deep natural reservoirs of water around Jabal Hafit, and through a network of ancient stone-walled underground passages distributed water to the villages. The existing channels were to be cleaned and repaired wherever the stonework had collapsed. He himself inspected the works on a regular basis, often appearing unannounced to see what progress was being made—a trait that was to become a characteristic of Shaikh Zayid. Work on the system was arduous and messy, and at times the Ruler's Representative was not averse to turning his own hand to the task. The message of this intense and sustained activity was clear to all the people of the oasis. Here, for the first time in living memory, was someone determined to arrest the decay and sense of drift in the oasis.[37]

Once the watercourses had been cleaned, it became clear that some of them had simply dried up permanently, as was quite common, and that the remainder were insufficient to supply adequate water for the growing population of the oasis. The solution was logical and inescapable—a new source needed to be found that could provide a wholly new supply. In later years, this would have been a matter of running a pipeline down from the mountains to the villages, a process demanding engineering skill but well within the bounds of normal practice. In the late 1940s, however, there was neither piping available in al Ain nor the money to pay for it. The only alternative was to mobilize the population and to build an *aflaj* on traditional lines.[38]

It was not a matter of the Ruler's Representative simply ordering the construction of the new channel but of persuading all the communities that it was in their joint interest to do so. Shaikh Zayid repeatedly visited each of the tribal leaders and their tribesmen over many months. Slowly, he wore down their objections, and they agreed to make the manpower available to build the new channel. A project on this scale had never been attempted within living memory, for most of the *aflaj* were many centuries old. Indeed, it was often said that few of the Arabs of the region had mastered the skills to build such a system. The building of al Saruj, the name given to the project, would prove such critics wrong.[39]

The scale of the task was massive. It meant excavating a tunnel often at a depth of 35 meters below ground, with a severely limited system of ventilation and lighting, in rock that was riddled with fissures. The tunnel would tap into an existing aquifer and then extend for approximately 1,500 meters underground before emerging at the surface. The irrigation system also required a steady and constant fall to allow the delivery of an even flow of water, neither too fast nor too slow.[40] The Bani Yas and their allies took the leading role in the excavation of the tunnel and the construction of the surface canal system for water distribution. It would be two decades before the entire system began to function.[41]

While the work on the al Saruj project was underway, Shaikh Zayid also undertook a complete reform of the water distribution system itself. Under the traditional arrangements, water was allowed to flow down the side channels from the main canal at set intervals and for prescribed periods. The aim was that water should be distributed equitably to those who were able to pay for the access rights. Over time, the system had become corrupted, as those with money were able to accumulate excessive rights of water access, which they then sold to others at a considerable profit. This meant that those without the money to pay these exorbitant rates were deprived of water altogether.

This situation went entirely against Shaikh Zayid's sense of equity. In his view, "falaj water coming out of the ground is a communal and universal right to be enjoyed by all those who live on the ground."[42] The ultimate source of this determination to provide free access to the water was rooted in his religious beliefs and his deep sense of honor.[43] As a result, while the work was being carried out on the new system, Shaikh Zayid put pressure on water owners to allow a more equitable distribution, initially without any effect. With the completion of the stages of the al Saruj project, however, he declared that the water from the new source would be for the poor alone and that those with existing water rights would not be entitled to benefit from it. With the prospect of water at a low cost, the lucrative market in *aflaj* rights began to wither and the monopolistic holders of water extraction permits saw that it would be in their interests to follow Shaikh Zayid's wishes. If they did not do so, they would be cut off from any share in the water flowing through the new resource. Accordingly, by the end of Shaikh Zayid's period of service in al Ain, water was freely available to all.

The water reform was a landmark in the history of Abu Dhabi, but the way in which Shaikh Zayid achieved such momentous progress is equally instructive.[44] Most telling was the force of example. By participating actively in the work of excavation, he demonstrated his personal commitment to the furtherance of the project. It is hard to imagine another man of his status in Abu Dhabi society working beside the Bedouin in the depths of the earth. News of what he was doing spread quickly through the tribes. Here was a leader who did not merely talk about action, but set to work himself. His example inspired others. He would never command the Bedouin as the Ruler's Representative, but they would follow wherever he led. He became 'their' Zayid. His power of personal persuasion and influence grew as the stories about him extended far and wide. The same pattern was followed in other areas. If a tribal leader was proving recalcitrant, Shaikh Zayid would visit him or welcome him to his own informal *majlis*, held under a tree beside his fort at al Miraijib. They would meet and talk, and the conversation might be repeated many times, sometimes extended over years. But eventually the objector would succumb to this gentle but persistent persuasion and begin to accept Shaikh Zayid's point of view.

In the case of water rights in al Ain, it took Shaikh Zayid almost two decades to achieve the full extent of his ambition for the people. Here, he first set the example by abandoning his own claim to rights over the water and then persuaded those closest to him to follow his lead. When a small group stood out against his wishes, he hinted at the ruin that faced them if they did not follow his request. None of those close to him in al Ain had any doubt about his capacity to make a harsh decision, for as a judge, he was as capable of handing down a stern sentence as any other ruler. But his first instinct was to seek the goodwill of others, to win them over to his way of thinking. By his lifestyle, he manifested trust in his people. He went freely among them, sometimes on camel or horse, later in a motorized vehicle designed for desert conditions. A young British political officer in the Trucial States, Julian Walker, made the following observation:

> Old bedu and villagers in rags, but with a proud and independent mien, would approach him either when his Landrover stopped or in the burasti in the afternoon. Calling him by name, they would tell him of the trouble they were having over camels, with their neighbours or with their water, and seek his help. He would listen to each case, sometimes discuss it with the Shaikhs around him, and then give a decision which would, if necessary, be recorded on a scrap of paper marked with his seal on the back... There was no Oriental splendour, only simple courtesy and dignity, and this was enhanced by the diffidence of a poor man seeking to break into our conversation for help from his ever-available Shaikh... Sitting around the fire in the evening, sipping tea as the men chatted, I

began to understand why Zaid had become so well liked and
respected, not only among his own followers, but also among the
tribes of the wide area around Buraimi [al Ain]. His courtesy, and
the informality of his justice, accorded well with the needs and
simple pride of the Arabs of the area.[45]

As a result, even tribes hostile to the Bani Yas respected Shaikh Zayid
as an individual, and he was able to go where no other member of his
family would have been so welcome. His policy of development for the
people began with the water reform but did not end there. Ultimately,
by the end of his tenure, he had brought education, medical care, a new
suq and better roads to the people of al Ain. Stories were told that he
would draw shapes in the sand with his camel stick – here a school, here
a hospital – at a time when such facilities were not available anywhere
in the entire region. And, in time, after he became Ruler in 1966, these
dreams became reality. His focus was, from the beginning, to improve
the people's standard of living.

Shaikh Zayid's style of governance was a novelty in Abu Dhabi.
Increasingly, Shaikh Shakhbut stayed aloof in the palace-fort on the
coast. Shaikh Zayid's other brothers visited him in al Ain, but did not
attract the same natural and unfeigned loyalty from the tribesmen as he
did.[46] His fame spread even among the tribes of Rub' al Khali, down
towards the southern coast of Arabia. The traveler Wilfred Thesiger had
heard of Shaikh Zayid long before he came to meet him at his camp:

> I had been looking forward to meeting him, for he had a great
> reputation among the Bedu. They liked him for his easy informal
> ways and his friendliness, and they respected his force of character,
> his shrewdness, and his physical strength. They said admiringly
> "Zayed is a Bedu. He knows about camels, can ride like one of us,
> can shoot, and knows how to fight."[47]

Thesiger stayed with Shaikh Zayid as his guest for a month, and saw
day-by-day how he had gained his reputation among the tribes, not just
as a Bedu "like one of us" but as a leader in the old tradition who had
a life-long claim upon their loyalty.

Regional Developments and
Shaikh Zayid's Expanding Role

The admiration and support of the tribesmen was to prove Shaikh Zayid's greatest asset in a crucial struggle for the status and independence of Abu Dhabi. At a time of regional turbulence and uncertainty, the tribal system could prove a source of instability. As Shaikh Zayid knew, the very nature of the tribesmen's desert lifestyle meant that they always lived on the edge of subsistence and that it was all too easy for them to revert to their earlier tradition of carrying out raids and seizing whatever they needed. As such, it was important for all the governments of the region to work together to keep the tribes under control. What happened when this curb was removed could be seen in the unnecessarily prolonged dispute between Abu Dhabi and Dubai from 1945 to 1948. What had begun as a minor border dispute before Shaikh Zayid took up office in al Ain grew rapidly into an extended conflict between the allied Bedouin tribes of both emirates, which neither Ruler could control or contain.[48] The quarrel was more of a prestige issue between the two Rulers than any concrete dispute between the two emirates. The area claimed by Dubai had no particular significance. Yet, neither Shaikh Shakhbut of Abu Dhabi nor Shaikh Sa'id of Dubai would back down, and neither Ruler could admit to any lack of control over their tribal supporters. Eventually, it was the younger leaders of the two emirates – Shaikh Zayid of Abu Dhabi and Shaikh Rashid of Dubai – who initiated the discussions that eventually led to peace.

As it would turn out, the only effective interlocutor with Abu Dhabi's tribal allies was Shaikh Zayid. He accompanied his brother to a meeting with the Ruler of Dubai on neutral ground in Sharjah and brought with him a pledge from the Al Manasir and the Al Bu Shamis tribes to observe a two-month truce. But this fragile peace broke down when Shaikh Shakhbut failed to compensate some tribes who had supported him in his campaign against Dubai, had suffered losses in the process and were thus threatening direct action to seek redress from the Dubai faction.[49] Shaikh Zayid went to the Al Manasir, this time accompanied by his brother Shaikh Hazza, in an attempt to secure the peace, but again without lasting success.[50] Gradually, raiding declined but it was not until 1948–1949 that the hostilities finally petered out.

The lesson drawn from these events was that tribal warfare, once unleashed, was hard to contain. Tribesmen were not like disciplined soldiers who fought or ceased to fight on command. Thus, even after the Rulers of Abu Dhabi and Dubai were willing to come to terms, repercussions of the tribal war still reverberated. As late as the summer of 1950, the Political Resident noted rumors that Shaikh Zayid, "the most forceful and manly character in the Shaikhdom," was massing armed men in a show of force against the dissident tribes.[51] This was not an attempt to re-open the war but rather to remind any tribes that through their continued raiding they would suffer severe retribution at his hands.

Shaikh Zayid played a peacemaker's role in this long dispute, but he also knew that the underlying problem was the tribesmen's lack of security. When his brother, the Ruler, refused to compensate them for what they had lost in his service, they had little alternative but to return to the practice of raiding. Out of this grew Shaikh Zayid's passionate conviction that the harsh conditions of the desert needed to be alleviated wherever possible. If any good came out of the tragic days of 1945–1948, it was the absolute determination on Shaikh Zayid's part that the two neighbors – Abu Dhabi and Dubai – should resolve any differences peacefully, as well as the belief that tribal war should never again be allowed to disturb the peace of the interior. To that end, as soon as he became Ruler, he began the process of settling the Bedouin and ensuring that they gained a stake in the community.[52]

Shaikh Zayid retained the respect of the tribes even when he needed to act against them. This honor and respect came to play a key role in the most severe test he faced as the Ruler's Representative in al Ain. Since there were no boundary lines drawn on the map, in accordance with international law, it was increasingly the allegiance of the inhabitants that determined borders. The tribes in al Dhafrah declared their loyalty to Abu Dhabi, but the Saudi government sought to find ways around this political reality. Here, the purpose of the years of assiduous 'tax collection' by Saudi agents became clear. It was claimed that these tribes that had paid the so-called *zakat* had thereby acknowledged Saudi rule. While this was not the case, sporadic attempts to build a claim continued for 20 years.

There were two periods of active contention, the first in the 1930s mentioned earlier in this chapter, and one that lasted over a much longer period from 1949 until the mid-1970s. Both disagreements concerned boundaries but did not involve the same border. In the 1930s, the focal point was the ownership of Khur al 'Udaid, an area of Abu Dhabi which had long been a point of contention. In 1949, the core issue was the ownership of a very large area of the desert lands of Abu Dhabi. There was also a claim by Saudi Arabia over some of the villages close to al Ain and over part of the same oasis complex fed by the waters from Jabal Hafit but which were under the suzerainty of the Sultan of Oman. Because the oasis complex was of such crucial importance, this became the focal point of the territorial dispute.

Initially, the argument was conducted between the British government and the government of Saudi Arabia, rather than directly between the Ruler of Abu Dhabi and the King of Saudi Arabia. The hidden force behind the enlarged claim of 1949 was the American oil company ARAMCO, which was anxious to secure the broadest possible expanse of oil-bearing land within the limit of its license from the Kingdom of Saudi Arabia. In fact, it was the ARAMCO research department in Dhahran that provided much of the documentation used to create the Saudi claim.[53] This process of manufacturing or marshaling evidence for a Saudi claim and producing a narrative was built around the need to make a case in international law. It bore no relation to the facts on the ground, to real allegiances or interests. The legal department of ARAMCO, faced with the challenge of making a political claim without any real substance or helpful documentation, had to set about creating the best case they could. It was an effective piece of work, couched in legal terminology but based on scraps of evidence and skirting the innumerable points of evidential weakness. The entire proposition was a fabrication rather than a factual representation.[54]

Shaikh Zayid intuitively grasped that the issue was that of loyalties and allegiance rather than treaty rights and legal argument. In a letter to the Political Officer, he stated, "[It is] clear to you what Turki [Turki Bin 'Utaishan, the Saudi commander] is doing in our country and with our subjects—giving them money, encouraging disobedience and making it worth their while to disown allegiance to us."[55] Shaikh Zayid had no doubt regarding Abu Dhabi's rights, which were known throughout the desert. Yet, in this case, these rights needed to be proved far away from the desert in an international court, which was a very different matter. Shaikh Zayid was able to provide testimony that the tribes, apart from a few renegades whose statements constituted much of the Saudi case, were loyal to Abu Dhabi. He noted, "We are still protecting and helping them, giving them what is good. Happiness and comfort, faith and freedom from worry."[56] In practice, the tribesmen stood behind 'their' Zayid as the Representative of the Ruler of Abu Dhabi. There was no doubt about the depth and steadfastness of their commitment. They 'belonged' to Abu Dhabi and not to Saudi Arabia.

In the 1930s, the first claim was formulated at the Royal Court in Riyadh, but it was only after the Second World War that King Abdul Aziz turned to the professional American lawyers of ARAMCO to assist him. In the interim, while the pressure from al Hasa diminished during the 1940s, it never ceased entirely. Tax collectors were still sent out into Abu Dhabi territory and concerted efforts were made to shore up support for the Saudi position among the uncommitted tribes. Meanwhile, Shaikh Zayid's success in keeping the peace around al Ain was noted when the PDTC survey team that explored the area in 1947 was able to work in complete security "without any opposition or interference by recalcitrant tribesmen or common robbers."[57] Nevertheless, the whole area became a point of contention in the search for oil between PDTC licensed by the Ruler of Abu Dhabi, and teams sent out by ARAMCO under the aegis of Saudi Arabia. In April 1949, a number of ARAMCO exploration groups were intercepted, and protests were made to the government in Riyadh. On April 26, 1949, the Saudi government responded that the ARAMCO parties were only working in Saudi territory, "as was borne out by the presence in the area of tribes owing allegiance to Saudi Arabia."[58]

Thus began a dispute that lasted a quarter of a century and was only brought to an end gradually by the patient diplomacy of Shaikh Zayid. Initially, from 1949 to the early 1960s, he was in the front line of defending Abu Dhabi against encroachment. For almost three years, the case was argued diplomatically, but in July 1952 the Saudis decided to establish a presence in Hamasah, a village that formed part of the Muscat portion of the oasis complex around al Ain. While the Sultan of Muscat gathered his array of tribesmen, the British sent a detachment of the Trucial Oman Scouts to al Ain as a measure of support for Shaikh Zayid.

Fearing a bloodbath, the British used diplomatic pressure to halt the advance of the Sultan's army. Looking back, it might have been better to allow the Sultan of Muscat to expel the interlopers by force from his village and territory. This would probably have settled the issue once and for all. However, the Foreign Office wanted to achieve a solution that would not alienate the Saudi authorities. As a result, two years of fruitless negotiation followed, during which time Shaikh Zayid was faced with the crucial problem of securing the loyalty of the tribes in al Ain. Tribal loyalties and traditional tribal territories were at the heart of the argument over allegiance. If the tribesmen agreed with the contention of the Riyadh government that they owed allegiance to King Abdul Aziz, as some had done, then it would prove very difficult to resist the Saudi claim that the area, which plainly included Abu Dhabi territory, was a part of Saudi Arabia and that the people who lived in that area and its vicinity bore allegiance to the Saudi King.[59] In retrospect, had Shaikh Zayid not been able to hold the main tribes loyal to Abu Dhabi at al Ain during the most critical phase of the dispute with Saudi Arabia, it is entirely possible that Abu Dhabi would have lost most of its present territory.

In the village of Hamasah, the Saudi Commander, Turki Bin 'Utaishan, provided food and money to any tribesmen and their families who would join him. In return, all those who accepted his hospitality had to declare their allegiance to the Saudi King. Meanwhile, in al Ain, economic resources were scarce, and Shaikh Zayid had little to offer to counter the food and money offered by the Saudis. Yet, despite the incentives offered to many tribesmen to switch allegiance, the vast majority of the Abu Dhabi tribes remained loyal to the Al Nahyan. For more than the two years during which the British government followed its diplomatic strategy, Shaikh Zayid continued and was able to sustain the morale of his people. The level of loyalty seems remarkable, but born in al Ain, a child of the oasis, they knew his reputation and were sure he would never abandon them. Every new ploy by the detachment in Hamasah was reported to him, and several direct attempts were made to suborn his own loyalty to his brother. All these overtures were spurned.

At the same time, the path of diplomacy in which the British had invested such high expectations proved a dead end. The International Tribunal in Geneva, to which Shaikh Zayid gave evidence that, in a desperate move, the Saudis in Hamasah had even tried to bribe him to betray Abu Dhabi, broke up in disarray on October 4, 1955.[60] Eventually, force appeared to be the only remaining option. On October 26, 1955, the Trucial Oman Scouts, supported by aircraft of the Royal Air Force and the forces of the Sultan of Muscat, captured the occupied village and expelled the Saudis. In the aftermath of the action, they found a huge war chest filled with rupees,[61] incriminating documents,[62] arms and ammunition.[63]

For two years and three months, Shaikh Zayid and his people were under siege. The blandishments emanating from Hamasah were ceaseless. During that time, although lacking similar resources, Shaikh Zayid embarked on a counter-strategy. He persuaded tribes that had wavered to the Saudi side to return to Abu Dhabi allegiance. He gathered intelligence and anticipated the moves that Turki Bin 'Utaishan would make. His greatest difficulty was keeping his tribesmen in check in order to avoid any acts of provocation that could possibly harm the Abu Dhabi case before the International Tribunal. In the light of all these tactics, despite being short of food and money, Shaikh Zayid fought a masterly campaign, consistently outmaneuvering his opponent. He denied the Saudis what they were convinced was certain victory.

It is essential to analyze the events of that victory in some detail, first because there is a unique and credible eyewitness account, and second because in this case one can see Shaikh Zayid at work at a moment of vital importance for the future of Abu Dhabi.[64] In terms of a military engagement, it was barely a skirmish—the forces involved were insignificant and no one was killed. Yet, the underlying tactical plan in Shaikh Zayid's mind and its strategic consequences were of considerable importance. For Edward Henderson, who was approached by the Political Resident to be his Personal Representative in the final sequence of events at Hamasah, the commanding figure as the Saudis were expelled on October 26 was Shaikh Zayid with his brother Hazza, "looking at the scene through their binoculars, with a group of their men standing near by."[65] As Henderson makes clear, Shaikh Zayid was close to the scene of the action, and his role was that of the general moving the units around on the battlefield. His whole discussion with Henderson was framed in those terms. Analyzing what he said and what he did, it is clear that all his actions were defined within a framework of strategic goals.

Shaikh Zayid had two opponents, linked but distinct. One was the Saudi government, whose motives were modern—economic advantage and an expansionist foreign policy. The other were the tribes, mostly outside the Bani Yas alliance, whose interest was traditional—freedom from constraint. The tribes were the means by which the Saudis could lay claim to Abu Dhabi's territory and, hence the long campaign by Riyadh to enlist them as Saudi subjects. Nor should it be forgotten that for all the apparently modern motives of the Saudi government, it had a strongly Bedouin perspective. Thus, it seems appropriate to understand the essential conflict in traditional and tribal terms rather than from a modernist perspective. Shaikh Zayid had to achieve two objectives: first, to expel the Saudis and to halt their long campaign of expansion, but in a way that did not outrage their Bedouin sense of honor; second, he had to persuade all the tribes around al Ain to regard Abu Dhabi as the predominant emirate in the region, as they had done in the days of his grandfather, Zayid the Great.[66] Some of the leaders of the tribes which were firmly in the Saudi camp had to be removed if this realignment was to take place. If a war was fought, the result would be the creation of a blood feud that might last for decades.

Thus, he was faced with a conundrum. He needed to play an active role and yet stand aside from the conflict, so that he could remain a 'man of honor' whom the tribes would accept and not a sworn enemy. During the two years of the Saudi occupation, he had kept open lines of communication – and certainly sources of military intelligence – to the opposing side. He was circumspect in what he said, not wanting to antagonize anyone with whom he might have to work in the future. To win the war, he had to appear disengaged from the fight.

Shaikh Zayid's objective was to restore the standing of Abu Dhabi among the tribes of the region to that which it had held in the days of his grandfather. Given his strategic need to appear detached, he was content to let the British publicly be seen to have expelled the Saudis from Hamasah. The danger had been ever present that the Foreign Office would find some way of evading its commitment to Abu Dhabi. Already, before the Second World War, the British had seriously considered pressuring Shaikh Shakhbut to offer a section of Abu Dhabi territory to appease the Saudis.[67] This kind of strategy was definitely unacceptable to Shaikh Zayid and the ruling family as a whole. Then the Foreign Office had tried diplomatic means, hoping for some kind of compromise, but this proved fruitless when the extent of the illicit activity by Bin 'Utaishan became clear. By using the Trucial Oman Scouts to expel the Saudis from Hamasah, the British were seen by the Bedouin to be feuding with the leaders in Riyadh.

In this case, Shaikh Zayid's instincts were pragmatic. He was well aware of his grandfather's skillful use of the British, as discussed in Chapter 2, to bring the Al Qubaisat tribe back into allegiance. His maternal grandfather belonged to the Al Qubaisat and he knew their history as well as he knew the history of the Bani Yas. He realized that to use a surrogate was always more politically astute than personal involvement. He had planned and choreographed his approach carefully in advance, as can be seen in Henderson's account of the events: "Sheikh Zayed turned to his brother, and had a long talk, at the end of which Sheikh Hazza turned to me: 'This is not our affair, as you know. Our people and our villagers are not directly involved.'"[68] This point was stressed more than once to Henderson. What Shaikh Zayid meant was that he did not want to become involved in a blood feud with the other tribes of the oasis complex that were not under his rule because that would merely have complicated the situation.

After the Saudi occupation, he faced the much more complex problem of regaining the allegiance of formerly hostile tribes. Unless he did so, there could never be true peace in the interior. Therefore, even as the crisis was unfolding, Shaikh Zayid was issuing guarantees of safe conduct to the pro-Saudi tribal leaders under the Sultan of Muscat's rule, so that they could come and talk with him and the Resident's representative. It soon became clear, however, that the dissident leaders would not accept the Sultan's government, and they would not meet his representatives. Shaikh Hazza, who was then accompanying Henderson and spoke for Shaikh Zayid, asked Henderson to repeat Shaikh Zayid's guarantee of their safety while they were on Abu Dhabi territory. With that reminder, negotiations moved forward. An emissary of the dissident leaders arrived and asked to speak to Henderson alone.[69] He stated that his uncles would never surrender to the Sultan, but Henderson made it clear that there was no alternative. The negotiations continued. Henderson then describes what followed:

> Shortly after half-past midnight…out of the darkness came the old Ford pick-up with no lights; and as it drew up in front of us I could see the figures of the three shaikhs and the driver crammed in the front, and a large group of their followers were in the back.
>
> They got down slowly and walked rather stiffly to where Shaikh Zayed was standing. They rubbed noses and spoke the greetings softly. Shaikh Zayed answered as quietly…[70]

It was at this time that the dissident shaikhs surrendered and agreed to go into exile in Saudi Arabia rather than surrender to the Sultan's forces. It was Shaikh Zayid's offer to do all he could that had avoided further bloodshed.[71] At the same time, a more significant event occurred. As Henderson recounts:

> The shaikhs remained standing looking utterly tired and dejected…Coffee was handed around and nothing was said until

from behind the shaikhs two men appeared. They were dressed in the usual long white robes and they wore dark cloaks; but I saw that their black head-ropes were round their necks like halters and their black and white headcloths were draped around their shoulders.

As they approached Shaikh Zayed they went down on their knees in the sand and started to crawl towards him…I then realised that they were the two heads of families who alone of all the people of Abu Dhabi had joined the Saudis during the three years of their presence in Hamasah.

It was a dramatic moment and I was full of curiosity as to Shaikh Zayed's reaction. As the first one reached him, and seemed to be trying to kiss his feet, Shaikh Zayed with the natural dignity which is especially his, stooped, took him by the shoulders, raised him and said: "Peace be unto you. You are forgiven and you may return to your house in peace."

He did the like with the second.

Both of them made for Shaikh Hazza who said with dignity in a soft voice. "You heard the brother's word. Go to your homes. He has forgiven you."

This dignified and decisive act of the shaikhs made a great impression on all of us.[72]

If any parallel was sought for this course of events, it would be Shaikh Zayid's grandfather's action at Khur al 'Udaid referred to earlier. The similarities are striking. There too, the Ruler used the British to fulfill his purpose, and there too, he brought the straying Bani Yas factions back into the fold. Moreover, the objectives in 1955 and in 1879 were completely congruent, for what was at stake in both cases was tribal unity.

Once the British agreed to remove the Saudis, the territorial issue was no longer Shaikh Zayid's principal concern. He focused, as he had throughout, on maintaining the territory and tribal dominance of Abu Dhabi. The symbolism of the scene that Henderson described is the restoration of the tribal system that had prevailed under Zayid the Great. The final challenge, the long Saudi attempt to suborn the tribes of the hinterland that had lasted from the 1920s to the 1950s, had been repulsed. With that danger overcome, there was no challenge to the restoration of the dominant power of Abu Dhabi. That was the significance of what Henderson witnessed, and that was clear to all the Arabs present on that fateful day. Even in victory, Shaikh Zayid's magnanimity extended to all. The dissident shaikhs were offered the choice of surrendering to the Sultan of Muscat or leaving immediately for exile, surrendering all their property in the oasis never to return. They chose immediate exile.

Building a Community Beyond al Ain

In general, it may be said that Shaikh Zayid inherited the mantle of his illustrious and respected grandfather, Shaikh Zayid the Great, whose memory remained an active force among the tribes. Zayid Bin Sultan was known among the tribes. He had sat with them, welcomed them to his *majlis*, settled their disputes and arbitrated between them. He was admired not just by the traditional allies of the Bani Yas but by other tribes as well.[73] He knew all the individual leaders and many of their followers. He knew who could be trusted and who could not. As a man of the desert, he watched and weighed all the daily comings and goings through the oasis and talked at length with visitors to his *majlis*. In accordance with desert tradition, he always wanted to know the news from any passing traveler.[74]

While Shaikh Zayid gained a great personal following among the people of al Ain, it was clear that he remained absolutely loyal to his brother the Ruler, although in the traditional fashion among the tribes he would not hesitate to express a disagreement if he felt it to be necessary. For his part, Shaikh Shakhbut was pleased to take the credit for his sagacious appointment of his brother in 1946, for in the space of a mere three years the position of Abu Dhabi in the region of al Ain was better than it had been for decades. Yet, areas of disagreement between the Ruler and his Representative in al Ain existed.[75] One, in particular, concerned the way in which the state's revenues were to be deployed. In the traditional system, the Ruler took a percentage of the profits of the pearl industry and licensed various other activities, such as fishing. From the 1930s, the oil companies had been making payments on an increasing scale for the rights to explore and extract, and even though oil had not yet been discovered, there was a steady flow of revenue from these sources.

It was Shaikh Zayid's contention that the income of the state should be used for the benefit of the people. His brother, on the other hand, believed that it was necessary to build up the state reserves, possibly to guard against another recession on the model of the 1930s that had proved so devastating. Neither attitude lacked merit, but they revealed the discrepancy in outlook between two generations.[76] Shaikh Shakhbut, who had ruled through the years of the Depression, like so many of his contemporaries elsewhere in the world, became extremely cautious of expenditure. Furthermore, he regarded many of the developments outside the Gulf, which stemmed from the post-war recovery, to be both dangerous and unwelcome. Shaikh Zayid was a much younger man during the Depression years and, although he had also suffered the extreme privations of all in Abu Dhabi during this period, he was imbued with a spirit of optimism for a better future. Progress and change held no fear for him.

It is difficult to find any criticism of Shaikh Zayid in all the written records,[77] except from external forces that had reason to fear his influence among the tribes.[78] His record in al Ain, in promoting tree planting and agriculture, encouraging education, and improving standards of health and housing, became a model for what could be achieved in Abu Dhabi as a whole, with available resources. After 1953, Shaikh Zayid also began to travel abroad. In particular, on a visit to Paris, he saw the great French public hospitals, which fired his determination to bring modern standards of health care to Abu Dhabi.[79]

Despite the 130 years of British presence in the region, Britain had, by its own admission, provided no funds for local development until this time.[80] It was only in the aftermath of the dispute with Saudi Arabia that some contributions began to be made, but these were negligible considering the length of British involvement and the dire development needs of the region. Nevertheless, these meager funds did allow Shaikh Zayid to expand some of his cherished projects. It was also a mark of the high esteem in which he was held by the British government that he was twice visited at al Ain by the Political Resident, Sir Bernard Burrows, once while the Saudis were still in occupation at Hamasah and once afterwards. Normally, the Resident arrived on a warship and stayed for a few days in Abu Dhabi, meeting the Ruler. No Resident had ever before made the arduous journey to al Ain.[81] But in the context of the confrontation with Saudi Arabia, this evidence of support was both welcome and significant. Burrows considered the visit in September 1953 most valuable, even if he was a little overwhelmed by Shaikh Zayid's generous hospitality.[82] Five years later, he returned to al Ain at Shaikh Zayid's invitation, this time accompanied by Lady Burrows. Together they toured the gardens of the oasis and saw the work carried out on the *falaj*. For Burrows, the evidence of considerable progress made since his previous visit, in the midst of the political crisis, was visible on every side.[83]

The Resident now saw with his own eyes what he had been reading in his officials' reports. The previous year he had sent a dispatch to London noting:

> The Political Officer was favourably impressed with conditions in Buraimi [al Ain]…Shaikh Zaid has had a new suq built at Al Ain; while the small school he opened at Muwaiqih four months ago under an energetic Muscati schoolmaster is proving a great success. Though at present there are only twelve pupils, their curriculum, which includes athletics, games and drill, has been carefully thought out and they appear to be progressing well.[84]

This attention to detail, on a matter so minor as the curriculum for 12 children, was typical of Shaikh Zayid. He knew that he had an important role to play in promoting his projects, supporting and monitoring them in order to achieve the desired results. That he was willing to do so was fortunate for the people of al Ain, as it would be for Abu Dhabi as a whole, in future years. The judgment in the Trucial

States Annual Report for 1956 contained one especially significant sentence: "The year has brought out, however, the overwhelming superiority of Sheikh Zayid in every way."[85] In this way, the local British officials indicated to the authorities in London that Shaikh Zayid was a man of substance and integrity—a great leader.

PART
II

THE
TRANSFORMATION

CHAPTER
4

The Imperative for Change

During the 1950s, the emirate of Abu Dhabi experienced disparate paces of development in the settlements of Abu Dhabi and al Ain. Edward Henderson described the island of Abu Dhabi as he had first seen it in 1948, accompanied by Wilfred Thesiger. They stayed in "the only substantial house on the seashore," Bait al Shamali. Recalling his visit, Henderson later wrote:

> Since the death of the great Zayed bin Khalifah in the early years of this century, trading from Abu Dhabi had gone down hill… The souk was tiny, and the majority of houses in which the inhabitants lived were of the palm-branch, *barasti* type. The foreshore of the island was three to four miles in length, and the town occupied only a tiny fraction of this. There was a thin scattered line of date palms just inland of the coast, and there was the cluster of huts which formed the town; then near the palm trees, the large fort.[1]

The Abu Dhabi settlement was to change very little during the ensuing decade. The Ruler's residence was enlarged after 1949, but it remained austere rather than luxurious. The creation of the Development Office by the British government promised change for the future, but in reality little evidence of development was seen in Abu Dhabi. Rather, the limited funds available were distributed between Shaikh Zayid's *falaj* program in al Ain, the building of a school in Sharjah and a new hospital building in Dubai.[2]

In sharp contrast, when he went to al Ain, Henderson noticed the tangible benefits being created by Shaikh Zayid's stewardship since he had become the Ruler's Representative there. Henderson gives the following description:

> …a brick house overlooking a garden…The rows of trees were intersected by irrigation channels, whose mud sluices would be broken and built up again systematically on a time-table to let the water run through by rotation every day or two in each part of the gardens. The water came from underground…springs that were, in some instances, as much as seven miles away under the foot of Jebel Hafit.[3]

There were markets in some of the villages, the newest and most flourishing being the one established by Shaikh Zayid in al Ain itself. Traders and buyers could do business freely and the markets grew rapidly, attracting commerce from afar.[4] Shaikh Zayid had also initiated the building of new roads that made it easier for traders to transport their goods to the coast and, from there, on to other regions of the world.[5]

The evident success of these developments, which were undertaken by Shaikh Zayid at his own expense, produced an unforeseen outcome. When in 1954, after 130 years in the region, the British government belatedly began to allocate limited resources for development, the enhancement of Shaikh Zayid's irrigation project topped the list. In a letter from the Foreign Office to the Treasury Department, the British official A.C.I. Samuel appended the following note:

> Not only is the project amply justified on economic grounds, but on political grounds also. The principal landowner of the region is Sheikh Zaid, brother of the Ruler of Abu Dhabi. Sheikh Zaid has been a tower of strength during our difficulties in Buraimi [al Ain], and we need to show our appreciation of his staunchness. According to the Political Resident, he would "appreciate nothing more than assistance in improving the supply of water to his gardens" [in al Ain].[6]

Visitors to al Ain would continue to contrast its relative development to that of Abu Dhabi throughout the 1950s and 1960s. At the end of October 1962, the Economic Secretary for the region, J.P. Tripp, visited Abu Dhabi. He spoke to the merchants and businessmen in the town and in the docks, from whom he received a torrent of complaints, all stemming from a lack of investment in development. Some leading foreign firms were losing £1,000 a month as a result. Tripp also went to meet Shaikh Zayid, who happened to be in town and mentioned the complaints of the merchants and traders.[7] Following a trip to al Ain, Tripp reported that he had found a great contrast between the bustle of al Ain and the absence of comparable activity in Abu Dhabi:

> Zaid has built a number of new shops which he has given to merchants rent-free. He has encouraged Persians and Indians to set up in business and as a result there seems to be more commercial activity in [al Ain] than in Abu Dhabi. Zaid told me that the number of tribesman [sic] coming up from Oman to sell their agricultural produce had increased significantly over the past few months.
>
> As regards agriculture, over 150 pumps have been installed during the past few months... Zaid was particularly proud of the increase in water in the Falajes on which he has been working for the past twelve years. The volume of water now delivered to the [al Ain] villages and gardens from these underground channels has been trebled in the past few years... It was encouraging to see... the children returning from school: this contrasted well with the absence of a school in Abu Dhabi. There were about seventy boys between the ages of seven and fifteen at school, which is staffed by Jordanians.[8]

For Tripp, the contrast between Abu Dhabi and al Ain could not have been more apparent. The former was a society fast falling apart, with rising discontent, one that could easily fall prey to outside agitators. At the same time, in al Ain, Tripp saw an active, bustling, happy town, where children were being educated. In the end, such an obvious contrast would ultimately provide the most powerful imperative for change in the emirate.

Despite the focus on development, the oasis continued to lack many amenities. The most pressing need was for a good doctor and effective health care. When a young girl was severely burnt in an accident, there was no hospital closer than Sharjah. Shaikh Zayid lent his own Land Rover to take the little girl across the desert to Sharjah, but she died on the way.[9] When his own mother, Shaikha Salamah, fell ill, a British doctor had to be rushed to al Ain.[10] These incidents made Shaikh Zayid all the more determined to ensure that the people of al Ain would receive access to proper medical services as soon as possible. In 1960, he encouraged the establishment of a missionary clinic in the oasis. In contrast, Abu Dhabi did not have its own hospital until 1967, after Shaikh Zayid became Ruler.

By the 1950s, a new political environment began to influence aspects of growth and development in the region. In the Arab world beyond the Gulf, everything was in flux. The old political structures, created in the aftermath of the First World War by the British and French, had been radically transformed in the years after the Second World War. First, British control over the oil industry in Iran by the Anglo–Iranian Oil Company was summarily terminated by the short-lived Nationalist government of Dr. Muhammad Mossadiq (1951–1953). The monarchy in Egypt, which began with Muhammad Ali in 1805, ended in 1952 with the deposition of King Faruq by the Free Officers Movement headed by Jamal Abdel Nasser. Four years later, Egypt successfully nationalized the Suez Canal and resisted a combined assault by France and Britain with Israeli collusion. President Nasser rapidly became an Arab hero, leading Egypt into a brief union with Syria by establishing the United Arab Republic between 1958 and 1961. In 1958, the new monarchy in Iraq, so carefully crafted by the Allies in 1921, was destroyed by a military coup. These sets of events, though rooted in local and national realities, revealed a common theme. In each case, the underlying objective was a transformation of Arab society, freeing it from European colonial rule.

From Cairo, the new *Voice of the Arabs* radio station broadcast a heady message: all Arabs everywhere were brothers and should join together in their struggle against Western imperialism. In the Gulf, these ideas had a muted but still powerful impact. The British, largely complacent during the early 1950s, became concerned with advancing 'Nasserism' after 1956.[11] The United States, alarmed by the global spread of Communism, tried to configure alliance systems that would resist the advance of the Soviet Union towards the Iranian and Arabian oilfields. Both Britain and the United States recognized that the Gulf's significance would be transformed by the likely discovery of oil, making the region attractive to outside powers and interests. For Britain in particular, it meant a dramatic revision of priorities, especially since Saudi Arabia was utilizing its oil revenues to strengthen its regional position. Recognizing its vulnerability, Britain would for the first time provide resources to improve living standards in the Trucial States.[12]

As Abu Dhabi looked likely to become an oil state with substantial revenues, Britain perceived the dangers for traditional governments in the Gulf. British officials believed that the old political structures could be preserved, because they were congruent with the needs of the region, but needed to be adapted to meet the demands of the new age.[13] Where once they had accepted the traditional patterns in the Trucial States, they now advocated modifications to suit changing circumstances. This apparent altruism had an underlying motive. Although there might be benefits to the peoples of the region, the focal objective was to ensure a new market for British goods. Viewed in their totality, the internal and external dynamics of change would exert powerful pressure on the Trucial States.

Shaikh Shakhbut's Resistance to Change

Although the widespread political turmoil mentioned above would play an important role, the most powerful catalysts for change were largely economic. It should be noted that even before the flow of oil revenues began in the 1960s, the financial resources of Abu Dhabi were already considerable. From 1940 onwards, the Ruler had been receiving an annual payment of Rs 100,000 for exploration rights.[14] In December 1950, an agreement with the Superior Oil Company provided for a payment of Rs 1.5 million and an annual fixed payment of Rs 1 million until oil was discovered.[15] Thus, in the early 1950s, the Ruler's coffers were fuller than they had ever been before, even at the height of the pearling boom before the First World War.

Yet, a state with potentially vast wealth perforce had a different role and status from that of a nation functioning at the level of subsistence. Oil was anticipated long before it became a reality, and its possible discovery had already distorted relationships with Abu Dhabi's closest neighbors.[16] There were many disappointments during the long and fruitless years of exploration before oil was finally discovered in significant quantities in the late 1950s. The scale of the first oil strike, which was to be processed through a new installation on Das Island, was more substantial than expected.[17] As a result, the new revenues would be sufficient to finance large-scale growth in the whole region, and Abu Dhabi was poised to acquire immense wealth for its own development.[18] Ultimately, the discovery of oil heralded a new era not only for Abu Dhabi but for all the states in the region.[19]

This prospect of oil wealth did not, however, initiate a process of change in Shaikh Shakhbut's outlook. He was careful by nature, always mindful after the experience of the Great Depression that good fortune was evanescent. He regarded the inexorable tide of social and economic change with growing trepidation.[20]

The conservatism and caution that defined his character grew stronger and, under pressure, his decisions became increasingly unpredictable. His relationship with the oil companies was a case in point. To the companies themselves, Shaikh Shakhbut initially displayed a reasonable attitude, determined to reach agreements. However, his mistrust of the companies' motives grew despite his high personal regard for many of the individual company representatives. He ensured that he was well informed by reading the newspapers and listening to the radio, keeping abreast of the political and economic developments of the day. He knew that the oil companies had to follow policy laid down by their management in London. His caution in respect of British policy and the interests of the oil companies was often amply justified. It is clear from the documents that the oil companies wanted to secure the best possible deal, and in their eagerness assumed that the Shaikh would accept whatever terms they proffered.[21] For Shaikh Shakhbut, this proposal represented a re-run of the 1930s when he had been urged by the British government to accept what he believed was a disadvantageous oil agreement. He had then achieved more satisfactory results by holding out for better terms despite strong pressure from British officials. Likewise in the 1950s, he had rejected British advice over the maritime exploration rights and had been vindicated by an arbitration award.

It was customary at the time, especially among the British, to criticize Shaikh Shakhbut for his supposed stubbornness and intransigence. This criticism must be interpreted with care. Frequently, the real cause of British complaints about the Ruler's inflexibility was simply that he would not comply with their agenda, which often ignored the interests of Abu Dhabi.[22] While the oil companies were more interested in keeping down the marginal cost of oil production, the British government was primarily anxious to preserve its own political position.[23]

Initially, Shaikh Shakhbut handled these matters on his own.[24] The negotiations developed without the advice of Shaikh Zayid, who was preoccupied in the early days of oil development with the affairs of al Ain and with the complex and persistent border concerns. However, the issue of oil became indicative of growing divergence in attitude between the two brothers. It was not that Shaikh Zayid favored the oil companies or the British government, but he had a clear and practical view of how oil revenues should be used in Abu Dhabi. The Ruler seemed wholly unwilling to address the imperatives for change, preferring to emphasize the need for vigilance over dealings with the British and the oil companies. Although his caution was largely justified, this approach obscured the higher issues at stake. In Shaikh Zayid's view, if the Ruler were to accept oil revenues, some plan had to be formulated for their proper allocation. The money could be reinvested abroad. Alternatively, it could be invested in infrastructure and social improvement. What was unthinkable was to accumulate it and not utilize it for public benefit. For Shaikh Zayid, the priorities were clear. The resources, or at least a large portion, should be invested in infrastructure and the advancement of the people.

Throughout the 1950s, it had already become increasingly apparent that Shaikh Zayid was a man of action. Though he had full authority over all of al Ain, with regard to the rest of the emirate he could only offer advice. The exception was when he acted for the Ruler during Shaikh Shakhbut's visits abroad.[25] On one such occasion, in the summer of 1960, with Shaikh Shakhbut on an official visit to London and other European cities for the duration of the summer, Shaikh Zayid, as Acting Ruler, immediately, and with a sense of urgency, began to put into effect long-standing plans for the building of roads and improvement of water resources. There was an element of risk in these actions, because the Ruler might have felt that, as Acting Ruler, Shaikh Zayid had overstepped his mandate by authorizing such a level of expenditure from public assets. Yet, as a confidential British source noted, "The Ruler of Abu Dhabi returned from his travels abroad on September 13 [1960]. Unexpectedly, he did not show any outward sign of dissatisfaction at Shaikh Zaid's expenditure on road development but continued the good work, albeit less energetically."[26] Significantly, the next monthly report stated:

> Having arrived back from his summer visit to the United Kingdom and Europe only three weeks previously, the Ruler of Abu Dhabi set off again, this time to the U.S., by way of Kuwait and the U.K. Rumour has it that he is seeking medical treatment for his eyes. In the meantime, dissatisfaction with Sheikh Shakhbut's unwillingness to finance development seems to be on the increase.[27]

There were definite limits to these initiatives undertaken by Shaikh Zayid. Following this episode, Shaikh Zayid told A.J.M. Craig from the Political Agency in Dubai that he had no further plans for development to be carried out in his brother's next absence, as the Ruler was unwilling to accept new ideas. As far as Shaikh Zayid was concerned:

> Shakhbut did not understand the value of anything new. Education, hospitals, public works—all had to be explained to him over and over again…[Zayid] himself had on occasion forced Shakhbut's hand by carrying out works without permission and risking his wrath; and once the storm had blown over Shakhbut had come to like the ideas and demanded to know why no one had suggested them before.[28]

Although Shaikh Shakhbut would not actively reverse Shaikh Zayid's projects by countermanding his orders, it appears clear that he was not going to offer his support either. On his return, he would frequently obstruct ongoing projects.[29] Craig added that he had also spoken to

Shaikh Khalid Bin Sultan, who stated that the whole family was dissatisfied with Shakhbut's attitude, since he would not spend any money and would not delegate any authority to them so that they could implement projects for which he himself lacked energy and interest.[30]

The historical record indicates that while the Ruler usually did not say outright in public that he would never sanction development, on many occasions, including the meetings of the Trucial States Council, he frequently questioned the benefits of wide-ranging development. Shaikh Shakhbut, while encouraging the general prospect of change, in the end only frustrated its fulfillment. Often, he would lead foreign companies to believe that he was about to make major investments with his growing resources, only to find fault with their proposals, their personnel or, most frequently, their financial arrangements.[31] Similarly, he would agree with the Political Agent or the Political Resident about the need to employ teachers, judges, skilled technicians, senior police officers, even a professional European secretary, and would then find some cause to dismiss them or undermine the initiatives.[32]

The Role of Shaikh Zayid in an Era of Change

Two polarities were beginning to emerge in Abu Dhabi during the late 1950s and into the 1960s—passivity on the side of Shaikh Shakhbut and activism on that of Shaikh Zayid. Shaikh Shakhbut had been the right man to calm the political turmoil of the 1920s, and in the first few years of his rule the tensions of the immediate past were defused. Yet, new challenges were emerging from the mid-1930s, notably the pressure emanating from Saudi Arabia, for which there were no easy solutions. Moreover, they were all inextricably linked. The territorial challenge meant that the Ruler of Abu Dhabi needed to secure support among his own people, and one means to do so was through the process of social and economic development. In essence, this was little more than the old tribal equation of loyalty and reward detailed in Chapter 1, now cast in a new guise. The connection was immediately perceived by Shaikh Zayid but elicited little response from Shaikh Shakhbut.

Had the two brothers both been resident in Abu Dhabi the distinction between them might well have engendered conflict, but the distance between them – Shaikh Shakhbut in the capital and his brother in al Ain – masked the contrast between passive and active government for many years. Nevertheless, although the growing political rift between them was concealed, it formed an undercurrent to unfolding events. What increasingly concerned Shaikh Zayid during his time in al Ain was the impact that frustrated reform and slow development would have on the Abu Dhabi emirate as a whole. For example, the consistent and effective control which he exercised over the hinterland of al Ain stood in stark contrast to the situation in Liwa, where the influence of Abu Dhabi was much less emphatic. When Martin Buckmaster, a Political Officer from Sharjah, visited al Ain prior to an exploratory visit to Liwa in 1952, he was impressed that Shaikh Hazza, Shaikh Zayid's brother, was "remarkably well informed," but he also recorded that Shaikh Zayid "admitted privately that he felt ashamed that none of the influential members of his family had visited Liwa before."[33]

In comparison with Al Nahyan power in al Ain, where Shaikh Zayid was in full command, the authority of the Ruler's Representative in the Liwa region, Ahmad Bin Fadhil, was much more constrained, although he carried out his duties as effectively as possible. The consequences would prove to be serious as Abu Dhabi's power in Liwa and the interior of the emirate declined. The intrusions by unlicensed oil exploration parties, as discussed in Chapter 3, were serious challenges to the authority of the Abu Dhabi government. Buckmaster considered it a significant incursion when he found track marks indicating illicit exploration by ARAMCO survey parties in Abu Dhabi territory.[34] So did Henderson, who noted that, from 1948 onwards, ARAMCO started to send out survey parties that made forays into Abu Dhabi territory. He even found one group almost on the Abu Dhabi–Dubai border, where their leader pretended he had lost his way.[35]

Shaikh Zayid knew that unless the Ruler of Abu Dhabi could exercise his control over the whole of his territory as effectively as he himself did in the region of al Ain, Abu Dhabi's sovereign rights would gradually be eroded. Shaikh Shakhbut's failure to attend to the needs of the tribes meant that support for Abu Dhabi was slowly diminishing, and despite everything that Shaikh Zayid was doing, the inability of the Ruler to act in support of his people was slowly destroying the state. While a raid by neighboring Bedouin was one thing, a succession of Western oil survey teams was entirely another. Shaikh Zayid's belief, buttressed by his experience in al Ain, was that the state's greatest strength lay in the loyalty of its people. Yet, he knew that the people expected reciprocity from their Rulers, and their loyalty merited financial support. Shaikh Zayid's own resources were overstretched in providing for his people in al Ain and he had nothing left to offer by way of support to the people of Liwa or other parts of Abu Dhabi. However, he sought from an early date to transfer whatever resources the state possessed for the benefit of the people. In this outlook, altruism blended with an acute political acumen. The traditional political system was based on the mutual interests of the Ruler and the people. If that essential equation was not maintained, then the effect on Abu Dhabi could be catastrophic.

By the early 1960s, the great danger within Abu Dhabi was that the people were becoming restive.[36] It was well known that other states in the region were doing more for their people than Abu Dhabi, and the Ruler, who lived a life of utmost frugality, was reluctant to invest the state's revenues in funding essential improvements.[37] The fissiparous tendencies of the tribal community, where tribes would simply move their abode and attach themselves to other Rulers, had started to emerge once again. The unity that Shaikh Zayid had managed to preserve for so long in al Ain, bonding the people together against offers of food and money, was beginning to fracture in Abu Dhabi itself.[38] The same was happening in Liwa and in other areas distant from Shaikh Zayid's personal influence.[39] Abu Dhabi was suddenly confronted with the prospect of instability.[40] The imbalance between popular expectations and the realities of state functioning had become acute. As a result, all the leading groups in the state – the prominent members of the ruling family, the British advisors, even companies with commercial interests in the development of Abu Dhabi – seemed unanimous in their opinion that change was imperative in the interests of development.

Indications of a possible shift in the structure of authority within the state had already appeared in the 1950s. A sense of collective responsibility in Abu Dhabi had begun to emerge. In the first oil company agreement, the Ruler alone was named, but in the 1950 concession it was specified that the Ruler was to be represented by "a three man committee composed of Hazza'a bin Sultan, Khaled bin Sultan and Za'id bin Sultan."[41] This signaled a potential shift in the governmental structure of Abu Dhabi, where the Ruler seemed willing to delegate some of his duties to his brothers. In practice, however, he seemed reluctant to implement the concession he had already made in principle. Yet, the involvement of his brothers in the running of the state continued to grow during the 1950s.[42]

The most important of these roles was representation on the new Trucial States Council which was established in 1952. It was clear by the early 1950s that many of the difficulties between the Rulers of all the Trucial States were occasioned by the lack of direct contact. The creation of the Council provided a forum where they could meet and talk, outside the strict limits of protocol and the rules of hospitality.[43] In the coming years, the Council was to play a crucial role in developing Shaikh Zayid's connections and political influence before he himself became Ruler.

Until the creation of the Council, the British government had only conferred with each Ruler individually, but it had become clear that there were political benefits in having a forum for general discussion. A consultative Council was clearly more open and democratic than the old system of private negotiation.[44] The British were becoming increasingly sensitive to accusations of 'imperialism' and were worried about the growing interest of the Arab League in the Lower Gulf.[45] The hope was that a common line of policy could be developed through the medium of the Council. Thus, the agenda was set by the Political Officer in Sharjah, who raised issues on which he sought the collective opinions of the Rulers. Although the Ruler of Abu Dhabi did not attend the first meeting, the initial discussion did set the tone for later events.[46] The principal issues discussed in March 1952 – cultured pearls, locust control and the Trucial States hospital in Dubai – were matters that affected all the emirates.[47]

In the early days, the meetings were stilted and constrained.[48] Shaikh Hazza and Shaikh Zayid both attended the meeting on April 25, 1953, but neither are recorded as having joined in the discussion. However, by the session of July 5, 1954, the presence of Shaikh Zayid had served to transform the character of the meetings and opened up a pattern of freer discussion. The meeting was held in the drawing room of the Agency Residence, converted into an improvised council chamber for the occasion.[49] Pirie Gordon, the Political Agent, noted that Shaikh Zayid, whom custom prevented from speaking in the formal meeting while the Ruler of Abu Dhabi was present, afterwards "took the opportunity privately to identify the State of Abu Dhabi wholeheartedly with the proceedings and decisions of the Council."[50]

Furthermore, a new rapport was developing within the Council among its younger and more energetic members. While Shaikh Zayid spoke forcefully behind the scenes for Abu Dhabi, Shaikh Rashid played an equally valuable and effective role for Dubai. Again as Pirie Gordon observed, "forbidden by Arab etiquette to assert himself in the presence of his father…[Shaikh Rashid] played so leading a part in discussion, [that it was considered desirable for the future] that the aged Ruler of Dubai should continue to be absent."[51]

The lasting collaboration between these two men, so fortuitous for the future of the region, developed from these meetings. A new Political Agent, J.P. Tripp, writing to the Acting Political Resident C.A. Gault in August 1955, observed that "Shaiks Rashid, Hazza and Zaid…appeared to be extremely friendly towards each other."[52] In subsequent Council meetings, the Rulers themselves began to observe that one of the functions of the Trucial States Council meetings was to allow them to meet effectively on neutral ground. "If Rulers did not meet, they could not get over past grudges. Council meetings had given them opportunities for seeing each other; the more they saw of each other, the more friendly they would become."[53]

The regular presence of Shaikh Zayid at the meetings of the Trucial States Council gave him considerable experience in dealing with the Rulers of the region and, more importantly, the opportunity to get to know their heirs and other sons. Although not a ruler himself, as the Ruler's Representative in al Ain he had an official status and on occasion was able to intervene decisively in the discussions, as for example over matters such as health and roads.[54] As a result of Shaikh Zayid's positive support for the objectives of the Council, over time Shaikh Shakhbut's own contribution became more engaged. At the meeting on November 17, 1953, the Ruler of Abu Dhabi allocated 4 percent of future oil revenues for development of the entire Trucial States region. Such an offer was the outcome of a sustained, persuasive effort by Shaikh Zayid.[55]

Shaikh Zayid's Challenge

While the Trucial States Council would prove a valuable forum for Shaikh Zayid, the problem of development and progress in Abu Dhabi remained. Shaikh Shakhbut continued to resist any large allocation of money that would advance the social and economic development of the emirate. As a result, from the early 1960s onwards, the difference between the two brothers became more obvious. Shaikh Zayid was increasingly perceived as a model of disciplined efficiency. There was a complete lack of rhetoric and arrogance in his manner and a quality of directness in his approach. All who met him appreciated Shaikh Zayid's intelligence and political acumen. He was conscientious in fulfilling his obligations, delivering whatever he undertook to accomplish. On many occasions, he voiced exasperation with his brother, not on his own account but because of the damage that was being sustained by Abu Dhabi. In a long and revealing private session with the Political Agent Colonel Hugh Boustead, he talked of his difficulties.[56] Boustead wrote to the Political Resident, Sir William Luce:

> Zaid spent over an hour with me on the evening of the 5th [October 1962]. He was consistently bitter about Shakhbut, and openly so in a way I have hardly seen him before...He said that while Shakhbut is here, there will be no development whether with or without an Advisor and that he did not feel that any staff will stay with him.[57] He said that his brother has set his mind

absolutely against development and is merely now playing with the development plans, with no intention of executing them. Although he said he is angry about Halul [a territorial dispute],[58] he is using it as lever to avoid talks on the administration…I asked him whether there is any possibility of matters improving when the oil came through, and he said "not at all." He has money to spare now for his people, but is unwilling to do anything.[59]

As Boustead perceived, something must have happened to make Shaikh Zayid so outspoken. One direct cause might have been the rapid deterioration in the living standards of the people in Abu Dhabi. Shaikh Zayid lived daily among the poor in al Ain and had known poverty at first hand. There was a growing realization on Shaikh Zayid's part that such deplorable conditions were unacceptable. This regrettable situation certainly went against his charitable concerns as well as his sense of equality.

Shaikh Zayid also realized the risks inherent in Shaikh Shakhbut's policy towards business, which he knew would only serve to drive away foreign companies.[60] Investment and innovation were crucial to the development of Abu Dhabi.[61] However, no one would invest in a country where bills were not paid and contracts were not honored. Furthermore, Shaikh Zayid was well aware that as money flooded into the coffers of Abu Dhabi, and as an increasing number of foreign entrepreneurs proffered schemes for its spending, his brother was becoming commensurately more fearful and anxious.

In April 1962, Boustead reported a frank conversation that Shaikh Zayid had had with Salim Ali Musa, an official at the Agency:

> Shaikh Zaid bin Sultan informed me this morning that Shaikh Shakhbut called him to the palace yesterday afternoon to tell him how angry he was to know that he, Zaid, had come to Abu Dhabi merely to get money. The Ruler said that he understood very well that not only Zaid, but all members of the ruling family want money and that he, Shakhbut…will hand over the power in order that they can run the country in the way they think fit.
>
> Sheikh Zaid said that Shakhbut in fact clearly meant that he, Zaid, should take over but Zaid added that "as I knew his

suggestion had no real intention behind it and is nothing more than play, I categorically refused."

Zaid then said that he had told Shakhbut that neither he nor anyone else of the ruling family were interested in taking over the money, or the power. But he added that "under your rule, there has been complete chaos, and as you are unwilling, at any time, to take advice, the only alternative is to leave things in your hands."

Zaid added, however, to Shakhbut that if he (Shakhbut) is interested in developing the State, then the only solution would be for him (Shakhbut) to engage proper employees to run the State, as is done in all the other Trucial States.

Zaid went on to tell the Ruler that he has never once consulted Zaid, or the members of the ruling family about anything concerning the development, or progress of Abu Dhabi, and that everything remained in a complete state of chaos. He added to Shakhbut that knowing him (Shakhbut), he did not anticipate any change or that he, the Ruler, would do anything.[62]

Shaikh Zayid then asked Ali Musa to report this conversation to the Political Agent, and he left for al Ain without bidding farewell to the Ruler.

By this time, the balance of power within the emirate of Abu Dhabi had shifted. The popularity of Shaikh Zayid far surpassed that of his brother, the Ruler. For most people, he was the hero who had saved Abu Dhabi by his resolute resistance to the Saudi incursion at al Ain. Although at that point Abu Dhabi had no telephones and few radio transmitters, communication by word of mouth, in the desert tradition, was extraordinarily efficient. Everyone on the coast knew about happenings in al Ain and vice versa. The British government, with many economic and strategic interests bound up with the success of Abu Dhabi had, after the military intervention at Hamasah, increasingly realized that Shaikh Zayid was the only hope for the future of Abu Dhabi. However, while in the period before 1947, British officials were inclined to intervene in a high-handed fashion in the affairs of the emirate, the new generations of officials coming to Abu Dhabi were much more circumspect. They knew that they could safely follow the lead and sense of direction created by Shaikh Zayid, and they were anxious that he should take an ever more active role. However, they would do nothing decisive to end the rule of Shaikh Shakhbut. The impetus for change had to come from Shaikh Zayid alone, and his reluctance to intervene was sometimes a frustration in itself for the British.

The Foreign Office records reveal a growing realization that Shaikh Zayid would make an ideal ruler. This was evident in the very long letter from the Political Resident to the Foreign Office on April 17, 1962, in which the Resident commented dispassionately on the report of Shaikh Zayid's meeting with Ali Musa:

> We are fortunate in having in Shaikh Zaid a man who, we believe, possesses many of the qualifications required of the Ruler of Abu Dhabi in the new era. He is well-liked and respected, both by his own people and by others. He is of a friendly, extrovert nature, fearless, outspoken, generous and anxious to help his people. In short, he is as different from his brother as chalk from cheese. This is not to say that he would be a compliant Ruler. He has all the pride and individuality of the Bedu and he could certainly not be pushed around by us or anyone else. But because he has the interests of his people at heart and because he has some realisation of the problems facing Abu Dhabi and would be ready to accept help in tackling them, we believe that he is a man with whom H.M.G. and others could do business to the benefit of the State. Finally, we have evidence to show that Shaikh Zaid's accession as Ruler would be welcomed both by the Family and by the people of Abu Dhabi generally, including the police force.[63]

Little more than a month later, in May 1962, faced with tremendous pressure and possible confrontation from several quarters, Shaikh Shakhbut agreed to the concessions demanded of him, such as a proper budget and development plans. However, no sooner had he conceded than he began to dissemble again. On the issue of education, for example, he had agreed to the employment of teachers from the Sudan. Once the agreement was secured with the Sudanese government, however, Shaikh Shakhbut began to find fault with the arrangement. Boustead, after a most unsuccessful meeting with the Ruler, called on Shaikh Zayid in the evening.

I had an hour with Zaid in the evening and told him straight out that the Sudan Government have put themselves out quite a lot, that they had the Ruler sign their appointments…Zaid said we must get them in any case and he would be responsible.[64]

Two weeks after his meeting with Boustead, Shaikh Shakhbut began to raise the issue of abdication. There was yet another remarkable exchange of views between the brothers and the Ruler. According to Shaikh Zayid, as Boustead later reported:

He [Shaikh Shakhbut] said that he had now decided to abdicate and said it was for Zaid and Khalid to run the state. He went on to say that he was sincere in handling the state for the good of all and then to complain that his brothers spent their time enjoying life in [al Ain] and asking him for money, and left him alone to deal with all the state affairs.

Zaid replied that they were perfectly prepared to help him at all times in the government affairs, provided he would let them do so…He said to the Ruler, "If you are sincere in your desire to work for the people in the State, you should not only seek but take the advices [sic] of the Political Agent and your Secretary and the staff who are appointed to work for the State." He then added that he and Khalid were perfectly prepared to carry on assisting the Ruler, provided that he, Shakhbut, would use them and give them responsibilities. He then made the point if the Ruler wished to abdicate, they could not stop him.

The Ruler's only reply was to criticise Zaid for spending money on shops, irrigation pumps, agricultural schemes, etc., in Buraimi [al Ain] to which Zaid replied that if the Ruler could produce any evidence from any corner that what he was doing in El Ain [sic] was not for the benefit of the people of Abu Dhabi, then he would admit his fault.

Zaid then again added, "If you wish to work sincerely for the people, allocate a budget for the State and take the money over and have it used for the State under proper financial arrangements…"

The Ruler then told Zaid that if he would arrange a budget for the Government, then the people would be aware of his income, which would be very shameful and could not be countenanced.

Zaid replied that this was the common practice in all states and that the revenues of the states and their budgets were normally known in the states and published in official papers, and that was the normal custom.[65]

As the pressure for change increased, Shaikh Shakhbut also grew more and more resentful about the negative comments being made about him in the world press, which was slowly becoming aware of the new oil wealth of Abu Dhabi.[66] Nothing could persuade Shaikh Shakhbut that there was no campaign to dishonor him. This fixity of thought and purpose was not new. Indeed, since the 1930s, generations of British officials had encountered Shaikh Shakhbut's obstinate countenance. Nevertheless, many admired him for his single-mindedness and were charmed by his personal affability. Nor was he behaving in a manner that would justify any direct and heavy-handed intervention. Abu Dhabi was at peace, and he was the legitimate Ruler, chosen by his family and accepted by the people. Any change in leadership could only take place through the action of the family.

The appointment of Boustead as the first Political Agent in Abu Dhabi at last gave Shaikh Zayid a means to deal with the government in London through a more senior official. He made it clear that he, his brothers Shaikhs Khalid and Hazza, the family and the people all wanted development. In his discussions with Boustead and other British officials, Shaikh Zayid emphasized that he had no desire to take power, but rather that he wanted his brother to take action for his own sake and that of the nation. In this he was successful, and he induced the British to use their influence with Shaikh Shakhbut. However, the results of their advocacy fell far short of his hopes and expectations.

The years between the first flow of oil in 1962 and the transfer of power in 1966 saw the beginnings of progress as envisioned by Shaikh Zayid, albeit at a much slower pace than he desired. He took advantage of every opportunity to promote development. He also sought to establish bonds with the Rulers and heirs in other Gulf states. The British authorities, stung by accusations from Arab countries that they were exploiting the Trucial States, were at last prepared to make some investment and to urge the Rulers to do likewise. Yet, in all these matters,

Shaikh Zayid stayed in the background. His brother was the Ruler and in public he maintained the natural deference expected from the younger for the elder. Moreover, he was mindful of the promise he had given in 1928, and he honored his word even though he was often urged to fulfill the popular aspirations by assuming power in the state. Meanwhile, torpor slowly settled over Abu Dhabi. After one occasion when it seemed likely that Shaikh Shakhbut would retire but then withdrew his decision, it was gradually accepted that Abu Dhabi's transition into the modern world would not materialize while Shaikh Shakhbut remained determined in his refusal to introduce much-needed development.[67]

Shaikh Zayid himself was acutely aware of how sensitive and difficult this time of transition would prove. Where once commercial relationships with the outside world had largely been conducted through the British government and most often with British firms, now Abu Dhabi was being virtually besieged by businessmen from France, the Federal Republic of Germany, Austria, Italy and the United States.[68] Moreover, as the magnitude of Abu Dhabi's oil wealth became clear, the United States government began taking an ever greater interest in the area. A widely circulated confidential paper by the American Consul General in Dhahran, John Evarts Horner, entitled "The Illusory Face of British Imperialism in the 'Arabian' Gulf" put the issue squarely. It envisaged a Gulf without British supervision and asked what the position of the United States should be. Horner concluded, "... a watching brief, for we are not dealing any longer with a congeries [sic] of minor fishing villages, but rather with an area rich in strategic oil."[69] It is not coincidental that in April 1964 a team from the US Consulate General made the journey by Land Rover from Dhahran through all the Trucial States. The members made a point of visiting al Ain and made personal visits to the Rulers throughout the region. This would have been the first contact for American diplomats with Shaikh Zayid in his own territory.

From then on, the US authorities in Washington as well as those based in Dhahran began to take a closer interest in the affairs of Abu Dhabi and the region in general.[70] They were increasingly well informed of the situation, partly from briefings circulated by the Foreign Office in London and partly from information gleaned at first hand by their own consular staff in Saudi Arabia and by the commanders of visiting US warships. Britain steadfastly resisted the notion that Washington should establish a consulate in the Trucial States, and became anxious about the number of US naval personnel based in Bahrain. They remained determined to preserve their position as the prime channel of foreign communication with Abu Dhabi. However, the State Department, especially in the aftermath of the Suez debacle, saw the need to develop an independent role in the Lower Gulf and began to extend its knowledge of the region. Nevertheless, it had to tread carefully to avoid alienating its Atlantic ally. For this reason, Horner did not make his visit and report until 1964. By then, however, the United States already sensed that the future of Abu Dhabi lay with Shaikh Zayid.

It is hard to imagine the pressures, both internal and external that were now being placed upon Shaikh Zayid. His elder brothers Shaikhs Khalid and Hazza had much more tense relations with the Ruler than he did himself. Time and again, he would be called upon to act as the peacemaker. Yet, his concern about the acute poverty of his own people in al Ain and of all the other tribes and townspeople in Abu Dhabi preoccupied him. Although he was being discreetly encouraged by the British government to assume control of the state, he firmly resisted pressure to take over the rulership of Abu Dhabi. Prudence, honor and justifiable caution restrained him. He did not favor his brother's style of management and often told him so in a very frank manner. Yet, he also knew the perils of contravening custom, first from the turbulence that had afflicted Abu Dhabi in his youth and more recently with regard to other states within the region. Furthermore, he had sworn to support his brother and it was not an oath that he would break lightly.

Thus, for four years between 1962 and 1966, Shaikh Zayid sought to ameliorate the conditions in Abu Dhabi and at the same time proceeded to implement his agenda for progress. Individuals with plans and ideas often discussed these with him before they met the Ruler himself. There was good reason to consult Shaikh Zayid for, if he knew about some proposed development, he would do whatever he could to further the project despite his brother's reservations.

It is a mistake to view the relationship between the two brothers in oppositional terms. From the early 1960s, Shaikh Zayid was recognized as the dynamic force in Abu Dhabi, yet there is no evidence that he had any ambition to assume the role of Ruler. At most, he wanted to assist his elder brother in bringing Abu Dhabi into the modern age. Had Shaikh Zayid wished, he could have assumed the position of Ruler at almost any point after 1962. In doing so, he would have had the support of his other brothers, the rest of the family and the people.[71]

Despite their constant disagreements over policy, there was also great mutual respect and trust between the two brothers. They shared many qualities—a love for the traditional desert life, for falconry and hunting, for poetry and lively debate. Neither man desired luxurious living nor the trappings of wealth, and at a deeper level there was a visceral trust between them. There was a special bond that Shaikh Shakhbut did not share with his other brothers. Lieutenant Colonel Edge, the British Police Commander, reported in 1962, "No male member of the family is allowed to sleep in the palace whilst Shaikh Shakhbut is in residence with the exception of Shaikh Zayid, he sleeps in a room over the entrance to the palace."[72] Indeed, Shakhbut would trust Zayid with his life.

Notwithstanding these deep affinities, however, they were essentially very different individuals. One fundamental difference was Shaikh Zayid's optimism, for he was invariably positive and confident, believing that the future would be better than the past. In contrast, his brother mourned the passing of a world that, harsh though it had been, was familiar to him.[73] Viewed with hindsight, it is possible to draw some conclusions as to the political consequences of this distinction. For Shaikh Zayid, the ideal solution was for his brother to transform his attitudes and implement reform. He strove to help Shaikh Shakhbut achieve that end. Yet, in his mind, he knew that it was becoming increasingly unlikely. At some point, therefore, he would have to contemplate the very scenario that he desired to avoid at almost any cost—persuading his brother to relinquish his position, and taking his place as the Ruler of Abu Dhabi for the benefit of the people and the country.

An Imperiled State

As Abu Dhabi languished, the danger of inaction grew. It was increasingly difficult to resist the argument being made in the Arab and international press that the contrast between Abu Dhabi's potential wealth and the plight of its citizens was disgraceful. However, the stasis could – and would – be ended only by those entrusted by custom with changing the Ruler. The Al Nahyan were responsible by tradition for proposing a new Ruler from within their family, if the situation warranted a change.[74] There were ample historical precedents. Additionally, there was the family accord of 1928 that guaranteed the personal security of the Ruler, a condition scrupulously observed by all concerned. During the summer of 1966, a decision was clearly emerging within the family that Shaikh Shakhbut should be replaced as Ruler, and the candidate universally favored to succeed him was Shaikh Zayid.

The only doubt about such a move was consistently expressed by Shaikh Zayid himself. A man of honor, he had sworn to support his brother and had fulfilled that obligation for almost 40 years. His desire for change was widely known and respected. The dilemma was the classic conflict between personal desire and public good. There seems little doubt that Shaikh Zayid's personal desires could be amply fulfilled by building a model community among his people in al Ain, close to the desert life that he had always loved. Politics and the administrative responsibilities of Abu Dhabi held no great allure for him, and he had no manifest personal ambition. It was duty alone that compelled him, over a period of many months, to quell his doubts and personal preferences and to agree that he would accept the role of Ruler if it were offered to him.

It was rumored at the time that the British government sought behind the scenes to replace Shaikh Shakhbut with Shaikh Zayid. There is nothing in the accounts of the period to indicate that this was the case. In fact, the archives and records show otherwise.[75] The frustration that the British felt with Shaikh Shakhbut was solely political. Individual officers liked and respected him, even to the extent of admiring his persistent defense of his own and his nation's rights against the British interest.[76] Yet the British were also increasingly concerned that his reluctance to make development decisions was becoming a liability to Abu Dhabi and undermining the emirate's credibility in the eyes of the international business community. Undoubtedly, they would have preferred a ruler who was more alert to the ways of the modern world, but the notion of a ruler of Abu Dhabi who would be 'pliant' in the hands of his British advisors was unfounded.

None of the documents suggest that Shaikh Zayid would comply with British wishes, unless he believed they served the interests of the people of Abu Dhabi.[77] Many reports exist concerning Shaikh Zayid in the years before he became Ruler, and none of them suggest that he had an especially accommodating nature. Almost all emphasize his sharp intellect, his political understanding of the people of Abu Dhabi and the region, as well as his commitment to social progress. Implicit within the reports is mutual trust, for British officials were able to talk candidly to Shaikh Zayid and to be trusted in return. That Britain would have welcomed the shift to a new ruler cannot be in doubt. Nor can there be any question as to the popular rejoicing that greeted Shaikh Zayid's accession to power in 1966.[78]

Within the family it was believed that eventually Shaikh Zayid would accept his destiny with humility, as the will of God and the will of his people. No one doubted that he would ensure that his brother, the former Ruler, would be treated with every respect, that he would receive ample financial provision, and that he and his property would remain secure. For it was clear that despite his frustration with Shaikh Shakhbut's policies, Shaikh Zayid's brotherly affection remained undiminished. For Shaikh Zayid to replace his brother as Ruler was a matter of last resort. Indeed, the universal hope within the family and outside was that Shaikh Shakhbut would resign, as he had intimated in 1954 and 1962, and allow the succession to take place naturally. However, this did not come to pass, and when the family finally fulfilled its traditional role, it did so with the nation's welfare in mind.

CHAPTER
5

A New Ruler Acclaimed

F ew leaders in modern times have come to power as reluctantly as
Shaikh Zayid Bin Sultan Al Nahyan. A deep sense of duty, coupled
with the absolute insistence of his family, impelled him to step into the
position of Ruler. Nevertheless, Shaikh Zayid's accession undoubtedly
reflected the wishes of the people of Abu Dhabi and marked a key
transition in the history of the emirate. It also proved the culmination
of a process that had been a decade or more in the making.

Even before Shaikh Shakhbut first intimated his intention to
resign in 1954, it was clear, both from within the family and within
the state, that Shaikh Zayid's leadership qualities had given him a
special status.[1] A visionary and a pragmatist, he was persuasive on
critical issues and succeeded even under difficult circumstances. This
was amply demonstrated when he convinced all the prominent families
in al Ain to curtail their all-important water rights for the common good.
The British authorities, for their part, liked and respected a man who
was both effective and decisive.[2] The other brothers of Shaikh Shakhbut
recognized that Shaikh Zayid, although the youngest, excelled in diplomatic skills. He was, thus, an ideal interlocutor for Abu Dhabi with
both the British government and the foreign companies which were
beginning to play a role in the emirate.

Shaikh Zayid was in his thirties when his brother Shaikh Shakhbut
first suggested that he might abdicate the rulership in his favor. From
that time onward, it had seemed increasingly likely that this would

eventually be the outcome, in accordance with the decision of the family and the clear will of the people of Abu Dhabi. Shaikh Zayid was destined to inherit the mantle of Zayid the Great. Yet, more than a decade was to elapse before the transfer of power actually took place.

During those difficult years, although Shaikh Zayid would speak forcefully in private to Shaikh Shakhbut, he would do nothing publicly to undermine the Ruler's position. Observers noted the formal respect that Shaikh Zayid accorded to his brother. The traveler Roderic Owen remembered witnessing a meeting between the two brothers. He recounts that after a difficult journey to al Ain in Shaikh Shakhbut's Cadillac, which was a less than ideal vehicle for the roadless conditions of the late 1950s, the car suddenly ran into what seemed to be an ambush. A group of men sitting by two Land Rovers abruptly got to their feet when they saw the Ruler's car and rushed towards it firing their rifles into the air. These were Shaikh Zayid's men and he was with them. A tall, powerfully built figure with a broad face and a direct look, it was clear that Shaikh Zayid commanded both their affection and loyalty. Owen observed that "in Sheikh Shakhbut's presence, he [Shaikh Zayid] was very much the younger brother, familiar but respectful... This personality, his behaviour showed, was at Sheikh Shakhbut's disposal."[3] Later, after a hunting party, Owen was able to observe the two brothers more closely. He noted:

> Sheikh Zaid was always the model of a younger brother, never dependent or obsequious, but never without a certain deference in his bearing. This gave me a great respect for him and more appreciation of Sheikh Shakhbut's importance. Day and night I was fortunate enough to be seeing what no expert however long old-established [sic] or knowledgeable had seen—the brothers together over a long period of time under a unique variety of circumstances.[4]

The outward manifestations of status and courtesy were important, and Shaikh Zayid never departed from the strict code of social behavior. Within the privacy of the family, he might allow his frustration to emerge and forthrightly and fearlessly urge his brother towards some course of action for public benefit. However, the basic pattern of honor and respect could not be broken. Within the traditional Arab families of the region, and most especially among the ruling families, the Ruler remained an embodiment of authority for all the junior members. While Rulers had retired from office in the past, as his ancestor Shaikh Shakhbut Bin Diyab had done in the nineteenth century, they always retained honored positions and were treated with deference. This was illustrated in the case of the eldest son of Shaikh Zayid the Great, Shaikh Khalifa Bin Zayid, who had indicated to the family that he did not wish to become Ruler, but was nonetheless highly respected as the patriarch of the family until his death in 1945.

Although accepted as a legitimate emergency practice within the tribal system, replacing a ruler was not an action undertaken lightly, as it represented a potentially serious disruption to tradition. The essential quality of tribal government was to avoid conflict and disharmony, unless it was absolutely inescapable. The ideal situation would have been for the Ruler to retain a position of honor while ceding power to his younger brother and a new generation of advisors who were more in tune with the new world that was emerging in Abu Dhabi with the advent of oil. In 1954 and 1962, when Shaikh Shakhbut had suggested that he might abdicate, Shaikh Zayid responded by urging his brother to embrace modernization in the interests of the state. Yet, even when the Ruler's approach to governance became increasingly detached from political reality, Shaikh Zayid's personal support never wavered.[5] Indeed, in 1954, when the Ruler first suggested that he should take his place, it was Shaikh Zayid who persuaded him to stay in office. As Burrows, the Political Resident in Bahrain, reported to London, "the outcome of a meeting between the brothers was the abandonment by Shaikh Shakhbut of his intention of abdicating."[6]

Shaikh Zayid's Dilemma

Despite Shaikh Shakhbut's occasional efforts to change his stand and effect development, these were never sustained. In all, Shaikh Zayid spent more than a decade trying to rectify an essentially impossible situation before finally accepting the rulership of Abu Dhabi on August 6, 1966. Why the accession took place at that particular point and not earlier requires some explanation.[7] Like so many transfers of power, it followed a period of partial amelioration, since under Shaikh Zayid's constant urging and guidance, his brother had reluctantly come to accept the need for limited change and reform. In the four years following 1962, when Shaikh Shakhbut had suggested that he might relinquish power, the Ruler proceeded to engage actively in many proposals for development. Indeed, from a position of inaction, the danger was that too many schemes were being initiated simultaneously. In almost all cases, however, the Ruler greeted ideas with alacrity, entered into serious and active discussions with companies and individuals, but subsequently created many difficulties as the projects moved towards fruition.

Thus, many worthwhile projects remained in abeyance. Abu Dhabi acquired a power station that was never completed because the Ruler fell into disagreement with the contractors.[8] This pattern was repeated in several instances, and Abu Dhabi witnessed many stalled projects as mute evidence of this impasse in government. Roads were planned but never built. A project for a water pipeline from al Ain to the coast almost failed because no decision was taken to employ the necessary consultants to carry out the preliminary planning and investigation work.

Politically, the most serious issue was the Ruler's vacillation on the question of an Abu Dhabi army. Shaikh Shakhbut thought that it would be valuable for the emirate to have its own army—not a purely ceremonial force as he had at first envisaged, but an active military formation, able to undertake the same kind of work as the Trucial Oman Scouts. After initial reluctance,[9] the British government saw merit in the proposal,[10] and made arrangements to depute British officers under normal terms of service and for the supply of equipment. However, as the scheme proceeded, with officers selected and equipment ordered, the Ruler began to raise a whole barrage of conditions and objections. He declared that he had initially been told that the British government would bear the cost of the officers and senior sergeants, and took great offense when he was shown correspondence that proved otherwise.[11] Up to that point, both the British and Shaikh Zayid had hoped, despite all the evidence to the contrary, that Shaikh Shakhbut would be able to adapt to the demands of the new era. When time and again it was proved otherwise, this realization led to a decisive turning point.

In practice, Shaikh Shakhbut's former resolute opposition to reform proved less problematic than his new strategy of bold advances and subsequent retreats from plans and commitments. As the influence of economic and political change in the region became more noticeable and business contacts with the international community increased, this vacillation began to affect the emirate's business image and development prospects. This in turn had an impact on local British officials, who were answerable to the authorities in London and had to explain the Ruler's frequently changeable stance. For Shaikh Zayid and those around him who were deeply committed to reform and development, the Ruler's arbitrary decisions and actions were ultimately undermining the social impetus for change and jeopardizing the whole program of modernization.[12]

Shaikh Zayid had three areas of special concern: social welfare, economic development and regional unity. He believed firmly that the people of Abu Dhabi should collectively benefit from the same higher standards as those living in al Ain under his authority had enjoyed for some time. In fact, Shaikh Shakhbut had long ceased to interfere in Shaikh Zayid's governance of al Ain. The Ruler had taken to living in the oasis, where life was better, instead of residing in the capital. Here, he was able to experience the benefits that progress and modernization could bring. Shaikh Shakhbut was especially appreciative of the benefits of modern medicine, both in his own case and for his immediate family.[13] Yet, he seemed incapable of taking the necessary decisions for development that would improve the living standards of the people of the entire state.

The Ruler's prolonged absences from the capital also had profoundly negative consequences. The more time he spent in al Ain, the less activity there was in Abu Dhabi. An absentee Ruler created a vacuum at a time when the increased volume of business made his presence all the more necessary. While in the oasis, he made no arrangements to delegate his authority in Abu Dhabi, nor did he give any instructions for government papers to be sent to him at al Ain. His inaccessibility meant that his office in Abu Dhabi was clogged with unanswered correspondence and unexamined documents, plans and proposals. No important decisions could be made in his absence.[14]

Shaikh Zayid's concern for development, as outlined in the previous chapter, existed within a wider political context. For Abu Dhabi to lag behind other states in the region in social and economic development would, in his view, become increasingly damaging over time. The true role for Abu Dhabi's Ruler was to provide effective leadership, both within the state and in the Lower Gulf as a whole.[15] Thus, two connected issues weighed heavily in Shaikh Zayid's mind: national interests and regional unity. Since the 1950s, he had fostered connections with the other states in the region through subtle personal diplomacy. Shaikh Zayid regularly attended the meetings of the Trucial States Council when not engaged in other business, and sometimes represented his brother when he was unable to attend. On other occasions, he had accompanied Shaikh Shakhbut and engaged in quiet discussions behind the scenes with the Rulers and heirs of the other emirates. The principle underlying these years of patient activity was simple. Shaikh Zayid believed that the future of the region lay in the individual emirates uniting as a group of free states for collective benefit. In the period before his accession to power, Shaikh Zayid demonstrated by virtue of his open and tolerant character the need to put aside historical and traditional enmities.[16]

Shaikh Zayid had long indicated that unity and cooperation within the region were his goals, and he never shifted from that position. He was convinced that Abu Dhabi, by virtue of its relative size, population and economic power was destined to play the leading part in such a development. Yet, he also believed firmly in sharing its growing wealth and benefits with the northern emirates for the ultimate benefit of all. Shaikh Zayid saw the Trucial States Council as a useful vehicle for advancing these ideas of unity. He favored initiatives that bridged the frontiers between the emirates, such as a single-passport system, workers' compensation and uniform standards of traffic control. He had pressed Shaikh Shakhbut to contribute to the finances of the Council, and he had supported the British attempts to transform it into a functioning and effective organization. However, the Ruler was highly adept at frustrating changes he did not favor.[17]

Precisely because of Shaikh Zayid's belief in the values of unity, he was deeply distressed when in 1965 Shaikh Shakhbut began to suggest that Abu Dhabi should exclude itself from negotiations towards a closer union.[18] The withdrawal or abstention from the deliberations of the Council at a crucial and sensitive stage of its development posed a serious threat to the future welfare of Abu Dhabi. Shaikh Shakhbut's declaration also came at a critical juncture, as the British had just agreed to relinquish the chairmanship of the Council. The new chairman would be one of the Rulers, elected by his peers. Hence, when the Trucial States Development Office (TSDO) was established, and associated with the Trucial States Council in 1965, the chairmanship of the Council should have been taken over by the Ruler of Abu Dhabi. Instead, Shaikh Shakhbut declined. Furthermore, he would make only the most minimal contribution of £25,000 to the TSDO, while Saudi Arabia was prepared to offer ten times that amount.[19] The Arab League offered even more. The Political Resident considered that the Ruler should be contributing about £1.5 million to the development of the region, given Abu Dhabi's key position and substantial oil revenues. However, Shaikh Shakhbut was not personally inclined to increase Abu Dhabi's contribution.[20] In the end, Shaikh Shakhbut raised his contribution to £75,000, but "he emphasized that this was as a gesture of friendship to the British Government..."[21]

For Shaikh Zayid, as for the British government, Abu Dhabi's position in the Council and the TSDO had significant political implications. The British had their own agenda. They feared that if the Arab League financed development in the Trucial States, as they had promised, then the British position would be weakened irreversibly.[22] Shaikh Zayid perceived the threat differently, in view of the emirate's past experience with Saudi Arabian policy.[23] Despite these divergent political concerns, the British and Shaikh Zayid had a common view on one issue—that Abu Dhabi could no longer afford to opt out of the development process, as the Ruler still intended to do. Abu Dhabi's

withdrawal from the TSDO discussions could have had severe consequences. Both Dubai and Sharjah had trade and educational facilities
not then available in Abu Dhabi. In Shaikh Zayid's view, moves
towards coordinated development might have proceeded without Abu
Dhabi, but it would have been to the great detriment of the emirate
itself and the region as a whole.

The issue of the Abu Dhabi army was another key matter. Shaikh
Zayid was acutely aware that Abu Dhabi would need the capacity to
defend itself and its interests in the future.[24] In the recapture of Hamasah
in 1955, he had seen how effective a small group of well-trained and
well-directed men could be.[25] He also admired the Trucial Oman Scouts,
but since this was a British formation and one that took its orders only
from London, it could not be deployed at the behest of the Ruler of
Abu Dhabi. In October 1965, Shaikh Zayid told A.T. Lamb, the Political
Agent in Abu Dhabi, that he had "spoken separately to Shakhbut about
the importance of getting British Army Officers to raise, train and
command the army…"[26] In the same report, Lamb also noted, "Zaid is
keen to have an army not only to defend Abu Dhabi, but to have a
well-run organisation which will contribute to the flow of wealth in
Abu Dhabi. Zaid sees the army as a deterrent to possible enemies…
and as an essential part of the government organisation…"[27]

This vision of the army's role, not publicly expressed before his
accession, is a clear indicator of the remarkable range and perspicacity
of Shaikh Zayid's thinking. He realized the significant role that the
army could play in Abu Dhabi's development. Well-informed as he was,
he would have been aware of the important part the army played in
Turkey and Iran, and of its key role in the transformation of Iraq. It was
obvious that such an army had to be under the firm political control of
the Ruler, although the employment of British senior commanders and
skilled instructors was vital. The potential part that the army could play
in generating a progressive climate was too great to ignore, a fact that
was already clear in Shaikh Zayid's mind by the end of 1965.

All these matters – confusion regarding the new army, uncertainty
over economic and social development, and vacillation over the role
of Abu Dhabi in the Trucial States Council – hinged on Shaikh

Shakhbut's capricious decisions. The year 1966 dawned with many commitments made by the Ruler. On January 1, 1966, Lamb gloomily concluded his Annual Review, "If Sheikh Shakhbut fails in 1966 to fulfil the promise he has shown at the end of 1965, the consequences could one day be serious…"[28] All concerned felt that they had almost exhausted the available options. Little more could be done to induce the Ruler to change his approach.[29]

There was a growing feeling that Abu Dhabi's predicament was reaching a critical point. It was hoped that Shaikh Shakhbut might still see the virtues of development during his proposed visit to Jordan in the spring of 1966. The British avidly supported the Ruler's official visit to King Hussein of Jordan. Their motive was straightforward. Lamb wrote to the British Ambassador in Amman:

> As you may know, our main task here is to persuade the Ruler to spend some of his oil income (which I estimate will amount to £25 million this year) on the development of his country, in his own, his people's and Her Majesty's Government's wider political interests. The Ruler has on three occasions in the past jibbed at taking the final step towards development. During the next few months we come again, and for the fourth time, to the crunch: contracts are due to be awarded for the first stage in the development of Abu Dhabi (a jetty or wharf; a road system; an international airport; a bridge to link Abu Dhabi with the mainland; electric power schemes for Abu Dhabi and Buraimi [al Ain] and a road to Buraimi [al Ain], not to mention a Palace-cum-Government offices). I hope that what he sees of Jordan's development will encourage him to press on with his own plans.[30]

While in Jordan, the Ruler was treated royally and he responded by making munificent public gifts—£200,000 for the relief of distress, and a further £500,000 for various projects. Lamb told him frankly on his return on April 28 that his gifts were more than generous and that his generosity abroad was now disproportionate in relation to what he was doing for his own people.[31] He was making these gifts at a time when the pay of both the police and the new Abu Dhabi Defence Force had been in arrears for months.

Under these circumstances, the visit to Jordan did more harm than good. The Ruler failed to make the desired connection between development in Jordan and what needed to be done in his own country. He continued to hesitate in respect of all development issues and he remained passive to the other states in the area. On all these issues, which were close to Shaikh Zayid's heart, he and his brother now held widely divergent views.

The Decision to Act

Late in April 1966, Shaikh Zayid planned to travel to Britain with his family to seek medical treatment for one of his sons. Lamb suggested that during the visit a senior official from the Foreign Office could call on Shaikh Zayid at his British residence. Lamb himself would be on leave in Britain during Shaikh Zayid's visit, and he suggested that he would brief the Foreign Office about the agenda for their talk when he arrived early in July 1966.[32]

Behind this new aspect of Shaikh Zayid's visit to Britain lay a material development that had taken place in Abu Dhabi around the middle of May 1966. Lamb wrote to the Political Resident, Sir William Luce, on May 21:

> Zaid asked me to go and see him on the evening of 17 May when he told me that on the previous evening there had been a flaming row between the Ruler and Shaikh Khalid. Zaid, Khalid and Mohammed bin Khalifah had stood together as they had intended…Khalid…demanded that Shakhbut set up a proper budget in which 20% or 25% of oil revenues would be allocated to the Ruling Family. Shakhbut asked Zaid and Mohammed bin Khalifah if they agreed with Khalid and when they replied that they did, he accused the three of forming a league (rabiṭat) against him. According to Zaid he told Shakhbut that they were not forming a league against him…since they were 'brothers' and…if they did not work together the Family and the State would fall apart. Zaid said that after this Shakhbut was quite nonplussed, made no further

comment and the conversation flowed into other channels while tempers cooled.

An important factor in bringing Zaid and Khalid to make this stand against the Ruler was, I think, the Ruler's recent gifts to Jordan which bore so little relation to what he was spending locally... Zaid's remarks, as quoted above, about the four 'brothers' standing together as a league are also, I think, an indication that the Family are beginning to realise that Shakhbut's behaviour is becoming [sic] to threaten the position of the Ruling Family as a whole.[33]

Later, Shaikh Shakhbut sent Shaikh Zayid two letters authorizing him as President of the new Finance Department to draw on accounts at the Ottoman and Eastern Banks. Shaikh Zayid was hence "empowered to sign cheques and authorise financial transactions on behalf of the Ruler." Lamb reported:

When Zaid showed me these letters he was delighted since he took it as an indication that Shakhbut was giving in to the wishes of the Family. He agreed with me however that the letters would not have any meaning unless there was a proper budget under which Zaid could make the necessary payments; otherwise he would have to go to the Ruler every time he wished to pay a bill and obtain the Ruler's authority... Zaid said that he was going to stay in Abu Dhabi for as long as it took him to obtain satisfaction from his brother in the matter of administration and financial control...[34]

Before Shaikh Zayid left for his visit to Britain, he had evidently talked with his brothers and with other members of the family.[35] He must have borne in mind that a budget, a proper financial structure and plans for development had already been promised in 1962 and that the Ruler continued to procrastinate on this issue even four years later.[36] In al Ain and elsewhere, discontent was being voiced against the state of affairs and even against the Ruler personally. Accordingly, when he reached Britain, Shaikh Zayid accepted a private meeting with Lamb and a senior Foreign Office official.[37] In the discussion that followed, Shaikh Zayid made it clear that there was pressure within the ruling family to change the rule of Shaikh Shakhbut. The British officials indicated that this would have to be the family's choice but that the British government would support whatever decision the family approved.[38] Shaikh Zayid indicated that once the family had reached a formal, united and binding decision, this would be conveyed to the British authorities in the region.[39]

When Shaikh Zayid returned to Abu Dhabi late in July 1966, he relayed the reassuring news that the British government would not interfere with the Al Nahyan family decision. In the months after the transfer of power, Shaikh Zayid conveyed to Lamb a full account of the ultimate pressures which caused the family to replace his brother. The narrative is indicative of his reluctance to act except in an extreme case, to protect the Al Nahyan:

> These pressures were, first, a serious family row in the early Summer of this year when Shaikh Zaid, Shaikh Khalid bin Sultan and Shaikh Muhammad bin Khalifa (the senior member of the Al Nahayyan) tried without success to persuade Shaikh Shakhbut to adopt more constructive policies, particularly financial and administrative. Secondly, Shaikh Zaid had brought home to him forcibly during his visit to the United Kingdom in June and July of this year that Abu Dhabi was a scandal in the eyes of the world. Thirdly, on his return to Abu Dhabi from the U.K. he found his brother still refused to countenance financial and administrative reform. The final pressure was applied to him by tribal leaders whom he found awaiting him in Buraimi [al Ain] after his return from the U.K. They threatened to take matters into their own hands.[40]

Thus, according to Shaikh Zayid, he was compelled, with the full approval and encouragement of the family, to replace Shaikh Shakhbut.

The days following Shaikh Zayid's return to Abu Dhabi, after the family had reached its formal decision and before Lamb returned from leave, provided the window of opportunity for the leadership transition. It was agreed that Glen Balfour-Paul, then Acting Political Resident, should jointly meet the Ruler with the Commander of the Trucial Oman Scouts, Colonel De Butts, on the morning of August 6, 1966. Accordingly, at 11.15 a.m. on that day, Balfour-Paul and De Butts sought an audience with the Ruler.[41]

None of the participants have left a detailed account of the content of that meeting, but the narratives in a number of sources are probably close to the truth.[42] The two visitors explained to the Ruler that it was in the best interests of the state that he should retire with honor. The Ruler demurred and expressed a desire to speak by telephone with Shaikh Zayid. The two brothers talked for almost an hour, with Shaikh Zayid reminding Shaikh Shakhbut that he had frequently expressed his desire to retire. Now was an opportunity to depart honorably. At the end of their conversation, Shaikh Zayid willingly acquiesced to all of Shaikh Shakhbut's requests concerning the manner of his departure. Shaikh Zayid was convinced that it was in his brother's interest to accept the change, since he himself said on many occasions that he was weary of his position as Ruler and its concomitant demands, particularly of an economic and developmental nature. Furthermore, there was clear public support for Shaikh Zayid's accession, to pave the way for the emirate's development and progress.

Nevertheless, Shaikh Zayid's affection and loyalty for his brother translated into concern for his well-being and safety. He later told Claud Morris, "It had reached a point when I had to satisfy my conscience that my brother would not only remain in good health, but also that others would not take advantage of his predicament."[43] This was a veiled allusion to the serious danger to which Shaikh Shakhbut was now vulnerable. On his return from England, Shaikh Zayid had come to realize the real danger faced by Shaikh Shakhbut from tribesmen who harbored feelings of resentment towards him. Shaikh Zayid thus undertook to protect his brother and his property against all harm. Only in this way, by persuading the Ruler to resign with dignity, did he feel that he was able to fulfill the promise given to their mother so many years before.

The inherent trust between the two brothers was now manifested. In the end, Shaikh Shakhbut agreed to leave the country immediately, and his brother reassured him that his exile would only be temporary. The Palace was cleared of all staff, and the Trucial Oman Scouts who guarded the Palace were also withdrawn. The Ruler's car was summoned and Shaikh Shakhbut drove slowly through the ranks of soldiers, who presented arms to him for the last time. On the airstrip outside the town, an RAF Pembroke aircraft was waiting, and at 2.50p.m. Shaikh Shakhbut Bin Sultan left the country he had ruled and in which he had preserved the peace for 38 years. The aircraft took him to Bahrain, where the Amir, Shaikh Isa Bin Salman, who had close ties with the ruling family of Abu Dhabi, greeted him. In the matter of Shaikh Shakhbut's eventual return, Shaikh Zayid fulfilled his promise. Following a period of transition in which the new government established itself, Shaikh Shakhbut was welcomed home. After a sojourn in the United Kingdom, Lebanon and Iran, he returned to his native land and people. He lived out his days as an honored member of the ruling family, remaining at his favorite residence in al Ain.

This transfer of power is rightly described as an evolution and not a revolution. Few shifts of authority within the region were handled so circumspectly and with such dignity. At its heart lay a new philosophy. It had come to the point where it was imperative to have someone "who could rule Abu Dhabi properly and who would cooperate with his neighbours."[44] For Shaikh Zayid, these were the two fundamental points: a government that could give impetus to the development of Abu Dhabi as well as build unity in the region.

A New Ruler Acclaimed

On August 6, 1966, Shaikh Zayid Bin Sultan Al Nahyan fulfilled what many had come to view as his destiny. When the people of Abu Dhabi heard the news, there was stunned surprise. Reports from all parts of Abu Dhabi soon indicated that Shaikh Zayid had carried out a smooth and successful transition in leadership.[45] He was in the prime of life, intelligent, universally respected, endowed with great wealth and a determination to spend the money for the benefit of his people.

Shaikh Zayid's accession also brought hope to many beyond the boundaries of Abu Dhabi. As Lamb perceptively remarked:

...Abu Dhabi is likely to prove too small a pond for Shaikh Zaid. His own declared policy is to respect the independence of the

Gulf States but to encourage friendship and co-operation among all of them by all means in his power. He sees himself as playing the major role in bringing this about and might well succeed in landing the part because of his real qualities…there is a chance, perhaps a good one, that Trucial States co-operation could be brought to fulfilment…In this council [the Trucial States Council] Abu Dhabi has played almost no part in the past; in the future it may well play a dominating part.[46]

It was to be expected that Shaikh Zayid would immediately launch a massive economic and social program for the benefit of his people. Instead, he first undertook two somewhat unexpected actions, but which had strong symbolic as well as practical importance.

His first act was to end generations of visceral hostility between Abu Dhabi and Qatar. For the first time in a generation, a Ruler of Qatar was welcomed in Abu Dhabi, and Shaikh Zayid himself paid a return visit to Doha. Shaikh Zayid demonstrated that needless antagonism between two neighbors had no place in his vision of the future and that disputes over boundaries should be settled by discussion and compromise. In the meantime, he had welcomed back those who had left during the rule of Shaikh Shakhbut, and for those who did not wish to return he also extended the hand of friendship whenever they cared to grasp it.[47]

The second act appears minor by comparison. Shaikh Zayid decreed that a new set of postage stamps bearing his image should be prepared for Abu Dhabi.[48] He considered it a matter of priority, and pressed the suppliers to produce the first new stamp. What Shaikh Zayid wished to demonstrate to his people was that a new and dynamic force governed the land and that the future was now bright.[49]

It was a new beginning in other senses as well. With the British, he had firm ties of friendship, but as Lamb recorded in a Despatch:

Although in conversation with me he has only once referred obliquely to this point, Shaikh Zaid is too intelligent and too acute an observer of world affairs to believe that H.M.G. will retain for ever their special position in the Gulf. He…wishes to put himself now in the best possible position to survive our withdrawal.[50]

Indeed, here was a Ruler with a keen political intuition, with leadership skills honed over 20 years and a clear vision for the future. Both Lamb and Shaikh Zayid knew that the future would be a clear break from the immediate past, with Abu Dhabi reaching a turning point. As they talked, both men were aware of new political trends. Each knew that Britain's power in the Gulf was waning, and that Shaikh Zayid was destined to be the leader in whatever political dispensation might follow.

CHAPTER
6

Building a New Abu Dhabi

The task that confronted the new Ruler from the day of his accession on August 6, 1966 was the monumental endeavor of creating a new society committed to change and progress. The enthusiasm that greeted his leadership in Abu Dhabi was sincere, but the new Ruler's pleasure at his people's welcome was tempered by the realization of the onerous responsibilities which lay ahead.[1] Following a period of turmoil, Shaikh Shakhbut Bin Sultan had succeeded in securing almost 40 years of peace. Much more would be expected of Shaikh Zayid Bin Sultan. The new Ruler's focus was pertinently on the economic and social advancement of the Abu Dhabi emirate and on furthering unity within the region. Shaikh Zayid's remark to a British visitor, John Daniels, reflects this sentiment: "I want five years' development to be achieved in one year."[2] However, as the new Ruler, he now faced political pressures from interest groups that had never confronted him directly while he had been the Ruler's Representative in al Ain.

The development plans created during 1965–1966 under Shaikh Shakhbut's rule were sound in that they incorporated all the necessary elements: roads, power generation, hospitals and other essential infrastructural projects. However, implementation had suffered because of a lack of leadership. As Ruler, Shaikh Zayid transformed the situation. New policy was formulated and projects implemented with energy and attention to detail. Shaikh Zayid had always argued for development to take place within a proper budgetary, ministerial and planning framework. His ascendancy gave him the opportunity to institute such plans and to see his aspirations, and those of his people, fulfilled.

As a result of the rapid changes, British officials were forced to re-evaluate their position. Previously, they had complained about the lack of progress; now they worried about too much being done at the same time.[3] Yet, the British authorities were aware that they were now dealing with a Ruler of singular purpose and determination, who was in full command of Abu Dhabi. They also began to note that there was a new and broader strategic context. Lamb commented on the British policy towards Abu Dhabi and its new Ruler:

> In considering our policy towards Shaikh Zaid, I think we should always bear in mind the following factors. To ignore them would, I fear, only lead us into unnecessary differences with him from which we might emerge as the loser. First, he is a man of the present day who looks at the world as it is, not as it was. Our own policy of modernising our relations with the Gulf Rulers should enable us to meet Shaikh Zaid's desire for an up-to-date inter-pretation of our relationship with him…Secondly, we must get away from regarding Abu Dhabi as just one of the Trucial States, comparable, for example to Umm al Qawain…We must accept that Abu Dhabi is an independent Shaikhdom whose area and wealth is greater than those of the six Trucial States put together… Thirdly, Shaikh Zaid is ready and eager to accept our advice and assistance in developing his state. We should give it for three reasons: it is in our financial and commercial interests; the ordered, reasonably rapid and successful development of Abu Dhabi is in our short-term political interest; and the development of Abu Dhabi to a point where it can find its proper place, but not as a second-class citizen, in a wider Arabian grouping, will be to our political advantage in the long-term, when the time comes for H.M.G. to retire from its special position in the Gulf.[4]

The tone and the nature of the political analysis were very different from the commentaries made by the British authorities in the past. It anticipated a time when Abu Dhabi, under Shaikh Zayid, would assume a role of leadership among the emirates, taking what Lamb described as "its proper place." The "up-to-date relationship" to which he also alluded was one in which the British could address serious and complex issues, rather than limited and trivial matters that had dominated previous discussions. Among the British officials, Lamb was the closest to Shaikh Zayid, and he achieved the deepest understanding of the subtlety of Shaikh Zayid's political thinking and his complete dedication to change. Lamb recognized the new Ruler's potential as the leader of the whole region from his first days in power.

Such recognition did not stop British officials, especially those in the Foreign Office in London, from arguing that the new Ruler's "reforming zeal, backed by oil revenues, may lead him to try to do too much too quickly," and that Abu Dhabi's rapid development, ahead of all its neighbors, may result in the creation of obstacles to cooperation between Abu Dhabi and the other Trucial States.[5] The British objected to Shaikh Zayid's program for rapid change, and worried constantly about its problems of management and cost. They consistently urged a slower pace of development.[6] The British government was itself wrestling with high inflation at home, and its officials focused on the single assumption that the underdeveloped structure could not withstand the pressure of so much rapid development and would, in economic terms, overheat.

While the pace of progress and growth may have had some repercussions, the new Ruler remained committed to the immediate and rapid advancement of his nation. In his view, the people had already waited too long. The conclusions of the British regarding costs, management and obstacles to regional cooperation might have seemed reasonable, given the new wealth and authority of Abu Dhabi. However, the Foreign Office officials failed to consider two important factors. One was the personality of Shaikh Zayid, whose commitment to progress by consensus went beyond mere words. Already in the first months of his rule, it was possible to discern Shaikh Zayid's funda-mental determination to encourage but not to coerce his fellow Rulers. This was a quality that would provide the essential cement for the young Federation a few years later. The second factor missed by Foreign Office officials was that although in strictly economic terms the British might have been correct, their thinking ignored the crucial political dimension that was uppermost in Shaikh Zayid's mind—the development of Abu Dhabi was to serve as a model for the entire region, an example of the kind of rapid progress that could be achieved given the political will.

While Lamb, as the Resident in Abu Dhabi, could sense the change in atmosphere, it was harder for the officials in London to grasp the new realities. Over the years, they had read many promises of improvement and transformation in Abu Dhabi, none of which had come to fruition. They found it hard to accept that an individual without formal education or a government apparatus behind him could accomplish what Shaikh Zayid promised. Moreover, although the British had for years proclaimed the benefits of and the need for social progress, they wished it to be channeled through a system under their control. In their view, the preferred vehicle for change should be the British-dominated Trucial States Development Office and not the individual initiative of a single Ruler.[7]

The British stance on Abu Dhabi's development plans can be explained partly by the previous experiences of British officials in the Gulf during the rule of Shaikh Shakhbut, when the Ruler had made grandiose plans and then resiled from them. Shaikh Shakhbut had also found many reasons to refuse payment to British companies that had become involved in the unfulfilled development process.[8] The British officials certainly did not believe that it was in the interests of Abu Dhabi for the process of development to falter under a new Ruler. However, they had a double responsibility—a duty to support the new Ruler but also to act on behalf of British companies at work in Abu Dhabi. These two interests were not always in harmony.

The Political Resident also recognized that the forces driving the program for change were both economic and political.[9] Infrastructural development carried a strong political message. Shaikh Zayid needed to demonstrate that Abu Dhabi was committed to initiating the sort of development then being offered by Saudi Arabia to the other Trucial Coast states. It was his mode of highlighting the new situation—Abu Dhabi would now be able to assume its proper leadership role in the Lower Gulf.[10] Furthermore, by financing virtually the entire budget of the Development Fund for all the Trucial States, Shaikh Zayid was able to demonstrate the tangible benefits of collaboration among the seven emirates. This vital political dimension, however, seems to have been ignored by many who viewed events in Abu Dhabi from the more distant perspective of Bahrain or, more distant still, London.[11]

In this context, Shaikh Zayid was well aware, from the tone of his many conversations with Lamb, that the relationship with Britain could not, and indeed should not, remain the same once Abu Dhabi had begun to move forward. While possible models for political evolution were Kuwait and Bahrain, neither of these was directly comparable to the situation in the Trucial States. In the emirates, the indigenous and traditional political structure remained strong, albeit starved of resources. Shaikh Zayid was completely convinced that the traditional polities had the strength and resilience to adapt to change, but he also realized that without social and economic development they could not resist external pressures. Therefore, it was politically imperative that the new Ruler should create evidence of visible change in Abu Dhabi, a transformation that owed nothing to outside influence.

The new spirit emanating from Abu Dhabi extended beyond the notice of just the British officials. At the time of Shaikh's Zayid's accession, the United States had no resident representative in Abu Dhabi. The British had always strongly resisted any suggestion that an American consul should be appointed. Nevertheless, the United States was keenly interested in developments in the region and gathered information from as many sources as possible. The US State Department records reveal that American interests and perspectives were rather different from those of their British ally. In 1966, the US Consul in Dhahran wrote a lengthy confidential memorandum to the State Department on political developments in Abu Dhabi. He observed:

> In addition to approving numerous contracts, Shaykh Zayid of Abu Dhabi is trying to create a government organization … Since replacing Shaykh Shakhbut as Ruler of Abu Dhabi in early August Shaykh Zayid has inevitably concentrated his efforts on the economic development of his backward shaykhdom, but he has also made some progress in the all-important political sphere. Inheriting

a practically non-existent governmental structure...Zayid wasted
no time in promulgating an official decree establishing the nucleus
of a governmental organization headed for the most part by
members of the al-Nahayyan family.[12]

A State Transformed: Shaikh Zayid's Plan of Action

From the outset, the scale of activity was unparalleled. The Draft
Budget of 1967 – in itself a profound innovation – recorded an income
of 47 million Bahraini dinars. Of this sum, 35 million were to be
allocated for the building of a new infrastructure. The entire projected
development totaled 39.25 million, including 4 million spent on
sewerage, 3 million on hospitals and clinics, and 3 million on the initial
stage of a harbor project, which for the first time would allow safe
access for large ships coming to Abu Dhabi. A sum of 3.75 million was
allocated for a housing program of 2,000 houses and an initial amount
of 0.5 million was allocated for education.[13] The burgeoning of the
economy can be judged by a number of measures, but perhaps the most
telling indicator of economic activity was the money in circulation and
in use. In June 1966, shortly before Shaikh Zayid took office, Abu
Dhabi adopted the Bahraini dinar as its unit of currency.[14] In 1966, there
were 2.4 million dinars in circulation in Abu Dhabi. By the following
year, that figure had more than doubled to 5.4 million.[15] By 1970, the
last full year before the creation of the United Arab Emirates and re-
monetarization, the figure had reached 13.6 million dinars.[16]

On March 20, 1968, Shaikh Zayid promulgated a Five-Year Plan
to detail a development strategy for Abu Dhabi. Clearly, it antedated
the political transformation engendered by the withdrawal of Britain in
1971, as well as the creation of the United Arab Emirates. However, in
the context of 1968, it was both a practical and a visionary program,
building on the successes of the rapid growth achieved between 1966
and 1968 and learning from the problems encountered in the process.
Some of the allocation priorities had changed from the Draft Budget
of 1967. The initial Budget had provided for the implementation of

plans that had been proposed prior to Shaikh Zayid's accession. These included projects that had been pending for years. Thus, the 1967 Budget contained an element of urgent remedial action, catching up with years of stalled development. The Five-Year Plan, by contrast, offered a more deliberate long-term strategy.

The new Plan contained a detailed budget and a comprehensive program allocated to each sector. The sum of 12.4 million dinars was allocated for education, with an emphasis on building a system of primary and secondary education throughout the emirate. A further 2.8 million was dedicated to industrial training units, with the long-term objective of reducing Abu Dhabi's dependence on external expertise. An allocation of 6.5 million was to be spent on a network of hospitals and dispensaries, while 13.4 million was provided for agricultural improvement, most of it for augmenting the water supply system, which was coming under increased pressure with substantially higher demands both in Abu Dhabi and in al Ain. Shaikh Zayid believed that the best way forward in agriculture was to develop new strains of crops and livestock that would be suitable for local conditions. Consequently, a network of agricultural research stations was established under the program, and these produced significant results over the years.

A social component underpinned many of the economic development projects. For example, central markets were opened for the first time in Abu Dhabi at the beginning of 1969. Following his practice in al Ain, Shaikh Zayid charged either token rents or no rents at all for the two hundred trading outlets in the central market. The establishment of markets provided several advantages, including allowing for safe and hygenic food distribution as well as creating structures through which standards could be controlled and maintained. This, coupled with the provision of a clean and safe water supply, meant that the problems of food and water-borne diseases found in many new cities could be largely eliminated. The general improvement also boosted agricultural production, a sector to which Shaikh Zayid accorded priority. By creating low-cost trading facilities, local producers could sell their produce at better prices than before. This move enabled the proprietors of the shops to launch into business with a minimum of investment.[17]

The intention was to propel Abu Dhabi forward rapidly, in accordance with a planned strategy, transforming it into a modern developed economy.[18] The targets were ambitious but, on the whole, realistic.[19] A substantial part of the plan focused on infrastructural development. More than 196 million dinars were dedicated to building roads, bridges, houses, urban facilities, and ports and airports. Much of the associated industrial development focused on improving output from the oil industry – the largest single item of the plan – and providing resources to sustain the vast building programs. One such scheme was the creation of a cement works to substitute imports with a commodity that could readily be produced in Abu Dhabi.[20]

The Five-Year Plan was based on a number of detailed studies and investigations carried out by foreign consultancy firms. Their task, defined by the Ruler, was to determine the necessary conditions for a program of sustained development. One immediate result of this new emphasis on analysis and planning was the establishment of the Council of Planning in late 1968, in order to implement the wide-ranging changes that the Ruler had initiated. The Council represented an ambitious attempt to provide a structure and a system of control where none had existed before. It began its work in May 1969 and was required to meet on a weekly basis. A number of subsidiary councils were created under its jurisdiction, with a wide range of committees covering detailed aspects of administration and finance. Soon, these subsidiary councils covered all the interests involved in the development program. Shaikh Zayid himself presided over the Council of Planning meetings whenever his workload allowed him to do so.

On the whole, Shaikh Zayid was cautious of 'expert advice.' His experience with British banks operating in Abu Dhabi and with other large British construction firms was that their advice reflected their own interests. However, the Ruler also recognized that, given the scale of what he proposed to accomplish in terms of development, he needed guidance. In this respect, he preferred to employ his own paid consultants, who were less likely to have divided loyalties. As he explained it to Lamb, he did not want a lot of experts running around his country. According to Lamb, Zayid was convinced of the need to build a strong base:

> ...the successful development of his State depended on his creating sound foundations: financial, administrative, economic, commercial, social and engineering. He had the finance required and could buy the engineering; but the other bases were weak or non-existent. Careful study and planning were required now, at the beginning of the new era inaugurated by his accession.[21]

Shaikh Zayid was well aware that this was a strategy fraught with risks as well as opportunities. In a short period, Abu Dhabi experienced a massive influx of consultants and foreign workers, all working on the development programs.

While rapid development was an imperative, it nevertheless had to be carefully managed. The injection of government funds into the economy risked inflation, with too much money chasing too few goods. Furthermore, there was the danger that the people themselves, who had grown up in a harsh environment, would be enfeebled by the sudden onrush of prosperity. However, while he had many models for the difficulties of rapid economic growth, Shaikh Zayid also knew his people well and believed that, as long as the program allowed them to enhance their own skills and provided opportunities for their individual betterment, they could withstand the pressure and pitfalls of rapid development. Thus, he allocated funds generously but judiciously.

The effective functioning of the councils and committees of the new administrative and economic structure owed much to Shaikh Zayid's capacity for tireless inspection and personal supervision. Frequently, the Ruler would appear on a building site or in an area of new development. He would be equipped with detailed knowledge of the day-to-day situation. If the case warranted it, he would demand to know, then and there, why a particular project was not proceeding according to plan or how an obstacle could be surmounted. Equally, he often came to praise good workmanship, rewarding those who carried out their duties with competence and dedication. Just as in al Ain, when he had worked alongside those laboring in the reconstruction of the irrigation system, now as Ruler of Abu Dhabi, he distrusted second-hand reports and preferred to judge things personally. His inspection tours made it clear that he viewed himself as a fellow worker in building the new Abu Dhabi. The Ruler's unannounced visits became legendary long before the mechanisms of press and publicity were available to report them.[22]

The speed and scale of change was unparalleled. A young Abu Dhabi resident, Mohammed Al Fahim, who left for Britain in 1964, recorded his observations on his return in 1967:

> As we drove into Abu Dhabi town from the airstrip I was amazed at the transformation that had taken place during my absence. The sleepy fishing village that I had left was now a bustling construction site. There were trucks, bulldozers, cars, and people everywhere – they were doing everything from building roads to laying cables – Abu Dhabi was a hive of activity…During the next five years the metamorphosis of Abu Dhabi occurred at lightning speed. In some sectors the incredible pace has still not let up. We skipped decades of slow development and simply jumped from the eighteenth century into the twentieth with one giant leap. We went from 'no tech' to 'high tech' in a matter of a few years. While it took most countries decades to develop communications and transportation systems for example, we did so in a very short time.[23]

Success depended on hard work. Many citizens of Abu Dhabi held several jobs concurrently, despite the fact that few had the education and experience to work in the new environment. The model for such dedication was Shaikh Zayid himself. The Ruler knew that unless he was seen to work harder and with more purpose than those under his authority, the development of Abu Dhabi would falter. He also knew that however much he sought to delegate, everyone – the people, the officials, even foreign governments – would ultimately take their lead from him.

The Need for State Institutions: Making Progress Permanent

Shaikh Zayid had succeeded during his days in al Ain by virtue of his political intuition and his constant desire to remain on top of events and developments. As Ruler, he continued to be assiduous in gleaning information from many sources, both local and international. Every meeting, every *majlis*, every newspaper or broadcast was absorbed and analyzed. He watched the complex evolution of British withdrawal from Aden followed by the civil war in Yemen and, closer to home, he observed the struggles that periodically convulsed Oman.

His years in al Ain had taught him that all judgments and policies are in some sense political. Even in the field of social welfare, where at times his actions have been presented as emerging solely from his well-known warmth and kindness, his program of development for the people has always been conceived within a political and diplomatic framework. His realization that Abu Dhabi could be a unifying force among the other emirates undoubtedly antedated his accession as Ruler of Abu Dhabi. Many of his decisions as Ruler echoed statements that he had made in the years before 1966. His ideas and plans were honed during that period of apprenticeship, giving his actions as Ruler a notable measure of confidence and a purposeful direction.

Most British observers caught only a glimpse of Shaikh Zayid's single-minded determination. None was privy to his full intentions. In retrospect, however, it is clear that every one of his decisions was an element in a coherent strategy. It is necessary, therefore, to consider his actions from August 1966 onwards in terms of the new polity that he had envisaged and which he gradually brought into existence. All his actions had a strong ethical base, yet they were also imbued with a clear political vision.[24]

Against this background, a new pattern emerges from his actions during the first two years of his rule. The Five-Year Plan was fundamentally a political act. In Shaikh Zayid's opinion, the benefits of rapid development far outweighed the risks being stressed by his British advisors. Aware of the rising instability in the region, he knew it was essential to consolidate the political structure within Abu Dhabi to win public confidence. He had already seen an exodus take place during his brother's rule. He was determined to reverse the trend and to make Abu Dhabi a magnet for those who had slipped from their loyalty to the Al Nahyan.[25] The strategy worked well and many people returned, some to work in the new projects and others to take advantage of the new opportunities that Abu Dhabi now had to offer.

Shaikh Zayid also saw the need to bind the Al Nahyan closely to the new system. His brother Shaikh Shakhbut had sustained the family peace for almost 40 years. Shaikh Zayid was determined to go further and make the family an effective instrument of government. While it was inevitable that some members of the family were stronger supporters of the new government than others, the new Ruler's policy was to integrate all of them into the new system. Thus, the administrative and depart-mental system that he created depended strongly on members of the family and others closely connected with the Al Nahyan, who were given positions of authority.[26] A less confident ruler would have been reluctant to dilute his power in this fashion, since such a move stood in stark contrast with previous practice.[27] However, just as in a parliamentary system, it was often more prudent to embrace as many elements as possible within a Cabinet rather than to isolate them.[28] By virtue of accepting these posts, the department heads manifested their loyalty and overt support for the new Ruler. Thus, these young men, representing powerful strands of authority within Abu Dhabi, were publicly honored by the Ruler by being entrusted with positions of significant responsibility and authority. However, though they were to be responsible for the effective and efficient running of their departments, Shaikh Zayid still retained undisputed political power and authority.

Shaikh Zayid also brought together a group of talented and highly educated young men to form his inner group of advisors. Pre-eminent among them was Ahmad Khalifa Al Suwaidi, a graduate of the Faculty of Economics and Political Science at Cairo University. His formal responsibilities, as head of the Emiri Court, soon developed to cover the field of major policy development and international relations. He was the Ruler's right-hand man, his 'eyes and ears,' someone whom he could trust implicitly. In the key field of economic development, Shaikh Zayid had two equally confident and reliable public servants in Mana Saeed Al Otaiba and Muhammad Habrush Al Suwaidi, both political-science graduates of Baghdad University. The former was assigned supervision over the crucial development of the petroleum industry, the economic powerhouse of Abu Dhabi and indeed the entire region, while the latter took control of the Department of Finance. This group of advisors was in close contact with Shaikh Zayid, often on a daily basis, in contrast to his meetings with the ministers, which were less frequent and governed by the constraints of protocol. Through this complex but efficient system of management, the Ruler often got to know about developments within the departments even before the information had formally been conveyed to the head of the relevant section.

By widening the political and economic structure, Shaikh Zayid gained a great deal. Any suggestion of nepotism or favoritism was only made by those who were completely ignorant of conditions in the region. Since the men appointed by the Ruler were identified publicly with the government, it was clear to the people of Abu Dhabi that their leaders were playing an active role. These prominent individuals had committed themselves by their involvement in a reformist administration rather than remaining detached from it.[29] Shaikh Zayid had made it clear with the creation of the departments, the Budget and the Five-Year Plan – the first within the region – that he intended to govern not in an autocratic fashion, but as a modern ruler. By retaining the final authority in his own hands or delegating power under the watchful eyes of his close and loyal supporters, however, he maintained both detailed knowledge of and strict supervision over the key areas of political and social development.

Another area that was to become a priority for Shaikh Zayid was providing opportunities to young men. Mohammed Al Fahim described how he and his brother benefited from this policy. His father wanted to send his sons to be educated in Britain, but he could not afford the cost of both the flight and fees.

> As it happened, Sheikh Zayed was in Abu Dhabi at the time and my father told him about his quandary. Sheikh Zayed immediately offered to pay for the airline tickets if my father paid

for the school fees and other expenses. The British Political Agent agreed to make the necessary arrangements. It was the cooperation of these three parties – our father, Sheikh Zayed and the British Political Agent – that enabled us to take advantage of this fantastic opportunity.[30]

This was an individual act of generosity, but it illustrated a central theme in Shaikh Zayid's concept of development, that of cooperation and partnership. He could easily have paid the entire cost, but he insisted that the family make some contribution for themselves, either financially or by hard work, giving them a stake in the enterprise. Subsequently, in an ongoing strategy to promote the education of UAE nationals, Shaikh Zayid would provide full scholarships for thousands to study at the best universities abroad.

In the years that followed, the Ruler became a source of benevolence to many within Abu Dhabi, but the resources he provided were intended to enable their recipients to better themselves. With a solid, well-built house rather than a tent or a *barasti* shelter, with water and sanitation, a desert dweller could raise his family in safe and healthy conditions, giving the next generation a better start in life than he himself had enjoyed. As one observer recorded:

> In addition to the monetary compensation, Sheikh Zayed also gave each Abu Dhabian three, and in some cases four, pieces of land. The first was for a home in the residential area, the second was to build a commercial building on one of the main streets in the centre of town, the third was an industrial site meant for a workshop or industrial project of some kind. In addition to these three pieces, the people of Liwa and outlying villages also received a gift of farmland as well as the necessary equipment to cultivate it including machinery, pumps, irrigation systems, even consultants and engineers to provide the necessary advice to make the land productive.[31]

Parallels may be drawn between the opening of the political system to accommodate the energy of the younger members of the Al Nahyan and the creation of opportunities for the people of Abu Dhabi. Both demanded hard work to make the most of the Ruler's magnanimity.

On Shaikh Zayid's part, it was an act both of generosity and extra-ordinary political sagacity because it gave every member of the nation an investment and a stake in the success of the new system.

Thus, Shaikh Zayid's guidance was evident in all fields of development. He seemed to have the ability to recall the progress and development of each individual family.[32] The Ruler would ask an individual in his *majlis* or on a visit how his business and his family were progressing, how his crops were growing, or what had happened to the trees that he had planted. While his concern was personal and benign, there was an underlying precept. Every citizen of Abu Dhabi was expected to use the benefits provided for him by the nation, not necessarily through business or trade but in some positive fashion. In a society where the family was paramount, the Ruler believed that the strength of the new nation would be built up through healthy children who would, in turn, raise families of their own.[33] His vision extended not over years but over decades. He knew that in the period after 1966 he was laying the foundation of a new society for future generations. While many of his advisors, perforce, took a shorter-term view, Shaikh Zayid's imagination was focused unwaveringly on the more distant future. What concerned him day by day was the means by which that long-term goal could be attained.

The External Environment: Britain's Decision to Withdraw

While internal economic and social development proceeded according to plan, the external environment remained in a state of flux. It is not known at what point Shaikh Zayid began to have doubts about the permanence of the British treaty relationship with Abu Dhabi and the other Trucial States, but he was well aware of the growing evidence of possible change. In the first place, British officials hinted about such a transformation soon after he took over as the Ruler of Abu Dhabi.[34] Second, the Labour government, which had come to power in Britain in 1964, was very different from the Conservative administrations with which both Shaikh Zayid and his predecessor had interacted.[35] 'Imperial' commitments were not popular within the Labour Party, and the government had embarked on an expensive program of social and economic regeneration.

Talk of British withdrawal was in the air long before it was first officially mooted as policy. Yet, the actual change occurred abruptly. By the mid-1960s, with the British economy weakening and a new Labour government committed to social expenditure, the budgets were scrutinized for possible savings. Defense expenditure, always regarded with suspicion by the Labour Party, became a prime target for cutbacks. A White Paper on Defence published on February 22, 1966 announced that substantial savings could be achieved by withdrawing from the British bases "east of Suez," though it suggested that the bases in the Gulf were to be protected and even given a more important role. However, by May 1967, within 10 months of Shaikh Zayid's accession, the plan had extended in concept to a withdrawal of troops from the Arabian Gulf as well.[36] Just prior to the official announcement on January 16, 1968, the British government informed the Rulers that it would resile on all its existing agreements and would withdraw entirely from its responsibilities in the Gulf by the end of 1971.[37]

This decision was to have momentous consequences for the region. Yet, there are few occasions in recent British political history when loyal friends and allies were treated so brusquely and so discourteously. No consideration was given to the Rulers' suggestions for transitional arrangements, which were publicly spurned.[38] The British government had always suggested that given the delicate politics of the region, the long arm of British military protection was essential. Both Abu Dhabi and Dubai were seeking to build up their own defense forces, but this development was still in its early stages. Some kind of transitional arrangement, at no cost to the British taxpayer and possibly funded by the emirates, would have sustained regional stability while the local forces were being strengthened.

There appeared to be little logic in this British policy. For some members of the Labour Party, cutting the ties with the Gulf seemed attractive as a final repudiation of Britain's colonial past. Moreover, the decision to withdraw the troops may have gained some support in Britain since the government was embroiled in a difficult encounter with its colonial past in Rhodesia and was experiencing an economic crisis at home. From the perspective of the Rulers of the emirates, however, the decision to sever defense ties was hasty and ill-conceived, particularly in view of the growing wealth and strategic importance of the Gulf. It seemed that a possible change of government after the general election that would take place shortly might reverse the policy as the Conservative opposition spoke up strongly in favor of retaining Britain's historic responsibilities in the region. Nevertheless, when the Conservatives were returned to power in June 1970, they broke their pre-election pledges and decided not to reverse the Labour Party decision, implementing the same timetable for troop withdrawal.[39] Thus, both major parties in the British political system opted to sever their nation's defense commitments to the peoples of the Arabian Gulf—Labour's political muddle and confusion was compounded by the unwelcome Conservative policy reversal.

Yet, despite the abruptness of the British withdrawal, in one sense it was timely. The states of the region, notably Abu Dhabi, had acquired a sense of their own destiny. Shaikh Zayid possessed both the resources and the political will to achieve solid and irrevocable change. In this process, it was now the British government that was being tepid in its enthusiasm and a barrier to progress. The time had come for Britain to bow out, a fact recognized by many within the Foreign Office.

Nevertheless, the British departure left many political issues unresolved. At the regional level, Abu Dhabi had disputed boundaries with its neighbors, Saudi Arabia, Qatar and, to a certain extent, Oman. Only one of the powerful states in the region, Iran, wholeheartedly welcomed British withdrawal. All the main Arab states in the Lower Gulf were concerned about Iranian expansion. The United States, faced with a changed balance of power, opted for a region dominated by its allies, Saudi Arabia and Iran. The idea, however, that stability in the Gulf after the departure of the British should now depend solely on the goodwill of Iran or Saudi Arabia was unacceptable to the other states on both practical and ideological grounds.

Throughout 1968 and 1969, the ultimate outcome of the British withdrawal remained largely unclear. The British plan was to cut rapidly all commitments to the Trucial States, preferring to bind them into a federation, as Britain had done in Africa and the West Indies. In this context, the British hoped that all the states in the Lower Gulf – Bahrain, Qatar and the seven emirates of the Trucial Coast – would become a single entity. Nevertheless, they feared that the differences between the Arab states over boundaries were so fundamental and the interests of the Trucial States so diverse that a working federation might be unattainable. Indeed, only a few years before, British officials had considered such a working union an impossibility, given the lack of a political and economic substructure.[40] By the late 1960s, however, a new element had emerged—the presence of a leader wholly committed to unity ruling over the largest of the Trucial States. That Ruler was Shaikh Zayid.

It is true to say that some of the other emirates feared that Shaikh Zayid would use Abu Dhabi's overwhelming and growing economic advantage to subordinate them. They also mistook his determination to build a strong armed force as the prelude to coercive action. Both fears proved groundless, and subsequent events reveal the sincerity of Shaikh Zayid's desire to create a union of equals. His belief in the need for Arab states to build a framework of mutual trust was already manifest. His earlier rapprochement with Qatar, as discussed in Chapter 5, eased what had previously been a troubled relationship. In the case of Oman, Shaikh Zayid went to great lengths to remove any doubts in the Sultan's mind about Abu Dhabi's intentions. The British Consul General in Muscat, D.C. Carden, wrote, "I think the Sultan…really is most grateful for Shaikh Zaid's words, and I hope Zaid's message will prove the starting point for closer relations in the coming years."[41]

Very quickly the local British officials came to recognize that Shaikh Zayid was a Ruler with the diplomatic skill to open channels of communication that had long been blocked or obstructed. In November 1966, the Political Resident, Sir Stewart Crawford, wrote to Lamb, "I mentioned…that there still remained some mistrust between the Ruling Families of Bahrain and Qatar and I thought that Shaikh

Zaid might have a valuable role to play in helping them to settle their differences in the interest of general co-operation."[42]

Shaikh Zayid's approach was to tackle issues directly. In theory, diplomatic relations with other countries remained the responsibility of the British government. However, he believed that through personal contact he could resolve issues, particularly with respect to foreign relations that had proved intractable under his predecessor, and for which British negotiation strategies had not been able to find a solution. He ardently wished to meet the Sultan of Muscat and Oman, who lived in seclusion in Salalah. Shaikh Zayid said that he did not mind where they met, provided they met soon.[43] He also took the initiative in arranging for an early meeting with King Faisal.[44] These endeavors reflected clearly Shaikh Zayid's desire to establish personal contact with the regional leaders, both to strengthen relations and to resolve outstanding grievances. Such strategies were important when seen within the context of the profound changes taking place in the Gulf. Moreover, as the Political Agent in Dubai, Balfour-Paul, observed, a partnership between Shaikh Zayid and Shaikh Rashid, based on their long record of concerted judgment and action, could lead the region in any direction they chose.[45]

Furthering the Transformation: The Road to Federation

Having announced its decision to leave the Gulf, the British government thus looked towards Shaikh Zayid to take the leading role in the development of the Gulf region. In the Political Agent's Annual Report for 1968, covering "the first of its last four years under British protection," C.J. Treadwell placed Shaikh Zayid at the center of the picture:

> In a sense a review of events in Abu Dhabi amounts to a report on the Ruler, Shaikh Zaid bin Sultan Al Nahayyan ... If, at the end of this surprising year, Abu Dhabi has emerged with honour, the credit is due in large measure to Shaikh Zaid. He must be

nominated Abu Dhabi Man of the Year and, barring accidents, he will carry the award for some years to come.

Since the chill January announcement of the withdrawal of British forces Shaikh Zaid has applied himself to the task of standing on his own two feet in the comparatively short time ahead…he accepted the British decision without question. Not for him the luxury of dreaming that withdrawal might after all be deferred. Though the question is academic I think it worth recording that any offer to extend our protection beyond 1971 would meet with sharp rejection from the Ruler. He may not have liked the decision but for him the die was instantly cast. So it is that throughout the year the Ruler was preoccupied with seeking means of ensuring future stability for Abu Dhabi in partnership with its neighbours after withdrawal…he believes that under his leadership and with its wealth, Abu Dhabi will emerge as the most important state in the area.[46]

The British authorities did not initially perceive how Shaikh Zayid would use the potential economic and political power of Abu Dhabi, anticipating that he might seek to put heavy pressure on his neighbors for his own gain. In fact, the reverse took place. Shaikh Zayid recognized from the outset that each of the other emirates (and indeed his other neighbors) had their own interests and agenda. Sharjah had benefited from the location of the British air base on its territory and had developed in areas of health and education. Dubai, under the remarkable leadership of Shaikh Rashid, had become the most economically advanced state in the region. Although Shaikh Zayid had established good working relationships on a personal basis with the Rulers of the region, based on mutual respect, he also recognized that where individuals could share the same views, states might be at variance. In the new context, where the specification of fixed boundaries had become of such vital economic importance, it required great skill to negotiate between and reconcile the particular interests of the individual emirates and the broader needs of the region as a whole.

It soon became evident that the new Ruler of Abu Dhabi was looking beyond the narrow interests of his own state and in the direction of general cooperation within the region. Shaikh Zayid himself stated that his policy was to foster friendship and cooperation among the nine Gulf states, and that he would pursue it with energy. Furthermore, he was recognized as an Arab Ruler whose knowledge and experience of his Arab neighbors would be invaluable in formulating policy.[47] He made it known that he would engage in personal diplomacy and would use his connections to address problems that would then be dealt with through the proper machinery of state. The Ruler was polite but forthright.[48]

The most sensitive issue was the relationship with Dubai. The personal bond between Shaikh Zayid and Shaikh Rashid had been forged and tested over the years.[49] On many occasions, a quiet understanding between the two leaders helped to settle disputes which might otherwise have festered. When Shaikh Zayid became Ruler, a boundary issue remained unresolved. This could have proved immensely damaging to the long-term relationship between the two emirates, as had happened in the past under previous rulers. The manner in which this problem was resolved, in a true spirit of compromise, reflects the stature of both men.

The core issue was oil exploration rights. While oil production had first been developed in Abu Dhabi, exploration was proceeding rapidly in many parts of the region, both on land and offshore. When Shaikh Zayid became the Ruler, test drilling was proceeding close to the border between Abu Dhabi and Dubai. This had already generated considerable ill-feeling in the last days of Shaikh Shakhbut's rule.[50] Shaikh Zayid, however, took a broader view of the issue. Lamb wrote in the first weeks of Shaikh Zayid's rule, "I have spoken to the Ruler of Abu Dhabi about relations between Abu Dhabi and Dubai and sought his views about a solution of the frontier problems which arose in the last few months of Sheikh Shakhbut's reign." Shaikh Zayid said that he would discuss the matter with Shaikh Rashid personally, and he "would try for a brotherly and neighbourly solution. If some give and take was required to arrive at a solution he would be ready to co-operate."[51]

The point that Shaikh Zayid stressed to Lamb was that he did not care what solution emerged to the problem. "[He] was prepared to accept any method of reaching a solution equally acceptable to Shaikh

Rashid. The first step was to have an exchange of views with Shaikh Rashid, who, the Ruler was certain, wanted a solution as much as he did." Lamb added that "It seems to me that Shaikh Zaid is approaching his talk with Shaikh Rashid…with a reasonably open mind," but Shaikh Zayid added that he must have his family's full support for any action he took in any matter.[52]

Shaikh Zayid realized that a resolution of the dispute with Dubai was not only in the interest of Abu Dhabi but also of the region as a whole. He thus agreed to a settlement to Dubai's advantage, through a minor exchange of territories. This proved the foundation on which both Rulers ultimately agreed to form a broader union of their emirates on February 18, 1968. The episode clearly revealed Shaikh Zayid's forthright approach and strategic vision. He placed great emphasis on integrity, and his words always reflected his actions. His talk was quiet but purposeful and his listener was left in no doubt as to his meaning and intention. The Political Agent in Dubai, D.A. Roberts, wrote about the first public meeting between the Rulers of Abu Dhabi and Dubai:

> All the evidence available to me, which includes conversations with both Zaid and Rashid, suggests that the visit has had the effect of improving relations between them at least for the moment. They both agreed on the desirability of mounting a Trucial States teacher-training operation although it is in fact uneconomic for the Trucial States to do it alone. They also agreed to coordinate their internal security work. On frontiers, if they did not settle the questions outright, they at least agreed on a programme of further discussions…[53]

Neither Shaikh Zayid nor Shaikh Rashid believed that the path to union would be easy or that long-standing rivalries could easily be suppressed. Abu Dhabi and Dubai were both very different entities, but the two Rulers had determined that they would act in the common interest rather than pursuing unilateral concerns. Nor did the two men see the process of union in exactly the same fashion.[54] Shaikh Rashid's approach was more in economic terms, with the insight that had made Dubai such an dynamic trading center. Shaikh Zayid, on the other hand, had a larger vision and possessed an extraordinary diplomatic flair, refined through years of handling sensitive issues at al Ain. He had been forced to learn patience during the long years of his brother's rule and to build loyalty when he had nothing to offer to those who supported him other than the force of his own personality. In all the documents that describe Shaikh Zayid, his quality of openness is much commented upon, but this transparency masked an adroitness in handling issues and individuals.[55]

In a world where the individual counted for more than structures or organizations, a man's reputation and sense of honor was the necessary lubricant of the political system. An honorable foe could be a more satisfactory partner than an untrustworthy friend. In Shaikh Zayid's case, disagreement over political or other issues would never erode established relationships of trust and honor.[56] Furthermore, his diplomacy and political acuity were such that he could successfully interact on a political level even where there was no bond of trust and honor. Shaikh Zayid was widely recognized as a man of deep integrity, whose word was his bond and who had the ability to establish peace where there had previously been discord.

Although, since the late nineteenth century, it had been fashionable to see history as a largely determinist and wholly inevitable process, several instances in more recent times prove that the role of the individual as a transforming influence cannot be denied.[57] Had Shaikh Shakhbut still been the Ruler of Abu Dhabi between 1968 and 1971, it seems unlikely that a lasting federation could have been formed under Abu Dhabi's leadership. In Shaikh Zayid, the region possessed a man committed to social and economic progress and a negotiator who was plainly interested in conciliation and not confrontation. Although he would not deviate from his fundamental principles, both in establishing his goals and in the means he used to reach them, he remained focused on his final objectives and was able to compromise on immediate benefits for the ultimate good. Finally, the growing oil wealth of Abu Dhabi meant that he had the economic resources to support his long-term objectives.

During the three years in which progress towards a federation was to be made, Shaikh Zayid's immediate priority was to build up the strength and infrastructure of Abu Dhabi. The emirate's social and economic development was all the more urgent because of the uncertainty of the immediate future. If all his aspirations to union failed, the Ruler had to ensure that Abu Dhabi could survive and prosper on its own. While ensuring progress for Abu Dhabi, Shaikh Zayid had to conduct delicate diplomatic maneuvers to achieve unification within the region. Shaikh Zayid's broad objectives were clear—social advancement and unity among the peoples of the region. But he knew that the context within which these had to be achieved was essentially political. The new Federation would have to exist in a political environment in which the two largest states in the region, Iran and Saudi Arabia, maintained claims over the new state's territory. The dynamics were such that these two regional powers may have offered political and economic assistance, but only in exchange for the subordination of the new federal state to their own interests. Shaikh Zayid would never accept such a proposal under any circumstances.

Shaikh Zayid envisaged the new Federation as truly independent, economically and politically secure, and with sufficient military power to deter a would-be aggressor. However, he also knew that the Federation's strongest defense lay in the promotion of friendship and mutual interests with other states. Nevertheless, despite the desire for friendship and cooperation, it was also clear that Shaikh Zayid would judge any offers of assistance to Abu Dhabi and the new Federation on merit, and that he would not compromise on their interests at any cost.[58] In this analysis, the role of the United Nations assumed a crucial importance in his thinking and that of his advisors. Once independent, the new Federation would be a full member of the community of nations and, although this provided no armed capacity, it provided a moral buttress. Later, he was to declare his faith in the "strengthening of cooperation and friendship between governments on the basis of the United Nations Charter and ideal international ethics, and all efforts towards establishing peace and justice for the benefit of the human race."[59]

As the prolonged negotiations began in 1968, Shaikh Zayid had a clarity of purpose. First, while he made it clear that he and Abu Dhabi were committed to unity, he allowed others to embark on an endless round of shuttle diplomacy. Here, Shaikh Zayid waited patiently for the other Rulers to determine their own means of collaboration, while stressing his commitment to work with them. As he watched, the negotiations came to a halt, immobilized by personal and political rivalries to the point that even the idea of a federation seemed to be doomed and beyond revival. Only then, when the low point had been reached, did Shaikh Zayid himself step forward to forge together the Federation of the United Arab Emirates.

PART
III

THE
UNION

CHAPTER
7

Birth of a Nation

Shaikh Zayid Bin Sultan saw his accession to the leadership of Abu Dhabi as an opportunity to translate his principles into action and carry forward his vision of unity, progress and development. He did not conceive his position of Ruler as the culmination of his political career, but rather as a platform from which to serve the people of Abu Dhabi. Furthermore, as projects began to transform the emirate and prosperity grew, it set the stage for his grand design to bring about greater regional unity and integration so that the benefits of progress could extend to all.

For Shaikh Zayid, the concept of unity possessed a strong moral dimension and was never a matter of mere political convenience. In his view, unity was a philosophical principle underlying the wholeness and integrity of human existence. It was like a river, swelling and gathering strength from different sources as it flowed. Shaikh Zayid saw it as axiomatic that political divisions should be broken down and that one by one the barriers to human progress – poverty, disease, lack of education – should be conquered. Division and fragmentation were a source of social weakness, and he believed wholeheartedly that a united Federation could achieve more than fragmented states. This broad vision was always implicit when Shaikh Zayid spoke of unity.[1] The establishment of the United Arab Emirates as a sovereign, independent state was the first step in a more inclusive union. While the UAE Federation was to be based on strong ethical as well as political principles, it was to be followed by greater regional integration and cooperation in the Gulf, and firmer relations with the whole Arab world.

Shaikh Zayid had understood the importance of unity since his youth in his father's *majlis*. He saw it first among the tribesmen who approached his father, each with his particular issues and concerns, but all united within the community of the tribe. This early image made an impression on him and would later develop into a central precept of his life. Many years later, he succinctly expressed the essence of his basic philosophy: "The sons of this region are [b]rothers, with one origin; their language is the same; their religion is the same; even the land they have lived on for thousands of years has always been one unit."[2] Shaikh Zayid envisaged a union among the peoples of the Gulf as providing a model of inspiration for the entire Arab world. If union could be achieved in this region, among tribes riven by deep antagonisms – some economic, some based on long-forgotten issues and quarrels, others on current animosities – it could succeed in other regions as well. If the peoples of the Gulf could find a basis for integration, then it should also be possible for other parts of the Arab world.

Shaikh Zayid was equally committed to progress, moved as he was by humanitarian considerations and a strong faith that inspired him to work for the common good. He later wrote, "Everything in life happens through the will of God Almighty, may He be praised. He directs and guides all…We must act and we must trust in God. From God comes all success."[3] Yet, he was convinced that unity was crucial to progress. Thus, the building of unity in the Gulf was part of a broader plan and Shaikh Zayid felt himself to be a humble instrument in this process. In this context, Shaikh Zayid observed:

> If God is pleased with someone born with the qualities of leadership, He will send him to a nation with which He is pleased. God will provide direction so that this leader may guide his nation along the true path…He will pave the way for leaders to arise among them [nations], to unite them for the common good, to raise the quality of life.[4]

While from Shaikh Zayid's perspective the idea of union was too important to be allowed to fail, it soon proved to be a most difficult undertaking. He noted the problems faced by the British-inspired federation created in South Yemen and took a strong signal from its ignominious collapse.[5] He wanted to create a successful and enduring union for the people, one from which they would derive real benefits, not one designed to satisfy British interests. Ever the realist, he recognized the complexities inherent in the transition from British protection to independent state. He knew why so few British officials believed that any union would survive intact.[6] He even accepted that their doubts had some justification.[7] For example, the experience of the Trucial States Council suggested that the fissiparous tendencies among the emirates would eventually result in the fragmentation of a fragile new state. Shaikh Zayid feared that the Ruler of each emirate would inevitably pursue the interests of his own state and not even consider the benefits of closer cooperation. In fact, between 1968 and 1971 most of the moves made towards federation seemed to confirm this concern. Although committed to the concept of union, the Rulers focused initially only on the immediate interests of their own people. Meanwhile, Shaikh Zayid gave priority to the strengthening of the economic infrastructure and social cohesion of Abu Dhabi. This would be an important building-block for the future of the union.

The process whereby the United Arab Emirates came into existence was extraordinarily complex. Apart from Shaikh Zayid, few of the other participants in the process – the British government, Iran, Saudi Arabia, the other states of the Lower Gulf – pursued any consistent policy. Many failures and few successes marked the three years of negotiation. But as early as April 1968, in a long talk with Edward Henderson, Shaikh Zayid outlined a plan that closely reflected the final outcome in 1971. He considered that in order for the Federation to endure it would need a firm purpose, and each emirate needed to have a stake in it. If it failed, social unrest was bound to follow. With Abu Dhabi as the principal contributor, its people would want to see the federal seat of government in their emirate. Yet, every emirate would be autonomous in internal affairs, despite a central Ministry for Defence and for Foreign Affairs.[8]

In the end, Shaikh Zayid proved to be the right leader in the right place at the right time. In addition to vision, strength and energy, he possessed a distinctive capacity for patient but persistent consultation aimed at reaching consensus. He also displayed a willingness to compromise and an ability to accommodate his adversaries to an extent that has seldom been seen elsewhere. The combined gifts of leadership that Shaikh Zayid demonstrated established a legacy that is unprecedented in the modern history of state-building.

On the Road to Federation

The quest for a new political framework began in mid-January 1968, when the British government suddenly announced that it was withdrawing its presence from the region. Despite the abruptness of the decision, the Rulers soon focused on the need to act collectively in the interest of their people.[9] For more than a century, the British presence had placed limitations on their endeavors. At the same time, British military power had served a protective and deterrent function against some of the more ambitious neighboring states. As such, the diplomacy of the powerful states in the region, notably Saudi Arabia, Iran and Iraq, had all been predicated on the continuing British role. But in 1968, that key element in the policy process was scheduled for removal by 1971, allowing little time for the states in the Gulf region to formulate a clear alternative. In retrospect, the creation of the United Arab Emirates as a sovereign state and the independence of Bahrain and Qatar represented a logical political progression. At the time, however, a stable and enduring outcome seemed highly unlikely. The potential for instability amply justifies the high premium that Shaikh Zayid placed on the development of mutual confidence, and the pursuit of harmony both in his state-building and in his diplomacy. Uniquely among his contemporary Rulers, Shaikh Zayid was in a position to judge the complexity of several factors that would ultimately determine the success or failure of the new Federation.[10]

The crucial first step came as a result of an underlying consensus being reached by Shaikh Zayid and Shaikh Rashid of Dubai. An initial bilateral agreement between the two Rulers created a union between Abu

Dhabi and Dubai on February 18, 1968. One critical factor that gave impetus to this agreement was the desire of both leaders to demonstrate to the other emirates how unity could work and prove beneficial.[11] Under this agreement, a single federal state would be formed with a common approach to foreign affairs, defense and security, medical and education services and citizenship.[12] To reinforce the fact that the agreement was more than a mere document, on the same day, the two states concluded an additional agreement on the demarcation of their maritime frontiers, which was of crucial importance to the potential development of Dubai's oil resources. This represented a voluntary concession by Abu Dubai to Dubai, a symbolic gesture that indicated how compromise could settle even long-standing disputes between the two emirates.

The bond between the two Rulers developed from the time that they had first worked together as younger delegates in the Trucial States Council, a mutual understanding based on a clear sense of each other's true qualities. This intrinsic trust remained unwavering throughout the formation of the UAE and thereafter. When the American Ambassador to Kuwait, William Stoltzfus, met Shaikh Rashid on June 4, 1972, he asked him how the new union was progressing, "Rashid indicated [that the] union [was] developing about as well as could be expected and considering it [sic] tender age. Zayid himself was [a] 'clean' person with good intentions, intelligent and amenable to reason."[13] The word 'clean' (*nazif*) denotes many qualities: truthful, honest, faithful, loyal, genuine, reliable, trustworthy and dependable. There is no doubt that Shaikh Zayid had just as high an opinion of Shaikh Rashid. Nevertheless, as may be expected of such strong personalities, they would not agree upon everything. However, there was a profound sense that they concurred on all the important issues and both firmly believed that intelligent compromise could resolve most problems. Thus, the accord between the two states was founded on a fundamental consensus between the two leaders.

Shaikh Zayid's approach to the Abu Dhabi–Dubai agreement was the first indication of how he intended to negotiate in the run-up to political union. Time and again, he showed that he was prepared to make a bold move whenever it served a higher goal. The significance of these two developments – the declaration of union and the settlement of a boundary issue – was recognized by regional leaders. In this context, the accord provided a first practical demonstration of a partial resolution of border problems, which had up to this point prevented effective cooperation between the emirates. Furthermore, it was a good-will gesture that would ultimately pave the way for a Federation not only between Abu Dhabi and Dubai but including the other emirates as well.[14] The element of popular will and the desire for unity were a potent but largely invisible force within the power structure of the region.[15] However, Shaikh Zayid recognized that they would ultimately be of vital importance in the emergence of a new state.[16]

The pioneering agreement between Abu Dhabi and Dubai envisaged an open union, with its responsibilities and benefits extendible to other states. Shaikh Zayid and Shaikh Rashid invited the Rulers of the other five Trucial States to join them—but made it clear that the link between Abu Dhabi and Dubai was fixed. Even if no other state joined, the Federation of Two would persist. Bahrain and Qatar were also invited to be part of the move toward greater unity. Once enunciated, the proposal for a wider union gained broad general support, and on February 27, 1968, an agreement was signed in Dubai by nine states to collaborate on the formation of a unified Federation. This agreement came into effect on March 30, 1968.

The Dubai Agreement, as it became known, was an optimistic aspiration rather than a practical agenda for union.[17] In their eagerness to reach a rapid accord, the participants had ignored the fundamental inter-state tensions that were already manifest on February 27, 1968. In reality, the accord was severely limited. Yet, despite this lack of any true consensus, it was probably the correct decision to reach an agreement in principle. In the spring of 1968, the people of the region, and others beyond, needed to see concrete evidence that the Rulers of the Gulf had responded positively to the broad initiative of Shaikh Zayid and Shaikh Rashid.

The agreement to form a Federation was widely welcomed in the Arab world, despite varying national interests.[18] Britain and the United States warmly welcomed the move. Iran, as might have been expected, was wholly opposed. Thus, less than two months after the British decision to withdraw, the problems of the region appeared to have been resolved, at least on the surface. Shaikh Zayid, in the meantime, was well aware of the difference between a signed agreement and a functioning political entity. His whole experience in Abu Dhabi had taught him to distrust a solution too readily conceded. However, with the central agreement with Dubai in place, he was content for other Rulers to tackle the difficult details of a working accord for a new union of the Lower Gulf.

The idea of a Federation of Nine was extremely ambitious. Among its advocates was the British government, which saw it as a neat solution to its post-imperial obligations.[19] Yet, too many inherent tensions existed for genuine success to be achieved. John Duke Anthony expressed the issues succinctly:

> After 1968, when negotiations started among all nine Lower Gulf emirates (including Bahrain and Qatar)...[an] important problem was the distribution of powers between the rulers and the Union government. Another was how the Union should operate...To a certain extent the polarization among the rulers over these issues reflected genuine differences of opinion, but in other ways it was the product of traditional rivalries along tribal and family lines.[20]

In practice, the main problems stemmed from Bahrain and Qatar. Both had a political agenda that diverged fundamentally from that of the other emirates. Bahrain's proposal for proportional representation would have resulted in domination over the smaller states.[21] Qatar had reservations from the start about the Abu Dhabi–Dubai union, and proposed a new federal structure.[22] A week after the initial agreement between Abu Dhabi and Dubai, Qatar unilaterally presented a plan whereby the five smaller emirates would be fused into a single United Arab Coast Emirate, with a single voice in the confederation. Understandably, the Rulers of Sharjah, Ajman, Ras al Khaimah, Umm al Qaiwain and Fujairah would not accept a proposal in which one of their number would be elevated as Ruler of the emirate, with his fellow Rulers demoted.

Despite evident resistance to its proposal, Qatar left the plan on the table, and its stance throughout the subsequent discussions was to urge for an agreement on lines it deemed acceptable. Following February's Dubai Agreement, and prior to the first meeting convened in Abu Dhabi on May 25, 1968, Qatar put forward a number of proposals in the meeting's agenda. Among them, the Qataris declared: "We should not wait until a charter is worked out, as the Dubai accord, being an interim charter, is adequate for the purposes of taking the major preliminary steps."[23] However, deep fissures were already apparent in the façade of common purpose, and a pattern soon emerged whereby Qatar's proposals met with united opposition, usually led by Bahrain.[24] Abu Dhabi's stance was to act as a mediator between what was rapidly emerging as a set of entrenched positions.[25]

Although Shaikh Zayid was aware of the contradictions in a possible union of nine emirates, he pursued this path because he believed in its utility. Referring to the May meeting, Henderson noted that it was Zayid who was willing to compromise in order to achieve the main objective and that he did much more to mend fences than to break them.[26] When in October 1969 the Supreme Council meeting ended in disarray, Treadwell, the Political Agent in Abu Dhabi, pointed out:

> Shaikh Zaid himself showed strength in character in pursuing the course he thought right. He could have sacrificed Bahrain and have gone on perhaps to become a leading member of a Union of eight… Instead, Shaikh Zaid elected to resist the moves against Bahrain, and in the process of doing so to suffer a break with Qatar, take a further step back from peace with Dubai and throw away the fruits of boundary agreements with both Emirates which were reached almost solely because of his own policy of conciliation. What spirit moved Shaikh Zayid to struggle against such odds to keep the nine together? It has been said that as Chairman he was anxious that all points on the agenda should be agreed … The more substantial a Union, the more easily could it present itself credibly to the outside world … I think we may be sure … that with his native wit and negotiating ability, the Ruler of Abu Dhabi will take a lead in re-kindling enthusiasm for a close association of states.[27]

Yet, in practice, the idea of a broad and all-embracing union in the area was becoming an obstacle to creating an effective political entity within the timetable set by the British for withdrawal by December 1971. Issues of security and defense were uppermost in the minds of the negotiators for the Federation of Nine. In part, this was because these were the only concerns that all the states had in common. Once Britain withdrew, they would have to take measures to enhance their own security and deal with territorial claims and counter-claims within the region.[28] Between 1968 and 1971, security issues remained a primary concern. In addition, Bahrain, although often in accord with the aims and desires of the other emirates, also sought to make its power, size and sophistication felt within the union. Furthermore, Bahrain was under pressure from Iran, which claimed the entire island as its historic territory, as well as other islands belonging to the northern emirates. The inclusion of Bahrain while this threat was unresolved might involve the new Federation in immediate hostilities with its powerful neighbor. In addition to the Iranian factor, Bahrain and Qatar continued to disagree on most issues. There were long-standing territorial disputes and economic rivalries between these two emirates that would not be overcome by joint membership of a larger federation.[29]

Shaikh Zayid was perhaps the only Ruler with a fixed and absolute commitment to achieve union. But it had to be an effective and practical union, not some fragile formulation that would collapse when confronted by the first serious challenge. It was difficult to have any great hope of ultimate success for a Federation of Nine. The disproportionate demands of Qatar in respect of the smaller emirates were unacceptable to their Rulers.[30] Moreover, although the power and weight of Bahrain might theoretically be an asset to the new Federation, its large population and advanced expertise in areas of education and administration could create an imbalance within the new structure. Well-qualified Bahrainis would quickly fill the ranks of the new administration and bureaucracy, inevitably causing local resentment. If Bahrain proved too dominant in the Federation, as its higher levels of expertise and population suggested it would, then the unity project might ultimately collapse.

From the outset, Abu Dhabi and its immediate neighbors believed that the most realistic option lay in a union restricted to the contiguous emirates that constituted the Trucial States. Their Rulers had been working together in the Trucial States Council for almost two decades and there already existed a degree of mutual interest and understanding. It was based on these principles that Shaikh Zayid had taken the first crucial step in forming the agreement with Dubai. Furthermore, because he recognized the importance of establishing trust and discovering mutual interests, he urged the Abu Dhabi delegation to resist the pressure to achieve quick solutions, and allow the other emirates time to reach a consensus.

From Nine to Seven: Resolving the Impasse

While Shaikh Zayid was not inactive in the negotiations between the spring of 1968 and the spring of 1971, he was content to bide his time. Effectively, negotiations for the Federation of Nine had reached an impasse in October 1969. Fresh attempts were made in June 1970 to regain momentum in the search for an agreement. It would prove to be a hopeless task. On June 13, 1970, the Bahraini delegation submitted a formal memorandum. The preamble to that memorandum declared:

> …more than two years have passed since the conclusion of the agreement regarding the union of Arab emirates, without the union between the emirates taking the required real and legal form as represented by the declaration of a federal state…and since we are passing through a decisive stage in the history of our Arab nation in general, and our Arabian Gulf in particular, we should, of necessity, begin taking fundamental resolutions pertaining to the concrete establishment of the union state.[31]

The Qatari delegation assumed that these observations of delay referred directly to their activity and replied vehemently.[32] The problems in the path of a Federation of Nine seemed to increase with every passing month, despite the efforts of Saudi Arabia and Kuwait. King Faisal's Special Envoy to Kuwait, Prince Nawwaf Bin Abdul Aziz, declared publicly that Saudi Arabia would not accept the failure of the negotiations: "The Saudi Arabian Kingdom will not accept a seven member union, and will exert efforts towards a nine member union."[33]

In mid-January 1971, perilously close to the anticipated date of British withdrawal, a team of senior representatives from Saudi Arabia and Kuwait paid another visit to all the emirates, meeting with each Ruler in turn. Shaikh Zayid issued an official statement after his meeting on January 18, 1971: "The government of Abu Dhabi welcomes the Saudi–Kuwait delegation and blesses its effort towards the establishment of the Union of Arab Emirates. These efforts coincide with the inevitable work which was, and still is, undertaken by Abu Dhabi for the establishment of the union on a sound foundation."[34]

However, whether the "sound foundation" was anticipated as the Federation of Nine or the Federation of Seven was becoming a meaningless question, as there still were no definitive moves towards any type of federation. On March 1, 1971, the pressure to achieve a solution intensified. After almost nine months of uncertainty, the British Foreign Secretary Sir Alec Douglas Home formally confirmed in the House of Commons that, in effect, the former Labour government's policy in the Gulf would be sustained.[35] British troops would be withdrawn in December 1971, and instead of the previous agreements for protection, Britain would offer a "treaty of friendship." Home, however, also made it clear that the British would transfer certain responsibilities only to a formally constituted federal authority, and although there was some ambiguity, the treaty of friendship was anticipated as being concluded with the newly functioning Federation.

In part, the announcement was designed to give impetus to the negotiators in the region, given that barely eight months remained before withdrawal. The British Representative in the region, Luce, once again visited all the Rulers and emphasized that the withdrawal of British forces would proceed no later than December 31, 1971, regardless of any unsettled issues. However, by the time of Luce's final visit early in June 1971, it was also clear that the prospect of the Federation of Nine was moribund as Bahrain and Qatar remained focused on their own interests. On August 14, 1971, Bahrain declared itself a sovereign and independent state, to be followed by Qatar on September 1. If the concept of a federation was to be preserved, it was imperative for the remaining seven emirates to reach an accord.

For three years, discussions had been held on a number of levels. There had been sessions at which representatives of the various states had met and talked. However, such discussions were always subject to revision by the governments, as the representatives had no plenipotentiary powers. Other discussions were held at the Deputy Ruler level and were more substantive. Finally, the Rulers of the seven emirates would meet, sometimes through the mechanism of the Trucial States Council, and their decisions had authority. Yet, the real momentum for change was in fact achieved through private negotiations between Rulers, sometimes on paper but more often face-to-face.

The nucleus of this more restricted union was the accord between Abu Dhabi and Dubai of February 18, 1968, which had prompted the moves towards union.[36] Neither Shaikh Zayid nor Shaikh Rashid believed that the path to even a Union of Seven would be smooth, or that long-standing rivalries could easily be suppressed. Abu Dhabi and Dubai, for example, were still very different societies. The northern emirates had also evolved in a manner different from their richer and more powerful southern neighbors. As already suggested, the two Rulers, albeit keen on the concept of union, perceived the objective differently. Shaikh Rashid maintained a perspective based on economic interest, traditionally Dubai's strength, which the Ruler led and managed with skill.[37] Shaikh Zayid's view had always been one of broader political and humanitarian interest, anchored firmly in an informed strategic vision. He too possessed the skills to reach his objective. A consummate leader, diplomat and negotiator, he was endowed with the political acumen, resilience and patience required to see the union come to fruition. However, the two Rulers had determined that they would act in the common interest rather than pursue parochial concerns, thus providing a model for their neighbors.

It was only in the last six months before British withdrawal that negotiations assumed a real urgency, and it was at this point that the role of Shaikh Zayid and of Abu Dhabi became even more pivotal. For over two years, Shaikh Zayid had observed the swing of ongoing negotiations. His role was always to conciliate and to prevent a breakdown in the discussions. The historian Frauke Heard-Bey has accurately characterized his attitude in 1968:

Abu Dhabi advocated proceeding slowly, allowing time to adjust to the new situation and to anticipate the consequences of each move. Abu Dhabi adopted a very cautious attitude towards the establishment of institutions at that time, realising how very difficult it could be to change certain functions once they had become institutionalised. The Abu Dhabi delegation wanted to concentrate on creating the right federation with, in due course, the right constitution on the basis of the experts' drafts and informal consultations among member States. It was less concerned about how the union would function in the interim period.[38]

At any point between 1968 and 1971, Shaikh Zayid's clearly stated opinion could have been decisive. His fellow Rulers had unanimously elected him as the President of the putative union. Abu Dhabi was designated as the capital of the new Federation. Without his support and goodwill, no federation could succeed. But he seemed content to allow the other states to take independent decisions. He had half hoped for the inclusion of Bahrain, with whom Abu Dhabi shared not only a currency but also many ties, but he appreciated the reasons why Bahrain might seek its own destiny. It was characteristic that he did not seek to dominate the discussions as he so easily could have done, both by virtue of his role as President and by the preponderant economic contribution that Abu Dhabi would make to the proposed federation. It seems likely that he had come to regard any federation as being only the first point in cooperation within the region and not its ultimate expression. This rendered the issue of a nine-state or seven-state federation immaterial. In Shaikh Zayid's view, wider cooperation would come at a later stage, as it did when the Gulf Cooperation Council (GCC) was formed a decade later.[39]

Indeed, it seems likely that Shaikh Zayid had, after witnessing the prolonged and acrimonious negotiations, come to regard the limited federation of the former Trucial States as being the *only* plausible option. The course of the discussions had indicated that this would be the most likely outcome. He had publicly advocated the principle of a larger union while it had remained even a remote possibility. However, as soon as it became obvious that both Qatar and Bahrain intended to follow their own path, he pressed with great energy for the creation of a smaller and more functional unit. There was also political acuity in choosing this option, because it was inevitable that Abu Dhabi's role in a smaller federation would be proportionally larger.

Once the responsibility for the creation of a new and solid political entity for the region devolved upon Shaikh Zayid in mid-1971, the moves for unity acquired a broader dimension. Shaikh Zayid believed that stability did not reside in artificial alliance systems, but in creating social and political units that enjoyed a natural harmony.[40] This would be a substantial development beyond what had already been proposed, and it seems remarkable that he was able to unite his fellow Rulers behind what amounted to a much more comprehensive plan. He was able to achieve this advance not only because he was the Ruler of the wealthiest state in the region, but also because he was universally accepted as a leader, trusted and honored by all the parties concerned.

With plans for the larger union effectively abandoned, Shaikh Zayid took the initiative. He invited the Rulers of the seven Trucial States to meet in Abu Dhabi for joint discussions with the aim of advancing an effective federation. On June 28 and 29, 1971, the Rulers of Dubai, Sharjah and Ras al Khaimah had a series of meetings with Shaikh Zayid. In one sense, these meetings were a disappointment, since the discussion focused largely on the terms by which the TSDO should be adapted to cover a broader range of functions. The proposals discussed at the meeting envisaged little more than a coordinating office, which might prove an obstacle to full unity, certainly in Shaikh Zayid's understanding of the concept.[41] He could not accept the lack of urgency displayed at the meeting. Even at the fully fledged meeting of the Trucial States Council summoned for July 10, 1971, it was clear that a majority of the emirates still favored a substantially autonomous arrangement. Indeed, the issue of the Federation of Seven was not even on the agenda. It seemed that only Shaikh Zayid recognized the need to produce a viable state structure before the withdrawal of Britain plunged the whole region into a state of potential disequilibrium. Nevertheless, while mostly disappointing, both meetings also served to clarify the distance that still remained to be bridged if a functioning state were to be created before the expiration of the British deadline.

In the immediate aftermath of each of the above meetings, Shaikh Zayid took decisive steps. First, on July 1, as Ruler of Abu Dhabi, he announced that a constitutional reform within Abu Dhabi would proceed independent of any agreed unification framework.[42] The unstated but well-understood subtext to this constitutional reform was that Abu Dhabi intended to move forward to statehood whether or not the other six emirates joined the proposed union. The plans for such a move had been in place for several months, but the date of the announcement is unlikely to have been coincidental. One of the first acts of the new cabinet was to establish, on July 8, 1971, the Abu Dhabi Fund for Arab Economic Development, with an initial capital of 50 million dinars.[43] Without Abu Dhabi, the chances of a successful federation were negligible. Shaikh Zayid's subliminal message was that independent statehood was preferable to an incomplete and weak union. At the same time, Abu Dhabi also pledged to make strenuous efforts to secure a comprehensive union of the emirates.

Second, on July 13, after three days of mostly fruitless discussion in the Trucial States Council, Shaikh Zayid for the first time posed the question directly.[44] He asked the Rulers of the other emirates whether they favored union or not. They were thus faced with a stark choice— a union on Shaikh Zayid's terms and with the full economic and security backing of Abu Dhabi or a situation in which Abu Dhabi would go ahead alone. All six Rulers chose unity. On that decisive day, Shaikh Zayid, echoing the precedent set by his grandfather and namesake, took firm control of the destiny of the region.

These combined moves in early July were evidence of Shaikh Zayid's determination to pursue the logic of an effective program for unity.[45] Shortly afterwards, it seems clear that Abu Dhabi, Dubai and Sharjah were in essence prepared to move forward together.[46] Thereafter, matters moved swiftly ahead. Detailed items were debated and voted upon. Abu Dhabi was designated as the federal capital of the new union, with a new capital planned for an area on the borders of Abu Dhabi and Dubai. The Provisional Constitution of the UAE stated that decisions in the Supreme Council on important issues were to be "by a majority of five of its members provided that this majority includes the votes of the Emirates of Abu Dhabi and Dubai. The minority shall be bound by the view of the said majority."[47] A National Consultative Council comprising forty members was proposed, with eight members each for Abu Dhabi and Dubai, six for Sharjah and Ras al Khaimah and four each for Ajman, Umm al Qaiwain and Fujairah. After a period of discussion, Ras al Khaimah decided that it could not accept a number of these conditions and, accordingly, opted to remain outside the Federation framework for the time being.[48]

Finally, on July 18, 1971, an agreement was reached among the remaining six emirates. On that day, each of the Rulers put their signatures to a common accord. They declared:

> In response to the desire of our Arab people, we, the Rulers of Abu Dhabi, Dubai, Sharjah, Ajman, Umm Al-Qaiwain and Fujairah, have resolved to establish a federal state under the name of the United Arab Emirates. On this blessed day a provisional constitution of the United Arab Emirates was signed. Conveying this happy news to the great Arab people, we pray the Almighty that this union shall be the nucleus for a full union to include the rest of the members of the family of sister emirates who, due to their current circumstances, were not able to sign this constitution.[49]

Shaikh Zayid had little use for 'empty political statements,' but he was scrupulous in his insistence that the written statement of the aims and objectives of the union reflect its genuine aspirations. Thus, the Provisional Constitution that was agreed upon was unique in its strong focus on the social and economic basis of the union, reflecting Shaikh Zayid's long-standing concern with these issues.

In reality, the level of development in the emirates varied widely from area to area, and it was therefore important to incorporate in the Constitution a fundamental commitment to issues of health, education and social welfare. Article 13 specified that both the federal government and the member emirates should cooperate to fulfill the specific obligations in these three vital fields. It was to be an area of joint responsibility, in which the federal government could act on its own initiative throughout the UAE.[50] It is clear that these areas were not to be a privilege restricted to the wealthy and advanced core emirates. The Constitution also declared: "The family is the basis of society. It is founded on morality, religion, ethics and patriotism. The law shall guarantee its existence, safeguard and protect it from corruption."[51] This was no empty promise, for Shaikh Zayid ensured that families were provided with the resources necessary to fulfill this central social function.[52]

Social welfare in a comprehensive form thus became a corner-stone of the Constitution, embodying Shaikh Zayid's personal vision of unity. Accordingly, the UAE Constitution declares:

> Society shall be responsible for protecting childhood and mother-hood and shall protect minors and others unable to look after themselves for any reason, such as illness or incapacity or old age or forced unemployment. It shall be responsible for assisting them and enabling them to help themselves for their own benefit and that of the community.[53]

Similarly, the Constitution states that education was to be the engine of national development: "Education shall be a fundamental factor for the progress of society. It shall be compulsory in its primary stage and free of charge at all stages, within the Union."[54]

Each of these Articles embodied principles which Shaikh Zayid considered central to the nation's welfare. The idea that society should improve from within, through a process of self-help, was an integral part of his pragmatic philosophy, developed over many years. Article 23 specified that the natural resources and wealth of each emirate was the public property of that emirate. However, in accordance with Shaikh Zayid's concern for the well-being of all the people of the emirates, the wealth of Abu Dhabi was to be used for the benefit of all UAE citizens. Thus, Abu Dhabi would become the engine of progress for the smaller and less wealthy northern emirates.[55]

The Constitution embodied the twin tracks in Shaikh Zayid's political thinking. The first was his concern with the improvement of the physical and educational condition of his people, for he believed that a nation that was ignorant and needy could never take pride in itself.

The second was the idea of unity, which he had pursued since his early years in al Ain.[56] Since the Arab peoples shared a common ancestry and were bound by family ties that Shaikh Zayid conceived as the central element of human society, the unity fostered among the former Trucial States was to serve as a model of what could be achieved by all Arabs through compromise and a desire for harmony.[57] As later events would show, for example in the establishment of the GCC in 1981, unity was the one principle that Shaikh Zayid placed above all else, and one that he has continued to pursue throughout his career.

In a report carried by Reuters on July 22, 1971, Shaikh Zayid said that the events of July 18 represented the most important step taken by the emirates towards a union founded on a secure base. He expressed satisfaction that in a short time the Rulers had been able to remove all the obstacles that had hindered agreement. Above all, he was reassured by the delight with which the people of the emirates had received the news of the formation of the union.[58] Characteristically, he minimized his own contribution to this outcome.

The United Arab Emirates Proclaimed

On December 2, 1971, a new flag was hoisted for the first time at the al Jamayra Palace in Dubai. Its colors – red, green, white and black – were all colors traditionally associated with the states that made up the new nation, the United Arab Emirates. Up to the last moment, it was hoped that Ras al Khaimah would join to form a union of seven emirates, but the state proclaimed on December 2, 1971 had only six members. Although the absence of Ras al Khaimah was regrettable, it did not alter the strong will and collective purpose of those emirates that had linked their destinies. They had chosen to stand united for mutual protection and benefit.

What was remarkable in Shaikh Zayid's formulation of the new nation, created in partnership with his fellow Rulers, all of whom stood with him before their new flag, was its mixture of elevated ethics and a profound understanding of the fundamental need for economic security and prosperity.[59] The complex process of state formation, after three years of indecision and shifting political ambitions, had been accomplished in four months. Although the firm decision for unity was made on July 18, 1971, by December 1, 1971, when Britain's responsibility for the former Trucial States ended, the new nation was ready to be launched. Not every aspect of the new nation was complete, but on December 2, 1971, the Supreme Council of the United Arab Emirates held its first meeting. The Rulers elected the Ruler of Abu Dhabi, Shaikh Zayid Bin Sultan Al Nahyan, as the first President, and the Ruler of Dubai, Shaikh Rashid Bin Sa'id Al Maktum as the first Vice President. This result, although widely expected, was the clearest possible manifestation of the linkage between Abu Dhabi and Dubai, which had been the cornerstone of the unity project from the outset. Article 49 of the Provisional Constitution made an accord between Abu Dhabi and Dubai essential to every major development in the new nation.[60] It was Shaikh Zayid and Shaikh Rashid who had stood together at the start of the union process, and the fundamental fact of the Federation was unambiguous. If Abu Dhabi and Dubai did not continue to act conjointly, the process of unity could never attain fruition.

This partnership between the two Rulers of Abu Dhabi and Dubai as the President and Vice President of the United Arab Emirates was the foundation on which the new state was built.[61] In the four months between the decision for unity and the declaration of the new state, Shaikh Zayid personally thrust ahead with the building of the infrastructure for the new state. He had decreed that all the resources, facilities and technical experience of Abu Dhabi should be placed at the disposal of the Federation until it was in a position to act on its own account.[62] By the time the first meeting of Abu Dhabi's own National Consultative Council was held on October 30, 1971, Shaikh Zayid was able to point publicly to the substantial progress that had been made in creating the administrative and organizational framework for the new state, which he stressed was the prime imperative for the entire region. Unity among the peoples of the former Trucial States was predestined, he said, and was a matter of importance not just for the peoples of the emirates but for the Arab world as a whole.[63]

Shaikh Zayid recognized the enormous task that lay ahead, not only in those four months but particularly after independence. One of the benefits of the Federation of Nine would have been that the skilled technicians and administrators that Bahrain possessed would have been at the disposal of the new union. It was therefore inevitable that the new nation would be dependent on external specialists until it could train and develop its own cadre of administrators. This lack of key personnel became apparent in many different sectors. For example, once the United Arab Emirates was born, the nation would need representatives overseas and at the United Nations. In November 1971, 40 men selected for their skills met under the leadership of Ahmad Khalifa Al Suwaidi, Abu Dhabi's Minister for Presidential Affairs, to be trained as future ambassadors and senior diplomats of the new nation. Even so, the new nation began its life with a Minister of Foreign Affairs and staff of three. At independence, the federal civil service had less than four thousand employees to fulfill all its functions. By 1976, demands for its services had driven this total up to 24,000.[64] The demand for good public administration in every sector of government meant a sustained drive to attract and train competent citizens to fill the many new posts available.

From the first moment that independence was in sight, Shaikh Zayid was convinced that the new nation would only survive and prosper if it implanted itself in the hearts and minds of its citizens in the same manner as the government of Abu Dhabi had done since his accession in 1966, by bringing great benefits to its citizens. He recognized that some of his fellow Rulers were suspicious of the idea of federation, and saw it as a challenge to their own authority.[65] His approach was to push forward with the reality of federation, without highlighting the points of contention. Thus, he was content to keep the Constitution as "provisional," the capital as "temporarily" located in Abu Dhabi, and leave to the individual emirates all residual powers not specifically allocated to the federal authority.

Shaikh Zayid saw the union of the disparate emirates as evolving over time, becoming stronger and more effective as the years passed. Nor was he concerned whether progress was achieved through federal

or emirate institutions. In fact, the central problem was more fundamental. In 1971, when the Federation was established, the people of the
emirates were still accustomed to a traditional form of authority, and
unused to the concept of dealing with a government bureaucracy, or
even considering themselves citizens of a sovereign state. To alter this
mindset, which had endured for centuries, and foster trust in state
institutions represented a complex challenge.[66] It was necessary to build
both a sense of national identity and a belief in the value of government
at the grassroots. The federal state would become effective in the eyes of
the people only when it was seen to meet their essential needs. It was
vital that the new government should achieve a string of quick successes.

Moreover, the federal government needed the clear support and
undoubted prestige which would follow from the new President's public
advocacy. Therefore, Shaikh Zayid, pre-eminently among the Rulers
of the emirates, spent a great deal of time promoting the message of
federation both in the hectic months leading up to independence and in
the years thereafter. The new President was careful to use the existing
substructure of tribal authority to convey the new developments to the
people. Traditional figures of authority were often given official roles in
the new administrative system, which allowed the Federation message to
be delivered through trusted voices. The aim was to integrate the long-
established structures of local and personal rule with the new institutions
of the state.

As the new nation began to make progress, the final piece was
put in place. The Ruler of Ras al Khaimah recognized that his decision
to remain outside the union and seek the support of other states for an
independent existence was politically and economically untenable. On
February 10, 1972, Ras al Khaimah was admitted to the United Arab
Emirates and accepted the Provisional Constitution in its entirety. This
fulfilled Shaikh Zayid's desire for a federation of all the Trucial States.
Even after December 2, 1971, he had not exerted any pressure on Ras
al Khaimah to join the union, accepting its decision to stay outside.
Once Ras al Khaimah's request for admission to the UAE Federation
was received, however, he greeted that decision with delight. The
Supreme Council followed his suggestion and unanimously welcomed

Ras al Khaimah's entry, which completed the formation of the United Arab Emirates.

Shaikh Zayid's initiative had allowed the creation of what J.E. Peterson, writing in 1988, described as "the Arab world's most successful unity scheme."[67] Peterson observed:

> All other attempts at Arab unity have been dismal failures. The UAE experiment differs from most of these in that it has been a real attempt at unification, rather than simply an empty political statement. Any attempt to explain the success of the UAE... would have to take into account the social, economic, and political similarities among members of the UAE...But the confederal structure of the union, though often overlooked, may have been just as important in ensuring a successful first fifteen years.[68]

The second day of December would thereafter be celebrated as National Day throughout the UAE, but February 10, 1972 was also a landmark. It illustrated the new President's key principle, that unity was a natural and evolutionary process, not a single political act. The astonishing result of Shaikh Zayid's patience, dedication, vision and belief in the value of compromise resulted in the formation of a nation unlike any other in the contemporary Arab world. Most importantly, he left no stone unturned in his efforts to ensure that the UAE would be structured in such a way as to be sustained long after the days of its founders. As he later remarked to his fellow Rulers:

> The Federation moves from one stage to another, and at every stage we have to review what has been done...so that we can continue the march and quicken the pace to meet the expectations of our people...Our Nation expects us to make it happy. It expects us to move it in the right direction.[69]

The hoisting of the flag on December 2, 1971 marked a historic moment and a new beginning. In the eyes of the people, Shaikh Zayid had justified their trust, but in his view he had merely performed his duty as leader of the nation.

CHAPTER 8

Sustaining the State

On a fine December day in 1971, a flag was added to the line of banners fluttering in the breeze outside the United Nations building in New York. It belonged to a new member-state, the United Arab Emirates.[1] Red, green, white and black, the flag incorporated colors associated with all the emirates that comprised the new union, without being specific to any particular one.[2] The emblem for the new state was chosen with equal care—on the one hand, the falcon, representing its heritage, and on the other, the dhows, symbolizing the maritime traditions of the emirates.[3]

A year later, on December 2, 1972, the UAE celebrated one year of independence. The first National Day evoked intense excitement and tangible pride in the new state's achievements. Most houses in Abu Dhabi flew the national flag, while enthusiastic crowds came into the streets to watch the defense forces marching by. Military aircraft flew overhead. Following the parade, young men representing all the emirates of the union appeared, striding rank after rank before the President and Vice President, the Supreme Council, the Council of Ministers, members of the Federal National Council and an array of foreign dignitaries who had gathered for the occasion. Later in the day, the new national anthem was performed for the first time.

This impressive display of national confidence masked the fact that the new Federation had faced a number of difficulties from the outset. On the one hand, there were external dangers as powerful neighbors either maintained claims over its territory or remained in actual occupation.[4] On the other hand, there were internal challenges, for the UAE comprised emirates that were at different stages of social and economic progress. While Abu Dhabi and Dubai were the most advanced, and Sharjah had a long tradition of education and health care, Ajman, Fujairah, Ras al Khaimah and Umm al Qaiwain were considerably less developed due to remoteness and paucity of resources. As a result, much of the federal government's activity over the first year was concentrated on building a proper infrastructure in these emirates. Furthermore, although the potential economic resources of the new state were very large, human resources were severely limited. This situation resulted in an enormous strain on the President and his small core of dedicated staff and advisors.[5]

Nevertheless, these challenges could not negate the great advantages enjoyed by the new state. The United Arab Emirates possessed in its new President a leader whose appeal extended well beyond his own emirate to the other emirates in the Federation. The loyalty of the people towards His Highness Shaikh Zayid Bin Sultan was not motivated by narrow interests, nor was it backed by military might, as in many other newly independent nations. Loyalty to him was sincere and based on a widespread appreciation of his unique qualities. The people believed in his integrity and trusted his commitment to use the enormous resources of Abu Dhabi for the benefit of all the other emirates.

The UAE's creation and its subsequent independence revealed the prospect of a greater degree of prosperity than ever before. From this point onward, Abu Dhabi's oil revenues would be channeled into the federal structure and benefit the whole community, especially those living in the disadvantaged northern emirates and in the desert regions. In this way, every UAE citizen began to acquire an individual stake and personal interest in the continuance and development of the new political system. There was popular conviction that, under Shaikh Zayid's guidance, what was already being achieved in Abu Dhabi could be replicated in every other emirate.

A key strength of the new government thus lay in its genuine and broad-based support. Neither the external threat of political subversion nor an internal spirit of separatism could promise any kind of equivalent benefit. Shaikh Zayid was convinced that the people would stand by him. He believed that his role was to safeguard the future of the new nation and to fulfill the aspirations of its people. A great leader is often described as the 'Father of the Nation.' In Shaikh Zayid's case, the title is wholly merited because without his energy and determination, the newly unified nation would not have come into existence. The scale of his task was immense, as this was an area characterized by resistance to suzerain authority, with each emirate being fiercely protective of its own identity and individual character. For this reason, the initial act of federation had itself been extremely difficult to accomplish. Next to the creation of the Federation, however, Shaikh Zayid's real challenge lay in making it work in practice. In attempting to foster a spirit of political unity, the weight of history was against him. There were no comparable precedents to serve as a reliable guide to action.

This third and final section of the book makes no attempt to chronicle the eventful and complex history of the United Arab Emirates since its establishment. What it seeks to do is to offer some explanation as to why a union with little chance of success at its inception has developed into a model polity both for the region and for the world at large. Some analysts have argued that its vast oil-based wealth gave the new state an advantage with which it was able to overcome existing social and political tensions. However, many other states have also possessed the advantage of an oil-exporting economy, and the mere fact of being an oil-rich state does not ensure or predetermine patterns of development. A more plausible explanation lies in the fact that, before 1971, there existed no unified state, no common institutions, and almost no political structure. The new United Arab Emirates was initially hampered by this lack of state mechanisms and structures. Paradoxically, however, this later proved to be an unexpected source of strength. State institutions were created to meet the special needs of the new, independent UAE rather than adapting the legacy of British administration to the new situation. More importantly, in this purpose-built nation, the new system was fashioned according to one master-plan envisaged by Shaikh Zayid Bin Sultan Al Nahyan.

The history of the United Arab Emirates can be approached from many different perspectives—economic, social and political. No single approach can be considered more valid than the other. The focus here, however, is on statecraft, and how Shaikh Zayid succeeded in establishing a new nation, the United Arab Emirates. His primary aim was not simply to create a new political entity but a state founded on certain principles and rooted firmly in popular approval. This underlying ethos can be described as a program of unity. It was not formally articulated or documented, but Shaikh Zayid referred constantly to its constituent elements in his public utterances. Its central premise was that unity enhanced national strength while division would weaken it. But the unity program went far beyond a simple political principle. Shaikh Zayid was determined that the ideals of unity should be implanted in the hearts and minds of all the citizens, so that they would begin to think of themselves as linked by this collective UAE identity, rather than the limited citizenship of the smaller states. In his view, the citizens of the UAE belonged not only to the emirate of their birth, but also to the wider union. All the positive qualities of local identity were harnessed in the construction of the larger, national identity. Being an Emirati provided them with rights that many had never enjoyed before, and possessing a UAE passport became a source of pride. Patriotism before the creation of the UAE had been largely a private matter, not publicly displayed. After 1971, however, Shaikh Zayid wanted the people to take visible pride in their new national status and their collective identity.

Thus, the unity program had no set boundaries or limits—it was infinite in concept. The measure of its success was the degree to which it could inspire in the people a feeling of belonging and commitment to their new nation. In a sense, Shaikh Zayid placed the onus on the people to nurture the concept of nationality for themselves. However, during the early stages of its development, he tended it assiduously. In interview after interview, he returned to the theme, pertinently highlighting the central issues, "We ourselves drew up the Federation plan not from expertise, but from faith, faith in our nation, in our country and in the necessity of unity."[6] He stressed, "Division is not natural to our people. In saying this, we are not speaking emotionally. It is an objective assessment."[7] These seeds, planted in the public mind, bore abundant fruit.

An Act of Faith

Shaikh Zayid's concept of the Federation was an act of faith. He knew all the legends of enmity between the ruling families of the region, which he had learned during his childhood years. But he had never allowed the divisive tendencies of the past to color his present relationships.[8] As a young man, and for the most part through the neutral forum provided by the Trucial States Council, he had slowly but surely gained the trust and respect of the Rulers and heirs of the region. By the 1960s, he was widely recognized as a man of honor, rooted in the Bedouin tradition, but also alert to the changes demanded by the modern world. His fellow Rulers might have continued to fear the dominant power of Abu Dhabi, but Shaikh Zayid as an individual always behaved without anger or rancor even toward those who opposed him. His approach was one of persuasion. He once said, "I do not impose unity on anyone. That would be tyranny. Each of us has opinions that differ from those of others. We exchange our views and melt them in one crucible and then extract their essence. That is our democracy; it is the democracy of unity."[9]

Shaikh Zayid also knew from the history of the region that anything less than a comprehensive and wholehearted union would ultimately disintegrate. The cohesive force of a strong and solid central core, and a common identity, was essential to counteract the centrifugal tendencies that had operated in the emirates over many centuries. Being in close contact with the people, he was convinced that they would readily accept the concept and ideals of union. Still, for the Federation to succeed over the long term, Shaikh Zayid was certain that the spirit of unity could never be imposed from the 'top down,' but rather needed to grow over time from the 'ground up.' It had to be a union based on the will of the people.

Shaikh Zayid's government created a harmonious integration of what many outsiders considered to be two irreconcilable elements. By convention, the concepts of 'popular will' and 'traditional government' are viewed as being diametrically opposed. While the former is associated with revolution, the latter contains the notions of immobility and stagnation. Both change and continuity had a role to play in his program. He scrupulously preserved the power, privileges and self-esteem of his fellow Rulers, reassuring them that the traditional forms of governance would continue. At the same time, he insisted that the economic and social benefits of unity belonged to all the people, providing them with the means to achieve the better lifestyle that they desired.

In retrospect, it is possible to discern a clear theme recurring through all Shaikh Zayid's decisions in the decades after 1971. While the different elements in his policy intertwined and interacted, two principal strands were always present. The first could be characterized as 'nation-building,' which was a process of internal legitimization. This involved treating the entity of the United Arab Emirates as a natural evolution of the region's history while at the same time acknowledging the individual characteristics of each emirate. The second strand might best be described as 'national security,' and encompassed the external dimensions of defense and international relations. The political developments that have occurred since 1971 may be viewed from the perspective of either, or both, principles. It is evident from all his pronouncements and the consistency of his policies that Shaikh Zayid sought to build a nation that possessed a strong ethical dimension. Yet, he knew that even the most ethically rooted nation had to survive in the harsh world of international politics. Thus, his policies were all designed to preserve, sustain and consolidate the nation while adhering to accepted principles.

From December 2, 1971, there was a newly founded federal state with its flag flying outside the United Nations, which had become a fully fledged member of the international community. Yet, statehood could not be achieved by the stroke of a pen. At the outset, the Federation was merely a disparate set of local populations owing allegiance to their respective Rulers and to a new and still nebulous entity, the United Arab Emirates. Shaikh Zayid's primary task was to build and instill that sense of national identity, to the extent that every citizen would feel a dual loyalty to their own emirate and also to the United Arab Emirates. He believed that the most effective means to achieve this was to make it clear to every citizen that each had a personal stake in the building of the new union and that it provided additional benefits rather than imposing new burdens.

For the President, the conundrum was how to achieve change and progress at an accelerated rate, while at the same time maintaining equilibrium, stability and social cohesion. In a nation where authority had been local and tribal, he needed to erect a system of government that would accommodate the needs of the modern world. The hardest task would be to convert a society poised on the fringes of survival into a modern state with all the necessary facilities where people would continue to work with drive and energy. For this, Shaikh Zayid saw national pride and national identity as being the most effective mobilizing forces.

The regional models of rapid development and economic transformation were Saudi Arabia and Iran, and neither provided an appropriate example for the United Arab Emirates. The 'White Revolution' instituted by Shah Muhammad Reza was an act of state policy forced on the people by governmental authority. It lacked popular roots. In Saudi Arabia, the creation of concrete institutions had been a slow process, and in 1971 the governmental structure was still inchoate.[10] Therefore, instead of following either of these models, Shaikh Zayid developed his own approach. In a society that had experienced only forms of personal rule, he added a framework of federal institutions to further strengthen the infant state. He constructed a form of dual governance, in which new federal organizations operated alongside the traditional institutions of each emirate. Rather than replacing existing local structures, Shaikh Zayid added new ministries or departments. His new institutions were well funded and capable of generating change and progress. Yet, he made no attempt to centralize all the sources of authority, and in many areas the federal system did not impinge at all on the local structure existing in each emirate.[11]

To the typical Western political theorist, this might appear an unwieldy bureaucratic and administrative superstructure. However, this was neither a Western capitalist model nor a socialist-style command economy. The role of the federal system was to provide a plan for development and progress. In individual and family terms, by accommodating as many young men as possible within the career structure of the state, Shaikh Zayid created a professional cadre that owed its loyalty and career prospects to the new United Arab Emirates. The posts offered in the new federal administration were not sinecures, but represented positions with real tasks.[12] Shaikh Zayid knew that loyalty to him as an individual was an insufficient foundation for the state and would prevent the development of any strong national loyalties. He rejected the idea of a 'personality cult,' which was against all the tenets of Islam and was also alien to the tribal system. Instead, he was determined to develop the federal government as a unifying institution and to provide career opportunities for young citizens, who then would gradually become adept at fulfilling the tasks of a modern state. By this means, he could create an enduring structure for the new society based on the rule of law. These men and women would become the archetypal 'UAE citizens' committed to the future development of the Federation.

All subsequent physical and social developments were made with this ultimate objective in mind. While the physical infrastructure could be improved in a short timespan, it was obvious to Shaikh Zayid that the corresponding social changes would take much longer. He had presided over rapid social changes during his years as Ruler of Abu Dhabi and was well aware of the time needed for reforms to take hold in a traditional and historically rooted culture. Moreover, in his years at al Ain, he had learnt that it is impossible to change the fundamentals of human nature, and that it is difficult to alter social customs. Nevertheless, he placed a great deal of trust in the inherent adaptability of his people, a trait rooted in their traditions. While the environment and lifestyle made each emirate different from its neighbor, and each village unique, he viewed that diversity as being a fundamental asset of the new unity model that he set out to build.

Unlike modernizing rulers in other states, Shaikh Zayid saw no future in creating a nation that denied these basic differences.[13] Yet, he also recognized that these elements of local distinctiveness would probably diminish naturally over generations. Therefore, the creation of the new state was not so much a matter of discarding the old entities as building a new state system that would provide an effective mechanism of adaptation to the modern world.[14] To make the process of change secure and permanent, he needed the support of both the existing framework of power – his fellow Rulers – and the social base over which they ruled. In this context, the United Arab Emirates would ultimately acquire legitimation from two diverse sources. In the first place, it was from the individual Rulers of each of the emirates who acted together and formed the highest organ of the state, the Supreme Council. Gradually, it was the Rulers themselves who came to realize that, far from challenging their position, the federal state could instead provide them with strong institutional and ideological support. Second, legitimacy stemmed from the loyalty and allegiance of the people. From their perspective, the UAE Federation conferred extensive advantages that were previously absent and laid no new or unacceptable constraints on its citizens.[15]

In addition to national pride and national identity, there were two other aspects, from Shaikh Zayid's point of view, that would symbolize the unity of the new nation and in practical terms advance its development. First was the value of work. While Shaikh Zayid was committed to sharing the proceeds of national resources with the people, he was aware that a future national identity could not be based solely on the receipt of oil revenues.[16] Being a man of action himself, Shaikh Zayid knew about the corrupting dangers of idleness. As a result, what he wanted was to create a new society which not only secured the welfare of all but provided the means whereby his people could economically sustain themselves by their own efforts. Second, Shaikh Zayid's vision encompassed both men and women. The role of his own mother in securing the stability of Abu Dhabi was well known and honored. His wife, Her Highness Shaikha Fatima Bint Mubarak, came to play a key role in the development of women's rights within the UAE. Like

Shaikh Zayid himself, Shaikha Fatima sought to build institutions that would last rather than relying solely on the power of the individual.[17]

The emphasis on the institutionalization of the state is a clear manifestation of Shaikh Zayid's recognition that the key to a nation's steady progress is to implement necessary change while maintaining the continuity that is essential for stability. This is exemplified in the way he skillfully integrated modern state structures with time-tested traditional systems. "Never total change, never total continuity" is a phrase that the historian L. Carl Brown has applied to Middle East history. It also succinctly expresses the central dynamic of Shaikh Zayid's policy. By an adroit blend of change and continuity, Shaikh Zayid was able to frame everyday political practice in terms of long-term goals rather than immediate expediency.

Political and Social Evolution

From 1971, Shaikh Zayid identified twin priorities in his domestic policy. First, he needed to ensure the political will and momentum for the development of the nation at the highest levels in the state. Second, he needed to ensure that the benefits of nationhood were visible to all the peoples of the Federation. These priorities were combined in a series of extensive federal programs. The first federal budget was proposed in February 1972, and a month later, barely three months after the proclamation of the new state, the Council of Ministers announced federal development initiatives amounting to six million dinars. Many of the initial projects focused on the building of public housing units and the development of utilities, including electricity and communication infrastructure.[18] In 1971, connections between the various emirates were still rudimentary and it was evident that a basic structure needed to be laid in place. This meant building road, air and telecommunication links.

The road-building program was perhaps the most solid evidence of the nation's determination to bind the emirates together. In June 1972, it was decided to expand the road between Dubai and Sharjah into a dual carriageway, one of the first elements of a road-building policy that developed steadily over the succeeding years. An observer, Malcolm C. Peck, wrote in 1986:

> The growth of physical infrastructure has been matched by the increase in communications. Communications have in a short span of time been revolutionized, a fact of great political as well as economic importance, because they serve to knit together the separate, frequently contentious emirates…various parts of the country have been linked by a first class road system. Abu Dhabi, Dubai, Sharjah and Ras al-Khaimah all have airports that service both international and domestic flights…Several major modern seaports have come into being since UAE independence.[19]

At the same time, Shaikh Zayid envisaged the development of a comprehensive social infrastructure. In a nation where hitherto there had been few schools, no higher education, and only rudimentary health care, this meant providing the facilities that would ensure that the succeeding generations would grow healthy and well educated. A comprehensive strategy of infrastructural projects was immediately put into operation. Over time and in this manner, the northern emirates, with their meager resources, would have access to the national wealth, which would bring them closer to the position of the more prosperous emirates. As such, the tried and tested programs of health, housing, urban development and education that had proved so successful in Abu Dhabi were extended systematically to the entire nation.

Meanwhile, some outside observers characterized the rapid construction taking place in the new state as too much and too fast. This reflected British attitudes before independence towards Shaikh Zayid's program in Abu Dhabi.[20] But such a perspective overlooked the political philosophy underpinning so much of Shaikh Zayid's thought. He wanted people in the new union to experience the benefits of development. A building program produced a cascade of desirable consequences. It created employment, enhanced property values and provided visible evidence of progress.

Furthermore, it was essential that all of the emirates should manifestly and rapidly benefit from the process, rather than be apportioned few resources that would provide a mere trickle of development without substantial improvement in living standards. As the main challenge of building unity lay in the political sphere, the President was content to see each emirate channel its energies positively in building roads, housing, ports and airports. It was also important that every individual should develop a stake in the success of the new political structure. Therefore, even ordinary citizens and their families needed to experience directly the advantages conferred by the Federation.

It was also a matter of principle for Shaikh Zayid that the new nation should be able to achieve self-sufficiency in food production, and thus to produce on a greater scale than had been possible in the past. He had clear memories of the harrowing deprivation that he had seen both as a child and as a young man. His long-standing commitment to the environment, which has grown and strengthened with the passing of time, had its effective origins in the first years after independence.[21] In the very first weeks of the newly independent state, the United Nations Food and Agricultural Organization (FAO) was invited, at Shaikh Zayid's insistence, to make a comprehensive survey of the agricultural potential of the new nation.[22] A mission from the FAO Office for the Near East, headed by Dr. Muhammed A. Nour, visited the UAE for the first time in January 1972, and had talks with Shaikh Zayid and a number of ministers. In February 1973, an eleven-member team arrived to carry out a detailed survey, and subsequently produced a comprehensive report. The team recommended:

> In view of the physical resource constraints that limit agricultural development in general, it is the view of the Mission that the United Arab Emirates should not launch on a course of massive effort to expand agriculture into a place of dominance in the country's economy. The goal, rather, should be to have a small but highly specialized and efficient agriculture. This means concentration on a relatively limited number of priority efforts.[23]

The consequences of this report were substantial and in many ways epitomized Shaikh Zayid's vision of development better than the mushroom growth of the cities and general urban development.

While Shaikh Zayid took an interest in all the major development projects underway across the country, he was most strongly committed to those involving agriculture and afforestation. His first objective was to create an agricultural base that would allow the UAE to become increasingly self-sufficient in agricultural produce.[24] By following the FAO strategy of specific and targeted development, overall agricultural production in the UAE increased by about 200 percent from 1977 to 1981, with some sectors showing even more dramatic increases.[25] Much of this growth was a consequence of improved methods of production, selection of better strains and varieties, enhanced irrigation, and extended technical education and support for the farming sector. More efficient marketing and storage meant that the wastage inherent in the old system was reduced considerably and, as the road network developed, farmers were able to reach more distant markets with their produce. The UAE became a leader in agricultural innovation, with money being invested in the existing research station at Digdaga in Ras al Khaimah and at al Ain.[26] On al Sa'adiyat Island in Abu Dhabi, the Arid and Semi Arid Lands Research Center achieved remarkable results in growing crops under controlled conditions.[27]

Shaikh Zayid's second objective was to minimize the negative effects of sand erosion and desertification. By late 1981, he had planted some four million trees—mostly acacia, eucalyptus and palm trees, all of which were irrigated daily, many with recycled and treated sewage water. He created a number of nurseries that provided the saplings for the afforestation project.[28] The initial FAO report stressed the vital importance of tackling the basic problems of aridity, vegetation destruction and sand dune fixation in the UAE, and the research team suggested a further detailed study. Tree planting on the scale undertaken by Shaikh Zayid had the effect of engendering a major and benign change in the environment.[29] The results were also immediate and visible. As Queen Elizabeth II of the United Kingdom observed in a public address on a visit to the UAE in 1979, "Your dreams in transforming the desert into a green land have been achieved."[30]

The growth of the United Arab Emirates is usually depicted as an urban revolution, and indeed those changes were extraordinarily dramatic in the first years after independence. However, the planned and coordinated development of the community, combining both social and economic progress and investing in improving the conditions of the poorest citizens and least developed areas, albeit less dramatic, was a more typical outcome of Shaikh Zayid's policy. His interest in afforestation epitomizes his outlook. The ecological benefits of tree planting were manifest, but it also produced an alteration in what might be called the psychological or cultural environment. Shaikh Zayid's forests have transformed a desert land into a network of verdant oases, which have become sanctuaries for the human spirit. This metamorphosis was planned, efficiently organized and systematically executed on the basis of sound scientific principles. However, it also had an ethical dimension. Just as Shaikh Zayid hoped that the new state would be a model for what cooperation and collaboration could achieve, he wished to demonstrate also that by taking a long-term view it was possible to transform the environment. The growth of the forests was a metaphor for the growth of the new Federation. Shaikh Zayid remarked:

> Our objective is to build a new generation, which will be able to shoulder its responsibilities and continue the march of progress in its land. My duty is to provide all the basic elements for a life of dignity for each citizen. Belief, work and faith are the foundation for success.[31]

Forces Against Unity

In retrospect, it is easy to over-emphasize the triumph of harmony and common interest. There were certainly those who opposed the extension of federal power and, at each stage, Shaikh Zayid had to cajole and persuade those who were reluctant to move forward.[32] Beyond the broader framework within which the Federation could initially establish itself, Shaikh Zayid was aware that there were several details that would require constant adjustment and attention in order to ensure its success. Eventually, a strong and effective federal government would be essential. The creation of a viable federal structure would take time, however, in view of the fact that it would be perceived as a threat by many of the fiercely independent emirates.[33] Shaikh Zayid's ultimate skill thus lay in preserving essential support for the federal program despite the occasional reluctance of the other Rulers.

The first operational and effective element of the United Arab Emirates was the national military. As part of the transfer of power from the British government on December 22, 1971, Shaikh Zayid signed an agreement through which command of the Trucial Oman Scouts was to be transferred to the United Arab Emirates, thereby laying the foundation for the new Federal Defence Forces.[34] A week later, the British government formally handed over command to the new UAE Minister of Defence, General Shaikh Muhammad Bin Rashid Al Maktum.

In January 1972, soon after its inception, the new force was put to the test with the need to restore the legitimate government in Sharjah. After a coup attempt had resulted in the death of the Ruler, Shaikh Khalid Bin Muhammad Al Qassimi, the federal army, acting on the orders of the Supreme Council and under the provisions of the Constitution, joined loyal Sharjah forces under the Ruler's brother to force the conspirators to surrender. At the same time, the Supreme Council declared that it recognized Shaikh Sultan Bin Muhammad Al Qassimi as the legitimate Ruler of Sharjah. This would prove to be a wise move as in future years Shaikh Sultan would became a strong bulwark of the Federation and a staunch supporter of Shaikh Zayid's concept of unity.[35]

In a sense, it was fortuitous that the federal institutions had to act so decisively in the first days of the new state. This made it clear to all skeptics of the Federation's effectiveness or viability that, although untried, the system worked well. The resolute action taken by Shaikh Zayid and the Supreme Council impressed foreign observers and governments. As noted by one observer, "In crushing the coup attempt the UAA [UAE] was thus able to demonstrate its capacity successfully to survive the first major threat to its internal authority."[36] That this strong test of federal authority came so quickly and in such a sensitive area as tribal succession served to reinforce a powerful message to the people of the United Arab Emirates. Earlier in the century, and well within living memory, violence had been used to enforce a change of ruler. The rights of the ruling families to determine the succession were jealously guarded, and when the British had previously intervened in matters of succession it was often (and rightly) resented as external interference. Now, the Rulers of the region had joined together and established which Ruler should be accepted as Sharjah's representative in the Supreme Council.[37] By acting collectively, the Rulers had managed to resolve a problem that had been the bane of the emirates through the previous decades of the twentieth century.[38] While the British were in place, the Rulers had observed a policy of non-intervention in each other's states. Free from British influence, they now felt an obligation to intervene when it was necessary for the well-being of the Federation as a whole. By this single, decisive act, they showed that the Council could act resolutely.

Despite this display of the effectiveness of federal institutions, however, the subsequent growth of the Federation also produced tensions. The extension of federal power was inevitably seen by some of the states as circumscribing their own power and freedom of action. The Provisional Constitution of 1971 was scheduled to remain in force for a five-year period, as were the terms of office for the President and Vice President, although there existed no limit on renewal. Shortly before his first term as President was due to end in December 1976, Shaikh Zayid surprised the nation in August by publicly declaring that he did not wish to serve for a second term of office. He did not explain why he wished to withdraw from the leadership of a political structure formed according to his principles, but in UAE political circles, where such issues were widely discussed, there was no doubt as to his reasons. Shaikh Zayid believed that some of his fellow Rulers did not share his active commitment to federalism and unity, and he was not willing to be the token President of a paralyzed federation. There was no suggestion that Abu Dhabi would withdraw in any sense from the Federation, merely that Shaikh Zayid would become, once again, first among equals with the other members of the Supreme Council, which would have to elect a new President.[39]

The causes of this crisis were complex, but they centered on the role of the Union Defence Force within the new state and thus affected the heart of the unity program. Shaikh Zayid's view was that the Federal Defence Forces should epitomize the unity of the state that it served. The Sharjah coup made it clear at an early stage in the Federation's history that a state which could not defend itself against internal and external threats could not survive. By taking such decisive and immediate action as it had done in this case, the new state gained a great deal of credibility. While the defense structure of the new state appeared to promote unity, the fact that not all the emirates were willing to merge their forces under a single federal military command served as an issue that tested the basic character of that unity. In this context, the internal and external dimensions of Shaikh Zayid's policy intersected, and his handling of the problem demonstrated his acute political sensitivity.

For Shaikh Zayid, the Federal Defence Forces served a dual role: on the one hand, a purely practical function to protect the nation from external aggression, and on the other, an emblem of progress. From the mid-1960s, Shaikh Zayid had seen that the armed forces could provide a model of advanced development in the new state. Military logic dictated a unity in command and equipment, and for Shaikh Zayid, lack of unity in the armed forces reflected adversely on the unity project as a whole. For this principle, he was willing to renounce his position as President.

When news of his decision reached the people of the UAE, overwhelming popular support, in the press and on the streets, made it clear that the people did not wish him to resign. Such sentiment was not an orchestrated demonstration, but represented a spontaneous expression of popular feeling. It also made it clear to those Rulers who preferred a loose federation to an ever closer union that popular sentiment was on the side of Shaikh Zayid.[40] In the end, a compromise was reached within the Supreme Council regarding the unification of the security and defense forces, with the addition of a clause to the Provisional Constitution about the federal government's prerogative over such matters.[41] This consensus, as well as the stated commitment by the other Rulers to the federation cause, allowed Shaikh Zayid to withdraw his proposed resignation and accept a second term as President of the UAE.

A very similar set of issues on the future of the union emerged in 1979, with the same unambiguous and almost unanimous popular support for unity. While the debate once again focused on the basic issues relating to federal and local powers, this time the debate over the direction the state should take effectively ended with the appointment of the Ruler of Dubai, Shaikh Rashid, as Prime Minister in 1979. The Ruler of Dubai was an extremely sagacious and effective leader who had worked closely with Shaikh Zayid since the 1950s. But, until this point, he had favored a much looser approach to union than that advocated by the majority of citizens. In this view, he had support among some of the Rulers of the northern emirates, who were concerned about the changing balance between the power of the federal government and those of the individual emirates.

Such disequilibrium was not Shaikh Zayid's concept of the union. From the beginning, he had seen the new state as a partnership between the individual emirates and the federal state. A public memorandum issued by the Council of Ministers and the Federal National Council in the spring of 1979 specifically focused on the need to make the Federation more governable and its institutions more responsive.[42] It was accompanied by large public demonstrations demanding full unity among the emirates.[43] Yet, while it became clear that some of the imbalances between the federal state and the individual emirates needed to be addressed, Shaikh Zayid and the other Rulers had no desire to abandon the dual structure that was fundamental to the Constitution of the UAE. Crucially, Shaikh Rashid agreed to act as Prime Minister and to head a new government, which was formed in July 1979.

This decision restored the partnership between Shaikh Zayid and Shaikh Rashid which had spearheaded the move towards union in 1968. The policy they now worked out between them allowed Shaikh Rashid to contribute his formidable personal experience and the managerial skills available in Dubai to the service of the union ideal. Part of his task would be to ensure that the delicate balance of authority and responsibility between each emirate and the Federation could be maintained. By accepting the post of Prime Minister, in addition to that of Vice President, Shaikh Rashid publicly joined in Shaikh Zayid's concept of the Federation. Shaikh Rashid stated that he considered the assignment to be a huge responsibility that required the full cooperation of all union members.[44] His voice carried great weight, especially with the Rulers of the smaller emirates, and his clear backing also had a wide public impact. His support lifted an enormous burden from the shoulders of Shaikh Zayid. It is perhaps no coincidence that Shaikh Zayid's development of his international role followed Shaikh Rashid's assumption of supervision over the day-to-day administration of the ministerial portfolios.

It was tragic, therefore, that shortly after his appointment as Prime Minister Shaikh Rashid fell ill. His failing health during the 1980s meant that he could no longer play an active role, as he had wished. However, the principle had been set that a developed state required an organized managerial structure. The system established after 1979 has endured in all its essentials until the present day. Shaikh Rashid's death in 1990 deprived the UAE of one of its founding fathers. Shaikh Zayid and Shaikh Rashid were both strongly committed to peace and harmony and to building their respective emirates, and, after 1971, the nation. Their approach of settling any issue between them by discussion rather than confrontation set a clear example for their fellow Rulers and for every citizen. The UAE was fortunate to possess simultaneously a visionary and inspirational leader in the person of Shaikh Zayid and an organizer and skillful manager in the person of Shaikh Rashid, at the formative period in its history.

With Shaikh Rashid as Prime Minister and the principle of military unity established and reinforced, Shaikh Zayid was prepared to operate pragmatically. In practice, the armed forces would function as a single body in a situation of emergency, and over time the problem of interoperability of equipment would diminish. The structure of unity would exist on paper, while those individual emirates that so desired could consider that their own units remained under their command. What had once been a divisive issue weakened and withered with time. Throughout, Shaikh Zayid's line of policy never wavered, but he was prepared to wait for evolution, not revolution, to realize his aspiration.

The early incident in Sharjah served as a reminder that in the future path of the Federation events would often unfold such that their impact could not always be predicted. In some aspects of his nation-building role, Shaikh Zayid could put forward a detailed plan. In matters such as communications and social policy, he had a grand strategy that was systematically implemented. In other areas, such as international relations and the politics of internal consolidation, he showed a mastery of tactical improvisation, responding to the rapidly changing nuances of the moment. He believed in planning where it was appropriate, but his instincts were always towards flexibility and pragmatism. Years later he observed:

> Dangers change from time to time, a friend may become an enemy and an enemy a friend. Life is inconstant and always changing. So it is with health and the weather. One must therefore be prepared for the unexpected and take precautions and preventive measures against any changes that may appear. It is better to prepare before an event, not after it.[45]

The political crises of 1976 and 1979 marked a decisive turning point in the national debate over unity. Whereas in 1976, Shaikh Zayid had felt compelled to offer to relinquish the presidency in order to sustain the unity program, in 1981, when his second term as President ended, this was no longer necessary. The President accepted a new five-year term without demur and the renewal of the Provisional Constitution, which had provoked so many debates in 1976, was also passed without dissent.

Overall, it seems clear that even if the momentum towards the further institutionalization of the Federation seemed sometimes to slow to a crawl, it never came to a standstill.[46] More important, it never went into reverse. With the wholehearted support of the people behind him, Shaikh Zayid's ideal of the 'UAE citizen' – loyal to his emirate, but also loyal to the whole nation – slowly but surely emerged and provided the state with a wholly new base of legitimacy.[47] This development has continued steadily year by year.

Shaikh Zayid at a meeting between Shaikh Shakhbut, then Ruler of Abu Dhabi, and the Sultan of Muscat, in December 1955 in the al Ain oasis.

Shaikh Zayid at the Trucial States Council. The TSC, founded in 1952, became the first effective forum for meetings between the Rulers of the emirates.

In 1966 the United States government was eager to know more about the new Ruler of Abu Dhabi and commissioned this photograph for their archives.

Shaikh Zayid with A.T. Lamb, who was Political Agent at the time of
his accession in 1966. Lamb held the new Ruler in great esteem.

Shaikh Zayid shortly after he became Ruler, with members of the new
Abu Dhabi Defence Force.

National Day, December 2, 1971. His Highness Shaikh Zayid with His Highness
Shaikh Rashid of Dubai and Their Highnesses the Rulers of the other emirates
on the momentous occasion of the establishment of the UAE Federation.

H.H. Shaikh Zayid reading the *Al Ittihad* newspaper. He has always been an avid reader, eager to remain well informed over a broad range of issues, national and international.

H.H. Shaikh Zayid has always been a visionary and a planner. Many stories are told of the sketches he drew in the sands of al Ain depicting his ideal city.

H.H. Shaikh Zayid with a favorite falcon. For him falconry is an integral part of Arab heritage.
He wrote in *Falconry as a Sport*, "There is a proverb which says, rightly or wrongly, that we
see others through the mirror of our own individuality, and myself I feel that this proverb is
near the truth. By following this sport, we are, after all, induced to remember our genuine
Arab traditions and to hold fast to our ancient virtues and moral code."

H.H. Shaikh Zayid has always manifested a deep empathy with young people, seeing in them the future of the UAE. Accordingly, he has given priority to providing them with the best educational, sports and recreational facilities for their intellectual, physical and social development.

H.H. Shaikh Zayid presiding over the first meeting of the Gulf Cooperation Council in Abu Dhabi in May 1981. The Council represented the fulfilment of his life-long desire for peaceful collaboration among the peoples of the region.

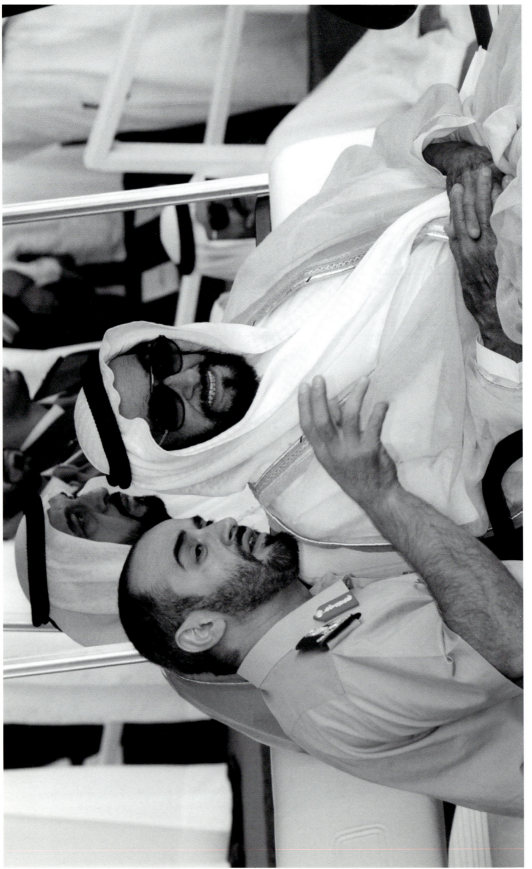

H.H. Shaikh Zayid Bin Sultan Al Nahyan, President of the United Arab Emirates and Supreme Commander of the UAE Armed Forces, with H.H. Shaikh Khalifa Bin Zayid Al Nahyan, Abu Dhabi Crown Prince and Deputy Supreme Commander of the UAE Armed Forces, and H.H. Lt. General Staff Pilot Shaikh Muhammad Bin Zayid Al Nahyan, Abu Dhabi Deputy Crown Prince and Chief of Staff of the UAE Armed Forces, attending a field demonstration at the International Defence Exhibition and Conference, IDEX 2003.

The Union Consolidated

In his analysis of federalism in the UAE in 1988, J.E. Peterson assessed both the positive factors leading to greater federalization and the negative factors working against it. On the positive side, his list includes the homogeneity of UAE society, the unifying effects of external threats, financial necessity and effective federal institutions. On the negative side, he lists traditional rivalries between the emirates, the indebtedness of the smaller emirates, economic domination by Abu Dhabi, armed forces that were autonomous and not under effective federal control, the dependence on expatriates, the issue of the sovereign balance between emirates and the federal government, and the 'temporary' Constitution.[48] Nevertheless, his overall 'balance sheet' was positive. "The long term gives cause for a rather optimistic outlook."[49]

What Peterson excluded from his tally was the impact of Shaikh Zayid's personality, which proved the most valuable asset of the new state. Throughout the first years of the UAE, in his speeches and interviews, through his appeals to the people, and by his example, the President provided a model for how the new state should operate—by consensus, openly, and for the common good. For the people of the new union, from the dawn of its federal history, Shaikh Zayid was rightly seen as the embodiment of the nation and the principal focus for trust and loyalty.

Between 1971 and 1981, the people knew that he had met the challenges of creating a new nation, and by the 1980s they considered the idea of unity irreversible. The pace and scope of the unity program did not perhaps extend as far as Shaikh Zayid desired, but by then the idea of the union breaking asunder was unthinkable. Moreover, Shaikh Zayid was able to carry the ideals of unity forward into a wider Arab arena, as he had always aspired to do. By February 1981, Shaikh Zayid was not only President of the UAE but the first President Designate of the new Gulf Cooperation Council. The idea of joint action, which in 1981 was essentially secure at the UAE level, had been adopted by the Arabian Gulf states for their collective benefit.

Until the early 1980s, Shaikh Zayid possessed few effective structures of government to which he could confidently devolve responsibilities.[50] It was not until the mid-1980s that state institutions had matured and needed less of his active intervention. By then, however, most of the core internal political issues had also been resolved.[51] Certainly, there was still a need to defend the ideals of national unity, but by this time the key battles had been won. Similarly, the program of social and economic development was unfolding year by year. Freed from these responsibilities, Shaikh Zayid was able to devote himself more completely to the role of the statesman, increasingly fulfilling the double role of mediator in inter-state conflicts and active advocate for the Arab and Islamic cause on the world stage. Of course, he continued to visit his people and keep in touch with their concerns and interests. However, the functioning of the state apparatus no longer hinged upon him, as it had done in the first decade of the nation's existence. It was a great measure of Shaikh Zayid's success that he had appointed a body of reliable men to continue his mission, a group comprising leaders, managers and administrators who could confidently carry out the tasks that he entrusted to them.

Gradually, then, a new generation was growing up that did not know what life was like before the creation of the UAE. This was becoming a political factor as early as the mid-1980s. For this generation, and for most of their parents, the federal government was seen primarily as a distributor of benefits to the people and a guarantor of their freedom and prosperity. This view of the nation was most effectively presented through the national media, comprising press, radio and television. The emblems of nationhood,[52] which included the national currency,[53] a national flag, national postage stamps,[54] and even a national football team,[55] each in their own way came to symbolize the entire nation.

The decade from 1971 to 1981 presents many examples of Shaikh Zayid's capacity to anticipate and be prepared for whatever issue emerged. When forcefulness was needed, he would be assertive, but when a diplomatic approach was required, he would use the right words. Many commented on his composure during a crisis, but he would observe philosophically that events were in the hands of God.[56] Underlying all his actions, whether planning a long-term strategy or reacting to a rapidly changing situation, was an unwavering consistency. Shaikh

Zayid always held true to his goals and vision. The growth of the United Arab Emirates over three decades has provided concrete evidence of the principles fought for by Shaikh Zayid and his people in its first formative decade. Such phenomenal progress was not achieved without struggle, for it took place in a region and among states which few imagined could ever act so purposefully for their common good.

Building a new nation – Abu Dhabi and then the UAE – involved challenges that had been experienced by no other society. The dynamic force in Abu Dhabi and the UAE was Shaikh Zayid, but he was acutely aware of the dangers of putting the entire responsibility for the new society upon a single leader. Hence, the new polity that he created embodied principles long cherished in Islamic societies:

> A ruling family, held together and sustained by strong ties of [family and] tribal loyalty…But to make it [a political entity] permanent, in lands of ancient culture and jaded loyalty, more was needed…The power of the state rests on and is exercised through well-established and well-organized institutions and social orders—army, bureaucracy, judiciary, and men of religion, with well-defined powers and functions, with regular recruitment and hierarchic promotion.[57]

These principles had been observed in Islamic governments many centuries before Shaikh Zayid sought to create the new UAE. But the need for a core philosophy, a system of values that would guide all the activities of state, was clear to him.[58] These ethical principles he found in his own life as a Muslim, and those principles animated all the activities described in this chapter. He was forming a new state, the UAE, but it was part of a broader strategy that envisioned this state as a force for good in the Gulf, and in the Arab and Islamic world at large, and ultimately as a positive contributor to the whole of humanity.

CHAPTER
9

Defense and Preservation

As a nation possessing vast reserves of oil, the United Arab Emirates had to defend its valuable natural resources from its inception. External rather than internal threats posed the most immediate danger to the new state. For the UAE, challenges to its new-found independence came from the more populous neighboring states as well as more distant powers, such as the United States and the Soviet Union. Each of these powers was seeking to extend its influence over the region and over the fledgling state. Such challenges compounded the complexities of internal consolidation and exacerbated the tasks of building the state and strengthening the Federation. Furthermore, on National Day 1971, the UAE was not yet well equipped to defend itself. The strategic vision of Shaikh Zayid Bin Sultan and his remarkable ability to out-maneuver potential enemies were crucial in protecting the new state from disaster.

Shaikh Zayid knew that the challenges of defending first Abu Dhabi and later the UAE were complex. He responded by developing a policy that operated along three axes. First, national security depended on forging a united nation. He knew from history that more citadels were betrayed from within than were ever taken by force. Thus, fostering popular support for the new state and securing the commitment of his fellow Rulers was absolutely essential. Second, he needed to ensure that any potential aggressor realized that an assault on the UAE and its resources would exact a high price. This required armed forces of high caliber and, above all, units that were well equipped. The British had always sought to limit the possession of sophisticated military equipment by local Rulers.[1] Third, he needed to enhance the credibility and international integrity of the nation, so that the UAE could take its rightful place in the world community and be regarded by the rest of the world as a force for good and as a nation worthy of protection and support through the mechanism of international law and the United Nations. None of these elements could be implemented in isolation.

Securing national unity and identity, a process initiated on December 2, 1971, has been a continuous endeavor. There are no rules and few models for constructing a national identity, and Shaikh Zayid knew that the peoples of the emirates would not offer their loyalty without good reason. To that end, they needed to know the issues at stake and the plans for the future. By concentrating his energies on education and establishing a strong communications network, Shaikh Zayid was able to provide the people with visible evidence of the benefits of unity and federation.[2] Knowledge contributed to a sense of national pride and optimism. At the same time, the federal government's role in furthering national development was fully reported, and this, in turn, projected a positive image of its work.

Shaikh Zayid employed all the available methods of communication to present this economic and social progress to the people. By establishing effective communication channels, it was possible to spread the unmistakable message that unity brought benefit to all. Shaikh Zayid understood the key role that media services could play in building national identity, and he used every opportunity to speak to the public. He would appear even at minor events to deliver a major address because it served as a platform from which he could reiterate the message of unity and relay that message, particularly to the women and young people of the state. Among the tribes of al Ain, he had from childhood been 'their Zayid.' Now, through radio and television, he achieved the same rapport with the people of the UAE as a whole. He was 'their Zayid, their President.'[3]

Shaikh Zayid's personal characteristics made him highly effective in his political and diplomatic roles. On all issues, he has consistently refrained from acting impulsively, preferring to take his time and weigh his options. Conciliation rather than the use of force has been his unwavering goal, and this provided a consistent theme in his foreign policy. At the opening session of the Federal National Council on February 12, 1972, Shaikh Zayid stated that it was the foreign policy of the UAE to "cooperate with all nations and peoples on the basis of the principles of the UN Charter and the highest universal ethics."[4] Despite his preference for a conciliatory approach, however, he was determined that UAE interests would not be placed in jeopardy.[5]

Shaikh Zayid's approach has produced a high degree of coherence in the foreign policy of the UAE. The principles laid down in December 1972, on the occasion of the first anniversary of the foundation of the UAE, have remained the basis for the country's diplomacy until the present day:

> Our foreign policy sets four objectives: maintaining good relations and cooperation between the UAE and neighboring nations and settling disputes that may arise in future by cordial, peaceful means, abiding by the UAE's commitment toward the Arab world and preliminary and fundamental Arab conventions; improving Islamic solidarity and cooperation with Muslim states in all spheres; and maintaining fruitful cooperation with all nations in all fields to establish security, peace and progress.[6]

These principles would often be repeated throughout the next three decades, and Shaikh Zayid has never wavered from them. By the end of the twentieth century, as a result of Zayid's outward-looking policies, the UAE maintained diplomatic relations with more than 140 countries and had over 40 embassies abroad.[7]

The Armed Forces and the Nation

As the United Arab Emirates Federation began to acquire a broad popular base and the possession of national citizenship took on the value of something to be prized and therefore protected, defense and security issues became a primary national concern. This was particularly the case as the external pressures on the new state began to grow steadily. For Shaikh Zayid, the guidelines for developing a strong defense have been to protect the country's sovereignty, defend its natural resources and forge ties with other nations capable of enhancing UAE security. While he always preferred diplomacy, he was both realistic and pragmatic, and knew that diplomacy was most effective when supported by a strong defense force that could act as a deterrent.

Historically, the local system of national defense had its origins in the Abu Dhabi Defence Force (ADDF), established in 1965 in line with Shaikh Shakhbut's desire to have an army loyal to Abu Dhabi, rather than depending on the Trucial Oman Scouts, which were under British control. The British government eventually accepted the idea of the ADDF, realizing that it implied a reduction in expenditure on the Scouts, since the ADDF would be funded by Abu Dhabi.[8] Shaikh Zayid was deeply involved in these plans from the outset,[9] often tempering his brother's ambitions with his pragmatism.[10]

As early as September 1965, Lamb had noted Shaikh Zayid's striking perception, even before he became Ruler of Abu Dhabi, of the central importance of defense:

> Zaid is keen to have an army not only to defend Abu Dhabi but to have a well-run organisation which will contribute to the flow of wealth in Abu Dhabi. Zaid sees the army as a deterrent against possible enemies ("Everybody will think we have three times as much as we have") and as an essential part of the government organisation about which I have written separately to the Political Resident.[11]

Shaikh Zayid did not view military power in terms of personal protection or actual conflict. From the outset, his perception of the military's role in national development was political and strategic. He saw the armed forces as a source of skill and technical sophistication in an under-resourced nation, as well as an instrument of international policy.

When he became Ruler of Abu Dhabi, in addition to his priority for social spending, he took immediate steps to strengthen the defense of the emirate. As early as November 1966, with his military advisor, Colonel Wilson, Shaikh Zayid was planning to develop an Abu Dhabi

Air Force, with the purchase of three aircraft and support services.[12] As far as the ADDF was concerned, the initial plan anticipated a small force of 250, growing to about 500. Under Shaikh Zayid, however, there was an immediate and dramatic increase in the scale and manpower of the force. In the five years from 1966 to 1971, the ADDF increased to almost 10,000 men, and Shaikh Zayid was able to establish a close liaison with the Trucial Oman Scouts.

By 1970, the ADDF had acquired armored vehicles and even artillery for the first time. Shaikh Zayid also upgraded the tiny air force with British jet aircraft (Hawker Hunters), delivered in 1970, which were designed to act both as fighters and provide support in a ground attack.[13] Moreover, he negotiated with the French government for the supply of modern Mirage aircraft.[14] Although some of the other emirates also began to develop their armed forces, the scale was nothing compared to that of Abu Dhabi.[15]

In the complex negotiations that led to the birth of the United Arab Emirates, military issues were a central concern for Shaikh Zayid.[16] With larger states flanking the new nation, he understood the need for a large and well-equipped armed force to provide a credible defense. He remarked that if the Federation was strong, potential enemies would be deterred and the UAE would be able to defend itself.[17] He also made it clear that the ADDF was not merely for the benefit of Abu Dhabi but for all the emirates of the region. Henderson asked him what would happen if attempts for the comprehensive Federation proved a failure. Shaikh Zayid replied emphatically that he would continue with as many states as would join him of the seven but he would only defend those who joined the Federation. He would assist in their development but he would not defend them unless they were members.[18] Shaikh Zayid plainly saw the ADDF as the core of a future UAE national force intended for the protection of the Federation as a whole and its vital interests.[19]

Furthermore, Shaikh Zayid knew that without adequate defense no state could hope to maintain its sovereign status. In the private analysis of the Political Resident, Crawford:

> Sheikh Zaid sees his security as best assured by building up his
> own defence force, which he is doing, by broadening his political
> base, to cover the whole of the Trucial States, and by looking
> elsewhere in the Middle East for political support. He is encouraged
> in the Trucial States by the genuine popular support that exists
> there for a Trucial States Union, by his own popular personality
> with the bedu part of the States population, by the magnetic
> power of his wealth…[20]

Crawford concluded in his advice to the Foreign Office, "Sheikh Zaid's
resources are likely, in the end if he is left in peace, to enable him to
achieve what he wants."[21]

Shaikh Zayid's strategic analysis was also acute. He found
unacceptable the growing British and American vision that a condo-
minium of Saudi Arabia and Iran should replace the departing British
power in the Gulf. In this respect, he told Lamb, the Political Agent in
Abu Dhabi, that he was certain that the Rulers of the Trucial States, as
well as the people, would want a sovereign, independent state which
would not need external protection. If Kuwait had succeeded in this, so
could the Trucial States.[22]

Following the successful launch of the UAE Federation in 1971,
Shaikh Zayid knew that it was essential to integrate the command,
control and equipment of all the existing forces. He rightly believed
that the armed forces should be a symbol of the nation's unity and not
display its differences. An initial step was to restructure the former
Trucial Oman Scouts into the Union Defence Force (UDF), based in
Sharjah. This unit quickly acquired advanced equipment, and worked
closely with the ADDF. Still, there remained no fewer than five
defense units in the region, including those of Dubai, Sharjah and Ras
al Khaimah in addition to the two mentioned above.

The role of these units was to defend their respective emirates.
In accordance with the Provisional Constitution, however, they would
also be jointly responsible for the protection of the Federation. As the
largest unit, the ADDF began to make the necessary transition into a
force capable of defending the whole nation. Indeed, given the relative
scale of the different units involved, Shaikh Zayid could have entrusted

national protection to Abu Dhabi and the UDF alone. Yet, from the outset, he was determined that the armed forces of the new state should embody the central principle of unity that was implicit in all his plans. This presented the armed forces with a challenge of meeting two seemingly divergent objectives. In the first place, they were engaged in a process of expansion that paralleled the enormous advances in civil society. In the second place, they would need to take the decisions towards consolidation and integration, which could prove difficult.

While Shaikh Zayid was aware of the problem implicit in his decision, he believed the matter could not be ignored. He recognized that division between the different defense forces within the UAE might pose serious challenges to the effective protection of the nation. In military terms, such a fragmented structure was fraught with danger and could prove debilitating in operational terms. There was no uniformity of equipment, procurement, strategy, command or training.[23] In political terms, fragmentation might provide an impetus to separatism. It conveyed a negative signal. In reality, the immediate problem was the fact that the military forces were simply inadequate in numbers and equipment for the new tasks that confronted them. It was, therefore, agreed that the armed forces of the new nation, which no longer had the British shield of protection, required a substantial increase in striking power and effectiveness. The defense forces of all individual states expanded to some degree in the years following the birth of the Federation, but only that of Abu Dhabi acquired substantial air and maritime forces, while the UDF and training establishments were also enlarged.[24]

It was not until the summer of 1975 that the Supreme Council finally made the decision to address the issue of command. It ordered an initial study aimed at the unification of the armed forces of all the emirates.[25] During June and July 1975, a succession of high-level Arab military advisors came to the UAE to study the implications of military unification. Their report provided a framework within which unity in the armed forces could be developed.[26] On October 21, Shaikh Zayid spoke to local journalists. He was unambiguous and stated that stability could only be secured through a unified structure for defense and security.

His speech generated an immediate response. On November 4, 1975, the Ruler of Sharjah, Dr. Shaikh Sultan Bin Muhammad announced that in the interests of national unity the Sharjah National Guard would be fully merged into the national defense system. Two days later, he also announced that the UAE flag would replace the flag of Sharjah. His aim was to show that Sharjah's future lay within the national structure of the UAE and that his emirate's interests would best be served by this voluntary renunciation. The act was symbolic and its message was directed to the other emirates. Shaikh Zayid publicly commended the Ruler of Sharjah for his support. Equally important was that the tide of public opinion was firmly in support of the unified force. This move gained momentum and, on May 6, 1976, the Supreme Defence Council, representing all the emirates and chaired by Shaikh Zayid, finally announced the merger of the defense forces of the different emirates into a single armed forces structure.[27]

The analyst Erik Peterson characterized this development in the following way: "The political structure of the UAE...was a vital factor in the military affairs of that country. Owing to the nature of the federation that evolved between the emirates of the UAE, the development of armed forces was a function of the evolving political process."[28] Yet, while the decision of the Supreme Defence Council called for the forces of each emirate to be incorporated into the national armed forces, it also allowed each defense unit to play an internal role within its respective emirate.

In essence, the question remained whether the 'local' defense forces existed primarily to serve the interests of the whole nation or of the individual emirate. On this issue, the Constitution was ambiguous and this resulted in a polarization in the views of different emirates. While Shaikh Zayid was primarily concerned with the practical issues of military effectiveness, he also did not want local formations to emerge as symbols of separatism. However, while the military logic was inescapable, the symbolic importance of the local forces to some of the emirates turned the issue into a test of the principle of union. The right to maintain their own forces soon became a totem of each emirate's individual identity.

As a result, the UAE Armed Forces remained the main zone of contention on ways to develop the structure of the nation. Many attempts were made to resolve the issue. During late 1976 and early 1977, directives were issued for the transformation of the armed forces into a new regional structure, under a common supreme command.[29] On January 31, 1978, Shaikh Zayid ordered that the integration of the armed forces should be completed. The decree merged all the forces into a single structure, cancelled the arrangement of regional headquarters, and converted the regional forces along functional lines into brigades under a common command.[30]

A unified command proved harder to achieve than was anticipated, but within what was formerly the ADDF and the UDF, which incorporated the majority of the armed units in the state, it developed rapidly. Thus, the UAE successfully created a common all-arms structure in a relatively short time and with unexpected ease. The remaining tasks were mainly technical rather than political. During the 1980s, the UAE Armed Forces concentrated on developing a senior officer corps, training and support systems, an *esprit de corps* and a procurement system that was capable of specifying the right kind of equipment for the strategic and environmental circumstances of the UAE.

Shaikh Zayid's response to this incipient crisis was measured and politically adroit. In speech after speech, he made it clear that national unity and military unity must go hand in hand.[31] Shaikh Zayid never relinquished the notion of a wholly unified military system. At the same time, as in numerous earlier instances, he was content to allow it to run its course and to develop inexorably. He never allowed his own passionate belief in the need for unity to sway his judgment and appeared willing to wait for the Rulers of each emirate to relinquish military independence voluntarily.

The developments in the armed forces in many ways reflect the transformations – economic, political and social – that have taken place in the nation over a period of three decades.[32] They provide a succinct and convenient measure of national change and progress that is often obscured in the complexity of internal and external events. From the beginning, Shaikh Zayid saw the armed forces as an instrument of policy, not war, whose essential consequence was social benefit in terms of unity. In this context, the US Ambassador Philip J. Griffin observed in a telegram to Washington in June 1972, "In [the] case of [the] attempted coup in Sharjah, [the] UDF and [the] more powerful ADDF joined forces to preserve internal order and stability in [the] UAE. This is [an] encouraging sign in [the] nation-building process."[33]

In time, Shaikh Zayid also realized that there was a new role for the military, which came strongly into focus in the 1990s. Peacekeeping forces were a valuable means by which the UAE could contribute to international security. UAE forces participated in the growing number of peacekeeping operations throughout the world, and it seems likely that this will form an increasingly important and appropriate role for the UAE in future years. Peacekeeping was the fundamental task of the UAE Armed Forces, as defined by Shaikh Zayid. While he always insisted that the UAE Armed Forces would resist aggression, he was equally emphatic that they would never be used in an aggressive role:

> Building a strong army of high combat ability was never meant for invasion or fighting but rather for defending [our] terrain, honor and homeland which has bestowed dignity on this people. We are for peace, neighborliness and friendship. The need for a strong army, however, remains constant and persistent. Such an army is for self defense rather than for invasion and fighting.[34]

With this military ethos, the UAE Armed Forces were ideally suited to roles of conflict resolution and to the reduction of tension. In the Lebanon and Somalia peacekeeping operations, the UAE Forces played an important role, being acceptable to all the parties in the dispute. Not only did they come from an avowedly Muslim country, but also one which possessed an outstanding record of pacific relations with its neighbors. In the operations in Kosovo and in Albania, beginning in April 1999, the UAE troops also revealed an exceptional capacity for providing humanitarian aid in a manner that preserved the dignity and independent spirit of its recipients. However, in the allied operation for the liberation of Kuwait, in January and February 1991, the performance of the UAE Armed Forces made it clear that its involvement in peacekeeping had in no way undermined its war-fighting capacity. UAE fighter planes flew 123 sorties against Iraq, and the UAE was among the first to enter and help liberate Kuwait during the ground attack from February 24 to 27, 1991.[35]

Shaikh Zayid's personal involvement in international reconciliation and the UAE's national contribution to global emergencies and crises have resulted in the development of armed forces equipped to meet any eventuality. In the modern world, military forces do much more than prepare for war, and the UAE Armed Forces provide an example of a military organization designed for the needs of the new millennium.[36]

Statesmanship

Military preparedness was the first pillar of national security, and Shaikh Zayid exerted much effort to ensure that the United Arab Emirates presented an image of military strength and resourcefulness. However, he knew that the UAE Armed Forces were primarily a means to deter aggression, and that the second pillar of national security was the protection afforded by the international community. Following the UAE's admission to the United Nations within days of the new nation's foundation, he recognized that the whole structure of international collaboration could be used to sustain and protect the infant state. The United Nations, regional and area groupings, and Arab and Islamic organizations all provided forums where the voice of the United Arab Emirates could be heard. He had seen from his earliest days in al Ain that politics is based on a network of mutual obligations. In entering the international arena, the UAE would assume obligations, but these would be more than offset by the 'debts of honor' that other nations incurred to the UAE in return. The international system was not very different in nature from the tribal structures he knew so well.

Before 1971, Abu Dhabi had no direct responsibility for its diplomacy and international relations. These, by treaty, had been the responsibility of the British government, and it is not surprising that these were conducted with British interests taking precedence over local concerns. This is not to say that the British government failed entirely to consider the interests of the Arab populations, but it did so only within the broader context of what would be to Britain's benefit. Thus, while the British defended the territory of Abu Dhabi against foreign claims by both diplomatic and military means, it was done in the expectation that the potential oil resources of Abu Dhabi would form part of Britain's strategic resources.[37]

Shaikh Zayid was a political pragmatist in his dealings with the British authorities. He accepted the idea of duality—that a political relationship between two nations could embrace both accord and discord. It is also clear that his careful and painstaking plan for the future relationships within the region antedated the creation of the UAE. To understand his ultimate objectives, it is necessary to examine their development from the mid-1960s.

When Shaikh Zayid became Ruler in 1966, he already possessed a great deal of knowledge about the forces that shaped international politics. He was aware that Abu Dhabi had two larger and more powerful neighbors, and that only peaceful relations with both would form a tenable basis for a long-term policy.[38] With Saudi Arabia, there was a bitter history of difficult relations dating back over 30 years, and Shaikh Zayid was determined to resolve this dangerous antagonism. He knew that decades of mistrust could not be brushed aside in an instant and that it was necessary to build mutual trust and confidence. King Faisal had been embroiled in the dispute for more than three decades; he had served as his father's Foreign Minister for many years, and his resolution in this issue was even firmer than that of King Abdul Aziz. Although his attention had been diverted by other political considerations over the years, he was not going to yield easily in his determination to see an outcome favorable to Saudi Arabia. However, Shaikh Zayid believed that if the discussions could be released from the 'dead hand' of British diplomacy, it would be possible to build an effective working relationship.

In April 1967, Shaikh Zayid visited King Faisal in Jeddah. King Faisal appreciated Shaikh Zayid's careful and respectful tone, as he spoke of King Faisal as 'his father.'[39] The King also referred to the problems over territory as being a matter between Arab brothers.

However, the long-standing antagonism could not be resolved at a stroke, and the meeting ended in an impasse. Shaikh Zayid felt that British diplomacy had hindered rather than helped at the meeting.[40] He was thereafter determined to follow his own path in the negotiations, jettisoning the cautious approach of British diplomacy that had proven fruitless for so long. His own objectives were straightforward. At the time, Saudi Arabia claimed the area around al Ain. The oasis area was crucial to the future of the emirate, and therefore could not be yielded. All other matters could be negotiated.[41]

Shaikh Zayid's stance at his first meeting in 1967 was that the issue was not a matter of lines on the map, but of honor and mutual confidence. While the British government had always argued in terms of verifiable boundaries, Shaikh Zayid sustained his discussions in a different register. He knew that it would be impossible for Abu Dhabi and subsequently the UAE to be secure while remaining at odds with its neighbor. Thus, he worked hard to overcome the decades of antagonism on the Saudi side based on their perception of British double-dealing.[42] It took seven years of steady effort to ensure that King Faisal recognized him as a man of his word. Once, during the course of a meeting, when the discussion turned to boundaries and tension rose, Shaikh Zayid said that the King was a brother Arab and welcome in his land, and that his 'boundary' ran beneath his chair in the palace in Abu Dhabi. By that he meant that talk of 'boundaries' between Arab brothers was meaningless.[43]

From the moment he became President of the UAE, Shaikh Zayid sought the role of conciliator and peacemaker. Above all, he made it clear that he longed for a good relationship between his country and Saudi Arabia. He ignored many difficulties that resulted from the Saudi unwillingness to recognize the new Federation as an entity, but continued to work patiently to improve relations. Then, once the atmosphere of antagonism had calmed down, he was able to demonstrate the benefits of a unified stance to both nations. After all, both were Arab nations, committed to Islam and playing a key role in the international economy through their oil industries. In practice, their joint interests far outweighed the matters that separated them. In essence, this was the same logic that he presented to his fellow Rulers in the process of building unity within the United Arab Emirates.[44]

A key factor in building rapport between the UAE and Saudi Arabia was Shaikh Zayid's leading role in the Arab oil boycott of 1973. On October 17, 1973, a phased reduction of 5 percent per month in oil supplies to the United States was agreed upon, although Shaikh Zayid wished to go much further. He was the first Ruler to give effect to the ultimatum delivered to President Nixon by the Arab oil producers to halt the dispatch of arms to Israel or face an embargo on oil shipments to the United States.[45] The speed and force of Shaikh Zayid's response to Washington's rearming of Israel took US policy makers by surprise, and his principled action inspired the other Arab oil producers in the region to follow suit.[46] On the following day, Shaikh Zayid authorized the complete cessation of all UAE oil supplies to the United States. It amounted to some 15–20 percent of US oil supplies from the Arabian Gulf. The decision was taken at a time when Abu Dhabi, the principal source of UAE oil, had a current-account deficit.[47] However, Shaikh Zayid felt that it was morally imperative for the Arabs to act with resolution. He knew that a 5 percent cut would be interpreted in the West as a mere face-saving political gesture, while an all-out use of the oil weapon, on the other hand, would indicate the depth and seriousness of their intentions.

The other Arab oil producers quickly fell in line behind the UAE initiative. The Western nations in general, and the United States in particular, came to realize that impolitic support of Israel carried a price, and the increase in oil prices that followed the October War markedly increased the leverage of the Arab oil producers. The role of Shaikh Zayid in this development was central. His strategic sense was unerring at a time when other Arab leaders could not perceive the fundamental issues that were at stake. In his view, all the Arabs were involved in this conflict, not just the 'front-line states.' Oil was a weapon like any other, but the West believed that the Arabs would never use this ultimate deterrent. By strategically deploying this weapon on October 18, 1973, Shaikh Zayid transformed the shape of world politics.[48] For the first time, the power that lay in Arab hands was openly demonstrated.[49]

Through his actions, he showed that he would pursue the cause of Arab brotherhood, whatever the cost in monetary terms.[50] This dedication to common concerns greatly impressed King Faisal.

Support for the united Arab cause incidentally resulted in further defusing tensions between Saudi Arabia and the UAE. The sense of solidarity forged at this point between the two leaders soon bore fruit, and this climate of mutual trust provided the political backdrop for the August 1974 settlement between the UAE and Saudi Arabia.[51] After the October War, Shaikh Zayid's reputation as a conciliator had become widely known in the Arab world, and in August 1974 he successfully mediated in a dispute between Egypt and Libya.[52] Shortly afterwards, heartened by this success, he visited King Faisal in Jeddah and witnessed the success of his concerted efforts over many years to achieve a reconciliation with Saudi Arabia. He reached an agreement that ended the hostile relations between the two nations.[53] While many details remained to be worked out and a joint technical commission was established for this purpose, the essence of the agreement was that the future lay in building friendship and cooperation[54] between the two nations.[55]

The significance of this agreement was profound. Without a resolution of this long-standing quarrel, joint Arab action in the Gulf may never have been possible. From that point on, it was accepted that the basic relationship between the UAE and Saudi Arabia was one of Arab brotherhood. There were many occasions when the two nations took different positions on political issues, but the essential accord was never breached.[56] Shaikh Zayid was shocked by the tragic death of King Faisal in the year after their agreement, and he did everything in his power to build a supportive relationship with his successors King Khalid and King Fahd. The atmosphere in the Gulf of mutual confidence and common concern brought the two nations together in the formation of the Gulf Cooperation Council in 1981.[57] Thus, within a decade, Shaikh Zayid had transformed the core relationship with Saudi Arabia from embattled antagonism to joint involvement in a program to build peace and concerted action in the region.[58]

Shaikh Zayid applied a similar approach to the troubling relations with Iran. Coinciding with the establishment of the UAE and on the heels of the British withdrawal from the Gulf region, Iran unilaterally occupied the two Tunb islands belonging to Ras al Khaimah as well as asserted a claim to Sharjah's island of Abu Musa in November 1971.[59] After December 2, 1971, Shaikh Zayid, as the UAE President, assumed responsibility for the islands, since Ras al Khaimah and Sharjah were now two constituent elements of the Federation. From his point of view, the Iranian actions were unacceptable, since the island's historic sovereignty had always been Arab. Even the Memorandum of Understanding (MOU) regarding the island of Abu Musa was seen as an agreement concluded under duress and thus could not be viewed as having settled any issue of sovereignty.

Based on his own strong conviction, and aware of the popular sentiment inside the UAE against Iranian control, Shaikh Zayid chose a prudent course that clearly asserted UAE rights to the islands but refrained from any action that might be seen as justification for the use of force. While protesting the Iranian aggression and building an international case to have the islands returned to UAE sovereignty, he stressed the country's commitment to cordial relations between the neighboring states and his willingness to solve any disputes in a fair and open manner. In a statement to journalists in 1981, Shaikh Zayid declared:

> Our method...is to present legal evidence and documents and through joint consultation and mutual understanding so that each gets its due and the Arab entitlement reverts to its people. Our position on the islands is clear and simple. These islands are part and parcel of the United Arab Emirates and its possessions.[60]

Shaikh Zayid maintained his approach even after Iran further violated the sovereignty of Abu Musa with its unilateral takeover of the whole island and the forced eviction of UAE nationals in 1992. On December 2, 1993, in a speech on the 22nd National Day, Shaikh Zayid stated:

> We have announced our readiness and true wish for a direct dialogue with Iran over the occupation of the three islands that belong to the UAE. We still call for dialogue and peaceful means to end this occupation and return the three islands to the sovereignty

of the UAE, according to international laws and norms and the principles of neighborly relations and mutual respect between countries.[61]

Throughout, Shaikh Zayid never wavered from his intention to solve the dispute through peaceful channels, direct dialogue, arbitration or referral to the International Court of Justice. Undaunted by Iranian actions, while steadfastly committed to seeing the islands returned, he firmly believes that time will once again prove his chosen course of action to be correct. In January 2000, Shaikh Zayid noted:

> The UAE has pursued clear policies to end the occupation of the UAE's three islands of the Greater and Lesser Tunb and Abu Musa, by peaceful means through the holding of serious and direct negotiations, referring the issue to international arbitration, or the International Court of Justice. However, the continued occupation of the three islands by Iran contradicts the clear, peaceful direction of the GCC states and the continued calls and initiatives to Iran to end the occupation in accordance with international laws and principles and in line with our historic ties, friendships and mutual interests…a response from Iran…will ensure the security and stability of the region based on fraternal relations, good neighborliness and understanding.[62]

Thus, while the issue remains unresolved even after 30 years of independence, Shaikh Zayid's principles and guidelines for settling the dispute have stayed the same throughout.

Shaikh Zayid's achievement can best be explained in terms of Winston Churchill's observation, made in the context of the Cold War, "To jaw-jaw is always better than war-war."[63] His foreign policy has been exceptionally successful. Shaikh Zayid has combined consistency of principle with a remarkable flexibility of practice. He has always sought, first, to persuade potential enemies that war brings no benefits, and second, that mutual interests can often be served by collaboration. His humanitarian projects have a pragmatic political rationale as well as a purely ethical dimension. Few would have imagined in 1971 that a Middle Eastern nation, so small in numbers, albeit economically strong, could acquire such weight and influence in the international arena. His subtle personal diplomacy, which exists in parallel with the official foreign policy of the UAE, has provided an unofficial 'back channel' of communication between hostile parties. As an interlocutor between adversaries he speaks in private with absolute truth and equal forthrightness. As a result, his words carry considerable weight.

Establishing Gulf Cooperation

Shaikh Zayid always sought to unite as many people as possible in his vision of the future. The political motivation for creating the 'second pillar' of security has been outlined above. This policy developed in four directions after 1971: first, the creation of unity among the emirates of the UAE; second, the development of a sense of common interest and purpose among the states of the Gulf area;[64] third, the generation of coordinated and common action among all the Arab peoples; fourth, the enhancement of the common welfare of humanity, both on a governmental level – often through the structures of the United Nations – and on a personal basis.[65] These elements in his policy can be traced back at least to the mid-1960s, perhaps even earlier. All were long-term objectives and Shaikh Zayid had no illusions that any of them would be accomplished quickly or easily.[66] Sometimes, the slow pace of progress taxed his patience, and he would speak forthrightly to that effect. But despite this natural urge to achieve rapid results, he maintained the same steady and systematic approach to progress in all fields of development.[67] There has been a consistency of policy, means and objectives extending over a period of three decades.

Although each of these elements may be considered in isolation, in reality they were interconnected, reflecting considerable interplay. Progress in one area could often lead to advance in another. Thus, political consolidation in the UAE helped to further the cause of joint activity in the Gulf, starting with the Saudi Arabian agreement of August 1974. This agreement strengthened the confidence of the Gulf states that they could and would act in concert, a conviction that eventually led to the Gulf Cooperation Council in 1981. Any dispassionate analysis of the evidence suggests that such an outcome – collective inter-state action embracing all six Arab Gulf states – would have been inconceivable had the relationship between the UAE and Saudi Arabia remained on the level of veiled hostility that still existed in 1971. The common link in these positive developments was Shaikh Zayid's desire for unity. The concept of unity operated successfully on multiple levels, and became the driving force for progress along all four lines of development—the unification of the UAE, the development of a common purpose among the Gulf states, the generation of coordinated action among the Arab peoples, and the welfare of humanity.

Shaikh Zayid realized that for generations the political tradition in the Gulf had been based on suspicion and rivalry. Over the years, he had learned that the only means to diminish mutual antipathy was by personal discussion. Often the occasion for interaction was unimportant—an invitation to a camel race, wedding or festival, or even a congratulatory letter in celebration of some achievement. By whatever means possible, he extended the hand of peace and friendship. What he sought was that individuals should meet, sit together and talk. This was the tradition of the *majlis*, which was fundamental to the Arab style of governance in the Gulf.[68] In the regional climate of suspicion, it was not necessarily a safe or wise option, which is why many rulers isolated themselves in their fortresses. Yet, Shaikh Zayid knew that any interaction or meeting required mutual trust. Without risk, there could be no gain and no advance. During his years at al Ain, every time that he had visited the encampment of a shaikh with a hostile or uncertain disposition, he had put himself at risk. Nevertheless, through these contacts, which extended over many years, he eroded the wall of mistrust with which many of the tribal leaders in the region protected themselves. It was in this new context of mutual trust that in 1973 and 1974, with his full support and encouragement, Gulf foreign ministers met to explore the creation of a political and economic plan for the Arab Gulf states.[69]

In the years after the October War, Shaikh Zayid became increasingly concerned about the growing US involvement and foreign military presence in the area, attributable later in part to the Iranian Revolution and the war between Iran and Iraq. Under President Nixon, the United States had created a twin-track approach to 'protecting' the Gulf, by providing military aid to Iran and Saudi Arabia to check any possible Soviet advance on the oilfields.[70] However, the United States had lost one of its tracks with the fall of the Shah, thus leaving only Saudi Arabia.[71] After the Soviet invasion of Afghanistan in 1979 and Soviet involvement in Ethiopia, the US government became preoccupied with the possibility of an increased Soviet threat to its economic and strategic interests in the region. President Carter told Congress in his State of the Union address barely a month after the Soviet invasion of Afghanistan, "An attempt by any outside force to gain control of the … Gulf region will be regarded as an assault on the vital interests of the United States of America, and such an assault will be repelled by any means necessary, including military force."[72] To fill the gap, the United States increased its naval forces in the Indian Ocean and the Arabian Gulf and also formed a Rapid Deployment Force, which would allow US forces to intervene directly in the region, using pre-positioned equipment.

For Shaikh Zayid, the projection of superpower conflict into the region was a matter of deep concern.[73] His approach towards the superpowers was to pursue a balanced policy by maintaining cordial relations with both, without getting pulled into either orbit. Still, he perceived the threat as coming more from the United States than from the Soviet Union, although he utterly condemned the Soviet invasion of Afghanistan in 1979. He did not believe that US activity was disinterested and feared that once they were in place, American troops might never leave. So far, the twin-track policy had involved the traditional local, Islamic powers of the region. However, the Rapid Deployment Force was a wholly US entity. Thus, while he recognized the need for defense, he saw it as imperative that the Arab states of the Gulf should be ready to do their own part rather than rely on surrogates. As he saw it, the only reasonable option was for the states in the region to provide for their own security. In March 1976, Shaikh Zayid stated:

> Everyone who has wealth will always be the target of the greedy. It is difficult to know from which direction that avaricious one will approach you. You may suspect the one coming from the East but

the danger draws near to you from the West or vice versa. The
people of the Gulf have got capabilities, wealth and awareness. They
are capable of filling any vacuum and of shouldering responsibility
for their country and their land.[74]

The principle was unambiguous, "The people of the Gulf are the
defenders of the Gulf."[75]

Despite these pressing concerns, the GCC was not formed purely
out of military necessity. Its origins antedated the political changes – the
Iranian Revolution, the Russian invasion of Afghanistan, the Iran–Iraq
War – that provided the impetus for new defensive arrangements.[76]
Throughout the late 1970s, the states in the area had slowly begun to
take steps towards joint action. In December 1978, the Crown Prince
and Prime Minister of Kuwait, Shaikh Sa'ad Al Abdullah Al Salim Al
Sabah, had held meetings with each of the Arab states in the region.
Each of the governments manifested a set of common interests that made
it clear that some kind of permanent organization would be welcomed.

The communiqué of the meeting held in Abu Dhabi with the
Kuwaiti Crown Prince expressed many of Shaikh Zayid's long-held
beliefs, "The two sides agreed on the need for a collective and speedy
move to realize unity of the Arab Gulf states emanating from their
religious and natural linkage and to achieve aspirations of their people
for progress and prosperity."[77] Discussions moved ahead rapidly at a
meeting of the Arab Gulf states held during the Arab Summit in
Amman, Jordan in November 1980, and more intensively during the
Islamic Conference held in Taif, Saudi Arabia in January 1981. During
February and March 1981, the Gulf Foreign Ministers met in a series
of sessions, working hard to produce the framework for an effective and
long-lasting structure.

Shaikh Zayid, mindful of the failed and formulaic unions previously
created in the Arab world, had insisted from the outset that this was to
be a vital and active organization, with a real capacity for development.
As he expressed it:

> Gulf unity is not merely intended as a declaration of unity reflected
> in the creation of a single state having one flag and a national
> anthem, but what is needed is the laying down of foundations of

unity relying on sound political, cultural, social and economic principles. These principles will enable Gulf unity to hold out in the face of challenges and will help to withstand external storms and pressures.[78]

Ultimately, the Preamble to the Charter of the Gulf Cooperation Council, signed by all the Gulf states on May 25, 1981 in Abu Dhabi, reflected Shaikh Zayid's insight. The objectives listed in Article 4 bore the hallmark of his dedication to a pragmatic activism. The Council was committed to "effect co-ordination, integration, and inter-connection between member states in all fields in order to achieve unity between them." Unity, *ittihad*, was the hallmark of Shaikh Zayid's work, the principle which he had worked for 10 years to achieve within the UAE. Now that same objective had expanded, as he had always wished, into the broader Arab domain. It was no mere coincidence that Shaikh Zayid was chosen by acclamation as the first President of the GCC Supreme Council and that he was the first Head of State to sign the Charter.

The Secretary General, Abdullah Bishara, in his elaboration of the GCC founding principles, revealed how closely it followed the model which Shaikh Zayid had created for the UAE:

> Despite the fact that the GCC Charter does not contain a clear-cut political theory, there is consensus on some form of confederacy between its six member states. Every Arab country is keen to maintain its special characteristics, independence and legislative authorities, while at the same time a strong desire exists among these states to promote their regional potential within one framework. There is common agreement that, acting under the umbrella of the Council, they will be able to pool their political, economic and other efforts in a confederal manner.[79]

However, just as the UAE was still evolving slowly, and not without difficulty, towards an ever closer union, so too Shaikh Zayid recognized that the broader union in the Gulf would take some time to be fully achieved. Although the need for defense cooperation was becoming a pressing need, he was insistent that the long-term civil elements of integration should proceed as quickly as possible. As a result, the two civil directorates made the most rapid progress.[80] Increasingly, the member-states came to see that the only path forward was that which Shaikh Zayid had advanced consistently in speech after speech. He declared:

> Our security policy, as we have mentioned, is based on the necessity for cooperation by the countries of the region themselves to resist any danger that threatens our security…This region is very important and indeed vital to the world and its economy. Perhaps, the main factor that provides security for the Gulf region is that it remains remote from the Super Power struggle.[81]

This emphasis on keeping the superpower rivalry out of the region formed the core of his policy, for he had seen what had happened to nations that had allowed themselves to be drawn into supporting one or the other.[82] The UAE's policy thus became the basis for the GCC stance on international relations.

Shaikh Zayid's support for the principles of unity in the Gulf has never wavered, but as an institution the GCC has not developed as far or as fast as he would have wished. As with other regional groupings, there are both enthusiasts and skeptics. While Shaikh Zayid's enthusiasm remains undiminished, he believes in allowing the development of the GCC to take its own course, just as in the case of the UAE Federation. Time, he believes, will inevitably bring fulfillment to his vision. To further the process, he has adopted the same techniques – media presentation, personal advocacy, rallying of public opinion – which were effective in building a constituency for the unity program in the UAE. Indeed, the parallels between these two aspects of his political practice are notable. Thus, the key issues of integration in the UAE and the political and economic harmonization among the GCC states have both been approached in similar fashion. In both cases, Shaikh Zayid has adopted a cautious and gradualist approach. He believes that the GCC states can only come together of their own volition and recognition of self-interest. For this reason, he will not force unity any more than he sought to do so in the case of the United Arab Emirates. His voice is active and powerful in support of moves towards common action, and his silence and absence speak just as emphatically.

International Cooperation

Another element in Shaikh Zayid's policy is related to his consistent desire to make the UAE a full and effective member of the international community.[83] This objective also stemmed from the same blend of ethics and realism that determined all his actions. For Shaikh Zayid, the rest of the world should see the United Arab Emirates as a worthy steward of its God-given resources. He has always made use of the country's financial resources to support his diplomacy and his humanitarian concerns worldwide. He also wanted his own nation to be open and receptive to the whole world, an ambition fulfilled in the 1990s by the massive growth in tourism. This, in addition to the growing power of television, brought the UAE to the attention of a worldwide audience, presenting a positive image of a peaceful and friendly nation.[84]

In the years since the foundation of the UAE, the scope of Shaikh Zayid's activities has been extended and broadened. In his early years, as man of honor within the region he had been trusted by those engaged in local disputes. In later years, he enlarged that capacity into the international, Arab and Islamic dimension by becoming an active force in humanitarian projects. In addition to his role as a political mediator, he took the lead where no one else had the courage or the initiative to make an advance. By 1974, Abu Dhabi's foreign aid had reached a massive 28 percent of its total income, an unprecedented level.[85] Shaikh Zayid's approach to international involvement embraced the same basic principles as all his other activities. He was interested in long-term results although he responded immediately and generously to distress and human catastrophe.[86]

The project to reconstruct the ancient Marib Dam in Yemen exemplified the type of work that he thought most beneficial. In April 1982, the UAE offered $3 million for urgent flood relief efforts in Yemen. However, Shaikh Zayid realized that the answer to the problem was not short-term relief, and later in April he personally provided the funds to rebuild the Marib Dam and thus resolve the underlying problem. In 1984, further funds were provided by the UAE to continue the work, and on October 2 of that year Shaikh Zayid laid the foundation stone for a project that would end the devastation caused by floods and revitalize thousands of hectares of potentially good agricultural land. Two years later, he was able to inaugurate the dam, which had been completed ahead of schedule and brought manifold benefits to a vast tract of Yemen.[87]

Marib had all the ingredients of a 'Zayid project.' It benefited ordinary people and produced a dramatic improvement in their lifestyle. Its long-term benefit was agricultural, allowing them to be self-sustaining and to achieve dignity through work. Shaikh Zayid financed a further network of canals to distribute water to the fields, making the area a model of agricultural development, like so many of the projects he has sponsored in the UAE. Yet, the project also had a historical connection that was important to him, for Marib was the site of an ancient water system that had provided water more than a millennium before. Its rebirth was a symbol of the continuing vitality of the Arab heartland. At the dam's inauguration, Shaikh Zayid told the people of Yemen, "This dam which represents the Yemeni and the Arab peoples' great history symbolizes everything that tie the two countries together...[It is] not only decisive and historic but also a good example of what relations should be among brothers of the same family."[88] Shaikh Zayid continued his support for the Marib Dam project with a further agreement signed on November 25, 2002. The project is ultimately estimated to irrigate more than 10,000 hectares of crops.

The phrase "brothers of the same family" represented the essence of Shaikh Zayid's political thinking. The Islamic values of the family should, he believed, be carried forward into all relationships. He thought increasingly in terms of the 'brotherhood of mankind,' a concept that embraced and extended the values which had sustained him throughout his life. He had always dealt fairly and honorably with his own brothers, who were tied to him by connections of blood. He had always behaved towards his fellow Rulers in the region as 'Arab brothers.' He had pressed for the creation of the GCC based on the principles of Arab unity and brotherhood. When many Kuwaitis, fleeing from the Iraqi invasion, traveled to the UAE in August 1990, Shaikh Zayid not only provided them with accommodation and financial assistance but also exempted them from paying any medical fees. During the crisis, more than 66,000 Kuwaitis came to the UAE seeking refuge, which Shaikh Zayid extended with generous hospitality.[89] Thus, he consistently advanced the concept of human brotherhood both through direct aid and by his personal example.

His goals of national unity, public benefit, peace and security, and a dedication to human values he spelled out unambiguously, and there has been a consistency in his approach to each of these aspirations. The Shaikh Zayid method is based upon persuasion rather than coercion. His objectives are openly and frankly stated, and his belief that he will ultimately succeed is expressed with equal candor. And yet, rather as water dripping from the roof of a limestone cavern slowly but inexorably forms a stalagmite, so too Shaikh Zayid's policies have taken shape slowly by accretion. Rather than press too hard, thereby turning persuasion into coercion, he has stood back and allowed time to overcome obstacles and create a desire for unity and cooperation. This approach has been exemplified from the early days under the rule of Shaikh Shakhbut and during his own time as Ruler of Abu Dhabi. It has also been manifest in the process of the formation of the UAE Federation, through the establishment of the GCC, and continues in the present day.

An ethical policy is one in which considerations of any short-term gain are tempered by the expected long-term consequences. For Shaikh Zayid, ethics and politics do not exist in separate domains, and his holistic approach has been reflected in his unique vision and perspectives. Shaikh Zayid's remarkable personal qualities have unfolded in a rich life-experience: a long period of governing before attaining full power; a bedrock of popular support; economic security; and a political acumen attuned to the necessity and inevitability of change. These elements have provided the unique circumstances in which his ethical policies have been framed.

With United Strength

In 1953, the philosopher and historian Sir Isaiah Berlin published a study of political leadership entitled *The Hedgehog and the Fox*.[1] The book dealt with the role of 'great men' and their impact on the course of history. Berlin referred to what he considered the essential distinction between two types of human beings. First, there are those who 'know one big thing.' They construct their perceptions of the world, their thoughts and feelings on the basis of this 'one big idea.' As a result, their views are all-embracing and seamlessly integrated. The second type seeks to accomplish a multiplicity of objectives, some of which may be contradictory. Berlin assigned the Greek political thinker Plato and the eighteenth-century German philosopher Georg Hegel to the first category, while suggesting that the Greek philosopher Aristotle and the historian Herodotus belonged to the second. However, Berlin also recognized that some great men possessed the best of both.

Based on the analysis presented in this book, it is evident that Shaikh Zayid Bin Sultan Al Nahyan is a rare example of an exceptional individual who has succeeded in blending fundamental principles with pragmatism. He plainly 'knew one great thing,' which was that disunity had been the curse of the Arab peoples and the cause of their decline from their early triumphs. An empire that had once ruled supreme from Cordoba in the west to Kabul in the east had been irreversibly weakened by endless division and dissension. Shaikh Zayid could see the perils of disunity among his own people in the Arabian Gulf.

Shaikh Zayid also 'knew many things,' gleaned from the experiences of his early life, from watching and listening, from reading both newspapers and works of literature, as well as studying the character and demeanor of those whom he encountered. His immense capacity to assimilate information, his prodigious memory and his intimate knowledge of tribal culture and customs made it easy for him to move beyond the traditional and conditioned patterns of thought. Shaikh Zayid knew that Abu Dhabi could not survive in isolation while the rest of the Arab world advanced. He understood the dynamics of international power politics, and often surprised his interlocutors with his immediate grasp of complex issues. The consequence of 'knowing many things' was that Shaikh Zayid never attempted to force the events of the real world into some theoretical framework. Rather, he adapted the framework and structure to fit unfolding events. Yet, at no point did he allow his principles to be compromised or distorted.

This harmonious blending of principle and pragmatism has provided the conceptual basis upon which Shaikh Zayid built the United Arab Emirates. He belongs to that select group of statesmen in the annals of history who have succeeded in uniting a disparate population into a nation. The essence of his political art has been his intuitive judgment of when to steer the nation by the beacon of principle and when to follow the landmark of pragmatism. The consummate skill of this interplay distinguishes him from his contemporaries. In a longer historical perspective, it should place him in the small and exclusive category of charismatic nation-builders.

The fact that Shaikh Zayid built the new nation by persuasion and not by coercion has been a consistent theme of this book, but it bears repetition. Persuasion demands time, and leaders are often men in a hurry. As a result, force has too often been their ultimate recourse. Shaikh Zayid, however, has revealed himself as a true statesman by eschewing the use of pressure and force. He considered time and experience as the true engines of change. It is therefore the means by which he has achieved this nation-building that places him in the ranks of great statesmen. For while many leaders have founded their nations on armed victory, revolutionary struggle or military power, Shaikh Zayid has built the United Arab Emirates as a civil structure through peaceful means, tolerance and persuasion, and with a determined focus on the dignity of the human being. Moreover, instead of rejecting the diversity of the elements that make up the Federation, in pursuit of some theoretical and abstract form of unification, he has established a plural and open structure, rooted in traditional values.

Shaikh Zayid's strength of character, the universal respect which he commands, and the economic and social power at his disposal would have allowed him to impose any political solution he willed. Instead, he took up the exacting task of creating a nation by consensus. He followed the more difficult and winding route to nationhood because he believed that in reaching this goal he was fulfilling his duty towards his people. The example of peaceful development that he set and the model state which he created are an incomparable gift to the people of the United Arab Emirates.

Shaikh Zayid as Pragmatist and Visionary

Under Shaikh Zayid's guidance, the UAE has maintained a fine balance in the political structure between the autonomy of the individual emirates and the power of the federal state. This policy has allowed diversity to flourish without compromising the country's cohesive unity, a pattern that was observed by a group of academics from the University of Jordan who visited the UAE in early 2000. In a report, one of them noted:

> During my recent trip to the UAE what impressed me most, among other things, was the country's sense of focus. The various Emirates seem to have known exactly what they wanted to do, and each has done it, or is doing it. Dubai in business, Sharjah in culture and heritage, etc. It is not just money that stands behind progress, as some may hasten to assert. Rather it is good planning, good management and good focus.[2]

These three attributes – planning, management and focus – can be traced back to Shaikh Zayid's accession as Ruler of Abu Dhabi in

1966. His careful preservation of the robust diversity noted in the Jordanian report has facilitated and fostered the differentiated patterns of development that are characteristic of the UAE. Indeed, diversity lies at the heart of Shaikh Zayid's vision for the United Arab Emirates, one that has matured from his early experience of tribal politics. The latter, contrary to accepted opinion, has provided a flexible and adaptable matrix within which the new union could develop. However, diversity can be both a positive and a negative political force, sometimes leading to fragmentation and sectionalism. These dangers have been avoided largely due to the personality and policies of Shaikh Zayid. His political pragmatism has transformed the inchoate and often fissiparous dynamics of Arab tribal ideology into a force for cohesion.

'Trusting the people' is a slogan often voiced by political figures, who rarely abide by this dictum. Shaikh Zayid has not merely espoused the principle, but applied it with remarkable effect. No clearer example of his political sensitivity need be sought. From his experience both during his years in al Ain and later in Abu Dhabi, he knew that popular sentiment favored the path of progress that he advocated. Often, Shaikh Zayid encountered resistance to his plans not from the people but from certain vested interests. He has always been a true populist, regarding public service as the main duty of a political leader. Shaikh Zayid succeeded in persuading the peoples of all the emirates that unity would impart strength, while disunity would expose them to domination by external powers. This equation has been widely understood by the citizens of the United Arab Emirates in the years since 1971.

The ethos of the new nation developed gradually. At times, the process was slower than Shaikh Zayid might have desired, a fact to which he often alluded in his speeches and public comments. Yet, his capacity to wait patiently for change to evolve provided the UAE with a unique source of strength. The virtue of patience by itself, however, was not sufficient to have brought about the accomplishments of Shaikh Zayid. Other traits, characteristics and special conditions have contributed equally to his personal development and political outlook. All of these, although detailed earlier in this book, are worth high-lighting once again.

Shaikh Zayid was born into the Bedouin tradition and nurtured in the rigorous conditions of the desert environment during his formative years. He developed the habit of hard work, often laboring with his own hands, thereby acquiring the virtue of self-reliance. Shaikh Zayid first learned the art of governance in al Ain, where he successfully introduced significant reforms, despite the lack of administrative support. His leadership skills evolved over time as he rose from the position of a tribal Shaikh to that of Ruler's Representative. Thereafter, he was chosen by the ruling family to shoulder his responsibilities as the Ruler of Abu Dhabi. He transformed a traditional tribal society into a unified and a progressive nation. In recognition of his achievements, he was later elected as the President of the United Arab Emirates by his fellow Rulers.

Considered in its totality, Shaikh Zayid's life might be divided schematically into four different historical phases. First, there was a period of apprenticeship from the 1920s until 1966. During this time, he formed his scale of human values, developed his principles and political intuition. He learned through practical experience, participation and observation, activities which helped him to develop a resilient personality and to hone his political skills. Second, there was a period of accomplishment from 1966 to 1971. During this time, Shaikh Zayid put his principles into practice for Abu Dhabi as a whole, setting an example of tireless effort and personal involvement in the process of development.

The third stage, from 1971 until 1981, encompassed major change and political transformation. During this time, Shaikh Zayid was able to accomplish a long-cherished dream of forging unity among the peoples of the emirates. The UAE was created by mutual agreement and accord, and built upon solid foundations. Finally, the fourth phase from 1981 to the present day has witnessed a period of steady incremental development and consolidation under Shaikh Zayid's presidency. The problems of rapid and dramatic change have been resolved and the UAE has emerged as a mature and strong polity, respected in the world as a model of peaceful social and economic advancement. Congruent with Shaikh Zayid's vision of the value of unity was the concept of regional integration, which he championed through the establishment of the GCC, serving as its first President.[3] Gradually, the state has acquired a prominent role in the Arab and Islamic worlds as an active member in forums such as the Arab League and the Organization of the Islamic Conference (OIC). It has also made its mark on the wider international stage as a responsible member of the United Nations, through its participation in UN specialized agencies and peacekeeping operations.[4]

The process of development from 1971 to the present bears the indelible mark of Shaikh Zayid's political vision. Many new states created after 1945 made a positive start but later failed to match their initial promise. The same cannot be said of the United Arab Emirates. In its case, progress has been sure and steady, confounding the critics who initially gave the new state little chance of success. In one sense, the skeptics were justified in their predictions, for the odds were stacked against the new nation, and it seemed rational to anticipate failure. What they overlooked, however, was the unexpected factor of the remarkable personality of Shaikh Zayid that decisively changed the course of regional history.

Modernity and Progress in Partnership with the People

From his early days in al Ain as the Ruler's Representative, Shaikh Zayid had a clear notion of partnership with the people, from the most humble level to the higher echelons of society. While cooperation would surely bring success, disunity would ultimately result in failure. This idea, rooted in the harsh realities of the desert, later became fundamental to his concept of government. He saw the loyalty of the people to the Ruler as based on a sense of mutual commitment between the government and the governed. Often, it needed time and persuasion to convince the people to extend their wholehearted support. His legendary patience cannot be dismissed as a passive quality. Rather, it should be perceived as a measured anticipation of a favorable turn in events. Shaikh Zayid has always been an activist, constantly pressing forward to achieve his goals. However, he has chosen to accomplish these aims by ensuring genuine support and consensus, rather than relying on coercion and manipulation.

In al Ain, he learned how tribesmen led their lives, and how they could be led. A tribesman who freely gave his allegiance would be loyal unto death, but one who was forced into submission would only remain true as long as the Ruler had power over him. Shaikh Zayid bound his people to him with ties of trust and honor, and by doing so he reaped ample reward. He saw all relationships of a political nature as being essentially reciprocal. It was his duty to provide economic benefits to his people and improve the overall quality of life by providing health facilities, ensuring a decent livelihood, and providing for the welfare of the family.

In retrospect, Shaikh Zayid has pursued what were often traditional objectives, like the maintenance of family values and social cohesion, but through wholly modern mechanisms. This has countered many of the undoubtedly negative consequences of the Western model of development, while reaping the obvious benefits of the West's technological and economic advances. Maintaining the delicate balance has required the same management skills and long-term vision that have characterized the other aspects of his political activity. The dangers of untrammeled modernization were apparent to his brother Shaikh Shakhbut. Like his brother, Shaikh Zayid was aware of the dangers of change. Nevertheless, he was confident that the process of transformation could be accommodated and that its advantages would vastly outweigh any risks. The very nature of 'change' in the UAE has evolved over time. When Shaikh Zayid first became Ruler of Abu Dhabi, and through the early years of the UAE, the focus of change was necessarily upon building the basic structures of a modern society where none had existed before. Public utilities of a high standard, such as electrical power stations, roads, ports and airports, hospitals and schools, were built over the space of three decades, marking the success of development.

Over time, Shaikh Zayid's holistic principles gradually influenced many aspects of the economic and social life of the UAE. While oil, as the country's greatest natural resource, has transformed the country's fortunes, the inflow of oil revenues alone does not necessarily guarantee planned development or material benefits for the people. Shaikh Zayid always saw the resources of the state as held in trust for the people of the emirates. It was therefore to be generously and judiciously used to bring about tangible improvement in the living standards of the citizens. Accordingly, national oil revenues have been channeled to meet the needs of the population in all dimensions.

Since becoming a sovereign member of the community of nations, the UAE has seen dramatic improvements in all facets of life. Supported by oil production rates that increased from 253,000 barrels per day in 1972 to 1.9 million in 2002, nominal GDP has risen from 6.45 billion dirhams to 234 billion in 2001, a 40-fold increase.[5] At the same time, the percentage of non-oil exports to the GDP figure increased from 37 percent in 1972 to more than 70 percent in 2001.[6] As a result, the UAE has accomplished economic development that puts it on par with other high-income countries throughout the world.

More important than the simple economic statistics is the fact that under Shaikh Zayid's guidance and leadership the UAE has seen unprecedented social improvement and advancement. As such, there has been an unparalleled increase in the quality of life for the people. In terms of health care, for example, the UAE has gone from being a country with one of the highest child mortality rates in the 1960s to joining the ranks of those with the lowest levels by the turn of the century.[7] Current life-expectancy figures, as reported in the Arab Human Development Report 2002, rank the highest in the Arab World, and compare favorably with those of the most developed nations.[8] This has been achieved partly by making primary health care accessible even in remote villages.[9] Shaikh Zayid has also directed the construction of modern and well-equipped hospitals, which operate according to the highest world standards. By the year 2000, the UAE had over 60 public and private hospitals, 380 primary health care centers, 352 private clinics and 250 specialist clinics serving the country.[10]

An equally important aspect to the development of health care has been in the field of education. The Holy Koran enjoins all Muslims, men and women alike, to develop their minds. From that simple precept, Shaikh Zayid found his life-long commitment to the cause of learning, viewing intellectual development first as a key to human enlightenment and then as a determinant of sustainable growth for the nation. The nature and structure of education changed markedly over the years since he opened the first school at al Ain. As universal education developed throughout the world and populations benefited from the spread of knowledge, Shaikh Zayid ensured that the UAE's educational policies kept pace with global trends. While there existed only 20 schools in the emirates in 1962, and 74 schools at the time of the establishment of the Federation, by the year 2000 over 1,150 schools offered educational facilities to almost 650,000 students.[11] In 2001, the single largest allocation in the federal budget was for education.[12]

With the information revolution and renewed focus on knowledge creation as a key national asset, it became imperative for the young nation to recognize exceptional talent and provide facilities for its development. Shaikh Zayid has always fervently believed that the greatest use that the country can make of the wealth that it has been provided with is to invest it in the continuous education and training of its people. The objective of education is to nurture the versatile, confident, honorable individual who can fulfill Shaikh Zayid's vision of a new generation of leaders for the nation. Learning should not be based merely on the memorization of facts and the pursuit of grades, but rather should comprise the meaningful acquisition and application of knowledge. Learners should be equipped with the skills necessary to compete in the new economic order and meet global challenges effectively.

The awareness of the need to remain at the forefront of educational developments has led to a reassessment of the educational policy in the UAE and the establishment of a new education strategy – Vision 2020 – that will incorporate the most effective teaching and learning programs into all levels of schooling.[13] This transformation is in line with a standard that Shaikh Zayid has advanced since the early 1990s, that the UAE should be among the leaders in education not just within the region but also on the international level. By instituting programs such as Distinguished Student Scholarships (DSS), Shaikh Zayid has ensured that high academic achievers could be identified and given the opportunity to receive the best possible education at the finest universities abroad. Other new initiatives, such as the establishment of the Emirates National School as a world-class institution following an internationally recognized curriculum, equally mirror Shaikh Zayid's aspirations.

The UAE's emphasis on high-quality education is also in keeping with world trends that focus on the creation of human capital as the driving force of the economy. It is geared to the development of the UAE human resource capabilities to serve the country's current and future needs and reduce dependence on imported skills. With this in mind, the state has paid special attention to programs of emiratization, supported by institutions such as the Tanmia that coordinates human resource training, skills development and placement of nationals in the job market.[14]

The UAE's success in the development of human resources is reflected in the scientific and technological advances made by the country, which have attracted wide attention from scholars and intellectuals. The country has become a preferred venue for international conferences and gatherings that explore issues of global significance. The excellent physical, financial, technological and communications infrastructure offered by the United Arab Emirates has drawn foreign investors and entrepreneurs to its free-trade zones.[15] For the same reasons, the country has also played host to world-class sporting and cultural events and has become a popular tourist destination, further concretizing Shaikh Zayid's desire to see the UAE open to the world.[16]

The considerable investment being made in the fields of trade, tourism and in the commercial and industrial zones form an integral part of Shaikh Zayid's strategy of economic diversification.[17] Since oil is a finite resource with a volatile market, such diversification is essential for the sustainable development of the country in the long-term. There is a concerted effort to equip the country with a strong economic base, and enable it to prosper in an era when oil may no longer be the foundation of the economy. Such long-term strategic planning, as advocated by Shaikh Zayid, has been one of the primary factors ensuring progress for the United Arab Emirates Federation and continued benefits for its people.

Shaikh Zayid's deeds were not only a product of his boundless generosity but also based on sound calculations of what was most important for his people. He lived his life by the tenets of Islam, which gave him a sense of direction and a deep inner peace. His character had been formed in the fold of his family, first as a child and young man, and later as a father. The loyalty to family was the most powerful and durable bond, and he saw the nation that was created in 1971 as built upon those simple, but strong and unbreakable, family connections shared by all his people. He was determined to foster a society in which the family and childhood were honored and sustained.

It was Shaikh Zayid who worried about the burden of dowries and instituted the Marriage Fund so that young Emiratis could start their married lives together in dignity and financial security.[18] It was Shaikh Zayid who supported group weddings to cut the heavy financial burden of traditional celebrations. Moreover, it was Shaikh Zayid and his wife Shaikha Fatima who championed the development of women in a traditional society. In consonance with Islamic principles, and recognizing the importance of the empowerment of women for the growth of the nation, Shaikh Zayid ensured that women were provided with the same high-quality education as male nationals, from the primary level through to tertiary education. The enrollment rates for women at the UAE University and the Higher Colleges of Technology bears witness to the success of this program. In fact, the overwhelming response of women to pursue further education has led to the establishment of the Zayid University for women.

Educational equality has been underscored by the provision of equal employment opportunities for women in all sectors of the economy and state. Furthermore, under the chairmanship and patronage of Shaikha Fatima, several women's associations have come into being, such as the UAE Women's Federation, which provide a suitable venue for the enriching exchange of ideas and serve as a forum for the promotion of UAE culture and heritage. The UAE has participated in several high-profile international gatherings on the role of women in society, and presented a strong case for the emancipation of women, for their central role in the family, and their vital contribution to society and country.

It is this sense of partnership between the government and the people which underpins the idea of nationhood within the UAE. Thus, while the government has provided the necessary infrastructure, resources and opportunities, UAE citizens have been encouraged to engage actively in commercial and industrial endeavors that contribute to the economic growth of the country, through majority holdings in private enterprises.[19] The creation of what the social scientist Sally Findlow calls an 'enterprise ideology' distinguishes the UAE from many other states that have acquired wealth through oil or mineral extraction:

> The UAE government actively encourages, through numerous formal schemes as well as the promotion of an enterprise ideology, the participation of all citizens in helping to build a self-sustaining economy and infrastructure. In this sense, the role of will and collective endeavor, in creating a unified nation where there was none before, is quite apparent. That is not to say that wealth, and the informational resources and political power that money can buy, have not helped. At the same time a feeling of social solidarity is facilitated by the lasting bonds of family or tribal relations, within such a small native population among whom almost everyone feels that they know the ruler personally (or at least a member of the ruling families).[20]

The concept of citizens' rights and duties, and the strengthening of loyalty towards the Federation has perhaps been Shaikh Zayid's most valuable gift to his people. He made it possible for the citizens of the UAE to find a new and cohesive identity in a successful and modern state.[21] His popularity in all the emirates has grown since 1971. His energy and hard work are legendary, as is his generosity. Over the years, the bond of trust between the people and the Ruler has strengthened. It was the people who came out into the streets to beg him to remain President.[22] They attributed the good that has come to the nation and to them as individuals to 'their' Zayid. He was concerned with the realities of their lives, not the issues of some invisible Grand Policy.

Finally, it would not be fitting to end the discussion here without a reference to the important role that environmentalism plays in terms of Shaikh Zayid's thinking. On the occasion of the UAE's first Environment Day in 1998, Shaikh Zayid stated:

We cherish our environment because it is an integral part of our country, our history and our heritage. On land and in the sea, our forefathers lived and survived in this environment. They were able to do so only because they recognized the need to conserve it, to take from it only what they needed to live, and to preserve it for succeeding generations. With God's will, we will continue to work to protect our environment and our wildlife, as did our forefathers before us. It is a duty, and, if we fail, our children, rightly, will reproach us for squandering an essential part of their inheritance, and of our heritage.[23]

Shaikh Zayid had been aware of the intricate balance of human life and natural forces since his youth. In the years at al Ain he had observed that a tribe could only grow crops when there was water, or sustain livestock for which there was fodder. The essence of what later came to be called his environmentalism was based on the long observation of the interplay between the human and the natural world. As a result, he was aware that modernization and progress were essential but also carried a price.

Water has been a life-long concern of Shaikh Zayid, who grew up in a desert economy in which this resource was the most valuable asset. His first initiatives were in the *aflaj* of al Ain, then in bringing water by pipeline to Abu Dhabi itself. Later, as technology developed, the energy-rich UAE was able to take advantage of its long coastline to desalinate seawater on a large scale. As a result, the UAE now produces enough water to give its inhabitants the second-highest level of per capita consumption of clean water in the world.[24] But as Shaikh Zayid pressed forward with more water production by desalination, he knew the environmental cost of the process. The desolate salt flats (*sabkha*), 300km in length and 20km wide described in Chapter 1 were a product of natural change, but they only appeared some 4,000 years ago.[25] Desalinating water produces either high levels of sea salt or increased levels of salinity on land unless constant efforts are made to control and minimize this harmful by-product. The result of creating fresh water could, it is now realized, over time create new and wholly man-made *sabkha* on an enormous scale.

An environmentally negligent strategy would have produced precisely this outcome. However, Shaikh Zayid recognized the complexity of the problem. Without water there could be no modern life in the region, yet a careless approach to its production would ultimately lead precisely to greater desertification, a process that he was actively seeking to reverse. By example, exhortation, persuasion, and even when necessary by the sheer force of his personality, he insisted on careful and planned environmental regulation of water production in the UAE, implementing a program that is probably among the most advanced in the Arab world, and certainly the most forward-looking among those nations with desert environments.

The Federal Environment Agency, established in 1993, and Federal Law 24 of 1999 both implement Shaikh Zayid's environmental strategies. The 1999 Law highlights the need for environmental impact analysis and the need for policies of sustainable development in all new projects.[26] Institutions such as the Environmental Research and Wildlife Development Agency (ERWDA) and its Marine Environmental Research Center (MERC) have played an important role in the UAE's ecological development. The country has embarked on extensive environmental planning and conservation programs, such as the Sir Bani Yas fauna and flora reserve and its conservation program for the protection of indigenous species that are on the endangered list. The Sir Bani Yas project merited Shaikh Zayid the World Wildlife Fund Gold Panda Award in 1997.[27] The country is also active in marine and coastal resource management, based on the collection of reliable environmental data. Its forward-looking policy on such data has led to the announcement of the Abu Dhabi Global Environmental Data Initiative (AGEDI) at the 2002 World Summit on Sustainable Development, in Johannesburg, South Africa.[28]

Judicious use of resources has assisted the UAE's drive to combat desertification, which has always been one of Shaikh Zayid's primary concerns. Archaeological evidence shows that what is now arid waste in the Sahara once supported substantial populations. Likewise, some desert areas can, with proper management, be reclaimed. Shaikh Zayid's dream of making the desert green emanates from a deep knowledge of the oasis cultures of the region, and his holistic vision led to extensive programs of afforestation as well as the establishment of experimental farms, which have generated a substantial increase in national food production.[29] For many years, his determination to recover desert land went against conventional thinking that this was an economically unwise course of action, being marginal and unproductive in its impact. Twelve thousand wholly new farming units have been created since 1993, based on modern methods of cultivation and irrigation designed to use water to maximum effect and with minimum waste.[30]

However, these farms are not merely units of production. They are communities, with solid well-built houses, supporting families and providing livelihoods where none existed before. This is the image that Shaikh Zayid had in his mind, not figures of profit and loss on a balance sheet. Each one of these farms represents a new patch of green on the map where there had before only been scrub or sand. The greening of the desert was not some abstract ecological dream but evidence of better lives brought about through a partnership of hard work by those who lived on the land, and investment of resources by the state. This was the partnership that the new President of the UAE had promised to his people in 1971, a pledge he has amply fulfilled.

A Lasting Achievement

A careful perusal of all the available evidence leads to the conclusion that the new nation was fortunate to be guided by a great statesman. Shaikh Zayid's unshakable confidence in the future of the UAE as a Federation eventually persuaded the doubters, and his capabilities and determination sustained it through difficult times. The techniques of counter-factual history provide a means to isolate and assess his contribution.[31] No other individual possessed the unique blend of traits and qualities necessary to create the UAE and shape its development. In addition, Shaikh Zayid's willingness to share the wealth and resources of Abu Dhabi with the other emirates in the Federation meant that sustainable economic and social development of the whole nation could proceed at a uniform speed.

In retrospect, Shaikh Zayid's most remarkable capacity has been to reconcile the seemingly irreconcilable. He has achieved this paradoxical harmony by seeking the point of equilibrium within the spectrum of opposing forces. This principle he observed and learned as a child in the maelstrom of tribal politics, and he has applied that lesson effectively throughout his life. Thus, Shaikh Zayid has built a state which combines a strong tradition of leadership with an ambiance of partnership; where tradition and modernity, Bedouin values and urban culture co-exist; and where individual aspiration and social unity are not mutually exclusive. He has never forgotten the lessons about human nature that he absorbed as a child and young adult. The phenomenal progress that has been accomplished domestically, viewed in conjunction with the regional and global status accorded to the UAE, is a measure of Shaikh Zayid's achievement.

In this context, it is also essential to see an underlying ethical dimension. Islam has underpinned Shaikh Zayid's life from its first days. He was nurtured in an atmosphere that inculcated a strong faith. He derived strength from the values of Islam—trust in himself, and a set of principles that included simplicity, frankness, adaptability, patience, strong social values, justice, duty, self-denial and an earthy realism. His political philosophy grew from the same Islamic roots. He sought to understand the past and learn from its experiences. He also understood the wisdom of forgiveness, even when he had the power to exact retribution. He believed that antagonism produced nothing positive, while the hand of friendship could bridge discord. From history, he realized the importance of choosing efficient men to serve in the administration of the state. He considered the people of the UAE as belonging to one family, a concept to which he attached great importance:

> A family which is one lives in happiness, well-being and comfort, as long as its members are like one hand, co-operating, having affection for each other and sticking together. In all of that lies their happiness. On the other hand, should dissension appear amongst them and conflict take the place of harmony...they will all become wretched.[32]

For Shaikh Zayid, a worthy and righteous action does not mean acting apolitically. Indeed, his political vision is made more coherent by his underlying values. When the Bani Yas tribe acted with united strength, as it had under his grandfather, Shaikh Zayid the Great, it could accomplish great deeds. Disunited, it was like a flock in disarray, an easy victim for any predator. The meaning of unity, its power and creative force, was ingrained in him from his early days, and then reinforced by all that he heard, read and observed. This was the connecting chain that linked all his political actions and policies. Unity was not merely a word, but a principle of life. To strive for unity was a worthy and righteous act that would undoubtedly bring its true reward.

It is perhaps useful to fit Shaikh Zayid's strategies into a neutral and external model. In 1994, the Professor of Organizational Behavior and Change at Stanford University, Jerry I. Porras, and his colleague James C. Collins published the outcome of a six-year study of long-term institutional success.[33] They concluded that two principles determined the capacity for sustained and continuous development. Success required the preservation of core values, united inextricably with the need to stimulate progress. In their view, core values are the necessary condition for permanent progress:

> Our key framework concept, preserving the core/stimulating progress, will also become increasingly important in the twenty first century... the corporate bonding glue will increasingly become ideological. People still have a fundamental human need to belong to something that they can feel proud of. They have the fundamental need for guiding values and sense of purpose that gives their life and work meaning. They have a fundamental need for connection with other people, sharing with them the common bond of beliefs and aspirations.[34]

It is important to note the date of Porras and Collins' study. Shaikh Zayid's pragmatic approach anticipated their analysis by more than two decades. Their definitions of the prerequisites for success were not based on a study of the UAE, but they delineated, from a wholly different context, precisely the same core elements with which Shaikh Zayid has built a lasting new polity in the United Arab Emirates.

In many respects, the strategies by which Shaikh Zayid has succeeded in the UAE provide a more eloquent example of the process than the institutions on which the foregoing study is based. In particular, he showed that retaining control over the process of change, and diverting its energy and potential damage into positive channels, was the key factor in long-term development. Also in this respect, Shaikh Zayid formed his core values in his early experience and made it his life-long passion to be a force for positive change.

Here, a parallel may be drawn from the traditional sport of falconry. From his early days, Shaikh Zayid has been a passionate falconer. While few living creatures are quite so liberated and untamed as a bird of prey, falcons can be trained to work with man. They cannot be forced but they can be subtly persuaded. As Shaikh Zayid has stated, a falcon is trained by recognizing its particular qualities.

> He begins by offering the bird food while talking to it and gently stroking it. The bird continues to feed from the hand of the trainer, hearing his voice and feeling his hands without seeing him until it becomes calm and gains confidence in him…[35]

Each bird is different and must be treated as an individual. No hawk will come back to a trainer who does not treat it well or does not respond to its needs. Yet, with good training, a falcon or hawk will easily form a partnership with man. Although it cannot be wholly subdued, its wild energy can be channeled.

Shaikh Zayid did not fear the tumultuous power of change because he believed it could be turned into a positive force for public good. He also knew, to follow the metaphor of the falcon, that it could never be fully tamed. Thus, he has never trusted the forces of modernity to be wholly agents for good, unless constantly directed along the right path. In his political praxis, he has recognized and accepted that only constant care and attention will keep the pathway of progress open. For this reason, he returns again and again to the same central themes in his speeches and private discourse.

Shaikh Zayid's great skill has been to infuse his people with the vision of a bright future, to alert them to possible risks, but also to guide them in the effective use of the natural resources with which they have been endowed. They, in turn, have offered him their trust, honor and, overwhelmingly, their love and affection. In the light of all that has emerged about Shaikh Zayid's character in the course of this book, there seems little doubt that he would regard this as ample reward.

NOTES

INTRODUCTION

1   Three notable exceptions are the valuable studies by Muhammad Morsy Abdullah, Frauke Heard-Bey and Rosemarie Said Zahlan. See Bibliography. However, these only deal incidentally with Shaikh Zayid.

CHAPTER 1

1   Unpublished NARA (National Archives and Records Administration), American Consul (Dinsmore) Dhahran to Department of State, Pol 2: Trucial States, November 20, 1968, A-209.

2   Extracts from "Remarks on the Tribes, Trade and Resources around the Shore Line of the Persian Gulf," read before the Bombay Geographical Society, September 17, 1863 by Lt. Col. Lewis Pelly, Bombay Geographical Society Transactions xvii, 1983, reprinted in *Records of the Emirates*, Vol. 3 (Gerrards Cross: Archive Editions, 1990), 641.

3   Ibid.

4   See Ira M. Lapidus, *A History of Islamic Societies* (Cambridge: Cambridge University Press, 1988), 52–53.

5   The structure of British officialdom in the Arabian Gulf was unique within the system of British foreign and colonial relations. In the first place, Britain came to the Gulf through its Indian governmental structure to protect its perceived economic and strategic interests in the East. The Gulf was seen (until 1947) largely through the eyes of the 'Raj,' the Government of India. From the 1820s, the Government of India made treaties—the Maritime Truce (largely under the threat of British naval intervention) with the states of 'Outer Oman,' along the shores of the Arabian Gulf. These states, which now make up the United Arab Emirates, were then known as Trucial Oman or the Trucial States. They retained full internal self-government, but external relations (and disputes between Trucial States) were subject to a measure of British control. The senior official was the Political Resident in the Persian Gulf, with his base in Bushire, on the Iranian side of the Gulf. Over time, a number of lower level officials were appointed. The lowest level was the Political Officer, the next the Political Agent. Initially, all relations with the Trucial States were handled, on a day-to-day basis, by a local Arab Residency Agent, based in Sharjah. The center of British operations shifted over time to Bahrain, with the Political

Resident finally moving his office from Bushire to Bahrain after the Second World War, a move long planned but never executed earlier. From 1947, there was thus a parallel structure of Political Agent (Bahrain) and Political Resident in the Persian Gulf in Bahrain, each performing different functions. As the states of the Trucial Coast grew in importance, British Political Officers and later Political Agents were appointed to Sharjah, Dubai and finally Abu Dhabi. The central task allocated to all these officials was sustaining British interests and supporting the local Rulers, in that order. From the First World War onwards, the Gulf became a more politically sensitive area and the parochial concerns of the Government of India (and its perspective) were increasingly challenged by the administration in London. The Air Ministry (through the control of air routes east), the Colonial Office and the Foreign Office all began to claim an interest in the region. This was only resolved after 1947, when, with the demise of the Government of India, responsibility was definitively transferred to the Foreign Office. However, the 'old hands' of the Government of India continued to dominate the structure on the ground in the Gulf. It was not until 1953 that the first Foreign Office Political Resident, Sir Bernard Burrows, was appointed. The complexity and transitions in the outlined structure sustained two consistent elements. First, that Britain wanted as much control in the area as possible, but with the minimum commitment of resources, the minimum involvement in local affairs and the minimum expenditure. Second, although a full colonial structure was never seriously contemplated, British officials frequently forgot that they were not colonial administrators and sought to intervene in local matters beyond the strict limits of their responsibilities. They were often encouraged (or required) to do so by the government which employed them. In doing so, they came up against local Rulers, who were well versed in what the various treaties had established and were determined to resist infringement on their sovereign rights. In the vast archive produced by the British officials, this resistance to intrusion is often cast in the most negative light.

6   See Ibn Khaldun, whose analysis of Bedouin life in *The Muqaddimah* is still the framework within which later studies were constructed. Ibn Khaldun, *The Muqaddimah: An Introduction to History*, 3 Volumes, translated by Franz Rosenthal (London and Henley: Routledge and Kegan Paul, 1958).

7   Ibid., 258.

8   See Lila Abu-Lughod, *Veiled Sentiments: Honor and Poetry in a Bedouin Society* (Berkeley, CA: University of California Press, 1986), 79. "Autonomy or freedom is the standard by which status is measured and social hierarchy determined. It is the consistent element shaping the Bedouin ideology of social life, in which equality is nothing other than equality of autonomy— that is, equality of freedom from domination by or dependency on others.

This principle is clear in Bedouin political organization, the segmentary lineage model. Although anthropologists disagree on many other aspects of this system, there is consensus that the system has as its central feature the maximization of unit autonomy." The skill of Shaikh Zayid has been to adapt these social constants within a strategy of change and development.

9   Largely in the old Arabia Felix of the southwest. This, in contrast to Arabia Deserta, had some agriculture and embraced parts of the Hadramaut and Yemen; in some cases, Dhufar was also considered to be part of this region.

10 See Sultan Muhammad Al-Qasimi (ed.) *The Journals of David Seton in the Gulf, 1800–1809* (Exeter: University of Exeter Press, 1995), 28.

11 J.C. Wilkinson has traced the origins of the designation of the oasis complex as 'Buraimi,' saying that the "application of the name…seems to be a European practice. It may find its origins in 'Abd al-Wahāb's *Lam' al-Shihāb*, which, the writer believes was specifically compiled at second hand for the Indian Government's Resident in Baghdad in the early nineteenth century…The old name was Tu'ām or Taw'am …and this still survives in Tayma, the alternative name for al-'Ayn…" See J.C. Wilkinson, *Water and Tribal Settlement in South-East Arabia: A Study of the Aflāj of Oman* (Oxford: Oxford University Press, 1977), 33, note 1.

12 J.B. Kelly, *Eastern Arabian Frontiers* (London and New York, NY: Frederick Praeger, 1964), 25.

13 For trade links, see Janet Abu-Lughod, *Before European Hegemony: The World System A.D. 1250–1350* (New York, NY: Oxford University Press, 1989) and K.N. Chaudhuri, *Trade and Civilisation in the Indian Ocean: An Economic History from the Rise of Islam to 1750* (London: Cambridge University Press, 1985).

14 Wilfred Thesiger, *Arabian Sands* (London: Longmans, Green, 1959; reprint London: Penguin Books, 1991), 259 (page citations refer to the reprint edition).

15 See Kenneth W. Gleenie, "Evolution of the Emirate's Land Surface: An Introduction," in Edmund Ghareeb and Ibrahim Al Abed (eds) *Perspectives on the United Arab Emirates* (London: Trident Press, 1997), 27.

16 The geographer Dr. John C. Wilkinson, who studied one of the clans of the Bani Yas, suggested that the availability of water structured their society. See Wilkinson, *Water and Tribal Settlement in South-East Arabia*, 55–72.

17 This applies to surface aquifers that require replenishment from rainfall as opposed to the deep aquifers that feed the *aflaj* system of water supply to al Ain.

18 Clarence C. Mann, *Abu Dhabi: Birth of an Oil Shaikhdom* (Beirut: Khayats, 1969), 11.

19 "Scarcity of resources and, in relation to these resources, relative density of population have formed the most characteristic phenomenon of the region's

age-old economic pattern: the versatile tribesman. He is to be found throughout the area and throughout the ages. He spends the winter with his livestock in the desert and comes to the coast to fish in the summer in order to supplement his own and his animals' diet. He plants or harvests his dates and takes part in the pearling, or he sows and harvests his millet high up in the mountains and spends the hot months of the summer fishing at the coast, or he leads a caravan or steers a ship and then returns to engage in some quite different activity. In short, there have been at all times in this area not a few tribesmen, every one of whom knew all there was to know about camel-breeding, pearling, fishing or sailmaking." See Frauke Heard-Bey, *From Trucial States to United Arab Emirates: A Society in Transition*, second enlarged edition (London and New York, NY: Longman, 1996), 25–26.

20 Richard Tapper has expressed this issue succinctly: "Unfortunately, Middle Eastern indigenous categories (of which perhaps the commonest have to be translated as tribe are *qabila*, *tai'fa*, *quam*, and *il* [original italics]) are no more specific than are English terms such as 'family' or 'group.' Even in the most apparently consistent segmentary terminology, individual terms are ambiguous, not merely about level, but also in their connotations of functions or facets of identity-economic, political, kinship, and cultural. As with equivalents in English practice, the ambiguity of the terms and the flexibility of the system are of the essence in everyday negotiations of meaning and significance." See Richard Tapper, "Anthropologists, Historians, and Tribespeople on Tribe and State Formation in the Middle East," in Philip S. Khoury and Joseph Kostiner (eds) *Tribes and State Formation in the Middle East* (Berkeley, CA: University of California Press, 1990), 56.

21 The very word 'Arab' has had the sense of 'people of the desert,' from early times. The great scholar of the Bedouin Jibrail S. Jabbur notes that the word occurs more than 10 times in the Holy Koran in this sense. He goes on to point out that while of course not all Arabs live off the desert, it is the land in which they are formed. "The life of the Arabs has strong roots in nomadism; and even today the Arab sedentary mentality is firmly bonded to that of the Arab bedouin. Hence, anyone trying to…understand the peculiarities of the Arab mentality and the distinguishing features of Arab life must return to the sources of these traits and features in the desert and in bedouin life. The Arab does not know himself, or understand his unique qualities and the range of his capacity for development, if he does not know that the way he lives has its roots in the desert. The tribal spirit, and proceeding from it, family solidarity, ambitions of group leadership, personal inclinations, and disputes over access to authority and leadership—all these and other matters trace their origins back to the organization of the tribe and to the influence of bedouin life." Jabbur adds that many customs and

conventions that operate today have their origins in Bedouin life. He lists, among others, concepts of honor, hospitality, generosity, sanctity of the guest, chivalry and bravery. See Jibrail S. Jabbur, *The Bedouins and the Desert: Aspects of Nomadic Life in the Arab East*, translated by Lawrence I. Conrad, edited by Suhayl J. Jabbur and Lawrence I. Conrad (Albany, NY: State University of New York Press, 1995), 29, 32.

22 The Rwala and the Al Murrah are two examples where this is documented.

23 See, for example, the statements in 1924 by Dr. Paul Harrison, who had first-hand experience: "The organization of the Arabs into tribes and the institution of tribal government must be very ancient indeed. So far as I know, there is not the slightest trace anywhere of Arabs without such a tribal organization. There is nothing to prevent individual Arabs from electing to live in isolation but no such individuals are to be found. An Arab may occasionally leave one tribe and join another, but whether he lives in desert, inland oasis or coast community, the individual Arab owes his allegiance to the sheikh, or chief, of the group." Paul W. Harrison, M.D., *The Arab at Home* (New York, NY: Thomas Y. Crowell Company, 1924), 126. With the fragmentation of societies in modern times and the development of urban living, the universality of Harrison's statement is more uncertain. Yet even today, tribal identity remains a potent force.

24 It is, therefore, important to recognize that while the Bani Yas and the other tribes allied to them were pure Arab Muslims, it is a mistake to ascribe to them traditions and interests that rightly pertain to other Arabs who are located in vastly different circumstances.

25 The 'Lower Gulf' embraces Bahrain, Qatar, and the UAE.

26 The character of 'Buraimi' and 'al Ain' causes much confusion. The modern usage 'al Ain' is to be preferred, as it relates to the Abu Dhabi areas of the Buraimi oasis complex. However, where the original sources cited use the old term, 'Buraimi,' it will appear in the text following the normal academic practice of respecting the integrity of sources.

27 *The Buraimi Memorials 1955: United Kingdom*, Vol. 2, Annexes (Gerrards Cross: Archive Editions, 1987), 11, paragraph 19.

28 *The Buraimi Memorials 1955: Saudi Arabia*, Vol. 1, 3–4.

29 The structure of the Bani Yas is complex, and the observation of Richard Tapper (see note 20) on the ambiguity of terms, especially in translation, should be borne in mind. The Bani Yas are sometimes termed a tribe, with sections, sub-sections and sub-tribes. This implies a strongly segmentary model. It had tribal allies, and hence, it is described as the Bani Yas alliance. But it is also called a 'confederation,' both internally, encompassing the 'sub-tribes' of the Bani Yas, and externally, embracing the allied tribes. Unfortunately, the term 'confederation' has significant and ineradicable connotations in English that do not match the Arab tribal context. In this

book, the Bani Yas are described as a tribe, with the assumption that the groups within it, following the model of flexibility, do not all relate to each other in the same way. Joined with the allied tribes, which changed over time, it is collectively described as the Bani Yas alliance. No terminology exists in any European language that exactly matches the Arab reality, and the form chosen above provides the smallest degree of distortion.

30 Studies of the tribes vary considerably in their depth and coverage. The tribes of the Nafud and the Rub' al Khali have been most widely treated. The Rwala of the Nafud, for example, have been written about in English by Alois Musil and William Lancaster, who lived for considerable periods with the tribes. No non-Arab could ever fully understand the complexities both of tribal dialect and custom, but as Jabbur points out in *The Bedouins and the Desert*, 14–20, most of the Arab writers on the subject of desert peoples were government officials, whose role must have colored their relationships to some extent.

31 This tendency to split into smaller sub-groups has been reflected in a 'segmentary structure,' to provide a model for the way in which tribal polities function. While tribes do divide under environmental or social pressures, there is no single model that describes the way in which they will relate to each other. As a debate within anthropology, this is now largely played out. What is clear is that neither the original segmentary structure devised by Evans Pritchard, nor its modification by Ernest Gellner for Morocco have much relevance to the situation in the Arabian peninsula.

32 One calculation suggests that there are more than 10,000 clans, sub-tribes or sections. See Jabbur, *The Bedouins and the Desert*, 270.

33 The converse, the customary connections requiring mutual support or even vengeance against an enemy, are much more limited.

34 This extends and adapts the four categories of myths, memories, values and symbols proposed by Bassam Tibi. See Bassam Tibi, "The Simultaneity of the Unsimultaneous: Old Tribes and Imposed Nation-States in the Modern Middle East," in Khoury and Kostiner (eds) *Tribes and State Formation in the Middle East*, 142.

35 What concerns us here are not the theoretical analytical structures used by anthropologists to define the 'types' of connection, but those experiences of connection felt by individuals, i.e. the terms and concepts which individuals use "naturally and effortlessly" when talking of those close to them, terms which one would then "readily understand when similarly applied by others." These, then, are the everyday structures of life. The terms for 'brother' are a classic example. On the one hand, they can refer to the son of the same father, and sometimes to sons of the same mother; but they can also refer to *brother* in terms of common antecedents, or in more general terms, such as the *brotherhood of man*. They are frequently used in all these senses. See

Clifford Geertz, *Local Knowledge: Further Essays in Interpretative Anthropology* (New York, NY: Basic Books, 1983), 57.

36 See Mohammed Al-Fahim, *From Rags to Riches: A Story of Abu Dhabi* (London: The London Centre of Arab Studies, 1995), 26–27. For an important anthropological approach to the dynamics of hospitality, see Aida Sami Kanafani, "Aesthetics and Ritual in the United Arab Emirates," Ph.D. dissertation (University of Texas at Austin, 1979), 317–332.

37 See Alois Musil, *The Manners and Customs of the Rwala Bedouins* (New York, NY: American Geographical Society, 1928), 438–454.

38 Ibid., 471–472.

39 Lady Anne Blunt, *Bedouin Tribes of the Euphrates*, Vol. II (London: John Murray, 1879), 210.

40 See Jabbur, *The Bedouins and the Desert*, 315–316. A scholar of literature, he also points out, "In the literature of no other nation I know is such commitment to protect others raised to the grand and glorious levels that are conceded to it by…the Arab spirit in Arabic literature."

41 Frank Henderson Stewart, *Honor* (Chicago, IL: University of Chicago Press, 1994), 102.

42 Hence the term 'segmentary theory' used to describe this form of social organization.

43 See Paul Dresch, "The Significance of the Course Events take in Segmentary Systems," *American Ethnologist* 13, No. 2 (May 1986): 319.

44 For these cases, see Stewart, *Honor*, 83.

45 Steven Caton, "Power, Persuasion, and Language: A Critique of the Segmentary Model in the Middle East," *International Journal of Middle East Studies* 19, No. 1 (February 1987): 89.

46 Dale F. Eickelman, *The Middle East: An Anthropological Approach*, second edition (Englewood Cliffs, NJ: Prentice Hall, 1989), 136.

47 Hendrik van der Meulen suggests that they are "…a 'textbook' example of a tribal confederation, since its constituent parts originated from different back-grounds, histories and ways of livelihood." Hendrik van der Meulen, "The Role of Tribal and Kinship Ties in the Politics of the United Arab Emirates," Ph.D. dissertation (Fletcher School of Law and Diplomacy, 1997), 103.

48 Except of course for the pioneering work by Frauke Heard-Bey, *From Trucial States to United Arab Emirates*, and more recently the Ph.D. dissertation, "The Role of Tribal and Kinship Ties in the Politics of the United Arab Emirates," by Hendrik van der Meulen.

49 See note 29.

50 This is not to suggest that a strong genealogical identity based on descent of itself prevents change; after all, the Bani Yas have an immensely strong sense of family and descent. As Lila Abu-Lughod observed of the Awlad 'Ali, "I had also expected tent-dwelling pastoral nomads who lived quietly

with their herds but found instead that these same people who touted the joys of the desert lived in houses (even if they continued to pitch their tents next to them and spent most of their days in the tents), wore shiny wrist-watches…listened to radios and cassette players, and traveled in Toyota pickup trucks. Unlike me, they did not regard these as alarming signs that they were losing their identity as a cultural group, that they were no longer Bedouins, because they define themselves not primarily by a way of life, however much they value pastoral nomadism and the rigors of the desert, but by some key principles of social organization: genealogy and a tribal order based on the closeness of agnates (paternal relatives) and tied to a code of morality, that of honor and modesty. Their social universe is ordered by these ideological principles, which define individuals' identities and the quality of their relationships to others. These principles are gathered up in Awlad 'Ali notions of 'blood' (*dam*) [original italics], a multi-faceted concept with dense meanings and tremendous cultural force…" Lila Abu-Lughod, *Veiled Sentiments*, 40–41. But while all this was true of the Bani Yas, they managed to preserve an openness in building connections that seemed precluded (in practice) in many other tribal systems.

51   The Al Nahyan are also described, especially in British documents as the Al Bu Falah. For the tradition, see Abdullah Bin Salih Al-Mutawwa, *Al-gawahir wa al-lalya fi tarikh 'uman al-shamaliy*, translated as *Jewellery and Pearls in the History of Northern Oman* (Abu Dhabi: Juma al-Majid Centre for Culture and Heritage, 1994), 36.

52   *The Buraimi Memorials 1955: United Kingdom*, Vol. 1, Part 1, section D. The following section is in part a paraphrase of the material provided there. Hendrik van der Meulen's Ph.D. dissertation, "The Role of Tribal and Kinship Ties in the Politics of the United Arab Emirates," Appendices 1–3 provide a comprehensive overview. He suggests that there are as many as 27 major and minor clans, sections and sub-sections within the system; other estimates are 15 groups and sub-groups.

53   Ibid., 102.

54   Sections of tribes were called *batn* (phratry), sub-sections *fakhth* (moiety) and *ashirah* (clans). See Mohammed Suleiman El Taib, *Mawsu'at al-qaba'il al-arabiyya*, translated as *Encyclopaedia of Arab Tribes* (Cairo: Dar al-Fakr al-Arabi, 1996), Part 1, 21.

55   Edward Henderson, *This Strange Eventful History: Memoirs of Earlier Days in the UAE and Oman* (London: Quartet Books, 1988), 7.

56   Of course, a web of intermarriages in fact achieved this effect.

57   See Ibn Khaldun, *The Muqaddimah*, 249–274.

58   Mann, *Abu Dhabi*, 15.

59   Van der Meulen, "The Role of Tribal and Kinship Ties in the Politics of the United Arab Emirates," 163–167.

60 Musil, *The Manners and Customs of the Rwala Bedouins*, 471.

61 Bichr Farès, *L'honneur chez les Arabes avant l'Islam* (Paris: Librairie d'Amérique et d'Orient, 1932) cited in Paul Dresch, *Tribes, Government, and History in Yemen* (Oxford: Clarendon Press, 1993), 38. "C'est donc grâce aux éléments de l'honneur que les Arabes communaient dans les mêmes idées et fraternisaient dans les mêmes pratiques pour constituer ce qu'on appelle une société."

62 Peter Lienhardt, "The Authority of Shaykhs in the Gulf: An Essay in Nineteenth-Century History," *Arabian Studies* II (1975): 61–75.

63 Martin Buckmaster, then a young Political Officer, wrote, for example, "The great impression on me was their respect for Zayid. It became very clear how popular he was wherever he moved." Cited by Claud Morris, *The Desert Falcon: The story of H.H. Sheikh Zayed Bin Sultan Al Nahiyan, President of the United Arab Emirates* (London: Outline Series of Books, 1976), 36.

CHAPTER 2

1 Off the town of al Muharraq in Bahrain: this was the force sent to protect the refinery at Abadan from the Ottomans and which was then dispatched to capture Baghdad. See, "Administration Report for the Bahrain Agency for the Year 1914," reprinted in *Persian Gulf Administration Reports: 1873–1957*, Vol. VII (Gerrards Cross: Archive Editions, 1986), 58. See also David Fromkin, *A Peace to End all Peace: The Fall of the Ottoman Empire and the Creation of the Modern Middle East* (New York, NY: Henry Holt, 1989), 201–203.

2 See Michael Rice, *The Archaeology of the Arabian Gulf* (London: Routledge, 1994).

3 It is one of the fallacies of many Western histories that portray the Gulf as a remote area, cut off from the rest of the world. Gulf trade has always depended on external markets, and both traders and rulers of the area were always aware of the market conditions that prevailed. With that news came other information about the outside world. See Jack Goody, *The East in the West* (Cambridge: Cambridge University Press, 1996), 52 and Richard Hall, *Empires of the Monsoon: A History of the Indian Ocean and its Invaders* (London: Harper Collins, 1998), passim.

4 See Alan Villiers, "Some Aspects of the Arab Dhow Trade," reprinted in Louise E. Sweet (ed.) *Peoples and Cultures of the Middle East: An Anthropological Reader*, Vol. 1 (Garden City, NY: The Natural History Press, 1970), 155–172.

5 For a succinct statement of these issues, see Kamal Salibi, *A History of Arabia* (Beirut: Caravan Books, 1980), 131–180. As the anthropologist Peter

Lienhardt pointed out, the external contact would also have an impact on the political structure of the internal tribal relationships. For this, see Peter Lienhardt, *Shaikhdoms of Eastern Arabia*, edited by Ahmed Al-Shahi (Oxford: Palgrave Macmillan, 2001), 24–32.

6   The essence of this pattern was observed by Jacob Black-Michaud in another context: "…all conflicts over honor or acts of violence in any given case are designed to show that the protagonists react 'honorably' in all circumstances. Such conflicts may in the long run all be attributed to the same desire to acquire and demonstrate the possession of prestige, thereby reaffirming political status and reinforcing claims to leadership…The very versatility of the notion of honor is intrinsic to its function, which is to provide a zone of ambiguity, creating room for political maneuver. In feuding societies there are few hard and fast rules as to which actions are honorable and which are not. Individuals interpret the notion very much as they please and as circumstances permit, manipulating it in furtherance of their own political ends." See Jacob Black-Michaud, *Cohesive Force: Feud in the Mediterranean and Middle East* (New York, NY: St. Martin's Press, 1975), 178–179.

7   Most Arabian tribal conflicts and alliances were relatively short-lived. The Hinawi–Ghafiri conflict was much more akin to the feud structures of parts of Europe (for example Albania) or parts of North Africa where antagonism could remain fixed and rooted over many generations. However, the obverse of this destructive social power was the need and ability to construct long-lasting alliance systems, of which the Bani Yas system is the most notable example. See David M. Hart, "Clan, Lineage, Local Community and the Feud in a Rifian Tribe," reprinted in Sweet (ed.) *Peoples and Cultures of the Middle East*, Vol. 2, 3–75.

8   Frauke Heard-Bey, *From Trucial States to United Arab Emirates: A Society in Transition*, second enlarged edition (London and New York, NY: Longman, 1996), 276.

9   European historians would recognize the parallel pattern in the Guelf–Ghibelline contest that polarized medieval Germany and Italy. See *The Hutchinson Dictionary of World History* (Oxford: Helicon Publishing, 1993), 248–249.

10 This discussion is partly drawn from Heard-Bey, *From Trucial States to United Arab Emirates*, 276–277. In her analysis, Heard-Bey draws largely on the works by J.G. Lorimer and S.B. Miles. The traditional interpretation, for example, J.C. Wilkinson's *Water and Tribal Settlement in South-East Arabia: A Study of the Aflāj of Oman* (Oxford: Oxford University Press, 1977), 224–225, presents the 'civil war' in terms of descent group alliances (*shaff*). Thus, the Hinawi–Ghafiri polarities in this analysis could be reduced to: Hinawi equals 'Southern Arab' (Qahtani [Yamani]) and Ghafiri equals

'Northern Arab' (Nizari ['Adnani]). However, this simple breakdown does not describe the political reality on the ground and over time. See note 11 below.

11 The traditional interpretation would only make sense if the political system were exclusively governed by sectarian fanaticism on one hand and a rigid structure of tribal allegiance on the other. This provides an 'If X then Y' scenario. So, for example, if a tribe is of 'Adnani origin, then by definition it must be Ghafiri. But this fits neither the facts nor the development of the political situation in Oman. This was not a matter of tribal fanaticism but of interlocked politico-economic interests; indeed, the evolution of the latter did much to wash away a large part of any such residual tendencies. Scholars have produced lists of the tribes and genealogies corresponding to the Hinawi and Ghafiri blocs. It is immediately evident from these lists that the Ghafiri included almost as many Yamani tribes as 'Adnani. Likewise, the Hinawi included as many 'Adnani tribes as Yamani. Wilkinson noted (see note 10) that the emergence of the Hinawi and Ghafiri blocs with such mixed tribal origins was regarded as a remarkable political development in Oman. The reformulation of tribal connections resulted in new political alliances and allegiances. He pointed out that access to water resources (*al aflaj*) was of particular economic interest to some tribes that depended on them for survival. This group acted as a unit and joined either the Hinawi or Ghafiri on the basis of this economic interest, regardless of any tribal or religious affiliation. The reason for the association of Hinawi with tribes of Yamani origin and of Ghafiris with 'Adnani has to do with tribal leadership within the two groups. Muhammad Bin Nasser, leader of the Ghafiri, was born of an 'Adnani group with origins in the Hijaz and Najd; Khalaf Bin Mubarak Al Hinawi came from an Arab tribe that originated in Yemen. Their struggle for dominance in the whole of Oman was of long standing, but it entered a new stage with the civil wars that convulsed the region after the death of Imam Sultan Bin Sayf in 1718. See Wilkinson, *Water and Tribal Settlement in South-East Arabia*, 224–228.

12 See Muhammad Morsy Abdullah, *The United Arab Emirates: A Modern History*, new edition (Westerham Hill: Hurtwood Press, 1994), 110. "…two independent federations emerged at the end of the eighteenth century on the Coast of 'Omān: the Qawāsim federation, with its capital at Rās al-Khaimah, and the Banī Yās federation, centered on Abū Dhabī."

13 See Clarence C. Mann, *Abu Dhabi: Birth of an Oil Shaikhdom* (Beirut: Khayats, 1969), 20.

14 In one version, the island is called Umm Dhabi ('mother of the gazelle') rather than Abu Dhabi. See Hamdi Tammam, *Zayed bin Sultan Al-Nahayyan: The Leader and the March*, second revised edition (Tokyo: Dai Nippon Printing Company, 1983), 21.

15   About the role of the Al Nahyan in the Bani Yas, see Chapter 1.

16   Tammam, *Zayed bin Sultan Al-Nahayyan*, 21.

17   Shaikh Diyab was killed by a member of another branch of the Al Bu
     Falah, who had a grudge against him and plotted his death. His son Shaikh
     Shakhbut tried and executed the 10 conspirators, but the man who actually
     killed his father fled the country. See Alan de Lacy Rush, *Ruling Families
     of Arabia: United Arab Emirates*, Vol. 1 (Gerrards Cross: Archive Editions,
     1991), 31. This is the "Historical Sketch of the Beniyas Tribe of Arabs,"
     from the year 1761 to the close of 1831 prepared by Lt. S. Hennell etc.,
     and reprinted from the Records of the Bombay Government.

18   In some cases, the sheer numbers of these invaders made it impossible for
     separate tribes to defeat them. Then a group of tribes had to come together
     to resist the incursion. Such temporary alliances were unstable and hard to
     maintain, which is why the military advantage lay with the Wahhabis.

19   "I beg to report that on Sheikh Saeed bin Tahnoun and his forces taking
     up a position near Brymee [al Ain] a party of Awamir joined him to the
     number of 200 men: He then sent to the Naeem Syf bin Humood and
     their Allies to invite them to hasten to him for the purpose of prosecuting
     hostilities against...the Nedgdees...the Zowahir tribe tendered their
     allegiance and allied themselves with him and so likewise the Section of
     the Zowahir who were with Syf bin Ali deserted the latter and went over
     to Saeed bin Tahnoon. In short Saeed bin Tahnoon and his forces with all
     the Zowahir on the 4th May surrounded and attacked Syf bin Ali in his
     Fort...He fought for one day but receiving no assistance...he resigned his
     Authority into the hands of Saeed and vacated the Fort. The latter seized
     all his property as well as horses and camels and destroyed the Fort." *The
     Buraimi Memorials 1955: United Kingdom*, Vol. 2, Annex B, No. 11
     (Gerrards Cross: Archive Editions, 1987), 56–57.

20   A more recent example was Shaikh Khalifa Bin Zayid, who, after the death
     of his father, Zayid the Great, refused the offer of leadership of the Bani
     Yas, lived through a time of turmoil, and died in his nineties.

21   For these events, see "The Historical Sketch of the Beniyas Tribe," in
     Rush, *Ruling Families of Arabia*, 31–63.

22   Cited in Tammam, *Zayed bin Sultan Al-Nahayyan*, 33. For a full con-
     temporary account of the Ruler's intrepid qualities, see Rush, *Ruling
     Families of Arabia*, 27–65, reprinted from selections of the Records of
     the Bombay Government, No. XXIV, New Series 1856, 461–496. The
     Records of the Bombay Government should be read with care since they
     are based on hearsay and incorporate some true and some questionable
     material.

23   See *Records of the Emirates*, Vol. 1 (Gerrards Cross: Archive Editions, 1990),
     222, 547–549.

24 See Letter from Captain John Pepper, May 16, 1835. Reprinted in *Records of the Emirates*, Vol. 2, 35.

25 In this case, the new Ruler was not involved in the plot against his predecessor, but was chosen as his successor by the family after the coup was suppressed. Shaikh Khalifa and Shaikh Sultan were killed in an act of private vengeance by one 'Isa Bin Khalid and his family. See Rush, *Ruling Families of Arabia*, 55.

26 Ibid., 54. This is the "Conclusion to the Year 1853" recounting earlier events provided by Lt. H.F. Disbrowe.

27 Ibid., 55.

28 See Peter Lienhardt, "The Authority of Shaykhs in the Gulf: An Essay in Nineteenth-Century History," *Arabian Studies* II (1975), 61. This is a wide-ranging analysis that shows both the need for Rulers to gain implied or actual consent for their actions, and how they operated within a well-established system of political values.

29 He had left with his mother in 1845.

30 It is not easy to find an exact parallel to the structure of politics among the Bani Yas, for reasons outlined in the first chapter. Based on custom, tradition and immediate self-interest, it requires a systematic analysis in the manner of Sir Lewis Namier's *Structure of Politics at the Accession of George III* (London: Macmillan & Co., 1929). Namier's contention that 'interest' was the prime mover in the developed and mature system that existed in 1760 has been challenged but not overthrown.

31 The policy might be stated as follows: 1. To retain a secure base in the respect and affections of the Ruler's own people. 2. To follow an essentially peaceful policy binding more and more tribes as allies. When the Rulers followed this policy line, as with Zayid the Great and Zayid Bin Sultan, they achieved dramatic success.

32 Shaikh Zayid had prudently taken refuge in Dubai to escape the dangers of Abu Dhabi town. He was to rule jointly with his brother, but it was clear from the outset that he was to be the dominant partner.

33 See Lienhardt, "The Authority of Shaykhs in the Gulf." Lienhardt's Oxford D.Phil. thesis, reprinted in part in *Shaikhdoms of Eastern Arabia*, expands on his arguments, especially 165–227.

34 For this issue, see Chapter 1 and Alois Musil, *The Manners and Customs of the Rwala Bedouins* (New York, NY: American Geographical Society, 1928).

35 The encounter in which he killed Shaikh Khalid Bin Sultan single-handedly became a legend among the Bedouin.

36 See Abdullah, *The United Arab Emirates*, 97.

37 For this development, see Henry Rosenfeld, "The Social Composition of the Military in the Process of State Formation in the Arabian Desert," *Journal of the Royal Anthropological Society* 95 (1965): 75–86, 174–194.

38 This was the member of the Al Quraysh tribe recognized by the Ottoman government as the chief official in the Holy City. All members of the tribe were entitled to the title of 'Sharif' provided that they were also a direct descendant of the Prophet Muhammad (PBUH). Although the records do not specify the name of the Sharif, the date indicates that most probably it was Aun Al Rafiq. Also, see J.G. Lorimer, *Gazetteer of the Persian Gulf, Oman and Central Arabia*, Vol. 2 (Gerrards Cross: Archive Editions, 1986), 772. Lorimer notes that more than 20 years after he made the pilgrimage, in 1904 "he received a fine mare with trappings from the Sharīf of Makkah," so it is evident that the connection continued for a long period.

39 See Abdullah, *The United Arab Emirates*, 98.

40 See the Administration Report of the Persian Gulf Political Residency and Muscat Political Agency for 1891–92: "In former years … tribes would have invaded and plundered the country until their claims had been satisfied. Owing, however, to the good offices of the Chief of Abu Dhabi [Zayid the Great], the Beduins abstained from their usual course of action. Peace was established between the Chief of Abu Dhabi and the Al-Bu-Karuban section of the Naim at Bereymi [al Ain], and he married the daughter of the holder of that fort. All the Beni Ghafri tribes, including some hitherto considered as Jowasimi, such as the Beni Katab and the Beni Kaab, are said to fight now under the Abu Dhabi flag." Reprinted in *Records of the Emirates*, Vol. 4, 519. Clarence Mann sums up the whole issue succinctly: "Although Shaikh Zayed attempted to remain aloof from the continuous wars and establish himself as the arbitrator between the various shaikhdoms, he was drawn into many of the conflicts by his tribal commitments." See Mann, *Abu Dhabi*, 56.

41 For example, it was noted in the Administration Report of the Persian Gulf Political Residency and Muscat Political Agency for 1889–90: "In August a considerable section of the Al-Morrah tribe bound themselves by compact to act in concert with the Beni Yas against Katr raiders." See *Records of the Emirates*, Vol. 4, 508. Elsewhere, Mann noted that after his pilgrimage, Shaikh Zayid "made increased efforts to avoid participation in the various conflicts and whenever possible to establish peace between adversaries. In 1883 he was successful in settling a particularly widespread feud that involved Umm al-Qaiwain, 'Ajman, Ras al-Khaimah, Sharjah and the Nu'aim tribe." See Mann, *Abu Dhabi*, 57.

42 See Abdullah, *The United Arab Emirates*, 98.

43 See "Administration Report on the Persian Gulf Political Residency for 1905–1906," in *Persian Gulf Administration Reports*, Vol. VI, 11.

44 His relationship with the Al Dhawahir in al Ain was characterized by a move from military action to benevolence; both techniques secured the tribe as an ally rather than an enemy. See Lorimer, *Gazetteer of the Persian Gulf, Oman and Central Arabia*, Vol. 2, 770–772.

45 Lorimer calculated these at $75,500 of which pearling dues and other pearling revenues accounted for $62,000. Lorimer's comment on Zayid the Great is also interesting. "The present Shaikh...rules his principality absolutely within the limits to which his powers of coercion extend; and, though his control over the Bedouin portion of his subjects is incomplete, as is the case more or less in all Arab Shaikhdoms, his authority over them is unusually great. He is by far the most powerful personality in Trucial 'Omān at the present time..." His influence was described as "dominant" throughout the region. See Lorimer, *Gazetteer of the Persian Gulf, Oman and Central Arabia*, Vol. 7, 409.

46 Ibid., 410–411.

47 For a description of the structure of British officialdom in the Arabian Gulf, see Chapter 1, note 5.

48 See the report of Lt. Arnold Burrowes Kemball of his visit to the Trucial shaikhdoms in 1844, reprinted in *Records of the Emirates*, Vol. 2, 97–112.

49 The innovation came as an additional clause to Article 3 of the treaty. Up to that point, it had followed the lines of the Ten Year Truce of 1843, with the signatories binding themselves not to retaliate for any act of aggression, but to "inform the British Resident or the Commodore at Bassidore, who will forthwith take the necessary steps for obtaining reparation..." See *Records of the Emirates*, Vol. 2, 143.

50 In 1868, a British naval expedition anchored off Abu Dhabi and fined Zayid The Great for an attack he had made on Qatar in association with the Ruler of Bahrain and his men. This attack had a dubious legality since the treaty of 1853 only prohibited maritime war between signatories. Qatar was not part of the agreement. After this episode, he began to use the provisions of the maritime treaty of 1853 to his advantage rather than breaking its terms. See *Records of the Emirates*, Vol. 3, 527–560 for documents detailing these events.

51 For a good treatment of these issues, see Abdullah, *The United Arab Emirates*, 96–103. As he sums it up, "Abū Dhabī's dealings with the British and their representative...were remarkably untroubled."

52 However, Shaikh Zayid did not fall into the error of being pliant to all British requests. For example, on occasions he would act, as did the other Rulers in their openness, to approaches from external powers, like France and the Ottoman Empire. He also received emissaries from the court of Tehran, to the annoyance of the British Resident. However, there was nothing within the treaty of 1853 that prevented this activity.

53 "Administration Report on the Persian Gulf Political Residency for 1905–1906," in *Persian Gulf Administration Reports*, Vol. VI, 11.

54 See Abdullah, *The United Arab Emirates*, 96–98.

55 Their sole preoccupations on land were the slave trade and arms supply which were the cause of many conflicts with the tribal leaders.

56 They left in 1836, and more followed in 1845 and 1869.

57 London's objections came because the Ottoman government, which had occupied the al Hasa province in 1871, had formed a close connection with the Al Thani Rulers of neighboring Qatar. The Foreign Office hoped to extract the Al Thani from their Ottoman connection and was anxious that British support for Abu Dhabi over Khur al 'Udaid should not compromise these broader British interests. It was only after 1881 that the Foreign Office reversed its stand, and saw Abu Dhabi's possession of the settlement as beneficial to the British case against the Ottomans.

58 See "Memorandum on the causes of hostility between Shaikh Za'eed-bin-Khalifah, Chief of Abu-Dhabi and Shaikh Jasim-bin-Mohamed Thani, and the raids made by each of them on other tribesmen or dependents," reprinted in *Records of the Emirates*, Vol. 4, 327–330.

59 This tone of respect emerges in the long correspondence over Khur al 'Udaid, which finally resulted in a decision of the Government of India in 1877: "…the Governor-General in Council empowers you to use your best endeavours to promote a reunion between the colonists at Odeid and the main body of the Beni Yas tribe of Abuthabi, and further authorizes you to afford assistance, if necessary, to the Trucial Chief of Abuthabi in coercing the seceders." See *Records of the Emirates*, Vol. 4, 299.

60 See "Administration Report of the Trucial Coast of Oman for the Year 1909," reprinted in Rush, *Ruling Families of Arabia*, 92.

61 See "Relations of Trucial 'Omān with the Sultanate of 'Omān, 1892–1907," reprinted in Rush, *Ruling Families of Arabia*, 91. "…during the last ten years, the Sultan of 'Omān had been paying a cash subsidy of $3,000 per annum to the Shaikh of Abu Dhabi on condition of his restraining the Bedouin tribes…as far eastwards as 'Ibri in Dhāhirah and perhaps also in parts of Ruūs-al-Jibal, though all these belonged to the Sultanate, the influence wielded by Shaikh Zāid-bin-Khalīfah far outweighed that of Saiyid Faisal-bin-Turki [Sultan of Oman]."

62 See J.C. Wilkinson, *Arabia's Frontiers: The Story of Britain's Boundary Drawing in the Desert* (London: I.B. Tauris, 1991), 70–75.

63 In January 1879, the Political Resident, Lt. Col. Edward Charles Ross, wrote to the Government of India, "There can be no doubt the appearance of the Turks in the Persian Gulf, and their acquisition somewhat curtailed the sphere of British control and limited our influence correspondingly." See *Records of the Emirates*, Vol. 4, 323. Much of the British concern revolved around the arms trade in the Gulf that eventually ended up in British India or Afghanistan.

64 The Treaty is reprinted in *Records of the Emirates*, Vol. 4, 243.

65 From roughly 1900, the fear of 'declining influence' becomes stronger. The letter to the Political Resident of June 10, 1901 is unambiguous. It states

that the problem of declining influence had already been discussed at the highest levels in the Government of India. The issue was that, "…in Colonel Ross' day, not one of these Trucial Chiefs would have winked an eye without looking at him first and it was even more so under Sir L. Pelly." Lt. Col. Kemball, the Political Resident to whom this letter was addressed, was asked, "Does the Resident still act as promptly and authoritatively as before, when any of the Chiefs misbehave, and is his intervention as implicitly accepted? If not, is there any way in which we can assist him, and can you suggest any means, short of establishing a protectorate, to make it even clearer than it already is both to the Chiefs and to others on this coast [that] our interests and influence are predominant and that we mean to keep them so." Couched in the courteous language of British administration, this is virtually an order for the Resident to rule with a heavier hand— which he did. See *Records of the Emirates*, Vol. 5, 37–38.

66   Memorandum, November 19, 1898, reprinted in *Records of the Emirates*, Vol. 5, 26. See also the letter of April 15, 1902 to the Political Resident asking for suggestions as to "steps which might be taken to increase our influence." Ibid., 81.

67   See Hansard Parliamentary Debates, 4th series, May 5, 1903, reprinted in *Records of the Emirates*, Vol. 5, 106–119. "Within recent years, however, we, for the first time, see Russian and French gun-boats coming into the…Gulf. Russian, German, and French Consuls have been appointed to various posts…and Arabic leaflets vilifying British power are oftentimes disseminated among the tribes." (See page 108).

68   Ibid., 109–110. "…there is no doubt that in the Gulf…we are feeling very keenly the [commercial] competition of other Powers." And, as the Marquess of Lansdowne, the Secretary of State for Foreign Affairs, observed, "It is impossible, to my mind, to dissociate our commercial and our political interests." (See page 116).

69   This was styled a 'Durbar,' in the Indian manner.

70   For Curzon's tour of the Gulf see *Records of the Emirates*, Vol. 5, 125–181, specifically 133. The 1853 Treaty of Peace in Perpetuity talked only of "prosecution of our feuds by sea" and "a perfect maritime truce." See *Records of the Emirates*, Vol. 2, 142–143.

71   *Records of the Emirates*, Vol. 5, 133.

72   In his study, Muhammad Morsy Abdullah talks about the "positive British policy" advanced by Curzon and implemented by Cox. 'Status quo' was Curzon's term but in fact this was a substantial extension of the doctrine of control by a means short of declaring a protectorate, which had been rejected by the Foreign Office. See Abdullah, *The United Arab Emirates*, 27. The British authorities were determined to compile a complete history of their intervention in the region and retain control of the archive. In this respect,

two significant research projects were initiated in 1903. The first was the commission to Jerome A. Saldanha to examine, summarize and edit the documents relating to the affairs of the Gulf between 1600 and 1905, to be found in the State Papers held in Bombay. These were printed for official use in 1906 as *Selections from State Papers, Bombay*, commonly known as "Saldanha's Précis." The second was a major investigation entrusted to J.G. Lorimer to establish the current and historical facts concerning the peoples and geography of the region. This was printed as the *Gazetteer of the Persian Gulf, Oman and Central Arabia* between 1908 and 1915. Both were restricted in distribution, being regarded as highly sensitive strategic documents.

73 "Address delivered by His Excellency Lord Curzon, Viceroy and Governor-General of India, to the Trucial Chiefs of the Arab Coast, at a Public Durbar held at Shergah on the 21st November 1903," reprinted in *Records of the Emirates*, Vol. 5, 142.

74 See letter, Barnes to Kemball (Political Resident), June 10, 1901, reprinted in *Records of the Emirates*, Vol. 5, 36–37. "His Excellency the Viceroy remarked that if any foreign power commenced to tamper with these tribes, he would be prepared to bring them under our protectorate at once, whether they liked it or not. But that it was hardly advisable to do this, until we were obliged...unless we were prepared to constantly interfere in the Chiefs' internal affairs. In His Excellency's opinion, the real way to deal with these tribes is, by a judicious policy of overlordship, by occasional visits in a gunboat, and by smart reprisals...to acquire such an influence over them that the man, who has succeeded to a Chiefship, by whatever means, comes to us of his own accord and asks for our recognition...We can be guided by circumstances and do as we please."

75 T.C. Fowle (Political Resident, Bushire) to Aubrey Metcalfe (Secretary to the Government of India), March 17, 1939, reprinted in *Records of the Emirates*, Vol. 8, 60.

76 A status officially certified when in 1900 the Royal Navy was instructed to fire five salutes to Shaikh Zayid the Great, but only three for the other Rulers of the region.

77 The flag issue was a complex one: Shaikh Zayid the Great and other Shaikhs objected strongly to its political overtones. In the 1820 treaty, Article 3 depicted the flag of 'the friendly Arabs,' which was a white flag with a central rectangle in red. For the Arabic text of the document sent to the Rulers as a reminder, see *Records of the Emirates*, Vol. 5, 176.

78 See Abdullah, *The United Arab Emirates*, 99–101 for this whole episode.

79 Cox was appointed Acting Resident in April 1904 and confirmed as Resident pro. tem. until he was appointed Political Resident in January 1909.

80 This complex affair stemmed from the new young Ruler of one of the emirates (Umm al Qaiwain) seeking to overturn the established pattern of alliances and connections. He flouted the decision of a council of Shaikhs presided over by Zayid the Great. Therefore, the latter, in alliance with the Rulers of Dubai, Sharjah and Ajman, took action to enforce the traditional settlement. Cox appeared with two warships and insisted on settling the matter. In a memorandum to the Government of India, he justified his intervention on the grounds that there had been a technical breach of the maritime truce because Zayid the Great had sent some tribesmen he had detained to Abu Dhabi by sea. See *Records of the Emirates*, Vol. 5, 464–465. For this episode, also see Abdullah, *The United Arab Emirates*, 101–102.

81 See *Records of the Emirates*, Vol. 5, 37, 104.

82 Lorimer, *Gazetteer of the Persian Gulf, Oman and Central Arabia*, Vol. 2, 752.

83 Ibid., 752–753, for the September 1905 and subsequent April 1906 meetings.

84 Ibid., 753.

85 Letter of June 18, 1904 to L.W. Dane, Secretary to the Government of India, Simla, reprinted in Rush, *Ruling Families of Arabia*, 86–87.

86 See Abdullah, *The United Arab Emirates*, 32–38.

87 Ibid., 35. On this episode, see also Obaid A. Butti, "Imperialism, Tribal Structure, and the Development of Ruling Elites: A Socioeconomic History of the Trucial States between 1892 and 1939," Ph.D. dissertation (Georgetown University, 1992), 132–140.

88 This was the Anglo–Ottoman Draft Convention of 1913. It was never ratified because of the outbreak of the First World War, but the British later chose to act as if it had been formally agreed, arguing that all the substantive points had been agreed. The line agreed in this document became the Blue Line that bedeviled relations between Saudi Arabia and the British for so long.

89 October 27, 1913 and May 14, 1914 respectively. See *Records of the Emirates*, Vol. 7, 768.

90 In fact, it was 1922 before these agreements were concluded. See *Records of the Emirates*, Vol. 7, 778–782.

91 "It was thus extremely difficult for a ruler to maintain a stable relationship with the British authorities; he had to rely on his wits and political intuition." See Rosemarie Said Zahlan, *The Origins of the United Arab Emirates: A Political and Social History of the Trucial States* (London: Macmillan Press, 1978), 67.

92 Ibid., 26–27, 107.

93 In 1929, the Political Resident, Lt. Col. Cyril Barrett, wrote, "Before the unfortunate *Hyacinth* [original italics] incident of 1910 the personal influence of Sir Percy Cox had gone far to break down the barriers of reserve and suspicion; but the whole position gained was lost by that

unfortunate episode, and it has never been recovered." Barrett to Government of India, September 5, 1929, reprinted in *Records of the Emirates*, Vol. 7, 92.

94   This was stated in its most precise and succinct form in the lengthy *Memorandum respecting British Interests in the Persian Gulf*, of February 12, 1905: "If Great Britain has become, in any sense, the arbiter and guardian of the Gulf, it has not been through a restless ambition urging her on to the control of the waste places of the earth, but in obedience to the calls that have been made upon her in the past to enforce peace between warring tribes, to give a free course to trade, to hold back the arm of the marauder and the oppressor, to stand between the slave trader and his victim." This is simple casuistry, to say the least. The local tribes and their Rulers never asked for British intervention in any form. The "calls" came from interested British parties and not the people of the area. See *Records of the Emirates*, Vol. 5, 349.

95   Joel Beinin and Zachary Lockman, "1919: Labor Upsurge and National Revolution," reprinted in Albert H. Hourani, Philip S. Khoury and Mary C. Wilson (eds) *The Modern Middle East: A Reader* (Berkeley and Los Angeles, CA: University of California Press, 1993), 395–428.

96   For a succinct statement of these developments see William L. Cleveland, *A History of the Modern Middle East* (Boulder, CO: Westview Press, 1994), 181–212 and more fully in M.E. Yapp, *The Near East Since the First World War: A History to 1995*, second edition (London: Longman, 1996), 69–115.

97   Cox occupied the post from 1904 to November 1914. Between 1915 and 1927, seven different officers held the post temporarily. The first substantive Political Resident to be appointed after Cox was Lt. Col. Lionel Haworth in January 1927. He was replaced in November 1928 by Sir Frederick W. Johnston. In April 1929, he in turn was replaced by Lt. Col. Barrett, who served for only eight months until November 1929 and was then followed by Lt. Col. H.V. Biscoe, who died in office in 1932. For the dates of posting, see Zahlan, *The Origins of the United Arab Emirates*, 243–244. Barrett wrote during his tenure in 1929, "No successor has occupied the position of Sir Percy Cox, and during a recent flying boat visit to Abu Dhabi, Captain Prior was surprised to find that not even the name of a single successor of 'Kokus' is known in that town. This is due to lack of touch and this lack of touch was due first to the preoccupation of the war and subsequently to the withdrawal of the Resident's despatch vessel." See Barrett to Government of India, September 5, 1929, reprinted in *Records of the Emirates*, Vol. 7, 92.

98   These implications are suggested in a valuable study by Aida Sami Kanafani. She points out, "In the UAE both host and guest are involved in a power relationship aimed at absorbing each other in the visiting interaction… The guest seems to be subjected to a rite of passage by the host aimed at neutralizing the power of the guest and incorporating him within his

'goodwill.'" Not to be able to offer hospitality reduced the power and status of the Political Resident. Kanafani concludes, "Summarizing the power of the host and the power of the guest one may suggest that each element of the host–guest pole strives to have control over the visiting situation." Lack of a capacity for proper reciprocity was a serious handicap. See Aida Sami Kanafani, "Aesthetics and Ritual in the United Arab Emirates" Ph.D. dissertation (University of Texas at Austin, 1979), 318, 332.

99   Zahlan, *The Origins of the United Arab Emirates*, 27. See also note 97.

100 In January 1921, a commission was appointed to work out the best structure for dealing with the 'Middle East.' The consequent re-arrangement of responsibilities lasted until 1926, when it was re-organized again, and in 1928 the new arrangements were thrown into the melting-pot once more. See Abdullah, *The United Arab Emirates*, 40–42.

101 "Because British policy was so uncertain and idiosyncratic, not always conforming to the treaties (which were always binding on the rulers), the management of relations with the British was far from easy. The ruler could not safely predict how the British would react to a given question, mainly because it was often difficult for the British representatives themselves to know how London or Delhi would choose to interpret policy. Moreover, British policy in the Gulf was in a state of transition: what new courses of action the increased importance of the Coast demanded had not yet been fully decided." See Zahlan, *The Origins of the United Arab Emirates*, 66.

102 The idea of a protectorate was raised again, and again rejected. See *Records of the Emirates*, Vol. 5, 101–116.

103 See Zahlan, *The Origins of the United Arab Emirates*, 34.

104 *The Buraimi Memorials 1955: United Kingdom*, Vol. 1, 28.

105 J.B. Kelly, *Eastern Arabian Frontiers* (London and New York, NY: Frederick Praeger, 1964), 115–123.

106 The role of the elder son of Zayid the Great, Shaikh Khalifa Bin Zayid, who had refused the rulership on his own account, was crucial. When Shaikh Saqr Bin Zayid violently took power from his brother, Sultan, he sought to secure the persons of his nephews, Shakhbut, Hazza, Khalid and Zayid, who had sought refuge first with friendly tribes and later in neighboring states—Dubai, Qatar and Saudi Arabia. Failing to control or eliminate his nephews, Shaikh Saqr turned on his surviving brothers, Khalifa and Muhammad. As a result of his actions, the Al Nahyan family, finally united against turbulence and violence, came together in support of the sons of Shaikh Sultan. The new Ruler, Shaikh Shakhbut, ruled from 1928 with the manifest support of his uncles, specifically Khalifa Bin Zayid, while he concluded an agreement with his brothers never to use violence on each other, a pact imposed on all of them by their mother. On these events, see Zahlan, *The Origins of the United Arab Emirates*, 42–45.

107 See Residency Agent, Sharjah, to Political Resident, Bushire, and a report transmitted via G.C. Barrett, Political Agent, Bahrain. The Agent observed, "Zaid a small boy still at his mother's breast [this cannot be other than figurative] was taken by her to her father Butti in Baraimi [al Ain] where she is still living...Butti is one of the leaders of the Qubaisat section of the Bani Yas and this accounts for the enmity which this section bears to the present Shaikh of Abu Dhabi..." This is a hearsay report, but it seems to be accurate in essence. See Rush, *Ruling Families of Arabia*, 144.

108 See Tammam, *Zayed bin Sultan Al-Nahayyan*, 52. "Ever since his seventh year of age, Zayed used to chatter in his father's Majlis, grasping knowledge...He would never stop asking questions or seeking clarification."

109 It was during this time that Shaikh Zayid developed some of his life-long friendships, particularly with Al Shaiba Bin Hamil, Mubarak Bin Fadhil, Muhammad Bin Ahmad Al Otaiba and, later, Ahmad Khalifa Al Suwaidi. See Shaikh Zayid's later interview with the Egyptian journalist Wagi Abu Zahri in *Akhbar al-Yawm*, January 1973.

CHAPTER 3

1 Residency Agent, Sharjah, to Lt. Col. L. Haworth, Political Resident in the Persian Gulf, May 1, 1928, reprinted in *Records of the Emirates*, Vol. 7 (Gerrards Cross: Archive Editions, 1990), 194.

2 See Clarence C. Mann, *Abu Dhabi: Birth of an Oil Shaikhdom* (Beirut: Khayats, 1969), 72.

3 Cited in Rosemarie Said Zahlan, *The Origins of the United Arab Emirates: A Political and Social History of the Trucial States* (London: Macmillan Press, 1978), 181.

4 Percy Cox, "Some excursions in Oman," *Geographical Journal* LXVI (September 1925): 199.

5 It should be noted that Shaikh Zayid, during his time as the Ruler's Representative in al Ain, always found some means of making payments to the tribes, although he was perennially short of cash. He did this, for example, by borrowing money from local merchants on his own recognizance so the trust with the tribes could be maintained. See Frauke Heard-Bey, "Der Prozess der Staatswerdung in arabischen Ölexportländern," *Vierteljahreshefte für Zeitgeschichte* 23, No. 2 (April 1975), 182, note 59. In Shaikh Shakhbut's case, it was more a question of approach towards expenditure rather than an absolute lack of funds.

6 Still, as far as the author is concerned, "Sheikh Shakhbut is a hero of this book." See Roderic Owen, *The Golden Bubble: Arabian Gulf Documentary* (London: Collins, 1957), 93, 98.

7   See *Records of the Emirates*, Vol. 8, 73–87. Many currencies circulated in the Gulf, the most prized being the eighteenth-century Austrian Maria Theresa silver *thaler*. However, most payments were made in Indian rupees.

8   For the contract and financial arrangements, see *Records of the Emirates*, Vol. 8, 609–619.

9   Ibid., 641–662.

10 The Trucial Coast was not very desirable terrain for the oil companies. There were no immediately obvious oil-bearing geological formations, and given both the size of the exploration zone and the difficult working conditions it was a highly speculative venture. The search for oil cost the huge sum of £12 million before any onshore finds were made, and when found they were at a depth far greater than anywhere else in the area. The enthusiasts were the government in London, which was anxious to have a British firm in place before American (or other) companies could get additional concessions by dealing with the local Rulers. Although by treaty the British government could veto negotiations, if there were no British company willing and able to undertake exploration, they would not in practice have been able to prevent the Rulers agreeing terms with a non-British company. This had been the experience in Bahrain. Personal communication from David G. Heard OBE.

11 J.E. Peterson, in an important article, suggested that it was the role of the British over 150 years that served to concentrate power in the hands of a limited number of shaikhs. He also suggests that it was the revenue from oil wealth that allowed them to "consolidate their internal positions, as well as to advance their prestige at the expense of the Rulers of non-oil producing shaykhdoms." However, in the case of Shaikh Shakhbut, while he was aware of his potential power, he did not exploit it. See J.E. Peterson, "Tribes and Politics in Eastern Arabia," *Middle East Journal* 31, No. 3 (Summer 1977): 297–312, especially 303.

12 Cited in Zahlan, *The Origins of the United Arab Emirates*, 122–123.

13 Letter of 13th Ramadan 1364 (August 22, 1945) from Shaikh Shakhbut Bin Sultan Bin Zayed, Ruler of Abu Dhabi to the Political Agent, Bahrain, reprinted in *Records of the Emirates*, Vol. 8, 158.

14 See Telegram from the Political Resident, Bushire to the Secretary of State for India, London, dated May 8, 1939. "Shaikhs at present are under wholesome impression that we have right of jurisdiction over British subjects and non Moslem foreigners…An approach to Shaikhs however for <u>formal</u> [original emphasis] cession would probably destroy this impression and at any rate in the case of some of them would result in refusal to cede jurisdiction." Reprinted in *Records of the Emirates*, Vol. 8, 135. This matter was taken further in a letter from the Political Resident to the Secretary of State, of the same date. The Political Resident argued against any attempt to

extend Britain's formal powers on several grounds, "(1) the Shaikhs will not believe our object to be solely war legislation, (2) they may demand a quid pro quo [original emphasis], (3) the Shaikhs of Abu Dhabi, Sharjah and Ras al Khaimah are likely to refuse to cede the jurisdiction sought..." Ibid., 137.

15 His disillusion was crowned barely a year later, on December 21, 1946, when the government in London published the Trucial States Order which brought Abu Dhabi more firmly within the British orbit than ever before. For the text of the Order, see *Records of the Emirates*, Vol. 8, 169–192.

16 Shaikh Zayid remarked to Claud Morris that the war was "as a distant sound." See Claud Morris, *The Desert Falcon: The story of H.H. Sheikh Zayed Bin Sultan Al Nahiyan, President of the United Arab Emirates* (London: Outline Series of Books, 1976), 29.

17 As the Washington-based Middle East Institute, founded in 1946, expressed it in a statement issued and reissued over time, "The Second World War brought the United States to its major and enduring politico-strategic involvement with the Middle East. Strategically, the Middle East was a vast intercontinental crossroads between Eurasia and Africa along which were strewn the 'wells of power,' and it became a critical supply route, operated by the United States, for the delivery of war aid to the Soviet Union, especially through the...Gulf and Iran. Two events, coming on the heels of the Second World War, intensified the American involvement in the Middle East. First, Soviet moves in Iran and Turkey, and Soviet encouragement of guerrilla warfare in Greece, convinced President Truman that a new Soviet offensive in the Middle East was in the making...The second event was the collapse of British efforts to find a viable and acceptable compromise in the Palestine problem." J.E. Peterson (ed.) *American Interests in the Middle East* (Washington, DC: The Middle East Institute, 1969), 3–4.

18 He was, after all, an essential party to the family pact that guaranteed fraternal support for Shaikh Shakhbut.

19 This certainly proved the case during the 1950s. Shaikh Zayid argued for a league among all the brothers to ensure the security of Abu Dhabi, but the Ruler would not work with his brothers on this basis.

20 The reference here is to Shaikh Khalifa Bin Zayid.

21 Loch (Political Agent, Bahrain) to the Political Resident in Bushire, February 17, 1935, reprinted in *Records of the Emirates*, Vol. 8, 82–85.

22 See Administration Report of the Bahrain Agency and the Trucial Coast for the year 1944, reprinted in *Persian Gulf Administration Reports: 1873–1957*, Vol. X (Gerrards Cross: Archive Editions, 1986), 23.

23 In the days of super-highways, it is now not more than a two-hour journey. In the past, it was a rough and arduous track between Abu Dhabi and al Ain, a journey lasting several days. See Edward Henderson, *This Strange Eventful History: Memoirs of Earlier Days in the UAE and Oman* (Dubai: Motivate

Publishing, 1993 edition), 47–48; see also, Mohammed Al-Fahim, *From Rags to Riches: A Story of Abu Dhabi* (London: The London Centre of Arab Studies, 1995), 54. The population fluctuated from winter to summer, but it seems on anecdotal evidence to have suffered less of a decline than Abu Dhabi in the hard days of the 1930s. Accurate figures do not exist, although great efforts were made in the 1950s to construct precise totals.

24 See Henderson, *This Strange Eventful History*, 67–69.

25 Other tribes in the wider area of al Dhafrah included the Al Manahil, the Al Rashid and the Bani Ka'ab, as well as the Bani Qitab.

26 The Sultan's actual power in the area of al Ain was negligible because it was far away from his center of government and controlled by some of the tribes hostile to his family.

27 The territorial disputes of 1934 were not concerned with al Ain and the surrounding villages, although it became a focal point of the later claim in 1949.

28 This should not be confused with the Koranic duty to pay *zakat*, which was an obligation to be performed by each individual directly. While the Saudi government might collect the tax in its own territory, it tried to collect the tax from tribes in Abu Dhabi, which could not by any stretch of the imagination be considered Saudi subjects, under some more general precept. The two appendices dealing with *zakat* in the Saudi Memorial (1955) are contradictory. See *The Buraimi Memorials 1955: Saudi Arabia* (Gerrards Cross: Archive Editions, 1987), Appendix B, Parts 1 and 2, 291–327, especially 318–319, "Misuse of the Term Zakah."

29 Thomas to Political Resident, June 13, 1927, cited in Zahlan, *The Origins of the United Arab Emirates*, 85.

30 Unpublished FO 371/163205 33829, Lt. Col. Edge to Political Agency Abu Dhabi, March 23, 1962.

31 The case presented by the Saudi government to the International Tribunal in respect of Abu Dhabi was tendentious, depending on a concept of boundaries that was undermined by the full weight of the evidence. In some cases, copies of crucial documents could not be found in the Saudi archives, in others, claims of tribal allegiance were shown to be fanciful. Nothing more than a temporary conquest by Saudi raiders during the nineteenth century was established and this could not in law be viewed as a claim of rights. None of the documents produced undermined the rights of Abu Dhabi in al Dhafrah.

32 Zahlan, *The Origins of the United Arab Emirates*, 181–183.

33 This may explain why Shaikh Zayid was appointed as the Ruler's Representative in al Ain in 1946. Ahmad Bin Muhammad Bin Hilal Al Dhahiri was *wali* of Buraimi (al Ain), and after his death Ali Bin Ghanim was appointed *wali* of al Jimi, although he would prove not to be as

powerful as his predecessor. As a result, Ibrahim Bin 'Uthman, *wali* of al Ain, was given by Shaikh Shakhbut the authority to control the governors of Abu Dhabi villages in Buraimi up to 1946, when Shaikh Zayid took over. See J.B. Kelly, *Eastern Arabian Frontiers* (London and New York, NY: Frederick Praeger, 1964), 135.

34   See Administrative Report of the Bahrain Agency including the Trucial Coast and Qatar for the year 1945, reprinted in *Persian Gulf Administration Reports*, Vol. X, 25.

35   See "Trucial Coast News Report," No. 2 for the period ending January 31, 1946, reprinted in *Political Diaries of the Persian Gulf*, Vol. 17 (Gerrards Cross: Archive Editions, 1990), 21.

36   See "Trucial Coast News Report," No. 3 for the period ending February 15, 1946 in "Bahrain Intelligence Summary," No. 4 for the period February 16–28, 1946, reprinted in *Political Diaries of the Persian Gulf*, Vol. 17, 43.

37   By January 1956, the Political Resident was able to report to the Foreign Office in London, "Considerable work has been done on the falages in the Abu Dhabi sector of the oasis, and the volume of water reaching the gardens has increased appreciably." See FO 10101/1/56, Burrows (Political Resident) to Riches (Foreign Office), January 19, 1956, reprinted in *Political Diaries of the Persian Gulf*, Vol. 20, 79.

38   For an account of the work done on the *falaj* system see Julian Walker, *Tyro on the Trucial Coast* (Durham: The Memoir Club, 1999), 34–37 and 138–141.

39   Frauke Heard-Bey, *From Trucial States to United Arab Emirates: A Society in Transition*, second enlarged edition (London and New York, NY: Longman, 1996), 178–180.

40   See Hamdi Tammam, *Zayed bin Sultan Al-Nahayyan: The Leader and the March*, second revised edition (Tokyo: Dai Nippon Printing Company, 1983), 59.

41   Heard-Bey, *From Trucial States to United Arab Emirates*, 177–180.

42   Shaikh Zayid's words are cited by Tammam, *Zayed bin Sultan Al-Nahayyan*, 61.

43   Surah XIII: 17, "He sends down water from the cloud, then watercourses flow (with water) according to their measure." *Translation of the Meaning of the Holy Koran*, M.H. Shakhir (New York, NY, 1984).

44   He also had ideas for the application of technology to the task. Crawford, a representative of the Development Division of the British Middle East Office visited Buraimi (al Ain). Following his report, the Political Resident in Bahrain, Burrows, wrote to London, "For Buraimi [al Ain] Crawford concluded that the best hope lies in the development of the falaj system already being undertaken by Shaikh Zaid, by digging new wells and connecting them underground, and was impressed by Zaid's idea of employing a pneumatic drill for the work of hewing out the large underground channels."

See FO 10101/1/54, Burrows (Political Resident) to Fry (Foreign Office), January 4, 1954, reprinted in *Political Diaries of the Persian Gulf*, Vol. 19, 537.

45 Walker, *Tyro on the Trucial Coast*, 140–141.

46 His brother Shaikh Hazza was active in the Liwa oasis complex, although not, it seems, officially appointed, as was Shaikh Zayid in al Ain.

47 Wilfred Thesiger, *Arabian Sands* (London: Longmans, Green, 1959; reprint London: Penguin Books, 1991), 268–269 (page citations refer to the reprint edition).

48 The principal tribes involved included the Al Manasir on the Abu Dhabi side and the Bani Qitab on the Dubai side. See "Extract from Bahrain Intelligence Summary No. 15 for the period 1st to 15th August 1946," in *Records of the Emirates*, Vol. 8, 515. The Administration Reports of the Bahrain Agency including the Trucial Coast and Qatar reported that on the night of October 17, 1945, Dubai forces occupied Khur Ghanadhah with 300 men. In a boundary settlement of 1937, Khur Ghanadhah had not been included in Dubai's claim. Thus this move "amounted to an aggression against Abu Dhabi, and moreover as many of the armed men were transported by sea it also constituted a breach of the treaty of 1853 with His Majesty's Government which forbade aggression by sea." Reprinted in *Persian Gulf Administration Reports*, Vol. X, 24. The Dubai forces were removed on October 29, 1945 and Shaikh Shakhbut promised he would not take any retaliatory action. However, by that time the Al Manasir had already launched raids against Dubai, and did not see themselves as party to any agreement. In the following year, Shaikh Shakhbut admitted to the Political Agent that he had no control over his allies. The Dubai tribes retaliated and a battle ensued north of Liwa.

49 See "Summary of events during the month of May 1947," Hay (Political Resident) to Donaldson (Foreign Office), June 4, 1947, reprinted in *Political Diaries of the Persian Gulf*, Vol. 17, 424.

50 See "Bahrain Intelligence Summary" for the period February 16 to March 15, 1948, reprinted in *Political Diaries of the Persian Gulf*, Vol. 18, 44–45.

51 FO 101/9/50, Pelly (Political Resident, Bahrain) to Furlonge (Foreign Office), August 5, 1950, reprinted in *Political Diaries of the Persian Gulf*, Vol. 18, 622. This was a move directed against the Al Na'im tribe which would later be at the heart of the Saudi attempt to take over at al Ain.

52 See Rainer Cordes and Fred Scholz, *Bedouins, Wealth, and Change: A Study of Rural Development in the United Arab Emirates and the Sultanate of Oman* (Tokyo: The United Nations University, 1980), 34–48. This report observes: "The well-considered policy of the government with its goal of equal participation of all tribes has laid the foundation for a successful process of development" (p. 2). The authors also draw an important political conclusion: "It is the restoration of the principle of loyalty which must

be considered the stimulus for the socio-economic development of Abu Dhabi" (p. 29).

53   See, for example, Henderson, *This Strange Eventful History*, 107–114 and Kelly, *Eastern Arabian Frontiers*, 142–174.

54   When Saudi Arabia handed Britain a long list of "incidents" allegedly having occurred in the disputed area, R.C. Blackham of the Foreign Office noted, "There is no point in sending a considered reply to this catalogue of imagined grievances…" See Unpublished FO 371/104297 68852, Blackham (Foreign Office) to Pelham (Jedda), June 14, 1953.

55   See Unpublished FO 371/104302 68852, Translation of a letter from Shaikh Zaid to Political Officer dated 4th Ramadan.

56   Ibid.

57   See Administration Report for the Bahrain Agency including the Trucial States and Qatar for the year 1947, reprinted in *Persian Gulf Administration Reports*, Vol. X, 21.

58   See Kelly, *Eastern Arabian Frontiers*, 143.

59   Saudi reply, December 6, 1952 to British Note, November 22, 1951, cited in Kelly, *Eastern Arabian Frontiers*, 166.

60   The details of this attempt may be found in Kelly, *Eastern Arabian Frontiers*, 194–201. There were in fact four attempts. According to Kelly's account, on March 30, 1955, Abdullah Al Qurayshi, a Saudi agent, had met Shaikh Zayid and told him that the arbitration in Geneva would end in Saudi Arabia's favor and he would help himself by coming over to their side. If he did so, they would give him 50 percent of any profits from oil discovered in the area. On July 26, Al Qurayshi sent a messenger, one Ali Ibn Barak, and offered him a new car and Rs40,000 in cash. On August 4, it was Al Qurayshi who again approached Shaikh Zayid and again offered him as much as Rs400 million from any oil that might be found. Finally, on August 26, before he left for Geneva, Shaikh Zayid received a message that Al Qurayshi wished to present him with three pistols, which might be interpreted more as a threat than a bribe. There is no reason to doubt that the offer of a 50 percent share was genuine and would have been fulfilled, for this was the basis on which Saudi Arabia came to an agreement with Bahrain over a territorial dispute involving oil. From the Saudi perspective, it would have been money well spent. When all these attempts were revealed to the International Tribunal on September 11, it dealt a devastating blow to the Saudi case because they could produce no effective rebuttal against a battery of Abu Dhabi witnesses to the campaign of bribery. Their legal argument was exposed as founded on a basis of pressure, blackmail and bribery. It seems clear that Shaikh Zayid listened without comment to the Saudi official making these offers, luring him into damaging admissions. The campaign which Shaikh Zayid waged in the struggle for al Ain was based on good

intelligence and a realization that if he could amass evidence of Saudi malfeasance, then the case would be secured for Abu Dhabi. This proved to be correct. In the end, the Tribunal broke up when more and more evidence of illicit Saudi activity emerged. This left the option of military action, which Shaikh Zayid had long been convinced was the inevitable outcome.

61 More than Rs1.5 million had been sent to Hamasah over a period of seven months. When the village was captured, Rs159,000 were discovered and returned to Saudi Arabia with the comment that this seemed a very large sum for the upkeep of 15 men. Evidently, at least Rs1.25 million, probably much more, had been spent in bribes to tribesmen and local shaikhs. See Kelly, *Eastern Arabian Frontiers*, 204–206.

62 Ibid., 195. When Hamasah was captured, account books were found listing the recipients of many of the bribes, with dates of payment and amounts.

63 Ibid., 202. At least 1,300 modern rifles and 185,000 rounds of ammunition were sent to Hamasah and distributed. The vast quantity of ammunition in particular was a very destabilizing factor in the tribal area.

64 This is contained in the full edition of Edward Henderson's autobiography published in 1999. For the first time, significant new material on the occupation of Hamasah and Shaikh Zayid's role on that day has been revealed. This account is taken from Edward Henderson, *Arabian Destiny: The Complete Autobiography* (London: Motivate Publishing, 1999), 219–242.

65 Ibid., 219.

66 See Zahlan, *The Origins of the United Arab Emirates*, 131–135, for Zayid the Great's forceful approach in relation to the Al Na'im.

67 Ibid., 140. This was the Committee of Imperial Defence which recommended to the Foreign Office in 1938, "[W]ith a view to the settlement of the South Eastern Frontiers of Saudi Arabia on lines acceptable to Ibn Saud, the Foreign Office and the India Office should be authorized to take up the question of the cession by the Sheikh of Abu Dhabi of a strip of territory…"

68 Henderson, *Arabian Destiny*, 220.

69 Ibid., 223–224.

70 Ibid., 228–229.

71 Ibid., 220.

72 Ibid., 229–230.

73 His reputation extended beyond the area of al Ain. Through the medium of the Trucial States Council, which he often attended with Shaikh Shakhbut or as his representative, he came to know the Rulers and some of the heirs to the other Trucial States. In particular, he formed a good working relationship with the heir to Dubai, Shaikh Rashid Bin Sa'id. They had already had positive contacts while trying to calm the tense relationship between Abu Dhabi and Dubai (1945–1948) which had led to conflict between tribal allies. The resulting peace owed much to their efforts. The

Trucial States Council became a crucial forum where issues of progress could be discussed.

74   Henderson noted in November 1948, "He [Zayid] was by far the leading personality in the area, he was the key source of information in the whole region as to the doings of the tribes." See Henderson, *This Strange Eventful History*, 65.

75   Disputes between the two brothers were invariably about the Ruler's failure to allocate sufficient resources for the people of al Ain, not money to be used for Shaikh Zayid's own benefit or comfort.

76   To one listener, Shaikh Zayid explained his and his other brothers' view of Shaikh Shakhbut's financial policy. See FO 10154/39/54, Burrows (Political Resident, Bahrain) to Eden (Foreign Secretary, London), April 15, 1954, reprinted in *Records of the Emirates*, Vol. 9, 489.

77   In 1954, Shaikh Shakhbut was unjustly critical, saying that Shaikh Zayid was dealing with the British behind his back. Shaikh Hazza Bin Sultan declared that Shaikh Zayid had merely done what he was asked to do. Ibid., 491.

78   Like Bin Jilwi's men.

79   See Claud Morris, *The Desert Falcon*, 45. The Oasis Hospital opened in 1960. Shaikh Zayid also saw to it that the children of the oasis were provided with instruction in the Holy Koran.

80   In the "Historical Summary of Events in the Persian Gulf Shaikhdoms and the Sultanate of Muscat and Oman 1928–1953," the British acknowledged that, "no funds were made available for local development until 1953." See *Records of the Emirates*, Vol. 9, 25.

81   Major Cox had visited in 1902 but that was before he was appointed Political Resident. See *Records of the Emirates*, Vol. 5, 547–549.

82   See FO 10101/10/53, Burrows to Fry (Foreign Office, London), October 5, 1953, reprinted in *Political Diaries of the Persian Gulf*, Vol. 19, 497.

83   See "Trucial States Diary" for the period January 28 to February 27, 1958, reprinted in *Political Diaries of the Persian Gulf*, Vol. 20, 589. "His Excellency the Political Resident, accompanied by Lady Burrows … left Abu Dhabi, accompanied by the Commandant, Trucial Oman Scouts and the Political Officer Abu Dhabi, on January 30 for Buraimi [al Ain], where they remained, under canvas, until February 2 … In Buraimi [al Ain] H.E. and Lady Burrows toured the gardens and falajes of the oasis. On the evening of January 31, Shaikh Zaid entertained them to dinner, and the following evening His Excellency gave a dinner party for Shaikh Zaid, the Muscat Wali, and local notables."

84   "Trucial States Diary," No. 3 for the period March 1–31, 1957 reprinted in *Political Diaries of the Persian Gulf*, Vol. 20, 374–375.

85   See Trucial States Annual Report for 1956, reprinted in *Persian Gulf Administration Reports*, Vol. XI, 559.

CHAPTER 4

1 Edward Henderson, *This Strange Eventful History: Memoirs of Earlier Days in the UAE and Oman* (London: Quartet Books, 1988), 19–20.

2 See Frauke Heard-Bey, *From Trucial States to United Arab Emirates: A Society in Transition*, second enlarged edition (London and New York, NY: Longman, 1996), 317–321.

3 Henderson, *This Strange Eventful History*, 56.

4 See *The Buraimi Memorials 1955: United Kingdom*, Vol. 1 (Gerrards Cross: Archive Editions, 1987), 49–50. "The Oasis…is, in virtue of its size and fertility and the number of its inhabitants, one of the most important economic units of Eastern Arabia. In addition, however, it has an unique importance as a centre of communications, since it is united both with the port of Sohār on the Bātinah coast of the Gulf of 'Omān…and with Abu Dhabi town and the other Trucial Coast ports…by well-established routes across the intervening deserts." The same document pointed out that the oasis complex exported fruit, vegetables, lucerne and dates, and was a center for trade in rice, cloth, coffee and sugar.

5 See "Persian Gulf Monthly Report for the period July 3 to August 6, 1958," paragraph 16, reprinted in *Political Diaries of the Persian Gulf*, Vol. 20 (Gerrards Cross: Archive Editions, 1990), 670.

6 See FO EA 1105/1, A.C.I. Samuel (Foreign Office) to Col. W. Russell Edmunds (Treasury), January 15, 1954, reprinted in *Records of the Emirates*, Vol. 9 (Gerrards Cross: Archive Editions, 1990), 721–722. £4,000 for the improvement of water channels to the Buraimi (al Ain) oasis was the largest single sum allocated. Six years later, Edward Henderson noted that Shaikh Zayid "may have been spending as much as half a lakh [Rs 50,000] a year" on *falaj* maintenance. He further noted that the results of the work were very gratifying: "For example part of Al Muwaiqi's grove could only be watered once every five weeks, and over a third could not be watered at all…therefore the trees were dying. Now the whole can be watered about every three weeks. The other groves in the Abu Dhabi villages of the oasis now receive twice or three times the water they had previously, and Al 'ain village…may have many times its previous supply when new sources are linked up by underground channels which are now being constructed." He observed that this was part of a "general policy of Zaid's to improve the living of his people without cost to themselves, and it is remarkable that in a country where water is so expensive it should be given to the farmers free." See Unpublished FO 371/148916 33243, Henderson (Political Agency, Abu Dhabi) to Lamb (Political Residency, Bahrain), March 27, 1960.

7 See Unpublished FO 371/163025 33829, J.P. Tripp, Economic Secretary's Visit to Abu Dhabi, October 18–25, 1962.

8   Ibid., section on Buraimi (al Ain).

9   See Mohammed Al-Fahim, *From Rags to Riches: A Story of Abu Dhabi* (London: The London Centre of Arab Studies, 1995), 64.

10 See FO 10101/11/54, Richards (for B.A. Burrows, Political Resident, Bahrain) to Fry (Foreign Office, London), October 7, 1954, reprinted in *Political Diaries of the Persian Gulf*, Vol. 19, 628.

11 See, for example, Unpublished FO 371/148896, Annual Review of Events in the Persian Gulf for 1959. The language (used here of Kuwait) is readily applicable to the Lower Gulf. It talked of the "gathering momentum of governmental re-organisation" inspired by "'reformists' intoxicated by Nasserite and pan-Arab propaganda." Britain was also acutely aware of the challenge emanating from increased United States involvement in the Gulf. The Political Resident's Annual Report for 1948 noted, "the rulers seem, if anything, to be anxious to preserve their ties with His Majesty's Government to whom they owe their independent existence and there is no sign of any inclination to turn to the U.S.A. in the place of His Majesty's Government in spite of the display of American strength and wealth in the Gulf." Reprinted in *Persian Gulf Administration Reports: 1873–1957*, Vol. XI (Gerrards Cross: Archive Editions, 1986), 3. In subsequent years, Britain had to steer a course between the twin dangers of Arab nationalism and US money and power. In addition, it was concerned about the role of Saudi money and resources undermining the British position in the region.

12 The context in which this financing was achieved stemmed from a concern for increased Saudi influence. The Political Resident's Annual Report for 1953 noted, "The first small steps were taken during the year in the development of the Trucial Coast. It was remarked by Sir Roger Makins in his report in 1952 that we could not run the Gulf on the cheap and that the maintenance of our position here would require the expenditure of money. This fact was brought home to us by the significant volume of sympathy which the Saudis appeared in the early part of this year to be winning in the towns of the Trucial Coast other than Abu Dhabi…the Arab's respect for power effectively wielded led to a rise in the prestige of the Saudis with a corresponding drop in ours. It was therefore decided that something should be done to demonstrate in a concrete way the benefits of the special relation of the Shaikhdoms with Her Majesty's Government." See FO 10102/3/54, Burrows (Political Resident, Bahrain) to Eden (Secretary of State for Foreign Affairs, London), March 12, 1954, reprinted in *Persian Gulf Administration Reports*, Vol. XI, 367.

13 These demands included greater sensitivity to damage, which could emanate from accusations of 'colonialism' from other Arab countries, in particular Egypt after 1956. It became important to show that the British government was exercising proper stewardship in the Gulf.

14 See Agreement between PDTC and the Ruler of Abu Dhabi, January 11, 1939, Article 4 (b), reprinted in *Records of the Emirates*, Vol. 8, 609–619.

15 See Agreement dated December 2, 1950, between the Ruler of Abu Dhabi and the Superior Oil Company, reprinted in *Records of the Emirates*, Vol. 9, 579–604.

16 See Unpublished FO 371/156669 33473, "Persian Gulf Monthly Summary" for the period January 1–31, 1961, paragraph 14. "The Rulers of Abu Dhabi and Dubai have agreed in writing to accept a decision by Her Majesty's Government on the delimitation of their common frontier. This will allow Petroleum Development Trucial Coast to go ahead with the exploration of the frontier area which has been held up pending a settlement."

17 The letter from the Political Resident in Bahrain, Sir George Middleton to R.A. Beaumont in the Foreign Office in London on March 8, 1960, revealed the British dilemma. See Unpublished FO 371/149084 (1535/1), reprinted in *Records of the Emirates*, Vol. 12, 301. The oil company ADMA and its French partners planned the Das Island installation to handle 1.5 million tons per year in the first instance. But it was capable of expansion to 6 million tons a year. The company planned to start producing 1.5 million tons annually from 1962. They proposed to tell the Ruler of this planned production but not of the likely future development. On the financial side, the company was prepared to advance Shaikh Shakhbut an initial £250,000 in 1960 and a further £250,000 in 1961. By the end of 1962, his anticipated royalty income from production would total £1.25 million annually and would stay at that figure until 1965. These figures compared with advances of £37,500 that he had received in earlier years.

18 For example, if the figures quoted by Middleton in March 1960 were at all close to reality, then anticipated development fund resources would have been £50,000 a year.

19 The British government faced a fresh problem as the new oilfields opened up. While anxious to preserve its own position, it was concerned that the Rulers of the region should not sign away rights to the oil companies. It was not in the Rulers' long-term interests to concede extensive licenses. There was a lengthy correspondence to this effect that lasted into the spring of 1966, which concerned the efforts of the Political Agent in Abu Dhabi to persuade Shaikh Shakhbut to follow British advice. See Unpublished Correspondence in FO 371/185562 37516, especially letter 1534/66 from Lamb (Political Agent, Abu Dhabi) to Luce (Political Resident, Bahrain), May 21, 1966.

20 This would later impact on the admittance of foreign workers and technicians.

21 The advance of £250,000 that the company had been prepared to make in March had shrunk to £125,000 by October and this was not because of any change in market conditions. See Unpublished FO 149087 33405 (1535/1),

Middleton (Political Residency, Bahrain) to Beaumont (Foreign Office, London), October 31, 1960. Shaikh Shakhbut was concerned that the company wanted to alter the terms of the agreement to a 50/50 share basis, at variance with the original contract. Middleton shrewdly observed that "Shakbut will soon...suspect that the company is trying to get the better of him." For years, Shaikh Shakhbut had survived on an arrangement that paid him an annual sum whether any oil was found or not. Now, he was being offered a profit-sharing arrangement, which depended on the value of the oil found and sold. If profits were low or non-existent, he would be much worse off. He preferred the surety of fixed contractual payments to the promise of fabulous but possibly chimerical wealth in the future. He knew from the newspapers and the radio, as well as the knowledge of developments elsewhere in the region, that oil revenue was uncertain, and he was averse to risk.

22 For another view on Shaikh Shakhbut's approach, see Henderson's report to D.F. Hawley in December 1959. He observed (paragraph 11), "I have put things as I see them and the view I have expressed is generally in favour of Shakhbut. I feel that we have in the past tended to overstress his weaknesses, and in the process overlooked some of his good points; and in doing this I can see many instances where we have perhaps too readily dismissed the Abu Dhabi government as hopeless..." He went on to say that Shaikh Shakhbut was "a difficult man to get on with," but that his balanced attitude was a useful corrective to the more traditionally acidulous view of the Ruler. See Unpublished FO 371/148929 33243, Henderson (Political Agency, Abu Dhabi) to Hawley (Political Agent, Trucial States), December 29, 1959.

23 The British motive in pressing for 50/50 was political. If they did not show that oil was being developed in an area wholly under their control under the same terms as in other areas, they would be accused of colonial exploitation, with great political damage. They do not seem to have conveyed any sense of this dimension to Shaikh Shakhbut.

24 The 50/50 agreement in particular was enormously complex. Part of Shaikh Shakhbut's unwillingness to sign the agreement may well have stemmed from the fact that he had reservations about its legal intricacies.

25 On one occasion, the Ruler's elder son stood in for him. On another, Shaikh Shakhbut gave the authority to his brother Hazza. However, he trusted Shaikh Zayid and preferred that he should take his place.

26 See Unpublished FO 371/156669 33473, "Persian Gulf Monthly Summary," September 1961.

27 Ibid., October 1961.

28 See Unpublished FO 371/157033 33628 (1014/61), Craig (Political Agency, Dubai) to Tripp (Political Residency, Bahrain), October 18, 1961.

29 One reason was that Shaikh Shakhbut simply refused to pay the bills. For example, the Police Commander, Lt. Col. Edge, reported in March 1962 that "Clothing and spare parts ordered during the Ruler's absence in Europe 1961 was not acknowledged by him [as] he considers that the responsibility of Shaikh Zayid who was then in charge." See Unpublished FO 371/163025 33829, Edge to Political Agency Abu Dhabi, March 23, 1962.

30 See Unpublished FO 371/157033 33628 (1014/61), Craig to Tripp, October 18, 1961.

31 In March 1961, the "Monthly Summary" reported, "Shaikh Shakhbut has signed an agreement with Tennants Ltd., for the survey and rapid construction of a jetty in Abu Dhabi; he has also agreed with the Eastern Bank for the opening of a branch office there…" In the May report, however, it was noted, "Having broken off negotiations with Tennants last month for the construction of a deep water jetty, the Ruler of Abu Dhabi has now authorised Halcrows to obtain tenders for a coordinated development scheme comprising a jetty, roads, houses, suq improvements, exploration of water resources and airport facilities." Soon, he was encouraging the company, saying that he liked both schemes, one for £1 million and the other for £3.75 million. He also said that he liked the idea of raising a loan for this development, but that of course he refused to consider a loan "unless he was absolutely free to spend it as he wished." When told that was impossible, this scheme likewise foundered, with much ill-feeling on both sides. See Unpublished FO 371/156669 33473, "Persian Gulf Monthly Summaries" for March, May and June 1961.

32 Not all of those dismissed went quietly. His first Secretary, a young Arabist called Peter Lienhardt, was dismissed within three months of his arrival in April 1960. While he was the Ruler's personal choice, he was dismissed "ostensibly on the grounds that he had been disloyal and that there had been a lack of progress since his arrival. Lienhardt's riposte that if money were to be spent more freely progress might follow, was ill received." Ibid., June 1961, paragraph 15. Yet, it appeared as if Lienhardt was echoing the constant recommendations of the Ruler's own brother, Shaikh Zayid, suggesting infrastructure development and social expenditure. See Unpublished FO 371/157034 33628 (1104/61), Miles (Political Agency, Abu Dhabi) to Ford (Political Residency, Bahrain), April 18, 1961.

33 Buckmaster continued, "The head man of the settlement, Saif bin Musa… was particularly disgusted with the cavalier treatment he had received from Shaikh Shakhbut, who, when he had last visited him, sent him away with a mere 40 rupees." See M.S. Buckmaster's report of his "Tour of Liwa and Dhafara: March–May 1952," reprinted in Jane Priestland (ed.) *The Buraimi Dispute: Contemporary Documents 1950–1961*, Vol. 1. (Gerrards Cross: Archive Editions, 1992), 617–618.

34 Ibid., 616. "Among the track-marks were some which had clearly been made by a 10-ton lorry equipped with very wide balloon tyres—almost certainly…[an] ARAMCO vehicle. At this point the track swung almost due south. I followed it for a further ten miles, then decided to strike east as I had not enough fuel for too lengthy a journey. In nine miles I came across a set of some ten tracks, among them at least two ten-tonners…"

35 See Henderson, *This Strange Eventful History*, 81–82.

36 A report from the Assistant Political Agent in Abu Dhabi (S.J. Nuttall) to the Political Agent in Dubai (H.G. Balfour-Paul) from July 16, 1966, revealed the underlying seriousness of the situation. This involved the Abu Dhabi Defence Force that had not been paid. Their commander, Col. Wilson, distanced himself from the matter, saying that they were "Arab officers in an Arab army. He himself has done all that he can to get the men paid regularly; if the officers wish to approach [the] Ruler themselves, they are at liberty to do so." Nuttall minuted, "There is some wild and disloyal talk among these officers. At the moment it is no more than talk; but it is worth noting that there now exists in Abu Dhabi a trained and efficient body of men with a grudge against the Ruler. They are unlikely to take any action on their own account…" Unpublished FO 371/185578 35760 (1941/66).

37 The Annual Review of Events for 1965 in Abu Dhabi notes that the "…Ruler's reluctance to spend his increasing oil income (£10.7 million in 1965) is [a] cause of discontent of which labour unrest on Das Island in December is a symptom." Unpublished FO 371/185523 35441, Lamb to Luce, January 1, 1966.

38 Lamb reported a meeting described to him by Shaikh Zayid, at which the brothers had confronted the Ruler with the need to construct a proper development budget. There were profound disagreements. Shaikh Zayid told the Ruler directly that he and his other brothers were not "forming a league against him but it was essential that the four of them should form a league together since they were 'brothers' and the senior members of the Family and if they did not work together the Family and the State would fall apart. Zaid said that after this Shakhbut was quite nonplussed, made no further comment and the conversation flowed into other channels while tempers cooled." Unpublished FO 371/185578 35760 (1013/66), Lamb to Luce, May 21, 1966.

39 In an earlier period, the departure of one of Shaikh Shakhbut's key witnesses for Abu Dhabi's claim to Liwa (Ahmad Bin Fadhil) was thought by the British government to be extremely serious. See FO 10154/39/54, Burrows (Political Resident, Bahrain) to Eden (Secretary of State for Foreign Affairs), April 15, 1954, reprinted in *Records of the Emirates*, Vol. 9, 494.

40 The Annual Report for 1965 remarks, "Discontent is widespread among all sections of the population, whose thinking is affected by Arab Nationalist

propaganda from outside and criticism is aimed not only at the ruler personally but the whole Sheikhly system…" It concludes, prophetically, "If Sheikh Shakbut fails in 1966 to fulfil the promise he has shown at the end of 1965, the consequences could one day be serious, not only for him, but also for us." This document was widely circulated within the Foreign Office for information. See Unpublished FO 371/185523 35441, Lamb to Luce, January 1, 1966.

41   *Records of the Emirates*, Vol. 9, 581, Article 1(e). This was the first time as far as can be judged that any name other than that of the Ruler was included in a document of this type in Abu Dhabi.

42   Thus, at the first meeting of the Trucial States Council in March 1952, the Political Officer Sharjah, John Wilton, wrote to the Political Resident Bahrain, Sir Rupert Hay, that Shaikh Shakhbut had excused himself on the grounds that he was fasting, but sent his two sons to represent him. Wilton commented, "I was disappointed at his failure to come himself… Nor did I think that his choice of deputies was altogether fortunate, but in the absence of his brother Zaid in Liwa, Hazza' has been sent to Buraimi [al Ain], so that they may have been the best he could manage." The conclusion that can be drawn from his observations is that Shaikh Zayid would have been the natural and desired stand-in for the Ruler. Other than the Council, which the Ruler considered unimportant, the proposal for a delegation came to nothing in practice, and Shaikh Shakhbut kept all the lines of power in his own hands. See *Records of the Emirates*, Vol. 9, 173.

43   Wilton was instrumental in the formation of the Council. In his view, the first moves towards collective action by the Rulers came in the aftermath of the Abu Dhabi dispute in the late 1940s. The Ruler of Umm al Qaiwain played an active role in the mediation of the settlement, and the Political Officer in Sharjah at the time (Noel Jackson) invited all the Rulers to lunch to celebrate the settlement. Not all of them attended, but this was the first occasion on which a number of Rulers had met together since the time of Shaikh Zayid the Great. Later Wilton himself followed the same pattern, inviting the Rulers to meet and discuss common issues concerning succession in Kalba and Sharjah. He made it clear that the British government had no view as to the outcome, but the Rulers should come to their own conclusions. These meetings provided the inspiration for the formal creation of the Trucial States Council, which in turn was to develop into the Federation and lead to the creation of the UAE under Shaikh Zayid's leadership. Personal communication from Sir John Wilton, February 26, 2000.

44   At the third meeting of the Council on April 25, 1953, the Political Officer (Sharjah) rehearsed the public reasons for the creation of the Council. "The Political Officer began by recalling the purpose for which the Council had been formed, namely to promote direct discussion and consultation between

the Rulers as a means of solving their common problems." See "Minutes of the Third Meeting of the Trucial States Council," reprinted in *Records of the Emirates*, Vol. 9, 183.

45　The fear of 'Nasserism' was ever present. Thus, a year before the Suez intervention, the Political Resident wrote to the Foreign Secretary in London, "It has for some time been recognised that, as they exhausted other subjects of controversy with ourselves and with the Western powers, the Arab nationalists would sooner or later take an interest in the Persian Gulf... notably in the increase in Egyptian propaganda and penetration..." See FO 10103/5/56, Burrows to Selwyn Lloyd (Foreign Secretary), May 7, 1956, reprinted in *Persian Gulf Administration Reports*, Vol. XI, 441.

46　See note 42.

47　The British would use the meetings as a sounding board for gauging a collective sense of the Rulers' opinions. For example, the British sought the Rulers' collective guidance on the succession to the territory of Kalba. On this sensitive topic, they all refused to be drawn, saying that it was a matter for "the Jawasim only." The Rulers said "that the matter was in the hands of Her Majesty's Government, who would do what they saw best for the common interest. The Political Officer then said that Her Majesty's Government would value their advice, in order to achieve in Kalba a permanently acceptable and stable regime, not merely a further stage in the present unsatisfactory chain of events, but they would not be drawn." FO 0228/5/52, Political Agent Sharjah to Political Resident Bahrain, March 23, 1952, reprinted in *Records of the Emirates*, Vol. 9, 176–177.

48　The Political Agent in Sharjah wrote to the Political Resident, B.A. Burrows on December 1, 1953, "...the Council still has a long road to travel before it can hope to begin to fulfil the role of either consultative or legislative body or even perform the functions of a rudimentary Witenagemot for the Trucial Coast. For this there are various reasons the chief being that the idea and practice of free discussion in semi-formal assembly is outside the ken of all the participants while a degree of mutual distrust renders them inhibited from speaking freely in the presence of each other at the same time as the representatives of H.M.G.... All Rulers attend mainly as an act of courtesy to H.M.G. rather than by any choice of their own." FO 0228/20/53, December 1, 1953, reprinted in *Records of the Emirates*, Vol. 9, 189.

49　See FO 10110/13/54, Pirie Gordon (Political Agent, Dubai) to Burrows, July 5, 1954, reprinted in *Records of the Emirates*, Vol. 9, 201–204. Pirie Gordon, in his letter to the Political Resident, conveys the sense of transformation: "All seven of the effective Rulers were again present the only absentee being the aged Ruler of Dubai whose affairs have long been under the Regency of his son Shaikh Rashid. In addition... Shaikh Zaid bin Sultan who happened to be visiting his brother the Ruler of Abu Dhabi at the time … From the start it appeared … that many of the Rulers had lost much of their shyness which had characterised their behaviour at earlier sessions … Even the Ruler of Abu Dhabi … made several interventions in debate … Permission to smoke was requested by the Regent of Dubai, frequent pleasantries were exchanged, and an informal atmosphere achieved which led to a wholly desirable urge for conversation."

50 Ibid., 201.

51 Ibid., 204.

52 See Despatch No. 15, 10110/10/55 from J.P. Tripp (Political Agent, Dubai) to C.A. Gault (Acting Political Resident, Bahrain), August 27, 1955, reprinted in *Records of the Emirates*, Vol. 9, 223.

53 Minutes of the seventh meeting of the Trucial Council held in the Political Agency on August 23 and 24, 1955: The Ruler cited was Shaikh Saqr of Ras al Khaimah. Custom prevented Shaikh Zayid from speaking unless the Ruler of Abu Dhabi did so, but these opinions most certainly accorded with his own known views. Reprinted in *Records of the Emirates*, Vol. 9, 228.

54 Ibid., 237, Item 2 (c). A subject in point was the hiring of private doctors.

55 As the Political Resident expressed it in his Annual Report for 1953, "… the suggestion was made to Shaikh Shakhbut that he might, when oil was produced in commercial quantities and he was reaping the benefits, put 2% of his share of the profits at the disposal of the Trucial Council for the benefit of his neighbours not fortunate enough to have oil in their territory. Shakhbut in characteristically quixotic fashion replied by offering 4%." See FO 10102/3/54, Burrows to Eden, March 12, 1954, reprinted in *Persian Gulf Administration Reports*, Vol. XI, 367.

56 Boustead's testimony has to be read with some care. Born in 1895, Abu Dhabi was his final post before retirement and he took a deep personal dislike to Shaikh Shakhbut, of which his colleagues were aware. See Unpublished FO 371/163025 33829, Boustead (Political Agency, Abu Dhabi) to Luce, October 3, 1962, Holograph Annotation to Paragraph 11. But despite his aversion to Shaikh Shakhbut, he was trained to provide honest and accurate reports. No doubt he took the opportunity to present any evidence hostile to Shaikh Shakhbut and colored events more highly than was legitimate, but it seems unlikely that he actually invented negative stories in their entirety. By contrast, Boustead had a profound admiration for Shaikh Zayid. "I will not easily forget my first visit to Buraimi [al Ain] and my first meeting with Sheikh Zaid. It is impossible to meet him without immediately being taken by him … I was always astounded at the crowds who gathered around him … with the sort of reverence and attention due to a minor saint. He invariably had a kind word for everybody, and was most generous with his money. I was immediately struck by all that had been done in Al 'Ain, his home town, and in the Buraimi [al Ain] area, for the benefit of the people."

See Hugh Boustead, *The Wind of Morning: The Autobiography of Hugh Boustead* (London: Chatto and Windus, 1971), 233.

57 The scale of departures, to which the Ruler's attitude was 'Let them go,' was of enormous concern to Shaikh Zayid, who realized the political damage that this outflow was causing.

58 The dispute between Abu Dhabi and Qatar was fully summarized in an internal Bahrain Residency memorandum prepared for Sir George Middleton by M.R. Melhuish on January 31, 1959. Melhuish concluded his report with an apt summation of the problem. "The main difficulty seems to be that this dispute over the possession of an unimportant island has now roused such passion in the hearts of the two Rulers that it is impossible for them to think in any logical fashion..." See Unpublished FO 371/148958 33243, M.R. Melhuish, Confidential Minutes, January 31, 1959.

59 Unpublished FO 371/163025 33829, Confidential 1084, Boustead to Luce, April 7, 1962.

60 See Unpublished FO 371/157034 33628, Confidential 1102, R.O. Miles (Political Agency, Abu Dhabi) to J.A. Ford (Political Residency, Bahrain), May 24, 1961, which notes that Shaikh Zayid was in favor of a liberal policy towards foreign business while Shaikh Shakhbut was demanding the profit tax of 25 percent.

61 A secret memorandum by J.P. Tripp of October 27, 1962 noted, "Shaikh Zaid told me that the Ruler's policy of levying 25 per cent of the profits on merchants and firms doing business in Abu Dhabi was not only unnecessary...but was also creating hardship for the people of Abu Dhabi since it led to a mark-up of prices by this amount." See Unpublished FO 371/163025 33829, J.P. Tripp, Economic Secretary's Report of a Visit to Abu Dhabi, October 18–25.

62 Record of conversation enclosed in Unpublished FO 371/163025 33829, Boustead to Luce, April 9, 1962.

63 See Unpublished FO 371/163025 33829, Luce to Crawford (Foreign Office), April 17, 1962.

64 See Unpublished FO 371/163025 33829, Boustead to Luce, October 3, 1962.

65 See Unpublished FO 371/163025 33829, Boustead to Luce, October 17, 1962.

66 See Unpublished NARA, Pol 15-1, Trucial Oman A-75 from AmConsul Dhahran, James A. May, Acting Principal Officer to Department of State, August 28, 1963. Shaikh Shakhbut was profiled in both *Time* and *Life*. The former article was titled "Sheik Jackpot" and the latter "'O long of Life' drinks camel milk and runs on oil." Neither was unfriendly, if naive and undiplomatic, but the Ruler took extreme exception. The US Consul in Dhahran reported to the State Department, "Shakhbut was very irritated by this article and by some other in TIME. He approached the American Consul in

Dhahran and wrote to the magazines in question. [The Consul] [r]eceived a letter by personal messenger from the Ruler of Abu Dhabi, in which he expressed his unhappiness over several newspaper articles concerning himself which he considered untruthful and unfavorable, but which he did not identify by names or dates of publication. Subsequently, the acting British Political Resident, Francis Brown, stated that he believed Shakhbut was referring to articles that had appeared relatively recently in *Life* and *Time*. He went on to say that Shakhbut was also upset by a BBC *Panorama* program which was shown several months ago in the UK and the script of which reached Shakhbut's hands…A talk by Edward Attiya on the BBC Third Programme, which was reproduced in 'The Listener' had also made him 'hopping mad.'"

67 See FO 10154/39/54, Burrows to Eden, April 15, 1954, reprinted in *Records of the Emirates*, Vol. 9, 487–496.

68 Major firms from all these countries proposed large-scale projects to Shaikh Shakhbut in the period between 1962 and 1966. On the links with Germany, see Frauke Heard-Bey, "Germany and the Gulf before 1971," in Yousef Al-Hassan (ed.) *The Dialogue Between Civilizations: The UAE and Germany* (Amman: Friedrich Ebert Foundation, 1995), 9–33.

69 Unpublished NARA, American Consul, Dhahran, John Evarts Horner, February 19, 1964, to Department of State, Pol R Trucial States, A-174.

70 For example, the long analysis "Centrifugal and Centripetal Forces in the Trucial States," Unpublished NARA, Pol 2 Trucial States, A-115, American Consul, Dhahran (Arthur B. Allen) to Department of State, February 10, 1965.

71 Even Shaikh Shakhbut's own sons sometimes disagreed with his policies. See Unpublished FO 371/163025 33829, Lt. Col. Edge to Political Agent for Abu Dhabi, April 6, 1962.

72 See Unpublished FO 371/163025 33829. Lt. Col. Edge to Political Agency, Abu Dhabi, March 23, 1962. However, Shaikh Hazza's family had their own quarters in the fort.

73 Glen Balfour-Paul remarked about Shaikh Shakhbut's reluctance to open his country up to the world, "He saw that it would be the end of life as his people knew it. There were only a few thousand of them, and they lived the sort of life they were happy enough with." Quoted in Gerald Butt, *The Lion in the Sand: The British in the Middle East* (London: Bloomsbury, 1995), 115.

74 This was how Lamb interpreted the statement about the brothers standing together: "Zaid's remarks…about the four 'brothers' standing together as a league are also, I think, an indication that the family are [*sic*] beginning to realise that Shakbut's behaviour is becoming [*sic*] to threaten the position of the Ruling Family as a whole." Unpublished FO 371/185578 35760 (1013/66), Lamb to Luce, May 21, 1966.

75 Some of the documents are not accessible, but there is no indication in the other records covering that period, or even in the memories of those officers involved at the time, that there was any such conspiracy. Since many agencies of government would have been involved, it is likely that there would have been at least some trace, in the records of the military, the cabinet office, or the financial departments. Moreover, the records of the United States on Abu Dhabi, which are accessible, would have shed light on this matter. All the extant evidence suggests that the impetus for the change came from within the family and the change was accomplished in the traditional manner.

76 Lamb, one of the shrewdest of the British officials, wrote confidentially to the British Ambassador in Jordan before Shaikh Shakhbut paid a visit in 1966, "His long experience of power, combined with an autocratic temperament, has made him determined to remain in complete control of the country. Socially, he is a man of considerable charm, who commands considerable respect by sheer force of character. He has had no formal education, but is endowed with considerable intelligence and a powerful memory." Unpublished FO 371/185578 35760, Lamb to Parkes (British Ambassador to Jordan), April 16, 1966.

77 The agenda for discussions to be held during a private visit of Shaikh Zayid to London in June 1966 is very instructive, being based on a set of agreed positions. It was during this visit that Shaikh Zayid met Lamb, who was on leave, at the Shaikh's house, Hall Barn, near Beaconsfield. Concerning a discussion about a possible change of ruler in Abu Dhabi, Lamb stated that it was a matter for the family to decide and that the British government would not intervene in such a matter. Shaikh Zayid concurred that it was a family matter, closed the discussion, asking neither for British help nor approval, but it was plainly an issue that was uppermost in his mind. (Private communication from A.T. Lamb, December 1996).

78 Lamb reported, "He is everyone's idea of an Arab Shaikh, generous and extrovert, and for that reason is probably the most popular person in Abu Dhabi...Shaikh Zaid is well aware of the importance of development to the state." Unpublished FO 371/185578 35760, Lamb to Parkes, April 16, 1966.

CHAPTER 5

1   See FO 10154/39/54, Burrows (Political Resident, Bahrain) to Eden (Foreign Secretary), April 15, 1954, reprinted in *Records of the Emirates*, Vol. 9 (Gerrards Cross: Archive Editions, 1990), 487.

2   One good example of this was the response of A.J. Johnstone, from the Political Agency in Dubai to Shaikh Zayid. Johnstone needed a large amount

of detailed information on al Ain. At Johnstone's request, Shaikh Zayid secured the presence of several key individuals in al Ain whom the representative wished to interview. Furthermore, he provided clear assurances or categorical denials in respect of other issues that Johnstone inquired upon. Shaikh Zayid gave his answers in precisely the form that the British government could work with. Whenever asked, he produced useful evidence and circumstantial detail as requested. Johnstone was plainly satisfied with the meeting and treated Shaikh Zayid with considerable respect. He also recognized that this was not a man whom he could manipulate. See Unpublished FO 371/156678 33473 (1051/61), Johnstone (Political Agency, Dubai) to Jones (Arabian Department, Foreign Office), February 8, 1961.

3   Roderic Owen, *The Golden Bubble: Arabian Gulf Documentary* (London: Collins, 1957), 187.

4   Ibid., 209–210.

5   See Unpublished FO 371/163025 33829, Sir William Luce's "Record of discussions with Shaikh Zaid bin Sultan at Buraimi on May 22–23" (1962), paragraph 3: "I asked him who would succeed Shaikh Shakhbut should he cease to be Ruler. He replied that while he was not anxious to become Ruler, there was really no alternative at present, and he would have to accept the responsibility." Claud Morris notes that Shaikh Shakhbut was dissuaded from resigning by his son Sultan, who "…became the obstacle to the very retirement that in his heart his father already sought." See Claud Morris, *The Desert Falcon: The story of H.H. Sheikh Zayed Bin Sultan Al Nahiyan, President of the United Arab Emirates* (London: Outline Series of Books, 1976), 57.

6   At the time, Shaikh Zayid was heavily in debt because he had borrowed money to the extent of about half a lakh of rupees (Rs50,000) to pay subsidies to the tribes in al Ain. When Shaikh Shakhbut sent money via his son Sultan, it was done with great reticence. Yet, in the end, Shaikh Zayid accepted his brother's assurance that he would change and persuaded him to stay in office. See FO 10154/39/54, Burrows (Political Resident, Bahrain) to Eden (Foreign Secretary), April 15, 1954, reprinted in *Records of the Emirates*, Vol. 9, 487–496.

7   "By Family Consensus Rather Than by Revolution" is an accurate statement of the position. See Hamdi Tammam, *Zayed bin Sultan Al-Nahayyan: The Leader and the March*, second revised edition (Tokyo: Dai Nippon Printing Company, 1983), 72.

8   See Unpublished FO 371/185542 35656 referring to a draft of "The Trucial States: A Brief Economic Survey," by Dr. K.G. Fenelon, CBE.

9   See Unpublished FO 371/179929 35506 (BT 1202/4), T.F. Brenchley (Foreign Office) to F.J. Burlace (Ministry of Defence), May 3, 1965. "I am writing now to say that the political factors have changed, and we have

come to the conclusion that we must accept that the Ruler intends to have an army and that nothing is to be gained by further delay on our part."

10 See Unpublished FO 371/179929 35506 (1202/65), A.T. Lamb (Political Agent, Abu Dhabi) to H. Phillips (Political Residency, Bahrain), September 16, 1965. "It is in our interests, and also those of the Ruler, to see in Abu Dhabi a well-run and disciplined force whose allegiance is only to the Ruler. Our interests would be served since we could then rely upon such an army to co-operate with the Trucial Oman Scouts in the defence and internal security of Abu Dhabi and also in time to replace one of the Trucial Oman Scout's squadrons at a great saving to Her Majesty's Government. It would be in the Ruler's interest, and I think that this may well be on the Ruler's mind, because an army commanded by seconded British officers would be faithful to the Ruler; it would not be beholden to one of the Shaikhs, indulge in politics or act in any way contrary to the Ruler's interests." The economic point was a key factor for the British government.

11 See Unpublished FO 371/179929 35506, Telegram No. 727, Bahrain to Foreign Office and ditto Lamb (Abu Dhabi) to Phillips (Residency, Bahrain), September 11, 1965.

12 A case in point was the issue of the appointment of a Director of Finance. See Unpublished FO 371/185530 35390 (1013/66), Lamb to Luce (Political Resident, Bahrain), February 9, 1966. The same pattern recurred when an effort was made to provide the Ruler with better legal advice.

13 A British doctor, who was flown out specially, treated his mother and the Ruler was deeply grateful.

14 See Annual Review of Events in Abu Dhabi, 1965. "His handful of officials are obliged to refer virtually all decisions, particularly those involving expenditure, to him personally. His British Secretary, Mr. Clark, has virtually no influence over the Ruler, his advice is rarely asked and even more rarely followed." See Unpublished FO 371/185523 35441, Lamb to Luce, January 1, 1966.

15 The term 'Lower Gulf' was used by John Duke Anthony in his 1975 book and neatly encompasses Abu Dhabi, Ajman, Bahrain, Dubai, Fujairah, Qatar, Ras al Khaimah, Sharjah and Umm al Qaiwain. These never formed a single state but had many interests in common that were different to Kuwait in the north or Oman. See John Duke Anthony, *Arab States of the Lower Gulf: People, Politics, Petroleum* (Washington, DC: The Middle East Institute, 1975).

16 He was a tough and determined negotiator but he always had a higher goal, which he outlined openly at the beginning of a discussion. The view of Lamb expressed in a secret memorandum in November 1966 ("Assessment of the personality, policies, role of Shaikh Zaid bin Sultan Al Nahayyan") is revealing: "Beneath the outward appearance [of the European

ideal of the romantic Arab Shaikh] there is, however, another man: intelligent, patient and reasonable in argument, knowing what he wants to do (if not yet how to do it properly and effectively) and with all the acquisitive instincts of the bedu (for example, his successful war of nerves on the banks in Abu Dhabi to extract from them the payment of interest at 6½% on his current account). He has a statesmanlike grasp of the basic principles of rule and a pragmatic approach to international politics. He has an instinctive appreciation of the political needs of the Gulf States. His handling of his subjects has been brought to perfection by long years of practice (as Governor of Buraimi [al Ain])." See Unpublished FO 371/185529 35559 (1011/66), Confidential: Despatch No. 3 of November 5, 1966 from Lamb (Political Agent in Abu Dhabi) to Crawford (Political Resident in Bahrain). The issue of the banks to which Lamb alludes is a perfect illustration of Shaikh Zayid's pragmatic approach. The local banks had for some time given Shaikh Shakhbut only 3 percent interest (which the British authorities considered indefensible), but they had resolutely refused to offer more. Immediately after his accession, Shaikh Zayid let it be known that he expected to receive a better rate, to which the banks demurred. He did not seek to berate or pressure them, as his predecessor had done, but quietly began discussions with other banks for entry into Abu Dhabi, which quickly became known on the banking 'grapevine.' Soon after this, the new Ruler told his existing bankers without dissembling that he had received offers of a better rate of interest. They immediately agreed upon the 6.5 percent.

17 It should not be thought that his objections were entirely without reason. In 1954, the Political Resident pressed him strongly to appoint a British Advisor and improve his administration. Shaikh Shakhbut knew what that meant, from the troubled experience of his fellow Ruler, Shaikh Salman Bin Hamad of Bahrain, with his Advisor, Charles Belgrave. His government would no longer be answerable to him but to the Advisor, to the Political Agent (the British wanted to send a Political Agent to Abu Dhabi) and ultimately to the government in London. See FO 1053/5, Confidential No. 103, Samuel (Foreign Office) to Burrows (Political Resident, Bahrain), July 9, 1954, reprinted in *Records of the Emirates*, Vol. 9, 92–93.

18 See Unpublished FO 371/185523 35441, Annual Review of Events in Abu Dhabi, 1965. "Sheikh Shakhbut…evinced a continuing desire to disassociate himself completely from the other Trucial States. In early January [1965], when invited to contribute to the Trucial States Development Fund, he promised a mere £25,000…He supported warmly an idea discussed with him by the Political Resident in October [1965] for the federation of the Northern Trucial States, apparently seeing this as an opportunity to opt out of the Trucial States completely, and sent only a junior Sheikh to the Trucial Council meeting in November. When in

December [1965] he was formally invited by the other Rulers to be the first Arab Chairman of the Council he received the suggestion without enthusiasm and was still considering it as the year ended." He eventually turned down the invitation. His motives for changing his mind are not easy to discern, but his vacillation was one of the causes for growing British dissatisfaction with him as Ruler. See Unpublished FO 371/179915 33465 (1102/65), Lamb to Luce, November 28, 1965, paragraph 4, and subsequently, Unpublished FO 371/185524 35441 (1011/66C), Balfour-Paul to Luce, March 5, 1966.

19 See Unpublished FO 371/179916 35465, Confidential Telegram No. 370, Luce to Foreign Office, May 20, 1965.

20 Luce sent a telegram to Boustead in Abu Dhabi asking him to convey a personal message from the Political Resident to the Ruler, "I appeal to his wisdom and statesmanship…to seize this great opportunity to earn the admiration and gratitude of us all by contributing £one-and-a-half-million [original emphasis]." However, it appears that the message did not have the desired effect. See Unpublished FO 371/179916 35465, March 10, 1965.

21 See Unpublished FO 371/179916 35465, D. Slater (Political Agency, Abu Dhabi) to Luce, May 9, 1965.

22 The British preferred secretly to collaborate with Saudi Arabia in an effort to undermine this Arab League initiative. Crawford at the Foreign Office summed up the essential political issues for the Treasury, which would have had to meet the bill for greater British involvement in the region. "I should perhaps say something about the reasons why we are taking the Egyptian threat to the Gulf so seriously. It has always been one of Nasser's long-term objectives to liquidate the British position in the Gulf. There have recently been signs of an increase in subversive activities there. There have been the recent Bahrain riots, and there were less publicised disturbances at Sharjah and Dubai last winter, which have turned out to be the work of a group of Yemeni immigrants directed from outside. The Political Resident has recommended that if we are to maintain stability in the Gulf area we must resolutely resist the penetration of the Gulf by those hostile to our presence there. The Trucial States, which include the Royal Air-Force airfield at Sharjah, have always been an important element in our position in the Southern Gulf. This position is all the more important now that Abu Dhabi Marine Areas (in which British Petroleum is a two-thirds shareholder) have discovered very substantial reserves of oil in the Abu Dhabi off-shore area." See Unpublished FO 371/179916 35465, Crawford (Foreign Office) to P.S. Milner-Barry (Treasury), April 26, 1965.

23 "Zaid, for example, already thinks that Feisal [the Saudi King] has resumed a forward policy overland in order to secure what he can before the

Arab League make further inroads on the coast." See Unpublished FO 371/179916 35465, Luce to Thomson (Minister of State, Foreign Office), May 16, 1965.

24 He agreed with Shaikh Shakhbut's objective for a "local force who would co-operate at all times with the T.O.S. [Trucial Oman Scouts] and on equal footing and would be posted to appropriate stations in the area, such as Liwa, Buraimi [al Ain], Jebel Thanna, Tarif and would live under canvas or in huts as suitable…" See Unpublished FO 371/179929 35506, J.E.H. Boustead (Political Agent, Abu Dhabi) to Luce, March 27, 1965. This issue is dealt with more extensively in Chapter 8.

25 See pages 90–96.

26 See Unpublished FO 371/179929 35506 (1202/65), Lamb to Phillips, October 11, 1965.

27 Ibid.

28 See Annual Review of Events in Abu Dhabi, 1965 in Unpublished FO 371/185523 35441, Lamb to Luce, January 1, 1966.

29 See Unpublished FO 371/163025 33829, "Record of discussions with Shaikh Zaid bin Sultan at Buraimi on May 22–23" (1962).

30 Unpublished FO 371/185578 35760 (1033/66), Lamb to Sir R.W. Parkes (British Embassy, Amman), April 16, 1966.

31 Lamb concluded his letter by observing that he hoped that the Ruler would keep to his promise to be more circumspect in future, "since his current internal expenditure of not more than £25,000 a month does not match his recent gifts totalling £700,000 to Jordan." See Unpublished FO 371/185531 35590 (1033/66), Lamb to Luce, April 30, 1966.

32 Unpublished FO 371/185578 35760, Lamb to Weir, May 21, 1966.

33 Unpublished FO 371/185578 35760, Restricted, Lamb to Luce, May 21, 1966. Shaikh Zayid later observed, "I often came personally to my brother, always in a brotherly way, to advise on matters immediately concerning us. I wanted to guide him, so far as I could, for the benefit as I thought of Abu Dhabi as a whole. However, he would not listen. My other brothers often tried to persuade Sheikh Shakbut by argument, but I always felt it best to do things as quietly as possible and avoid any sense of pressure." Time and again, he was forced into the role of middleman. He told Shaikh Shakhbut, "If you want to make issue with one of your brothers, or want to blame them for something, don't blame them directly. Always try to use another of your brothers to approach in a friendly way the brother with whom you wish to take issue. Send a messenger. Make a bridge. But whatever you do, never blame directly or open your face to your brother in an aggressive way. If you do that, respect will inevitably be lost between you." He practiced what he preached. Although he would speak freely and firmly to Shaikh Shakhbut, he always remained composed and courteous. Afterwards, away from the

Ruler's presence, he would sometimes express his frustration. See Claud Morris, *The Desert Falcon*, 55–56.

34 Unpublished FO 371/185578 35760, Restricted, Lamb to Luce, May 21, 1966.

35 According to Claud Morris, Shaikh Ahmad Bin Hamid, the son of Shaikh Zayid's uncle, put the situation in this way, "Many factors compelled Sheikh Zayid to take power in 1966…Let us look at three. The first was the fact that the people were isolated, deprived of their land and its wealth. This was the main fact. They could not get at the resources needed for development. They had no access to it in any form. There was no availability of money to the people. The money simply came from the petrol company. It went into hoarding. The second fact was that the family as a whole, the principals of the Bani Yas tribe, were [*sic*] not happy at the way Sheikh Shakbut was administering the Emirates. The administration, to put it coldly, was not efficient. It had flaws, holes and deficiencies. The third fact was that neighbouring countries were blaming us for the situation in Abu Dhabi. Their complaint was that we were a wealthy country yet doing so little because we appeared to lack a man who could provide the leadership necessary to exploit our wealth with wisdom. Given those three factors, change was really inevitable." Cited in Claud Morris, *The Desert Falcon*, 53–54.

36 See Unpublished FO 371/163025 33829, "Record of discussions with Shaikh Zaid bin Sultan at Buraimi on May 22–23" (1962).

37 Lamb was to arrive in London on July 3, 1966.

38 Sir A.T. Lamb, private conversation, tape recorded, November 1996.

39 There is no available documentary record of these discussions, which were naturally secret. A number of British documents covering this period have been retained under conditions of security until 2007. However, they are unlikely to alter the overall understanding of events, which is that the initiative was taken by Shaikh Zayid to have an outline discussion while in the United Kingdom. The feedback received was sufficiently unambiguous for him to advise the family that the British would support such a move if they chose to make it.

40 See Unpublished FO 371/185529 35559, Despatch No. 3 of November 5, 1966, from the Political Agent in Abu Dhabi to the Political Resident in Bahrain.

41 The events of that day are recorded in Balfour-Paul's Despatch No. 20 of August 8, 1966, which remains inaccessible in the Public Record Office until 2007. In his study on *The End of Empire in the Middle East*, Balfour-Paul comments on the episode, "It fell to the author, as Acting Resident, to receive and act on the family's appeal." See Glen Balfour-Paul, *The End of Empire in the Middle East: Britain's Relinquishment of Power in her last three Arab Dependencies* (Cambridge: Cambridge University Press, 1991), 223, note 68.

42 Shaikh Shakhbut, Balfour-Paul and De Butts have not left accounts of the details of their meeting. Shaikh Zayid, of course, was not present at their encounter, but he later spoke at length to his brother by telephone. Shaikh Zayid gave an interview on the topic to Awad Al-Arshany. Al-Arshany's version appeared in his book *Zayid the Paladin who Conquered the Desert*, in Arabic (Cairo: 1980), 134–135.

43 See Claud Morris, *The Desert Falcon*, 70.

44 See Unpublished FO 371/185537 35590, Telegram No. 371, Luce to Foreign Office, June 8, 1966.

45 See Unpublished FO 371/185529 35559, Confidential Despatch No. 3 of November 5, 1966, from the Political Agent in Abu Dhabi to the Political Resident in Bahrain.

46 Ibid.

47 This was also to be his response to potentially divisive issues of dispute with Dubai over oil rights. Eventually, he would extend this principle to Saudi Arabia as well. Amity between Arab brothers was to be the touchstone of his policy, reiterated in speech after speech over the next three decades.

48 "The first definitive stamps of Abu Dhabi [bearing Shaikh Shakhbut's portrait] were withdrawn on the day Shaikh Zayed assumed responsibilities as Ruler." See Mahbub Jamal Zahedi, *Gulf Post: Story of Post in the Gulf* (Karachi, Pakistan: Sanaa Publications, 1994), 74.

49 See correspondence between August 10, 1966 and September 6, 1966, beginning with Unpublished FO 371/185560 35716 (1446), Melhuish (British Residency, Bahrain) to Nuttall (Political Agency, Abu Dhabi).

50 See Unpublished FO 371/185529 35559, Despatch No. 3 of November 5, 1966, from Melhuish (Political Residency, Bahrain) to Nuttall (Political Agency, Abu Dhabi).

CHAPTER 6

1 The American Consul in Dhahran visited Abu Dhabi and reported to the State Department on October 19, 1966, "The reactions of local observers as well as the reporting officer's own observations confirm that Shaykh Zayid has become extremely popular with all his subjects. While the prospect of sharing for the first time in the economic prosperity of their country accounts in great measure for the present euphoria of the population, Zayid's political decisions have also contributed to his popularity." See Unpublished National Archive Records Administration, American Consul Dhahran to Department of State, Airgram No. A-50, Subject: Political Developments in Abu Dhabi, October 19, 1966.

2   See John Daniels, *Abu Dhabi: A Portrait* (London: Longman, 1974), 54. This conversation took place shortly after Daniels' arrival in 1967.

3   There was a further dimension. They wanted the development effort to be focused through the TSDO under their steering hand and ultimate control. They could not prevent Shaikh Zayid following his own priorities under his own direction to develop Abu Dhabi, especially since he was funding the TSDO program as well, but they did not like it. Hence the change in tone.

4   See Unpublished FO 371/185529 35559, Despatch No. 3 (1011/66), A.T. Lamb (Political Agent, Abu Dhabi) to R.S. Crawford (Political Resident, Bahrain), paragraph 14, November 5, 1966.

5   See Unpublished FO 371/185529 35559, Confidential Memorandum, J.E. Marnham (Foreign Office) to Sir Roger Allen, December 6, 1966. Allen's holograph marginal note adds, "It is, I imagine, inevitable that Abu Dhabi should now try to dominate rather than cooperate with her small and much less wealthy neighbours." Events proved both of them wrong.

6   The Political Resident wrote to the Foreign Office on November 19, 1966, "The risks of things going off the rails in Abu Dhabi through Shaikh Zaid's impetuosity and desire for quick results before the development programme can be fitted into a proper economic and social framework are great. For example, if present trends continue, there is liable to be a raging inflation in Abu Dhabi which will have manifold damaging consequences, not only in Abu Dhabi but in the surrounding States; and this will hit us directly in various ways, including pressures on the T.O.S. to raise rates of pay to keep in line with the almost inevitable upward trend in the Abu Dhabi Defence Force." It should be noted that the Resident gave primacy to British economic interests, while Shaikh Zayid pressed for the development benefit necessary for the people of Abu Dhabi. See Unpublished FO 371/ 185540 35590, Crawford (Political Resident, Bahrain) to Marnham (Foreign Office), November 19, 1966.

7   The British authorities preferred to use the TSDO as a means to channel all development and aid. In response to a proposal for the United Nations to provide technical assistance, the Ministry of Overseas Development in London wrote, "While we welcome in principle the proposed U.N. technical assistance, we see possible snags ... We suggest it would be preferable if key officers ... although provided by U.N. [*sic*] should be responsible to the council and financed from the Development Fund rather than by the U.N. ... We fear that U.N. appointees might perhaps be led to negotiate separate projects with individual rulers without reference to the Council." See Unpublished FO 371/185535 35590, Outward Telegram Ministry of Overseas Development to Dubai and Bahrain, November 4, 1966.

8   For example, see the long correspondence in respect of Brian Colquhoun and Partners, Consulting Engineers, and of Wimpey, in Unpublished FO 371/185540 35590, between March 7 and November 20, 1966.

9   He wrote to Marnham at the Foreign Office that, in formulating any plans or advice, "we must be sure that these are based on the full understanding of the kind of circumstances in which he [Shaikh Zayid] will have to apply them." Unpublished FO 371/185540 35590, Crawford to Marnham, December 17, 1966.

10   Abu Dhabi was the largest and the richest of the states in the Lower Gulf.

11   Balfour-Paul observed that "... as a result of immersion in the local scene they [British officials abroad] tended to acquire a protective colouration and a pronounced sympathy for the people in whose destinies they were in one way or another involved." See Glen Balfour-Paul, *The End of Empire in the Middle East: Britain's Relinquishment of Power in her last three Arab Dependencies* (Cambridge: Cambridge University Press, 1991), 153. That was true, and he was no doubt speaking for himself as a participant; but the degree of perception was inevitably a personal quality. Some officers, to judge by their correspondence alone, were more acute than others. Moreover, careerism played its part. An officer was expected to reflect his own views but not to the detriment of policy determined from home. The cardinal sin in the Diplomatic Service was 'going native,' that is, reflecting the views of the locality against British policy. Officers were also wise to adopt the idiom and argot of the 'Office.' A good officer wrote tales and parables for his readers that would amuse and please. It was one of the ways in which an officer could impress his superiors and advance his career. But an officer would be wise invariably to preserve in his correspondence a sense of distance – and unvoiced superiority – over his contacts, even if they were Rulers. Thus, to understand what is being stated as 'fact' needs careful interpretation.

12   See Unpublished American Consul Dhahran to Department of State, Subject: Political Developments in Abu Dhabi, October 19, 1966.

13   A full account of the early developments in Abu Dhabi is given in *Two Glorious Years in the History of Abu Dhabi* (Beirut, n.d.), 53–101.

14   For details of the process and its implications see K.G. Fenelon, *The United Arab Emirates: An Economic and Social Survey*, second edition (London: Longman, 1976), 80–83.

15   *Two Glorious Years in the History of Abu Dhabi*, 203.

16   Ibid., 147. This generation of money was funded by the growth in oil with annual production rising from 12 million tons in 1966 to 32 million tons in 1970.

17   See Mana Saeed Al-Otaiba, *The Economy of Abu Dhabi: Ancient and Modern*, second edition (Beirut: Commercial & Industrial Press, 1973), 79–80.

18 This was not a 'Great Leap Forward' on the Chinese model of 1958–1962, based on an expectation of an economic transformation emerging from a social revolution in the countryside and little expertise. The Abu Dhabi model was based on adequate financing, allowing the employment of external specialists and resources to accomplish the ambitious targets.

19 The 5.9 million dinars provided for tourism and related issues included a project close to the Ruler's heart: a zoo, wherein animals indigenous to the region that were under threat could be preserved. That pioneering effort, like some of the agricultural stations, also acquired a significant research role over the years and an international reputation. A good example of this pioneer activity was the joint venture with the Environmental Research Laboratory of the University of Arizona in building the Arid Lands Research Center on the 'Isle of Happiness' (Sa'adiyat). See Unpublished NARA, Pol 7, Trucial States, Power/Water/Food Project in Abu Dhabi: Possible Visit by Shaykh Zayid to U.S., August 19, 1970. For the history of the Arid Lands Research Center, see Hassan Dawood Salman, "Technology Planning for the Post-Oil Era in the United Arab Emirates (UAE)," Ph.D. dissertation (University of Bradford, 1988), 213–227.

20 For this plan, see Al-Otaiba, *The Economy of Abu Dhabi*, 175–182.

21 Unpublished FO 371/185540 35590 (1103/66), Lamb to Balfour-Paul (Political Residency, Bahrain), November 15, 1966.

22 One of the reasons why the Ruler was keen to have a radio station in Abu Dhabi (something that once again the British considered unnecessary) was that it would be a means whereby his authority could be communicated more effectively to all those with whom he was not in personal contact.

23 See Mohammed Al-Fahim, *From Rags to Riches: A Story of Abu Dhabi* (London: The London Centre of Arab Studies, 1995), 136–137.

24 The American Consul in Dhahran reported, "As soon as Mr. Lamb returned from leave he called on Shaykh Zayid and was confronted with the question, 'Well, how do think I'm doing?' The PA replied that he thought he was doing a fine job but as to be expected he had made some mistakes. The Ruler agreed saying that he was aware that he had been criticised abroad for the way in which he has been handing out contract awards and spending money generally. However, he said he had been doing this not foolishly but by design. The reasons he gave were: (1) after sitting by for thirty-two years…it was only natural that he would spend money on projects which he thought should have been implemented long ago in the shaykhdom; (2) he told the PA he also had to show his people dramatically that he was different [from Shaikh Shakhbut]. The PA acknowledged that the spending spree was necessary under the circumstances but told Zayid it was now time to slow down and carefully plan for the future. The Ruler indicated he was perfectly agreeable to this approach and welcomed the advice of

the experts…" See Unpublished NARA, American Consul Dhahran to Department of State, Subject: Political Developments in Abu Dhabi, October 19, 1966.

25 Mohammed Al-Fahim recalled, "Thankfully, many Abu Dhabians who had left in the previous three decades began to trickle back after 1966. They brought with them a wealth of education, skills and work experience from the host countries – including Saudi Arabia, Qatar, Kuwait and Bahrain – in which they had lived and worked since their departure. They became valued contributors to what was being done at a time when every available hand was needed to help us move forward." See Al-Fahim, *From Rags to Riches*, 138.

26 See John Duke Anthony, *Arab States of the Lower Gulf: People, Politics, Petroleum* (Washington, DC: The Middle East Institute, 1975), 144–146.

27 Especially so since he could give valuable experience to a potential rival. His brother had always refused to include Shaikh Zayid and his brothers in government for that reason.

28 The creation of the first government departments in Abu Dhabi observed these innately political principles. Shaikh Zayid incorporated many strands of opinion and different elements within the family inside his government. The following list of personalities is indicative of this process. Shaikh Khalid Bin Sultan was appointed as Deputy Ruler of Abu Dhabi State and its dependencies; Shaikh Hamdan Bin Muhammad as Chairman of Public Works, Electricity, Water, Health and Education; Shaikh Mubarak Bin Muhammad became Director of Police and Public Security; Shaikh Tahnun Bin Muhammad was made President of the Department of Agriculture as well as Chairman of the al Ain Municipality; Shaikh Surur Bin Muhammad was appointed as President of the Law Court; while another doyen of the family of Shaikh Muhammad Bin Khalifa, Shaikh Saif Bin Muhammad, became President of the Land Registry and Municipalities Departments. The head of the Department of Finance was an external professional, but its Deputy Chief as well as Director of Customs, a developing portfolio, was Shaikh Muhammad Bin Khalid. Shaikh Ahmad Bin Hamid became Director of the Department of Labour, Social Affairs and the Civil Service. For a translation of the Emiri Decree No. 3 of September 1966, which led to the establishment of these departments, see Unpublished NARA, American Consul Dhahran, Subject: Political Developments in Abu Dhabi, October 19, 1966.

29 See Hendrik van der Meulen, "The Role of Tribal and Kinship Ties in the Politics of the United Arab Emirates," Ph.D. dissertation (Fletcher School of Law and Diplomacy, 1997).

30 See Al-Fahim, *From Rags to Riches*, 125–126.

31 Ibid., 140.

32   This is perhaps a consequence of growing up in an oral culture in which complex family narratives were the materials of history.

33   Hence his determination to improve health standards, especially in areas of obstetrics and child care. In this area, his wife Shaikha Fatima played an extremely important role in developing resources for the family, and providing a forceful example for the women of Abu Dhabi. Another area had to do with the Bedouin. The American Consul in Dhahran reported, "One of the first things that the new Ruler has told the British he would like to do is bring about the resettlement of the bedouin of Abu Dhabi. While he acknowledges this will not be an easy task, he has forcefully made the point that he does not consider the nomadic way of life appropriate for subjects of a state possessing the oil wealth of Abu Dhabi. Foraging for food and water as a regular way of life, Zayid has told the British, is degrading and means would have to be found to settle the bedouin in permanent quarters." See Unpublished NARA, American Consul Dhahran, Political Developments in Abu Dhabi, October 19, 1966.

34   The precise point at which Britain began to plan for withdrawal is uncertain. Glen Balfour-Paul suggests that there were rumors in Arab Nationalist circles as early as 1949 that Britain intended to 'federate' its interests in the Gulf. See "Persian Gulf Annual Review for 1950," reprinted in *Persian Gulf Administration Reports: 1873–1957*, Vol. XI (Gerrards Cross; Archive Editions, 1986), 119. One idea, which he appositely characterizes as 'grotesque,' was that Britain intended, as part of the construction of the Baghdad Pact (1955) to unify the Gulf States under the rule of Abdul-Ilah Bin Hussein, the Regent of Iraq. Certainly by 1951, the Political Resident (Hay) was anticipating full independence by the 1970s. Balfour-Paul suggests that the Trucial States Council was established in 1952 as a first tentative step towards union. By March 1954, Burrows was writing, "There is a long way to go before we achieve anything like integration but these steps are at least in the right direction." See FO 10102/3/54, Burrows (Political Resident, Bahrain) to Eden (Foreign Secretary), March 12, 1954, reprinted in *Persian Gulf Administration Reports*, 367. For a good treatment of these issues, see Balfour-Paul, *The End of Empire in the Middle East*, 112ff.

35   It also differed markedly from the Labour government that had held power from 1950 to 1951.

36   See Harold Wilson, *A Personal Record: The Labour Government, 1964–1970* (Boston, MA: Little, Brown and Company, 1971), 479–483.

37   At the same time, therefore, while one branch of the British government was seeking to determine the long-term social and economic structure of Abu Dhabi, another was contemplating abandoning any direct interest in the future of the nation. This ambiguity suggests the confusion and inconsistency that lay at the heart of British policy in the region. While the

burgeoning economic crisis was the root of the problem, part of the reason for the abrupt withdrawal was ideological. Britain was seeking to develop a new stance in the world, disencumbering itself from the vestiges of Empire. The means chosen by the Labour government were political rather than military, most notably in the case of its rebellious colony of Southern Rhodesia, which simply declared unilateral independence in 1965, after Britain had stated it would not resist the move to secession by force. The shadow of the Rhodesian situation dominated the thinking of the British government for the whole of its term of power. So too did an unexpected military commitment closer to home, when the government was forced to send troops to the province of Northern Ireland in 1968. Equally, the attack by Israel on its neighbors in 1967 hastened rather than hindered Britain's desire to remove itself from active involvement in the Middle East. Dennis Healey, at the time the British Defence Secretary, later wrote in his memoirs, "…hard experience compelled me to recognise that the growth of nationalism would have made it politically unwise for Britain to maintain a military presence in the Middle East and South East Asia, even if our economic situation permitted it." While Britain had a presence on the ground, it could not avoid being drawn into the confrontation between an expansive Israel and its Arab neighbors resisting the process. The Arab response to the war of June 1967 may well have been a subtle and largely invisible motive for British withdrawal. Shaikh Zayid was adept at reading the political signals of a changing balance within the region. See Dennis Healey, *The Time of My Life* (London: Michael Joseph, 1989), 299.

38   Healey also set the withdrawal into a still wider political context. He wrote that the British Cabinet "finally decided to apply for membership of the Common Market in May 1967. From that moment it was clear that we would leave Singapore and cut our remaining commitments in the Gulf." See Healey, *The Time of My Life*, 293. If this is the case, then the outburst by Healey on television in Britain when he publicly spurned the offer of the Rulers to meet the costs of the troops was not a crude off-the-cuff remark, but a desire to close the topic once and for all by a brusque and absolutely negative pronouncement.

39   See Balfour-Paul, *The End of Empire in the Middle East*, 123–131.

40   See, for example, Unpublished NARA, Pol 1, Trucial States – UK, No. A-228, American Embassy, Kuwait to Department of State, March 11, 1965, describing a possible shift in the British attitude towards the Arabian Gulf states.

41   See Unpublished FO 371/185531 35590, D.C. Carden (British Consulate General, Muscat) to Crawford (Political Resident, Bahrain), October 26, 1966.

42   See Unpublished FO 371/185531 35590, Crawford to Lamb, November 2, 1966. This dispute, over the hereditary lands of the Bahrain ruling family

in Zubara and over ownership of the Hawar Islands, had lasted over two generations.

43 See Unpublished FO 371/185531 35590, Lamb to Carden, December 12, 1966.

44 See Unpublished FO 371/185531 35590, Confidential Telegram, Bahrain to Foreign Office, Telegram no. 830, December 19, 1966. "P.A. [Political Agent] Abu Dhabi reports in a letter that Shaikh Zaid took initiative and raised with him subject of meeting with King Faisal. He authorised P.A. to say that he wanted an early meeting and that he was, in principle, prepared to meet the King at any place convenient to the latter. The conversation showed that Zaid would be prepared to go on the pilgrimage on his own initiative … [need to establish] the personal relations which seem to be the only way forward on the territorial issue."

45 See, for example, Unpublished FO 371/185525 35441 (1035/66), Lamb to Balfour-Paul (Political Agent, Dubai), October 12, 1966. "It does seem to me that Zaid is doing his best to use his own form of diplomacy to restore friendship among all the Trucial States and that he has fully in mind the importance of Shaikh Rashid in this."

46 See Unpublished FCO 8/1210/1, "Abu Dhabi: Annual Report for 1968," Treadwell (Political Agency, Abu Dhabi) to Crawford, January 4, 1969.

47 See Unpublished FO 371/185531 35590, Confidential Record of Conversation on October 26, 1966, between the Political Resident and the Ruler of Abu Dhabi.

48 For example, in response to the Political Resident Crawford's expressed desire that the Ruler improve relations with Saudi Arabia, "The Ruler replied that he held King Faisal in great esteem. Saudi Arabia was now a State with great wealth and standing but she did not seem to be able to distinguish between friends and enemies. Saudi Arabia's enemies lay to her west, not to her east and she should surely see that she had nothing to worry about from the east. What could Abu Dhabi, with its small population, do to harm to Saudi Arabia? Saudi Arabia seemed to wish to fight on two fronts when she need only fight on one. He agreed with the Political Resident that Saudi Arabia had a part to play in the affairs of the Arabian Peninsula but the initiative lay with her." Ibid.

49 When Shaikh Zayid came to power, there was initial concern in Dubai at the mode of his accession as Ruler. It was wrongly perceived as an act of British manipulation. However, the new Ruler's determination to work closely with his closest neighbor quickly dispelled these misperceptions.

50 See Unpublished FO 371/185537 35590 (1086/66C), M.S. Buckmaster (Political Agency, Dubai) to M.C.S. Weston (Foreign Office), November 9, 1966. It points out that the Abu Dhabi and Dubai interpretations of the boundary were not consonant.

51 See Unpublished FO 371/185537 35590 (1082/66), Lamb to Balfour-Paul (Political Residency, Bahrain), August 15, 1966.

52 See Unpublished FO 371/185537 35590 (1082/66), Lamb to Balfour-Paul, November 15, 1966.

53 See Unpublished FO 371/185531 35590 (1044/66), D.A. Roberts (Political Agent, Dubai) to Crawford (Political Resident, Bahrain), November 26, 1966.

54 The American view was succinct but correct. "Ultimate success of UAE quite clearly depends on willingness of Zayid and Rashid to cooperate... Evidence at moment is that both understand realities of situation and will gradually consult and coordinate more. Hopefully they will do so despite fact that respective outlooks...are poles apart..." See Unpublished NARA, Pol UAE-US, Stoltzfus (American Embassy, Kuwait) to Secretary of State (Washington), March 28, 1972, paragraph 7.

55 Many commented in exactly the same terms on US President Franklin Delano Roosevelt. Like Shaikh Zayid, the President seemed easy and amiable; petitioners left his presence convinced that they had been heard. But he, like Shaikh Zayid, had a set of higher objectives to which he adhered and all his actions were tempered by his sometimes invisible goals.

56 The issue of trust and honor was fundamental to Shaikh Zayid's capacity to work with both Shaikh Rashid of Dubai and with King Faisal of Saudi Arabia. In both cases, there were profound political divisions and disagreements. What, however, bridged the divide in both cases was the mutual trust in the honor and probity of the participants.

57 The role of Margaret Thatcher in relation to the Argentine invasion of the Falklands and later her role in stiffening the resistance to the Iraqi invasion of Kuwait are two recent examples.

58 In December 1966, for example, he received the Head of the United Arab Republic Educational Mission in Dubai, who offered assistance in improving Abu Dhabi's education system. "...the Ruler replied that he did not require any and had not yet turned his mind to education...the Egyptian asked him to say that he would require UAR assistance in the future; the Ruler replied that he...did not know that he would require assistance in the future." It was always unwise to pressure Shaikh Zayid in this way, and the Ruler proceeded to ask his visitor some extremely awkward and penetrating questions about Egypt's role in Yemen. "The Ruler then went on to lecture the Egyptian about the wickedness of an Arab State interfering in another Arab country's affairs..." See Unpublished FO 371/185531 35590 (1073/66), Lamb to Balfour-Paul, December 18, 1966. He was referring directly, of course, to Yemen, but also obliquely to the Egyptian presence in the Trucial States. The delegate complained to one of Shaikh Zayid's close associates, Khalaf Bin Otaiba, that Abu Dhabi was run by the British, "to which Khalaf replied that the British consultants, contractors and officials were servants

of the Ruler and took their orders from the latter. But they could approach the Ruler with advice and proposals just as Khalaf himself could, without fear, give his views to the Ruler. Could an Egyptian do the same with Nasser? Khalaf doubted it and ticked off the Egyptian for criticising the system of government in Abu Dhabi." Ibid.

59 Speech of H.H. Shaikh Zayid at the opening of the 8th Legislative Session, March 4, 1990, cited in Sheikh Zayed, *Hopes and Deeds* (Beirut: Book and Publishing Establishment, 1990), 151 (available in French and English).

CHAPTER 7

1 Indeed, in his hands the idea of unity became a well-articulated political and social philosophy. It grew naturally from his strong Islamic sensibility since the unity and harmony of Divine purpose found its strongest expression in the Holy Koran.

2 Shams Al-Din Al-Doaifi (ed.) *Sheikh Zayed: Leadership, The United Arab Emirates 1971–1987* (Beirut: Book and Publishing Establishment, n.d.), 115.

3 Ibid., 25.

4 Ibid.

5 "…federalism, as a sort of testamentary bequest from a dying empire, was by this time losing, or had already lost, credibility all over the place, wherever it was bequeathed [by the British government]." See Glen Balfour-Paul, *The End of Empire in the Middle East: Britain's Relinquishment of Power in her last three Arab Dependencies* (Cambridge: Cambridge University Press, 1991), 93–94.

6 Personal communications with Sir A.T. Lamb and Sir John Wilton.

7 The writer David Holden observed in 1966, "In short, there is no realistic possibility of the present Gulf rulers coming together of their own accord in any political grouping worth talking about." See David Holden, *Farewell to Arabia* (New York, NY: Walker and Company, 1966), 159.

8 See Unpublished FCO 08/11, Henderson (Political Agency, Abu Dhabi) to Crawford (Political Resident, Bahrain), April 4, 1968. "His analysis ran on these lines: if there was to be an effective union it would have to draw almost all its revenue from Abu Dhabi. The people of Abu Dhabi would not agree to the spending of such a very large part of their money by an organisation which was outside Abu Dhabi territory; therefore the key offices of the Union Headquarters must be in Abu Dhabi… States would be internally autonomous but for the purposes of Defence and Foreign Affairs they would have to be represented by one Minister of Defence and one Foreign Minister. Similarly there could only be one Commander in Chief and only one army headquarters… In favour of the scheme it can be

said that he is single-minded, resolute, courageous and does have the funds to achieve it."

9   The same British minister, Goronwy Roberts, who brought them the news of withdrawal had come two months earlier in November 1967 to tell them that Britain would continue its political and military role in the region. See Balfour-Paul, *The End of Empire in the Middle East*, 123–126. However, there is documentary evidence that in the same timeframe as Roberts was visiting the Rulers for the first time, Britain already had withdrawal firmly in mind. See Unpublished FCO 8/142, "The Minister of State's Visit to the Persian Gulf, November 1967," 6, section 11. "Ministers have agreed that it will probably not be in our interests to stay in the Gulf beyond the mid-1970's … They have also agreed that we should aim within this time to bring forward the States to separate independence (preferably as four units i.e. Bahrain, Qatar, Abu Dhabi & Dubai with the five smaller shaikhdoms merging in some form with either both [*sic*] of the latter), subject to any special arrangements any of them may wish or feel compelled to make with Saudi Arabia. Meanwhile, it has been agreed that we must avoid any public statement or leaks about our acceptance of this general time limit." Though the timetable was more extended than what actually transpired, the essential policy decision to withdraw seems to have been well advanced by November 1967.

10   See Balfour-Paul, *The End of Empire in the Middle East*, 137ff. The central issues in regional defense were complex. The geopolitics of the region after 1971 was dominated by three powerful, large and populous nations, all with oil resources, bordering the Arabian Gulf: Saudi Arabia, Iran and Iraq. In the search for a federal solution in the Lower Gulf, Iran and Saudi Arabia were the main actors, with Iraq in the wings. Both Iran and Saudi Arabia had claims over the territory of a number of the smaller states that had been under British protection and, in a situation where the balancing power of the British was removed, neither could have allowed the other to absorb the lands and resources of the smaller states bordering the Gulf. It was, as James A. Bill later presented it, "a rectangle of system-challenging tension in which each of the actors exists in a tenuous state of balanced conflict with each of the other actors." The Gulf system was, he noted, "highly unstable in nature. Misperceptions and miscalculations by any actor or combination of actors can lead directly to violence and to the system's collapse." See James A. Bill, "The Geometry of Instability in the Gulf: The Rectangle of Tension," in Jamal S. Al Suwaidi (ed.) *Iran and the Gulf: A Search for Stability*, The Emirates Center for Strategic Studies and Research, Abu Dhabi (London: I.B. Tauris, 1996), 109–110.

11   Through all the later negotiations, a central preoccupation of Shaikh Zayid was fixed from February 1968. See Unpublished FCO 8/9 57547,

Crawford (Political Resident, Bahrain) to Foreign Office, February 29, 1968. "Shaikh Zaid's object had been to protect his union with Dubai and he had not wanted a meeting of the nine at this stage. Their [Shaikh Zayid and Shaikh Rashid] own policy had been to demonstrate their co-operation and to avoid being the odd man out. Thus they had gone to the meeting [with the other Lower Gulf leaders] prepared to agree to anything – union, federation, or league of Gulf States – regardless of whether or not it had a chance of working." The centrality of the union with Dubai was never questioned throughout the period up to the creation of the UAE. Shaikh Rashid was forced by circumstances to play a more opaque diplomatic game than Shaikh Zayid. His political practice should be viewed in the light of a comment he once made to Balfour-Paul, at the time the Political Agent in Dubai. "But it doesn't matter if you don't understand what I say, it's what I don't say that matters." See Gerald Butt, *The Lion in the Sand: The British in the Middle East* (London: Bloomsbury, 1995), 114.

12 See Abdullah Omran Taryam, *The Establishment of the United Arab Emirates, 1950–85* (London: Croom Helm, 1987), 89ff. Taryam played an important role in the negotiations and was a trusted advisor to the Ruler of Sharjah. He collected a large body of material available nowhere else and interviewed a number of the participants. His book is an important source, but as he says with great candor, "Here I should point out in all honesty that I have deliberately suppressed certain pieces of information of the utmost confidentiality" (p. 8). Many of the archives now open add to or supplement his account, and further clarification will be possible in the future.

13 See Unpublished NARA, Pol 15-1, UAE, Kuwait 1036, Stoltzfus to Secretary of State, June 10, 1972.

14 See Taryam, *The Establishment of the United Arab Emirates, 1950–85*, 90.

15 The Political Agent in Dubai, David Roberts, noted, "The merchants of Dubai, who rejoiced at the Dubai/Abu Dhabi union regard the larger union as involving them in the affairs of Qatar and Bahrain, which they regard as 'distant.'" See Unpublished FCO 8/9 57547, Roberts to Crawford, March 6, 1968. The same theme and terminology emerged from a meeting with the Ruler of Fujairah. "I asked the Ruler of Fujairah on 2 March what his view was of the recent meeting of the 9 Rulers … He himself wished for union with Zaid … it was unity with Zaid that he really wanted. He regarded Qatar and Bahrain as 'distant people'…" Unpublished FCO 8/9 57547, Roberts to Balfour-Paul (Political Residency, Bahrain), March 7, 1968.

16 See note 8.

17 It seems clear that the accord between Shaikh Zayid and Shaikh Rashid was viewed by both Rulers as the prime agreement that would underpin any subsequent grouping. The Qatar perspective was that the subsequent agreement superseded the Abu Dhabi–Dubai accord. Shaikh Zayid's per-

ception, as reflected by Ahmad Al Suwaidi and reported by Lamb: "…the Ruler was far from satisfied with the new agreement which was certainly not as positively unifying as the Abu Dhabi/Dubai union but they would have to try and make it work…the general attitude seems to be that this union might well meet the same fate as that of South Arabia." See Unpublished FCO 8/9 57547, Lamb (Political Agent, Abu Dhabi) to Crawford, March 2, 1968. For a long detailed and cogent summary of the meeting, see Unpublished FCO 8/9 57547, Roberts to Crawford, March 6, 1968. Roberts states, "Rashid and Zaid went a good deal further than they had led anyone to believe. The Abu Dhabi/Dubai union, however, expressly envisaged a meeting of the Trucial States Rulers followed by a meeting with the Rulers of Bahrain and Qatar…the Ruler of Abu Dhabi was willing to come to any meeting at any time of any composition desired by the Ruler of Dubai but would on no account agree to the Ruler of Qatar's condition préalable [precondition, original emphasis] that Zaid and Rashid should issue a second communiqué stating that the Dubai/Abu Dhabi union was subject to ratification by the other seven Rulers." In the determination to stick to this fundamental basis, Shaikh Zayid was completely resolute.

18   The support extended to the federation project was of course grounded in the particular national interests of each country. Saudi Arabia, for example, saw the federation as a mechanism to resist the spread of Arab nationalism in the region as well as to limit the power of Abu Dhabi. This is why Saudi Arabia strongly supported the idea of the Federation of Nine, in which Bahrain and Qatar would act as a balancing weight to that of Abu Dhabi, instead of the proposal of a smaller Federation of Seven. Egypt, on the other hand, voiced its approval for the idea of a union of the Trucial States because it would promote the idea of greater Arab unity and, from its perspective, lead to the spread of Arab nationalism. For some of the transcripts from Arab broadcasts see Unpublished FCO 8/9 57547, March 1968.

19   However, it is also suggested that in fact Britain from the outset preferred the Federation of Seven, seeing great difficulties in joining Bahrain and Qatar to the Trucial States. See Frauke Heard-Bey, *From Trucial States to United Arab Emirates: A Society in Transition*, second enlarged edition (London and New York, NY: Longman, 1996), 368. There was certainly a good deal of skepticism on the part of the Political Resident and the Political Agents in Abu Dhabi, Dubai and Bahrain. See, for example, Unpublished FCO 8/9 57547, A.D. Parsons (Political Agency, Bahrain) to Crawford, March 2, 1968. Only a full examination of the archives through 1971, once released and available, will shed a more definitive light on the issue. Yet, it is already clear that British policy was not monolithic. Different officials resident in one or other of the states reflected a range of views, all 'British' and ultimately congruent. Of course, in both detail and

aspiration, there could be wide variations. Moreover, given that the policy of withdrawal had been advanced by a Labour government, and the Conservative administration had given strong assurances that it would not be put into effect if they won the general election of 1970, which they did, a degree of uncertainty and indefinition was inevitable.

20 "For example, the wealthy Rulers of Baḥrayn, Qaṭar, Abū Dhabi, and Dubayy... each favored his own emirate as the site for the permanent federal capital. To the disappointment of the first two shaykhdoms, Abū Dhabi was eventually chosen as the temporary capital for the first seven years, with the agreement that a permanent capital would be constructed on land donated by Abū Dhabi and Dubayy from both sides of their joint frontier..." See John Duke Anthony, "The Union of Arab Amirates," *Middle East Journal* 26, No. 3 (Summer 1972): 271–272.

21 Bahrain proposed in October 1970 that the representation on the Union Council should be based on population, a proposal opposed by the other parties, with Abu Dhabi abstaining. From this point onwards, the likelihood of Bahrain's participation was much reduced.

22 Parsons reported the view of the Ruler of Bahrain and his brother the Bahraini Prime Minister that "Shaikh Ahmed [of Qatar] had no objective at the meeting [of February 27–28] other than the destruction of the Dubai/Abu Dhabi union... it is of course quite normal that the agreement should mean different things, or nothing, to each of the participants at the same time." See Unpublished FCO 8/9 57547, Parsons to Crawford, March 2, 1968.

23 Cited in Taryam, *The Establishment of the United Arab Emirates*, 96.

24 See Unpublished FCO 8/9 57547, Confidential Telegram, Lamb to Foreign Office, March 19, 1968. "Sheikh Khalifa bin Sulman [Prime Minister of Bahrain] arrived here today... Sheikh Khalifa's attitude was vehemently anti-Qatari and warmly pro-Zaid whom he said was obviously leader of Trucial Oman."

25 See Taryam, *The Establishment of the United Arab Emirates*, 96–98.

26 Unpublished FCO 8/918/1 68945, Henderson (Political Agency, Doha) to Weir (Political Residency, Bahrain), May 13, 1969.

27 Unpublished FCO 8/924 69095, Treadwell (Political Agent, Abu Dhabi) to Crawford (Political Resident, Bahrain), November 2, 1969.

28 See Richard Schofield (ed.) *Territorial Foundations of the Gulf States* (London: UCL Press, 1994).

29 Specifically, the Al Khalifa claim to Zubara and Bahrain's ownership of the Hawar Island. On March 16, 2001, the International Court of Justice delivered its final judgment in the case concerning the territorial dispute between Qatar and Bahrain. The court ruled in favor of Bahrain's claim to sovereignty over the al Hawar Island while Qatar's claim to sovereignty

over the town of Zubarah and the small islands of Janan and Hadd Janan was accepted.

30 See, for example, Taryam, *The Establishment of the United Arab Emirates*, 137, citing the Qatar official statement of October 31, 1969.

31 Ibid., 147.

32 Ibid., 148.

33 Ibid., 161.

34 Ibid., 162.

35 See Balfour-Paul, *The End of Empire in the Middle East*, 128–133. His lapidary phrase "frantic manoeuvring to square the circle" might be applied to British policy as a whole. In retrospect, it seems extraordinary that the situation was in effect left 'open' between the Conservative election victory of June 1970 and March 1971, a period of almost nine months. No doubt the Rulers were kept informed, but until the parliamentary statement of March 1, 1971, nothing was finally determined. Having allowed matters to drift during this extended period, the original timetable allowed only nine months for a new political structure to be created. However, this judgment must be provisional until the Foreign Office and Cabinet Office papers for this period become available.

36 See the report of the long meeting between Lamb and Shaikh Zayid on March 5 in Abu Dhabi after the Ruler returned from al Ain. Lamb notes that he was impressed by the Ruler's zest and confidence. "He is in good form and is not allowing the disappointments [over unity] he has suffered…either to damage his relations with us or to make him 'retreat to his tent' as you feared. In short, he is quite ready to drive the three horses of UAE, Abu Dhabi/Dubai (and Trucial States) Union and the Trucial States Council together…I then asked the Ruler what steps he proposed to take to keep the Abu Dhabi/Dubai union together. He said that the best way was to get the other Trucial States to join it…It seemed to him that some of the Rulers at the recent meeting in Dubai were just not prepared to take into account what the people wanted. He could assure me that the people of the Trucial States wanted Trucial States unity under Abu Dhabi and Dubai but wanted no close alliance with Bahrain and Qatar. It seemed to him that Trucial States unity must be his main aim." See Unpublished FCO 8/9 57547, Lamb to Crawford, March 7, 1968. This was in fact the policy consistently followed by Shaikh Zayid down to the eventual creation of the UAE.

37 See Ali Ajjaj, "Social Development of the Pirate Coast," *Middle East Forum* 38, No. 7 (Summer 1962): 75–80.

38 See Heard-Bey, *From Trucial States to United Arab Emirates*, 347.

39 Appropriately, the founding conference for the GCC was held in Abu Dhabi in May 1981.

40 The failure of SEATO (South East Asia Treaty Organization) and similar structures supported his view.

41 Taryam described it aptly as "nothing more than a glorified public works department." See Taryam, *The Establishment of the United Arab Emirates*, 174.

42 A cabinet and ministerial substructure was appointed as well as a National Consultative Assembly of 50 members.

43 The date is sometimes given as July 16. See Ibrahim Al Abed, Paula Vine and Abdullah Al Jabali (eds) *Chronicle of Progress: UAE 1971–1996, 25 years of Development in the United Arab Emirates* (London: Trident Press, 1996), 13.

44 It had already been made clear in private meetings that Abu Dhabi would not accept a loose constitutional arrangement. If there was no general agreement, Abu Dhabi would either go its own way or it would unite with any other interested emirate. These were generally understood to be Dubai and Sharjah. See Taryam, *The Establishment of the United Arab Emirates*, 174–175.

45 The constitutional changes indicated the seriousness of Abu Dhabi's intention to create a structure outside the proposed union, while the development fund indicated the economic benefits that would come to those who followed its lead.

46 Dubai had a number of continuing concerns, but these were largely resolved in a series of private bilateral meetings in the first full week of July. The government of Dubai continued to express hopes that the Federation of Nine would be a possibility. A senior emissary declared, "Dubai agrees to the union, but requests waiting for some time, at least until our brothers in Qatar and Bahrain make up their mind finally regarding either union or independence." Abu Dhabi replied in essence that there was no time left, British withdrawal was fast approaching, and the risk of instability, if there was not at least some successor administration, was real. See Taryam, *The Establishment of the United Arab Emirates*, 173–174.

47 The Provisional Constitution of the United Arab Emirates, Article 49. Constitutional Amendment No. 1 of 1996 cancelled the word temporary wherever it may appear and made the document permanent. References here are to the Constitution of the United Arab Emirates published by the Federal National Council in 1997.

48 Ras al Khaimah objected to the dominance of Abu Dhabi and Dubai, and the principle that the balance of power should be held by the larger states.

49 Radio Abu Dhabi newscast, 1.30 p.m., July 18, 1971, cited in Taryam, *The Establishment of the United Arab Emirates*, 175–176.

50 See J.E. Peterson, "The Future of Federalism in the United Arab Emirates," in H. Richard Sindelar III and J.E. Peterson (eds) *Crosscurrents in the Gulf: Arab, Regional and Global Interests* (New York, NY: Routledge, 1988), 221. Peterson suggests that this overlap led to the weakness of the federal institutions relative to the institutions of the individual emirates. However,

it also meant that in a structure where power was ultimately reserved to the lower level, it allowed the central institutions to intervene in areas that could legitimately have been regarded as "states' rights."

51   Constitution of the United Arab Emirates, Article 15.

52   Initially, this support was based on a traditional appeal for assistance when young people married. The Ruler provided citizens with a place to live and a means to earn a living. Over the years, the pattern of generosity was to become both more systematized and acquire a more direct social purpose. Traditionally, marriages were formed both between and within tribes; the alliances followed well-established patterns. The parents of the young people played a vital role in seeking a suitable marriage partner for their children. However, as the society of the UAE became more open, the old customs began to change. Many more marriages were contracted with Arabs from other countries and with non-Arabs as well. This became a matter of concern to Shaikh Zayid, who saw the family as the basic social institution. He was determined to encourage marriages between UAE citizens and the prospect of citizens from different emirates marrying each other seemed an important means of cementing the unity and integrity of the nation. Accordingly, he created an element within the federal budget to finance a Marriage Fund that made grants of up to 70,000 dirhams to UAE men marrying UAE women. Eventually, the budget of the Marriage Fund advanced to more than one billion dirhams. Moreover, the Fund sought to lower the barriers to marriage that occurred when excessive dowries were demanded by the families of young women. It actively promoted the benefits of marriage between UAE nationals, especially to citizens studying abroad. See *Women in the UAE* (Abu Dhabi: The UAE Women's Federation, 1995), 51–54.

53   Constitution of the United Arab Emirates, Article 16.

54   Ibid., Article 17.

55   This vision was not exclusive to the UAE, as Shaikh Zayid declared at the first meeting of the National Council of the Federation. He observed, "…the Federal State joined the Arab League in order to share with its Arab brothers in the Arab cause and achieve its objective, perfectly aware that the people's fortune is related to the common fortune of the Arab nation." See Sheikh Zayed, *Hopes and Deeds* (Beirut: Book and Publishing Establishment, 1990), 20. See also Article 6 of the Constitution of the United Arab Emirates, which specifies, "The Union is a part of the Great Arab Nation, to which it is bound by ties of religion, language, history and common destiny. The people of the Union are one people, and one part of the Arab Nation."

56   For example, since 1946 Shaikh Zayid had believed in resolving disputes between 'Arab brothers' by discussion and sensible compromise. Thus, he

had won the support of tribal leaders and in particular developed a good working relationship with both Dubai and Oman.

57 See Article 6 of the Constitution of the United Arab Emirates.

58 Cited in Taryam, *The Establishment of the United Arab Emirates*, 176.

59 By 1968/69, Abu Dhabi was supplying 90 percent of the development budget for the Trucial States and Shaikh Zayid had made it clear that the financial resources of Abu Dhabi would be available to the new state. This sense of security did much to convince his fellow Rulers that the United Arab Emirates would be beneficial. See Muhammad Morsy Abdullah, *The United Arab Emirates: A Modern History* (Westerham Hill: Hurtwood Press, 1978), 81.

60 John Duke Anthony points out that this concentration of political power and authority in Abu Dhabi and Dubai was a matter of concern to some of the poorer shaikhdoms. However, it is difficult to see how it could have been otherwise. Abu Dhabi provided most of the financial resources for the new nation. While Shaikh Zayid was prepared to move slowly and steadily, he would never countenance Abu Dhabi being forced to accept a majority vote by the small emirates against Abu Dhabi's interest. See John Duke Anthony, *Arab States of the Lower Gulf: People, Politics, Petroleum* (Washington, DC: The Middle East Institute, 1975), 105–112.

61 In many ways, it paralleled the crucial partnership between the British Prime Minister Churchill and the US President Roosevelt in leading the Allied cause to victory in the Second World War. Just as in that partnership, both leaders in the UAE had strong personalities and quite distinct aims and objectives. They sometimes disagreed quite forcefully on political issues. But the unshakable strength of their accord and sense of common purpose allowed them ultimately to transcend disagreements.

62 See *Chronicle of Progress*, 13.

63 Ibid.

64 See J.E. Peterson, "The Future of Federalism in the United Arab Emirates," 212.

65 See Anthony, "The Union of Arab Amirates," 271–287.

66 See Mohammed Al-Fahim, *From Rags to Riches: A Story of Abu Dhabi* (London: The London Centre of Arab Studies, 1995), 152.

67 See J.E. Peterson, "The Future of Federalism in the United Arab Emirates," 198.

68 Ibid.

69 See *Sheikh Zayed: Leadership*, 48–49.

CHAPTER 8

1   The UAE was admitted to the United Nations on December 9, 1971 and the flag was hoisted for the first time on December 12.

2   Shaikh Zayid, knowledgeable about history and his family traditions, may well have been aware of the furore caused by the attempt of the British to impose a flag emblematic of the Qawasim in 1901. See Chapter 2.

3   The falcon was also the commonly used symbol for the emirate of Abu Dhabi.

4   For example, the border with Saudi Arabia was still unresolved and Iran had occupied three islands belonging to the UAE (Abu Musa and Greater and Lesser Tunb). Technically speaking, when two of the islands were annexed, Ras al Khaimah had not yet acceded to the Federation. However, with that emirate joining the Federation in early 1972, the dispute became a concern for the UAE as a whole. From this point onward, it has remained a central tenet of UAE policy to obtain the return of the islands by all peaceful means.

5   For example, Ahmad Khalifa Al Suwaidi. Al Suwaidi was responsible not only for building up the international connections of the new state in his capacity as the UAE's Foreign Minister, but also for developing much of the new internal administrative and economic system.

6   Shams Al-Din Al-Doaifi (ed.) *Sheikh Zayed: Leadership, The United Arab Emirates 1971–1987* (Beirut: Book and Publishing Establishment, n.d.), 41.

7   Ibid., 42.

8   He had already worked assiduously to establish good relations within the ruling family and within the wider Bani Yas alliances.

9   *Sheikh Zayed: Leadership*, 41. Similarly, in a speech to the Supreme Council in 1989, Shaikh Zayid stated, "I do not impose my views and I am not autocratic whether inside the Council or in society in general. If there are views which are opposed to mine, I would always modify to the more correct opinion because I believe that this is a virtue imposed by the good relations and the fruitful dialogue between the President and his brothers, the Rulers and the people." See *Gulf News*, January 10, 1989. Shaikh Zayid also followed the principle that unity could not be achieved by force in his regional diplomacy. In a message to Yemeni President Ali Abdullah Salih during that country's civil hostilities in 1994, Shaikh Zayid stated, "The use of force will not bring union. Unity cannot be imposed by force and arms. The language of force and military means for settling disputes is unacceptable and will not bring any good to the people of Yemen." See *Gulf News*, May 28, 1994.

10 The 'White Revolution' initiated by Shah Muhammad Reza in Iran never took root, while in Saudi Arabia excessive expenditure in the 1960s induced

an unbalanced economy that needed dramatic corrections under Faisal Bin Abdul-Aziz, first as Prime Minister and later as King. The smaller states – Bahrain and Qatar – were not directly comparable, nor was Kuwait. On the latter, see Jill Crystal, *Oil and Politics in the Gulf: Rulers and Merchants in Kuwait and Qatar* (New York, NY: Cambridge University Press, 1990).

11 The federal authorities had defined areas of responsibility under the Provisional Constitution, such as health and communications. In some areas, responsibilities were shared, for example in the administration of law.

12 The new positions were subject to selective entry and there was always fierce competition from all the emirates for positions in the federal administration.

13 Both Reza Khan in Iran and Atatürk in Turkey had coupled building a new state with destroying much of the old society.

14 The problems which Samuel Huntington observed in his work *Political Order in Changing Societies*, specifically Chapter 3, "Political Change in Traditional Polities," have not surfaced in the development of the UAE. The reason perhaps lies in Shaikh Zayid's capacity to fulfill the requirements specified by Huntington, "To cope successfully with modernization, a political system must be able, first, to innovate policy, that is, to promote social and economic reform by state action... the expansion of communications and education, the broadening of loyalties from family, village, and tribe to nation, the secularization of public life, the rationalization of authority structures, the promotion of functionally specific organizations, the substitution of achievement criteria for ascriptive ones, and the furthering of a more equitable distribution of material and symbolic resources" (p.140). However, this transformation was accomplished without breaching the existing structure of governance at the emirate level. Modernization existed alongside tradition. This is not, however, unparalleled. Huntington also observes that "In America, the ease of modernization within society precluded the modernization of political institutions. The United States thus combines the world's most modern society with one of the world's more antique polities" (p.129). A similar capacity to accommodate modernity and tradition within a single society is equally the achievement of the United Arab Emirates. See Samuel P. Huntington, *Political Order in Changing Societies* (New Haven, CT: Yale University Press, 1968). The mechanism that allowed this to take place was what has been called the 'rentier' economy, which allowed the new state to provide benefit and not burden to all its citizens. Moreover, as Jill Crystal has observed, "access to the state is a critical resource." In the UAE, this would refer to the new federal state. See Jill Crystal, "Sources of Power: Social Stratification and Political Influence in the Arabian Gulf" (unpublished paper presented to the Annual Meeting of the Middle East Studies Association in Portland, Oregon, October 1992), 19.

15 The Constitution gave citizens certain rights that they had never possessed before and federal regulations protected the people from commercial and

social exploitation. For example, only a national could own real property or a business. Foreign enterprise required a local sponsor or partner, and this became a means whereby many local families were able to develop business enterprises with minimum risk. In addition, citizens paid no federal taxes.

16 In an interview with All India Radio in 1984, Shaikh Zayid stated, "Till the discovery of oil, our people suffered centuries of isolation and poverty. It was our duty to try and compensate them by planning and executing the essential economic and political infrastructures that can enable them to lead their life in dignity and peace." The text of this interview is reprinted in *Khaleej Times*, December 4, 1984.

17 For example, with the creation of the Abu Dhabi Women's Association in February 1973, the aim was to establish a distinctive role for women in the society of the UAE. The success of these initiatives over more than 20 years has been remarkable. By 1997, the women of the UAE were to achieve the highest level of development in any Arab country, according to the Human Resources Development Report of the United Nations. See UAE Ministry of Information and Culture, *United Arab Emirates Yearbook 1997* (London: Trident Press, 1997), 190.

18 See Ibrahim Al Abed, Paula Vine and Abdullah Al Jabali (eds) *Chronicle of Progress: UAE 1971–1996, 25 years of Development in the United Arab Emirates* (London: Trident Press, 1996), 19.

19 See Malcolm C. Peck, *The United Arab Emirates: A Venture in Unity* (London: Croom Helm, 1986). The development in the UAE was more cohesive and more modest than the surge of growth that occurred in Iran at the same period. Some of the criticism – mostly focused on duplication and redundancy of facilities – was short-sighted. This same writer who commented adversely on the development of port facilities and airports in several of the emirates also pointed to the paralytic effect that inadequate ports were having on Iran. At one port, over 200 ships had to wait to deliver their cargoes, with an average waiting time of five months. Five percent of Iran's oil revenues were absorbed by the additional costs of these delays. Nothing of a similar nature occurred in the UAE, where there were relatively few bottlenecks. The infrastructure proved capable of dealing with a pace of development that few had anticipated. See J.B. Kelly, *Arabia, the Gulf and the West* (London: Basic Books, 1980), 197–200, 293.

20 Characterized as "overbuilding, prompted by interemirate rivalries" by one writer. See Peck, *The United Arab Emirates*, 100.

21 Of course, he had already revitalized al Ain by his work with irrigation and agriculture in the 1950s and 1960s.

22 See Food and Agricultural Organization of the United Nations, *Agricultural Development in the United Arab Emirates: Report on the Present Position,*

Prospects and Priorities (FAO Technical Advisory Service, Near East Regional Office, Cairo, 1973).

23   Ibid., 19. This proposal also suggested major improvements in fisheries, which were of great importance to the UAE.

24   "When one looks around today it is easy to see the results of his ongoing efforts in this field. The towns and cities throughout the Emirates abound with greenery, especially in Abu Dhabi and some of the islands—there have been an estimated 9 million trees planted since 1966. The transformation is beyond belief." See Mohammed Al-Fahim, *From Rags to Riches: A Story of Abu Dhabi* (London: The London Centre of Arab Studies, 1995), 154–155.

25   Between 1977 and 1981, fruit production rose from 38,000 tons to 146,000 tons, while egg production doubled over the same period and vegetable output went up four-fold.

26   More than 280 farms were established around al Ain.

27   Other research stations in Umm al Qaiwain and Dubai worked on dairy farming, to the extent that they were eventually able to supply a significant part of the population with dairy products. A poultry farm established in Fujairah was designed to satisfy a large part of national requirements.

28   One, at Bu Deeb, on the Abu Dhabi highway, sat astride a natural aquifer. Here, in 1981, 84,000 acacia seedlings were being grown, each irrigated daily with 2–3 gallons of water drawn from nine wells. In 1981, it cost 120 dirhams to plant and maintain each seedling for two years. See Peck, *The United Arab Emirates*, 107–108. Thus, the Bu Deeb nursery represented an investment of more than 10 million dirhams, and there was an increasing number of such establishments throughout the emirates.

29   See Food and Agricultural Organization of the United Nations, *Agricultural Development in the United Arab Emirates*. The tree roots served to bind the surface and subsoil and prevent erosion; transpiration through the leaves in suitable species improved the moisture balance in the atmosphere, while plantations reduced the ground temperature and acted as shelter belts, preventing surface erosion from the winds off the desert.

30   February 26, 1979. See *Chronicle of Progress*, 142. The scale of this development is remarkable. By May 1997, more than 4.5 percent of the terrain of the UAE was under forestry or agriculture, while more than 200 islands formerly barren were being recovered. The most advanced system of water recycling had been established, so that waste water could be used to irrigate farms and forestry. Mangroves, which grew sparsely along the coast, were planted in the shallows along the shoreline, providing a natural habitat for wildlife. See, "How Sheikh Zayed turned the Desert Green," *Christian Science Monitor*, May 27, 1997.

31   See *Sheikh Zayed: Leadership*, 99.

32 As President, he normally ruled with a very light hand. Even when he became aware that some Rulers were trying directly to undermine his policies, Shaikh Zayid decided not to move against them. Only when the situation became critical did he act, as when negotiations for the Federation plan were in imminent danger of collapse in 1971.

33 The core of the problem which Shaikh Zayid had faced was the fierce independence of the constituent emirates. Yet, he was able, because of the inchoate and unformed political structure of the UAE, to work around the problem. Assured of his support from the population at large, he was able to avoid confrontation and crisis.

34 The Abu Dhabi Defence Force (ADDF) was much larger and better equipped. The Trucial Oman Scouts, however, although less well-equipped, were a disciplined and highly effective land force and provided a key element in the Federal Defence Forces. Operationally, from the early days of Shaikh Zayid's rule in Abu Dhabi, the Scouts had already worked closely with ADDF and there was mutual respect and confidence between the two forces. Shaikh Zayid had proposed that the ADDF should work under the command and control of the Scouts on patrols of the desert, around Liwa and al Ain. After the handover from British command, they were renamed the Union Defence Force (UDF). See John Duke Anthony, *Arab States of the Lower Gulf: People, Politics, Petroleum* (Washington, DC: The Middle East Institute, 1975), 104.

35 The coup leader, Shaikh Saqr Bin Sultan (who had ruled Sharjah until he was removed in 1965 under British orders) opposed the agreement with Iran over Abu Musa and was believed to favor withdrawal from the Federation and a connection with Ras al Khaimah. See John Duke Anthony, "The Union of Arab Amirates," *Middle East Journal* 26, No. 3 (Summer 1972): 276–277.

36 Ibid., 277.

37 Presumably it was technically possible for the ruling family to select another Ruler, but he would not have been recognized by his brother Rulers, and he could not have taken his seat on the Supreme Council. In 1987, when there was a dispute over who had the right to Sharjah's seat on the Supreme Council, it was evident that while the Supreme Council could not determine the ruler of a state, it felt itself only able to declare who was entitled to the emirate's seat on the Council. This was analogous to the power formally exercised by the Political Resident to 'recognize' a new ruler. See *Middle East Contemporary Survey*, Vol. XI (Boulder, CO: 1987), 386–387.

38 When the Ruler of Fujairah died in 1974, he was succeeded by his son, Shaikh Hamad Bin Muhammad Al Sharqi. The succession was announced by the Supreme Council on September 18, 1974. In 1981, Shaikh Rashid Bin Ahmad succeeded his father as Ruler of Umm al Qaiwain. In 1990, Shaikh Maktum Bin Rashid succeeded his father,

Shaikh Rashid, in the same smooth and tranquil fashion. Eventually all the emirates followed Shaikh Zayid's example and formally designated a Crown Prince or Deputy Ruler.

39 In the debate over the renewal of his presidency in 1976, he made it clear that he would act decisively if necessary. The power of such action was not to coerce those who opposed him, but rather to withdraw himself from the area of contention. In this context, the hint of withdrawal was sufficient to settle the issue along the lines envisioned by Shaikh Zayid.

40 He also made it clear to the other Rulers that if they failed to follow his lead, they would have to follow their own path without his presence or support. Implicit was the threat that while Abu Dhabi could and would flourish outside the federal structure, the other smaller emirates would not. Without the wealth and prestige of Abu Dhabi underpinning them, their prosperity could vanish as quickly as it had come. Ultimately, of course, the real power behind Shaikh Zayid's ideal of unity was the knowledge that over time the obvious benefits of union would be persuasive enough in their own right. Above all, Shaikh Zayid trusted the people. In two situations of crisis in 1976 and 1979, it was the UAE citizens as a whole who rallied spontaneously around the President and the concept of unity. The unmistakable will of the people compelled those who doubted the appeal of the federal ideal to silence their opposition and support Shaikh Zayid.

41 *Chronicle of Progress*, 99–105.

42 See Frauke Heard-Bey, *From Trucial States to United Arab Emirates: A Society in Transition*, second enlarged edition (London and New York, NY: Longman, 1996), 407–410.

43 *Chronicle of Progress*, 142–144.

44 Ibid., 147.

45 Interview with the *New York Times*, June 1, 1998.

46 See J.E. Peterson, "The Future of Federalism in the United Arab Emirates," in H. Richard Sindelar III and J.E. Peterson (eds) *Crosscurrents in the Gulf: Arab, Regional and Global Interests* (New York, NY: Routledge, 1988), 216. "On the surface, at least, the process of federalization had slowed to an imperceptible crawl but no one questioned the underlying legitimacy of the federal state."

47 "The citizen is the real resource of this land, he is the most expensive resource of this country." See *Sheikh Zayed: Leadership*, 100.

48 The Constitution became permanent in 1996, while the armed forces were officially unified under one central command in December 1997.

49 J.E. Peterson, "The Future of Federalism in the United Arab Emirates," 210–227.

50 In 1971, his eldest son, Shaikh Khalifa, was still in his early twenties, his second son, Shaikh Sultan, in his teens and his third son, Shaikh

Muhammad, a boy of 11. In future years, they provided the essential close and solid support on which he could depend, but in 1971 this did not exist. While Shaikh Zayid had the support of other members of his family, the political picture was not transformed until his sons had the experience to work with him. Under the rule of his brother Shaikh Shakhbut, Shaikh Zayid had always urged the close involvement in government by members of the ruling family. In his own rule, he always used the talents of family members. With his own sons, he ensured that they were trained for the roles that they were to fulfill. He himself had learned the skills of a ruler in the long years as Ruler's Representative at al Ain, and he was determined that his own sons should also learn well. For example, Shaikh Khalifa held early responsibility, like his father, in al Ain, in the Abu Dhabi Defence Force, and as Prime Minister of Abu Dhabi. These were posts of responsibility, but they were also a means to learn the art of governance. He also ensured that they received an appropriate education. Shaikh Sultan attended the Royal Military Academy at Sandhurst, United Kingdom, and Shaikh Muhammad attended Sandhurst and Cambridge University. As his sons' experience of government deepened, they were able to provide increasingly effective assistance to Shaikh Zayid.

51 Analytically, we can see the internal and external axes of policy intersecting and interacting in a more active and complex fashion in the period 1971–1985 than in the subsequent period. A key determinant was the appointment of Shaikh Rashid Bin Sa'id as Prime Minister in 1979. By accepting the post, Shaikh Rashid publicly undertook to support the Federation. He was an extremely effective leader. However, his increasing ill-health during the 1980s meant that he could not play the pivotal role as he once had in the debate over the identity of the Federation as an ever closer union or a loose federation. The gradual weakening of this critical voice in the 1980s (which was sadly silenced by death in 1990) was a crucial factor.

52 The national anthem, the national emblem and the national flag were the subject of a nationwide public competition held in October 1971.

53 In May 1973, after a long transitional period, the new national currency – the dirham – replaced both the Bahraini dinar and the Qatari riyal, which had been adopted by different emirates. The creation of a single, secure and unitary national currency pegged to the US dollar under the control of a new UAE Currency Board was a crucial economic and political step. With the currency being fully convertible, it has had an enviable record of stability. As a result, the success of the dirham became an emblem of the success of the national economy.

54 A Union Postal Administration came into effect on August 1, 1972, replacing the stamps issued by each individual emirate. For the history and

stamps issued see Stanley Gibbons, *Stamp Catalogue: Part 19, The Middle East*, fifth edition (London: Stanley Gibbons Ltd., 1996), 594–609.

55   The UAE Football Association was established in 1971 and joined FIFA the following year. In 1974, it joined the Arab Football Association and the Asian Soccer Federation.

56   Hamdi Tammam described his "permanent calm" as the most characteristic feature of Zayid's personality. See Hamdi Tammam, *Zayed bin Sultan Al-Nahayyan: The Leader and the March*, second revised edition (Tokyo: Dai Nippon Printing Company, 1983), 311.

57   See Bernhard Lewis, *Islam in History: Ideas, People, and Events in the Middle East*, revised edition (Chicago, IL: Open Court Publishing Company, 1993), 206. Lewis is describing the Turkic elements that altered the traditional Islamic system, and became the reformed Islamic political system. It is striking how these elements recur in the structure created by Shaikh Zayid.

58   The view of Ira M. Lapidus is relevant here. "While there was no trans-ferable model of an Islamic State, Muslim societies were often based upon similar concepts, institutions and vocabularies. Generally, for Muslims, a Muslim ruler was the symbol of a legitimate regime, a guarantor that Muslim laws would be enforced, and the representative of the historic continuity of Muslim communities and their attachment to the Prophet [PBUH]. Muslims regarded states and empires as the ultimate protectors of worship, education and law. In times of war they expected protection…in times of peace, patronage for scholars and saints. The existence of a Muslim state assured its peoples that the civilized order of the world was being upheld." Lapidus further demonstrates in his lengthy and important work that over the centuries the 'rightly guided' Muslim state has taken many forms. See Ira M. Lapidus, *A History of Islamic Societies* (Cambridge: Cambridge University Press, 1988), 264–276.

CHAPTER 9

1   The British justified this by saying that local training was inadequate for the use of sophisticated material. However, in the post-British environ-ment, Shaikh Zayid knew that the UAE needed a threat capacity which depended on the possession of high-grade equipment.

2   Before 1971, education and literacy had been limited. In all the Trucial States in the early 1950s, school enrolment had never risen above 250 annually, but this had increased to over 3,000 just one decade later. In the first years of the UAE, more than 30,000 students were enrolled in schools, a figure that increased ten-fold by 1996–1997. Relevant statistics are cited

in Abdullah Mograby, "Human Development in the United Arab Emirates: Indicators and Challenges," in *Education and the Arab World* (Abu Dhabi: The Emirates Center for Strategic Studies and Research, 1999), 286–291. As a result, by 1994 adult literacy in the UAE, as measured by the United Nations, had risen to 78.6 percent, higher than all the other states in the region except Bahrain. See *UNDP Human Development Report 1997*, 146–147. This newly literate population was served by a multiplicity of channels of communication. A weekly newspaper, *Al Ittihad*, was published in Abu Dhabi from October 20, 1969, and later appeared as a daily. In 1970, another newspaper, *Al Khaleej*, first appeared in Sharjah. English-language newspapers such as *Emirates News* and *Khaleej Times* reported national news, in addition to a high proportion of international news, much of it drawn from external news agencies. The growing role played by the UAE in international affairs was prominently featured, and Emirati citizens began to gain a sense of the important role that their country was playing in Arab issues and in world events more generally. In addition, three other major Arabic newspapers began circulating after 1969. In Abu Dhabi, this included *Al Wahda* (1973), *Al Fajr* (1975), and in Dubai, *Al Bayan* (1980). English-language newspapers available included: *Emirates News* (Abu Dhabi—associated with *Al Ittihad*, August 1971); *Khaleej Times* (Dubai, 1978); *Gulf News* (Dubai, 1979); and *Gulf Today* (Sharjah, 1996). See Ahmad Nafadi, *Sahafit Al-Imarat: Al-Nash'ah wal Tattawur Al-Fanni wal Tarikhi*, translated as *The Press in the United Arab Emirates: Origins, Technical and Historical Development* (Abu Dhabi: Cultural Foundation, 1996).

3   This universal identification within the UAE of Shaikh Zayid as President helps to explain the outpouring of support regarding the events in 1976 and 1979 (See Chapter 8). By then, radio and television had established his popular persona.

4   *Majmu'at Khutab al Shaikh Zayid* (Abu Dhabi: n.d.), 14.

5   Sir William Luce, the Political Resident in the Gulf, had already noted in a 1962 report that while Shaikh Zayid preferred to settle disputes with his neighbors by meeting them face-to-face and talking things over, "he would not sacrifice Abu Dhabi interests for the sake of agreement." See Unpublished FO 371/163025, W.H. Luce (Political Resident, Bahrain) to A.R. Walmsley (Foreign Office), March 30, 1962.

6   UAE Ministry of Information and Culture, *Majmu'at Tasriha Ahadith wa Tashrihat Sahib al Sumu al Shaikh Zayid bin Sultan al-Nahyan* (Abu Dhabi: n.d.), 30–31.

7   UAE Ministry of Information and Culture, *United Arab Emirates Yearbook 1997* (London: Trident Press, 1997), 58.

8   See Unpublished FO 371/179929 35506, Lamb (Political Resident, Abu Dhabi) to Phillips (British Residency, Bahrain), September 16, 1965.

9   Lamb noted in a conversation with Shaikh Zayid, "Zaid told me that he had spoken separately to Shakhbut about the importance of getting British Army officers to raise, train and command the army…" Thus, Shaikh Zayid clearly saw that an army was not just a matter or ordering equipment, but meant getting the right troops as well as logistic supplies, a long-term training process, and building up a proper structure of command. See Unpublished FO 371/179929 35506, Lamb to Phillips, October 11, 1965.

10   For example, in a key meeting held on October 11, 1965, Shaikh Zayid had clear views on the realities behind organizing camel patrols and engaged in detailed explanations to his brother about how a modern force should be organized and structured. See Ibid. Shaikh Zayid was then sent to the UK to purchase equipment for the Abu Dhabi Defence Force. See Unpublished FO 371/185578 35760, Weir (Foreign Office) to Thompson (Minister of State, Foreign Office), June 29, 1966.

11   Unpublished FO 371/179929 35506, Lamb to Phillips, October 11, 1965.

12   See Unpublished FO 371/185553 35716, Lamb to Balfour-Paul (British Residency, Bahrain), November 5, 1966.

13   The purchase of the British Hawker aircraft encountered some contractual difficulties which were resolved after Shaikh Zayid took a firm stand. In a report about a meeting with Shaikh Zayid attended by Major P. Sincock, Annex A to 165/2 MAO dated September 16, 1969, it is noted, "He also felt that he had been 'conned'… into spending money unnecessarily and also 'done' by Hawkers over the Hunter deal." Hawkers had submitted much larger bills than had at first been anticipated, pleading unexpected costs. Shaikh Zayid's view was that he had not changed his specification and they had had the chance to state their price, so now they should stick to it. In this context, he found the French companies much easier to deal with. See Unpublished FCO 8/1242, "Record of Audience with Shaikh Zaid, 13 Sep 1969."

14   Information drawn from *Strategic Survey 1972* (London: International Institute for Strategic Studies, 1973). See also Table 1 in John Duke Anthony, *Arab States of the Lower Gulf: People, Politics, Petroleum* (Washington, DC: The Middle East Institute, 1975), 105.

15   Dubai continued to preserve an individual and independent arms procurement policy. The emirate bought British and Italian armored vehicles that differed from those supplied to the Abu Dhabi Defence Force and the Union Defence Force.

16   See Unpublished FCO 8/11 57547, E.F. Henderson (Political Agent, Abu Dhabi) to Sir Stewart Crawford (Political Resident, Bahrain), April 4, 1968.

17   Ibid.

18   Ibid.

19 Ibid. The contrary view sometimes expressed to the British officials that Shaikh Zayid intended to use his large forces to overawe his fellow Rulers in the Trucial States was not sustained by events. His own analysis was later narrated by Henderson, "Zaid countered every protest of mine by saying that if he got no cooperation he would go it alone with as big an army as he needed … In favour of this scheme it can be said that he is single-minded, resolute, courageous and does have the funds to achieve it. His argument that the loose union of the Seven, with no drive in it will fail is to me valid … If the Union fails, he says the people will be angry, there will be revolutions and those Shaikhs who cannot stand alone, will be wiped out."

20 Unpublished FCO 8/14, Sir Stewart Crawford, Despatch of June 12, 1968 printed at FO/CO/WH, Appendix Section 3.

21 Ibid.

22 See Unpublished FCO8/49, A.T. Lamb to Sir Stewart Crawford, January 20, 1968.

23 At the same time, Shaikh Zayid shrewdly observed in April 1976 "that unifying the sources of weapons supplied to Arab Gulf military forces would serve to weaken these armies since it places them under the control of a monopoly." See Ibrahim Al Abed, Paula Vine and Abdullah Al Jabali (eds) *Chronicle of Progress: UAE 1971–1996, 25 years of Development in the United Arab Emirates* (London: Trident Press, 1996), 94. The significance of this statement should not be overlooked. The issue of supply coordination has been used repeatedly to criticize the UAE policy of seeking supplies from several sources. See Anthony H. Cordesman, *Bahrain, Oman, Qatar, and the UAE: Challenges of Security* (Boulder, CO: Westview Press, 1997), 378–380. The unstated assumption behind Cordesman's work is that the UAE should standardize with US equipment, because all future defense activity will only take place in the context of a US-supported posture. Cordesman ignores the fact that Israel is seen as a threat by Arab nations but not by the US. Shaikh Zayid has been well aware that US supply decisions are conditioned by their contingent effect on Israel. He also observed in 1975, talking of his sophisticated Mirage fighters, "… if there's another confrontation with Israel, one of the Arab front line states may need them and we would then be in a position to turn them over. This is a common struggle; during the October War, Kuwait contributed forces. If there is a next time, perhaps we will also contribute forces." See Shaikh Zayid's interview in *Newsweek*, March 10, 1975. A dispassionate assessment of the risks of a sole supplier may be found in John Duke Anthony, "The Gulf Cooperation Council: A New Framework for Policy Coordination," in H. Richard Sindelar III and J.E. Peterson (eds) *Crosscurrents in the Gulf: Arab, Regional and Global Interests* (New York, NY: Routledge, 1988), 56. "A common arms acquisition policy would require all six states to purchase their weapons and long-term, follow-on training and

support systems from a single source. As a consequence, the GCC would become intimately and critically dependent on one supplier, something which very few, if any, countries…would be prepared to do…An equally, if not more important, consideration is that such a relationship inevitably would be perceived as a *de facto* alliance and would send important – and undoubtedly, controversial – political messages throughout the Middle East and international community." Although the 1990–1991 Gulf War has increased the need to function as part of an alliance system, it has not extinguished the need for the UAE to have the potential for an independent military and foreign policy.

24 For example, the Zayid Military College in al Ain graduated its first officer class in April 1973. See *Chronicle of Progress*, 42.

25 Ibid., 82.

26 Ibid., 86.

27 Ibid., 95. The Supreme Council made an amendment to the Provisional Constitution that gave the Federation the sole right to establish land, naval and air forces.

28 See Erik R. Peterson, *The Gulf Cooperation Council: Search for Unity in a Dynamic Region* (Boulder, CO: Westview Press, 1988), 72.

29 The Western Region was to be centered on Abu Dhabi, the Central Region on Dubai, and the Northern Region on Ras al Khaimah.

30 See *Chronicle of Progress*, 126.

31 In practice, he ensured that the efficiency of the national forces was maintained at all times, in effect by marginalizing the local forces that were not fully integrated within the national command structure. These became an increasing financial burden to the individual emirates, a costly symbol of a local independence that had less and less resonance with the public at large.

32 Almost every issue in civil society has had its echo in the military: national versus emirate forces; the role of women in society; the role of expatriates; the need for technical innovation; skills and training issues; the development of effective economic mechanisms (offsets); technology transfer, etc.

33 See Unpublished NARA, Griffin, AmEmbassy, Abu Dhabi to Secretary of State, WashDC, Pol 23–8 UAE (Abu Dhabi) 1560, June 12, 1972.

34 UAE Ministry of Information and Culture, *United Arab Emirates Yearbook 1998* (in Arabic) (London: Trident Press), 130.

35 While initially supportive of the embargo imposed by the international community on Iraq following the 1990–1991 Gulf War, Shaikh Zayid became increasingly frustrated when the embargo failed to meet its objectives. He became particularly distressed that the Iraqi people – fellow Arabs – were suffering deprivations that appeared only to get worse as time moved on. While Shaikh Zayid was committed to defending Kuwait and participating

in deterrence efforts vis-à-vis Iraq (as, for example, during the October 1994 crisis), at the same time he maintained, "It has become a duty that the suffering of the Iraqi people should be brought to an end." See "Zayed calls for end to Iraq embargo," *Gulf News*, October 17, 1995. By 1997, the UAE, with Shaikh Zayid's support, began taking direct action to help the Iraqi people. Thirty-five tons of food and medicines were collected and delivered to Iraq in January 1997, while another 500 tons followed the next month. See UAE Ministry of Information and Culture, *United Arab Emirates Yearbook 1997*, 56.

36 Well equipped, a strong ethos of command, professional rather than conscript-based, and non-aligned are all necessary qualities which match the profile of the UAE Armed Forces.

37 Note the report of John N. Gatch Jr on his meeting with British officials in the year before Shaikh Zayid's accession. "Arthur Paul, who describes himself as the Chief of the 6-man Gulf States East Section of the Foreign Office 'Research' organisation (comparable to the Bureau of Intelligence and Research in the US State Department), in his words, is currently visiting Kuwait as part of an area wide tour. During the course of a discussion on the state of the Middle East politics in general, Mr. Paul indicated that the idea of confederation or inter-governmental grouping of any sort in the area was no longer considered feasible…by him as a solution to the UK's problems in the Gulf. He further indicated that the logical ultimate 'solution' to the problem of filling the UK vacuum, which will occur in a matter of time, is the entrance of Saudi Arabia…as the dominant force in the area. He illustrated his point by making the statement, 'if the UK presence in Abu Dhabi leaves, then the logical successor to us is Saudi Arabia.'" See Unpublished NARA, American Embassy Kuwait to Department of State, Pol 1, Trucial States–UK, No. A-228, March 11, 1965.

38 Saudi Arabia and Iran. He was also concerned with restoring good relations with Qatar. The US Weekly Summary noted, "The coolness that has for so long characterized Abu Dhabi's relations with its neighbor Qatar is rapidly disappearing due to the close, brotherly affection that seems to be developing between the Ruler, Sheikh Zayed and Sheikh Khalifa bin Mohammed [*sic*] Al-Thani, the Deputy Ruler of Qatar. According to the British, the two have long been friends, but their relationship since Zayed assumed the rule has now blossomed into a full scale political love affair. The British are hoping to seize this propitious moment to win the agreement of the Abu Dhabians and Qataris to an amicable settlement of their historical onshore boundary disputes. Once the land boundaries have been established with acceptable reference points, HMG would then take the thornier question of the off-shore demarcation lines between the two states. Comment: Settlement of the Abu Dhabi–Qatar boundary dispute could provide the impetus for a more

conciliatory approach by other Gulf state Rulers with respect to their own territorial claims." See Unpublished NARA, Weekly Summaries Eastern Province, Bahrain and Trucial States, No. 15, October 12, 1966. The reference to "Sheikh Khalifa bin Mohammed Al-Thani" in the quote is incorrect as the Deputy Ruler at the time was Shaikh Khalifa Bin Hamad Al Thani. As far as Shaikh Zayid is concerned, Iraq also featured in his thinking, but his main concerns were with those states with which he shared direct land or maritime boundaries.

39   See Unpublished NARA, AmEmbassy Jidda to DOS, Incoming Telegram, April 18, 1967, 017004, Confidential Jidda 4296. "Zayed handled himself well while here. He approached Faisal as son to Father, told [the] King that anything he possessed was at Faisal's disposal, that he looked on [the] King as his 'Protector' and that Saudi Arabia would be first country to which he turned in [the] event of trouble…if nothing else, good personal rapport was developed between Faisal and Zayed as result of [the] visit which should offer something to build on."

40   See Unpublished NARA, AmEmbassy Jidda to DOS, Incoming Telegram, April 17, 1967, 015896, Confidential Jidda 4282. "Zayed reportedly not entirely happy about inconclusive results of [the] visit and now blames British for not having paved the way more with Faisal in making it clear that Buraimi [al Ain] is Abu Dhabi territory. Man [British Ambassador to Saudi Arabia] described Zayed as 'Frosty' to him at airport departure."

41   For example, Saudi Arabia was insistent on 'access to the Gulf' at Khur al 'Udaid, which had also long been a source of conflict with Qatar. Shaikh Zayid was prepared to negotiate on non-core issues in the interests of a general settlement.

42   King Abdul Aziz had once (memorably) remarked that "the British were people of 'but'. They made statements and gave you assurances but always added at the end 'but'." See Unpublished NARA 611.86/3-2350 [J] Rives Child to DOS, March 23, 1950, reporting his meeting with King Abdul Aziz. That is to say, in his view, the British were evasive and never serious in their negotiations.

43   There is no documentary source for this story, but knowledge of it is so widespread that it is unlikely to be wholly fanciful.

44   In January 1973, the US Ambassador to Abu Dhabi forwarded an account of a revealing meeting with the French Chargé d'Affaires: "Newly assigned French Charge d'affaires Jean Bellivier, who from his previous experience in Jidda claims a certain familiarity with the Saudi–Abu Dhabi border problem, commented to me recently that it was his impression from discussions with UAE and Abu Dhabi officials since his arrival that Shaikh Zayid will likely avoid any serious negotiations on the border dispute until he can confront the Saudis from a position of relative strength. Zayid, according to Bellivier, feels

the only way King Faisal will treat him with respect, i.e. not try to impose a settlement as he would on an erring minor tribal chieftain, is for the UAE (i.e. Abu Dhabi) to acquire a modern and strong enough local military capability to deter the Saudis from actually seizing territory [*sic*] or intimidating him through military action. Thus, Zayid intends to continue his policy of expanding and equipping the Abu Dhabi Defense Force (ADDF), so it will possess the capability of repulsing any military move the Saudis may attempt against the UAE. In terms of equipment, Bellivier felt that Zayid would have little inclination to bargain seriously with the Saudis until his mini army has at the minimum an effective air and armor capability. I took the occasion to inquire of Bellivier as to the projected timing of the Mirage jet fighter deliveries. He explained the problem was Abu Dhabi had ordered aircraft that were not built yet. First deliveries of the 12 planes were not expected, he said, before December 1973." See Unpublished NARA, AmEmbassy, Abu Dhabi to Department of State, Pol 32-1, Saud-UAE, January 29, 1973. One significance of this dispatch is that it makes clear that the Mirage fighters would be the latest model and probably superior to the Saudi equipment.

45 J.B. Kelly, *Arabia, the Gulf and the West* (London: Basic Books, 1980), 397.

46 Perhaps it should not have been a surprise, since on October 12, 1973, the chairmen of the four principal US oil companies sent a memorandum to President Nixon stating, "any action of the U.S. government at this time in terms of increased military aid to Israel will have a critical and adverse effect on our relations with the moderate Arab oil-producing countries." Cited in Kelly, *Arabia, the Gulf and the West*, 396.

47 For the chronology of these events, see *Chronicle of Progress*, 51–52.

48 The impact of Shaikh Zayid's move was lost on many, but not on J.B. Kelly. In his entertaining but acidulous account of the events of 1973, he at least saw the significance of the events: "To the Arabs, the peculiar conjunction of economic circumstances since the autumn of 1973 has offered a singular opportunity to behave as though the power and grandeur of the Umayyad and Abbasid caliphates had been restored." See Kelly, *Arabia, the Gulf and the West*, 395–457, particularly 423.

49 "Following the cease-fire [in 1973], Israel pulled her forces out of Egypt west of the Suez Canal and then evacuated a wide strip of Sinai…The reason for this evacuation of captured territory – so uncharacteristic of the Israelis – was a remarkable shift of American support away from Israel and towards Egypt, prompted perhaps by realisation that supplies of oil from Arab states was more vital to US prosperity than the intransigence of an expansionist Jewish state." See Otto von Pivka, *Armies of the Middle East* (Cambridge: Patrick Stephens Ltd., 1979), 47.

50 Shaikh Zayid provided £100 million for the support of Egypt and Syria at the cost of raising the money through the London money market. He also led the way with a complete boycott of oil supplies to allies of Israel.

51 We shall not know the full background to these events until the archives are available for these years, but the weight of current evidence and the chronology suggests the vital importance of the lower level of tension between the two Arab neighbors. Many other political factors entered into the decision, but the successful conclusion depended on King Faisal, who had every incentive – economic, political, prestige – not to settle for less than his maximum claim. It was easy to talk of 'honor' but it seems plausible that he was impressed by Shaikh Zayid's translation of the rhetoric of honor into practice with his costly support of the Arab cause. It was well known that Abu Dhabi at that time was in the midst of a financial crisis, and Shaikh Zayid openly admitted that he had to mortgage his future oil revenues to London banks in order to raise the cash sums required to support the Arab cause.

52 See Anthony, *Arab States of the Lower Gulf*, 152.

53 Many reports suggest the content of the agreement, but the terms and underlying understandings have never been published. The most balanced account is to be found in Anthony, *Arab States of the Lower Gulf*, 148–149. Significantly, he sets the agreement into its true context. "By the mid-1970s, neither Saudi Arabia nor Abu Dhabi were any longer considering a possible confrontation with one another over the areas in dispute. [This was a vital outcome of Shaikh Zayid's 'confidence-building measures.'] Both states increasingly shared an overriding interest in the perpetuation of traditional rule in the area and in the establishment of a UAA [UAE] capable of defending itself against external threats. Accordingly, in a move widely interpreted as a sincere effort to end the conflict, high officials from both states agreed to a formula on July 29, 1974, whereby the issues in dispute between them were resolved peacefully. [The agreements were initialed by Shaikh Zayid and Prince Fahd Bin Abdul Aziz, the Saudi Deputy Prime Minister, on July 29. However, the formula was only made substantive when Shaikh Zayid and King Faisal reached their accord on August 21, 1974.] According to the formula, the two states acknowledged in principle that Abu Dhabi sovereignty would be recognized over six of the villages in the Buraymi Oasis region [the remainder were in Oman] previously claimed by Saudi Arabia; that the rich Zararah (Shaybah) oilfield previously in dispute would be divided between them, and that Saudi Arabia would obtain an outlet to the Gulf through Abu Dhabi in the Khawr al-'Udayd area. The ratification of the accord paved the way for the establishment of diplomatic relations between these two states and has facilitated coordination of joint policies towards such questions as oil and regional security." Anthony, a non-partisan academic observer, was in the

UAE shortly after the agreement was made and spoke to many senior officials. It is likely that his judgment is the closest that exists to a statement of the facts and their context. Although the details of the agreement were modified in the subsequent period of technical adjustment, the essence remained as had been agreed between Shaikh Zayid and King Faisal. The outcome was, as Professor Richard Schofield observed, "…Saudi Arabia's full claim to sovereignty over the oasis was in effect relinquished by the 1974 agreement with Abu Dhabi." See Richard Schofield, "Borders and Territoriality in the Gulf and Arabian Peninsula during the Twentieth Century," in Richard Schofield (ed.) *Territorial Foundations of the Gulf States* (London: UCL Press, 1994), 44.

54   On December 3, 1974, Shaikh Zayid again visited King Faisal to discuss future plans, and a week later, a large delegation led by Ahmad Khalifa Al Suwaidi arrived to make plans for cooperation and coordination in political and economic areas as well as in education, information and agriculture. This completed the range of topics discussed by the two Rulers. See *Chronicle of Progress*, 71–72.

55   Shaikh Zayid's main objective was a context of security in which the UAE could develop, and this he achieved. His second objective was the promotion of regional unity and amity, which was also achieved. His third aim was to remove the claim that Saudi Arabia had made to the region of al Ain, and this he achieved. The details of boundaries were not to be settled at that meeting and were the subject of subsequent negotiation at a lower level. But peace and friendship were what he sought to accomplish, realizing that British wrangling over 'lines on the map' had achieved nothing over the space of 35 years. From this point on, relations between the UAE and its neighbor could be normalized. Both Rulers knew that their common interests were greater than their differences.

The continuance of the long antagonism between Abu Dhabi and Saudi Arabia had many causes, but in part it was because the Saudis believed the British had dishonored them. In preparing their response to the Saudi claim in the 1930s, the British government had insisted that King Abdul Aziz ruled Najd under Ottoman authority. This was a view that they firmly maintained over 30 years. Thus, they claimed in the Memorial submitted by the government of the United Kingdom: "Ibn Sa'ūd also acknowledged the suzerainty of the Turkish Government, but allowed himself to seize the coastal province of Hasa…This done, however, he hastened to submit again to Turkish suzerainty; and, early in 1914, he entered into a formal agreement with the Turkish Government, accepting appointment as the Turkish Wāli of Najd." Reprinted in *The Buraimi Memorials 1955: United Kingdom*, Vol. 1 (Gerrards Cross: Archive Editions, 1987), 9, clause 13. However, King Abdul Aziz had been the sworn enemy of the Ottomans, whom he had expelled from al Hasa in 1913. Moreover, in 1902 he had repossessed Najd by expelling the Al Rashid, who were allies of the Ottomans. That the British government based their case on Abu Dhabi's behalf upon the subservient status of the House of Saud to their Ottoman enemy was an insulting suggestion. See *The Buraimi Memorials 1955: Saudi Arabia*, Vol. 1, Part V, paragraphs 20 and 21, 398–399. Thus, in recognizing the duality of the Saudi claim, Shaikh Zayid responded in terms that it was not a matter of land but of honor. This King Faisal himself had stated. Shaikh Zayid refused to discuss the demeaning details of boundaries, but he addressed the dimension ignored by the British government. This may have proved a key to unlocking the long dispute. Shaikh Zayid, in his words, on this and other occasions acknowledged the reality of paramount Saudi power in the region, and thus redressed this slight. This enabled him to secure withdrawal of the Saudi claim to al Ain. For the historical background, see J.C. Wilkinson, *Arabia's Frontiers: The Story of Britain's Boundary Drawing in the Desert* (London: I.B. Tauris, 1991), passim.

56 See Robert Litwak, *Security in the Persian Gulf 2: Sources of Inter-State Conflict* (London: International Institute for Strategic Studies, 1981), 54. "The 1974 Agreement, accompanied by Saudi Arabia's extension of diplomatic recognition to the United Arab Emirates (UAE), was the prelude to a period of improved relations between the two countries. In 1974 and 1975 it was reported from various quarters that serious technical defects in the supporting maps and documents to the agreement might precipitate a revival of the dispute. Despite the questions arising from the ambiguities of the 1974 understanding, bilateral relations remained close in 1976–77 owing to Abu Dhabi's acquiescence to the Saudi line on oil pricing at the turbulent December 1976 OPEC conference in Doha." The two countries also had an interest in containing subversion, especially in Oman, with the steady rise of the Popular Front for the Liberation of Oman and the Arab Gulf (PFLOAG).

57 The role played by Kuwait as a mediator between Saudi Arabia and the UAE both before and after the foundation of the UAE was an important and honorable one. Before 1971, Kuwait made an important contribution in terms of developing education in the region by making large contributions without expectation of any political return. As a result, Kuwait was trusted as an impartial advisor. In the political crisis of 1979, it was the Kuwaiti mediator who formally proposed the appointment of Shaikh Rashid as Prime Minister, which proved the key to unlocking the domestic political impasse. See Anthony, *Arab States of the Lower Gulf*, 32–33.

58 "Saudi Arabia led the way toward greater cooperation among the Arab Gulf states, apart from Iraq, in the 1970s…" See Mazher A. Hameed, *Saudi Arabia, the West and the Security of the Gulf* (London: Croom Helm, 1986), 14.

59 Britain, which was in its very last days of control of emirates foreign policy, acquiesced in the Iranian move, leaving the UAE, when it became fully sovereign, with a *fait accompli*.

60 Statement to *Al-Anwar* newspaper, quoted in Shams Al-Din Al-Doaifi (ed.) *Sheikh Zayed: Leadership, The United Arab Emirates 1971–1987* (Beirut: Book and Publishing Establishment, n.d.), 262.

61 *Chronicle of Progress*, 372–373.

62 Speech at the opening of the Federal National Council session on January 30, 2000, quoted in UAE Ministry of Information and Culture, *The Emirates Daily Digest*, No. 019, January 31, 2000.

63 Observation made at a White House lunch, June 26, 1954. See *Bartlett's Familiar Quotations* (Boston: Little Brown, 1992), 622. Shaikh Zayid said much the same thing to Lee Dinsmore in 1972: "Better solve problems talking than shooting." See Unpublished NARA, Pol 15-1, UAE, Dhahran 318, February 16, 1972.

64 He thought principally in terms of the Arab states of the region: Saudi Arabia, Oman, Kuwait, Bahrain and Qatar. He did not ignore either Iran or Iraq, but recognized that binding them to common action would be much more difficult.

65 Here, his pioneering commitment to ecological issues finds a place. The degree to which he was promoting and funding long-term research and development programs in the fields of natural history, ecology and the environment so many years in advance of other international leaders is worthy of note.

66 See, for example, Unpublished FO 371/163025 33829, Luce (Political Resident, Bahrain) to Walmsley (Foreign Office, London), March 30, 1962. "On March 15 he told Salim [Ali Musa]…that he did not approve of his brother's attitude towards his neighbours. If he (Zaid) were in charge he would meet his neighbours and try and make sensible arrangements about any disputes which existed instead of leaving everything to H.M.G. Zaid's character being what it is, I think he means this, though he would not sacrifice Abu Dhabi interests merely for the sake of agreement."

67 See Unpublished NARA, Pol 15-1, UAE, Dhahran 318, February 16, 1972.

68 See J.C. Matejka, "Political Participation in the Arab World: The Majlis Mechanism," Ph.D. dissertation (University of Texas at Austin, 1983).

69 Erik R. Peterson, *The Gulf Cooperation Council*, 51. Peterson, in turn, drew his information from Anthony H. Cordesman, *The Gulf and the Search for Strategic Stability* (Boulder, CO: Westview Press, 1984), 625, as well as Joseph A. Kechichian, "The Gulf Cooperation Council: Search for Security in the Persian Gulf," Ph.D. dissertation (University of Virginia, 1985), 18. It was against this background, on January 21, 1973, that the UAE Ministry of Foreign Affairs was host to a meeting for diplomats from the

UAE and other Gulf states. See *Chronicle of Progress*, 37. On September 3, 1973, Shaikh Zayid, who was visiting the Rulers in the area, was able to announce a range of further moves to deepen collaboration between "the brother States of the Arab Gulf." Ibid., 49.

70 Henry Kissinger had stated, "The vacuum left by British withdrawal, now menaced by Soviet intrusion and radical momentum, would be filled by a local power friendly to us." See Michael A. Palmer, *Guardians of the Gulf* (New York, NY: The Free Press, 1992), 88.

71 In the US plan, Saudi Arabia had only figured as a makeweight. "*Pax Persiana* was to replace *Pax Britannica*." See Emile A. Nakhleh, *Arab–American Relations in the Persian Gulf* (Washington, DC: American Enterprise Institute for Public Policy Research, 1975), 38.

72 Quoted in Palmer, *Guardians of the Gulf*, 106.

73 See Abdul Kassim Mansur (pseud.), "The Military Balance in the Persian Gulf: Who will Guard the Gulf States from their Guardians?" *Armed Forces Journal International*, November 1980.

74 See *Sheikh Zayed: Leadership*, 143.

75 Ibid.

76 "…the Iran–Iraq war in particular was not the single overriding factor in the inception of the GCC, as some have suggested, though it certainly was an important catalyst." See Erik R. Peterson, *The Gulf Cooperation Council*, 99.

77 Ibid., 98.

78 Ibid., 99.

79 Ibid., 102.

80 These comprised the Economic and the Environment and Human Resources Directorates. The Economic Directorate was charged with harmonizing fiscal affairs, energy, trade and industry, agriculture and hydroponics, transport and communication. The Environment and Human Resources Directorate was entrusted with education, health, human resources, social affairs, environmental protection, culture, youth and sports. Ibid., 174–177. "Soon after the formation of the organization, GCC officials decided to emphasize the centrality of economic cooperation to the GCC's entire program. Economic integration, because it stressed concrete and specific mutual interests between the member states, was viewed as the most appropriate avenue to achieve higher degrees of cooperation in the political as well as defense and security domains." For example, between 1981 and 1987, the Gulf Standards and Measures Organization (GSMO) produced 53 standards that became operative in all the GCC countries. These were detailed requirements that affected everyday life at all levels of society. Moreover, the habit and custom of working together was directly fostered by the GCC. Between June 1981 and the end of February 1988, ministers and officials from all

the six countries met on no less than 102 occasions to push forward the program of economic collaboration.

81 See *Sheikh Zayed: Leadership*, 137.

82 "Who," he asked, "empowered the superpowers to interfere in our affairs? When the U.S.A. forms the rapid deployment force for the region, it is encouraging the Soviet Union to intervene as well. Consequently, we become the field for the superpowers' disputes." Ibid., 146.

83 Ibid., 249.

84 Moreover, Shaikh Zayid believed that sporting ties and links were a useful means of fostering international understanding, and he took pride both in the UAE teams and individuals that participated in international events. The construction of a range of outstanding sporting facilities meant that international events could be held for the first time in the territory of the United Arab Emirates.

85 Frauke Heard-Bey, *From Trucial States to United Arab Emirates: A Society in Transition*, second enlarged edition (London and New York, NY: Longman, 1996), 381.

86 For example, in December 1987, he donated $1 million to the families of those who had died in the Palestinian *intifada*. See *Chronicle of Progress*, 287.

87 See *Chronicle of Progress*, 186, 229, 270.

88 See Association of Popular Heritage Revival, *Zayed: the Glorious* (Dubai: Association of Popular Heritage Revival, n.d.), 133.

89 Heard-Bey, *From Trucial States to United Arab Emirates*, 390 and *Chronicle of Progress*, 323.

CHAPTER 10

1 Isaiah Berlin, *The Hedgehog and the Fox: An essay on Tolstoy's view of history* (London: Phoenix, 1999 reprint).

2 Dr. Ahmad Y. Majdoubeh, "View from Academia," *Jordan Times*, April 7–8, 2000, 5.

3 For a brief discussion of Shaikh Zayid's role and the establishment of the Gulf Cooperation Council see William A. Rugh, *Diplomacy and Defense Policy of the United Arab Emirates*, Emirates Lecture Series 38 (Abu Dhabi: The Emirates Center for Strategic Studies and Research, 2002), 45–48.

4 UAE Ministry of Information and Culture, *United Arab Emirates Yearbook 2002* (London: Trident Press, 2002), 94–95.

5 See Ali Tawfik Al Sadik, "Evolution and Performance of the United Arab Emirates Economy 1972–1995," in Edmund Ghareeb and Ibrahim Al Abed (eds) *Perspectives on the United Arab Emirates* (London: Trident Press,

1997), 211–213. Also *Gulf News*, September 9, 2002. The UAE production capacity is actually higher, and stands at 2.6 million barrels per day, but current OPEC production agreements limit the UAE to 1.9 million.

6   Ibid.

7   Hans Rosling, *Health Development in the United Arab Emirates from a Global Perspective*, Emirates Lecture Series 23 (Abu Dhabi: The Emirates Center for Strategic Studies and Research, 1999), 2–3.

8   *The Arab Human Development Report 2002* (New York, NY: United Nations Development Program, 2002), 143.

9   "Standard of healthcare service high in UAE," *Khaleej Times*, September 9, 2002.

10   UAE Ministry of Information and Culture, *United Arab Emirates Yearbook 2002*, 230–232.

11   Ibid., 208.

12   Ibid., 107.

13   The strategy is outlined in the UAE Ministry of Information and Culture, *United Arab Emirates Yearbook 2002*, 208–209.

14   Ibid., 218–220.

15   There are currently 12 free zones operating in the country and their share in non-oil exports has increased to 57 percent in 2000. In total, 3,000 companies work out of the free zones with a trade volume of around $8 billion. See UAE Ministry of Information and Culture, *United Arab Emirates Yearbook 2002*, 126–133.

16   Ibid., 154–162.

17   The non-oil sector accounted for slightly over 70 percent of the country's GDP in 2001. In addition to significant strides being made over the years in terms of industrial development, other sectors, such as banking, insurance, construction, trade and real estate, have experienced growth rates over the past several years. See *Gulf News*, September 9, 2002 as well as UAE Ministry of Information and Culture, *United Arab Emirates Yearbook 2002*, 148–152.

18   Until the end of 2000, a total number of 25,143 beneficiaries received assistance through the Marriage Fund. See UAE Ministry of Information and Culture, *United Arab Emirates Yearbook 2002*, 228–229.

19   See the section on the business environment in the UAE Ministry of Information and Culture, *United Arab Emirates Yearbook 2002*, 110–114.

20   Sally Findlow, *The United Arab Emirates: Nationalism and Arab-Islamic Identity* (Abu Dhabi: The Emirates Center for Strategic Studies and Research, 2000), Emirates Occasional Papers 39, 20–21. She successfully distinguishes the special character of the UAE from other similar states that have been given the title 'rentier states.' In this the role of active participation is crucial.

21   Ibid., 30–31.

22 See the discussion in Chapter 8.

23 UAE Ministry of Information and Culture, *United Arab Emirates Yearbook 2002*, 20.

24 Ibid., 178. The United States had the largest per-capita consumption.

25 Simon Aspinall, "Environmental development and protection in the UAE," in Ibrahim Al Abed and Peter Hellyer (eds) *United Arab Emirates: A New Perspective* (London: Trident Press, 2001), 280.

26 More dramatic for the UAE public – and for the wider world – was the establishment of the Zayid International Prize for the Environment in the same year, with a wide and imaginative remit. Under the patronage of the Crown Prince of Dubai, this is an award of major international importance. It is presented every two years in Dubai on the advice of an International Board of Referees. The scale of the award alone – $1 million in 2001 – puts it on a par with the Nobel Prizes.

27 UAE Ministry of Information and Culture, *United Arab Emirates Yearbook 1997* (London: Trident Press, 1997), 18.

28 See *Gulf News*, September 4, 2002.

29 See UAE Ministry of Information and Culture, *United Arab Emirates Yearbook 2002*, 164–165.

30 There were 5 million date palms in the UAE in 1986; by 1997, this had increased five-fold. Ministry of Agriculture figures cited in Aspinall, "Environmental development protection in the UAE," 287. Other calculations give a figure of 18 million date palms in 1980 and 40 million in 2000. See UAE Ministry of Information and Culture, *United Arab Emirates Yearbook 2002*, 165.

31 In the 1990s, the technique of counter-factual history became popular. Historians began to speculate, how would the world be different if the known facts of history were to be changed. Once these issues were regarded as the province of the historical novelist, but now serious and reputable specialists published answers to such questions as "What would have happened if the North had lost the Civil War in the United States?" See Niall Ferguson (ed.) *Virtual History: Alternatives and Counterfactuals* (London: Picador, 1990), 1–90.

32 Shams Al-Din Al-Doaifi (ed.) *Sheikh Zayed: Leadership, The United Arab Emirates 1971–1987* (Beirut: Book and Publishing Establishment, n.d.), 258.

33 Porras and Collins used long-run business as the focus for their research, but the same principles apply to state development. See James C. Collins and Jerry I. Porras, *Built to Last: Successful Habits of Visionary Companies* (New York, NY: Harper Business, 1994).

34 Ibid., 228.

35 Sheikh Zaid bin Sultan Al-Nahayan, *Falconry as a Sport: our Arab heritage* (Westerham, Kent: Westerham Press, 1976), 17–19.

Abdullah, Muhammad Morsy. *The United Arab Emirates: A Modern History*. New edition. Westerham Hill: Hurtwood Press, 1994.

Abu-Lughod, Janet. *Before European Hegemony: The World System A.D. 1250–1350*. New York, NY: Oxford University Press, 1989.

Abu-Lughod, Lila. *Veiled Sentiments: Honor and Poetry in a Bedouin Society*. Berkeley, CA: University of California Press, 1986.

Ahmad, Abdelhamid Muhammad. "The Seven Trucial states." *Orient* 5 (1964): 97–102.

Ahmed, Akbar S. and David M. Hart, eds. *Islam in Tribal Societies*. London: Routledge and Kegan Paul, 1984.

Ajjaj, Ali. "Social Development of the Pirate Coast." *Middle East Forum* 38 (Summer 1962): 75–80.

Al-Abed, Ibrahim and Peter Hellyer, eds. *United Arab Emirates: A New Perspective*. London: Trident Press, 2001.

Al-Abed, Ibrahim, Paula Vine and Abdullah Al Jabali, eds. *Chronicle of Progress: UAE 1971–1996, 25 years of Development in the United Arab Emirates*. London: Trident Press, 1996.

Al-Arshany, Awad. *Zayed the Paladin who Conquered the Desert* (in Arabic). Cairo: 1980.

Al-Doaifi, Shams Al-Din, ed. *Sheikh Zayed: Leadership, The United Arab Emirates 1971–1987*. Beirut: Book and Publishing Establishment, n.d.

Al-Fahim, Mohammed. *From Rags to Riches: A Story of Abu Dhabi*. London: The London Centre of Arab Studies, 1995.

Al-Faris, Abdulrazak F. *The Economy of Abu Dhabi*. Abu Dhabi: Crown Prince Court, Research & Studies Division Publications, 2001.

Al-Haj, Abdullah Juma. "The Formation of the Political Elite of the United Arab Emirates." Ph.D. dissertation, University of Reading, 1990.

Al-Hassan, Yousef, ed. *The Dialogue Between Civilizations: The UAE and Germany*. Amman: Friedrich Ebert Foundation, 1995.

Al-Marayati, Abid, ed. *The Middle East: Its Governments and Politics*. Belmont, MA: Duxbury Press, 1972.

Al-Mulla, Farid Ahmad. "Systemic and Domestic Factors as Determinants of the Gulf Emirates' Foreign Policies." Ph.D. dissertation, University of Sussex, 1982.

Al-Musfir, Muhammad Salih. "The United Arab Emirates: An Assessment of Federalism in a Developing Polity." Ph.D. dissertation, State University of New York at Binghamton, 1984.

Al-Mutawwa, Abdullah Bin Salih. *Al-gawahir wa al-lalya fi tarikh 'uman al-shamaliy (Jewellery and Pearls in the History of Northern Oman)*. Abu Dhabi: Juma al-Majid Centre for Culture and Heritage, 1994.

Al-Nabeh, Najat. "United Arab Emirates (UAE): Regional and Global Dimensions." Ph.D. dissertation, Claremont Graduate School, 1984.

Al-Nahayan, Sheikh Zaid bin Sultan. *Falconry as a Sport: our Arab heritage.* Westerham, Kent: Westerham Press, 1976.

— "Arms and the oil: Interview with Zayed bin Sultan al-Nahayan." *Newsweek* 85 (March 10, 1975).

Al-Naqeeb, Khaldoun Hasan. *Society and State in the Gulf and Arab Peninsula.* London: Routledge, 1990.

Al-Otaiba, Mana Saeed. *The Economy of Abu Dhabi: Ancient and Modern.* Second edition. Beirut: Commercial & Industrial Press, 1973.

Al-Qasimi, Sultan Muhammad. *Power Struggles and Trade in the Gulf 1620–1820.* Exeter: Short Run Press, 1999.

— (ed.) *The Journals of David Seton in the Gulf, 1800–1809.* Exeter: University of Exeter Press, 1995.

— *The Myth of Arab Piracy in the Gulf.* Second edition. London: Routledge, 1988.

Al-Sagri, Saleh Hamad. "Britain and the Arab Emirates, 1820–1956." Ph.D. dissertation, University of Kent, 1988.

Al-Sayegh, Fatima. "Domestic Politics in the United Arab Emirates: Social and Economic Policies, 1990–2000." In *Iran, Iraq, and the Arab Gulf States.* Edited by Joseph A. Kechichian. New York, NY: Palgrave, 2001: 161–176.

— "American Missionaries in the UAE Region in the Twentieth Century." *Middle Eastern Studies* 32 (January 1998): 120–139.

— "The Merchant's Role in a Changing Society: The Case of Dubai 1900–1990." *Middle Eastern Studies* 34 (January 1996): 87–102.

Al-Shamlan, Abdulrahman Rashid. "The Evolution of National Boundaries in the Southeastern Arabian Peninsula: 1934–1955." Ph.D. dissertation, University of Michigan, 1987.

Al-Shamsi, Saeed M. "The Al-Buraimi Dispute: A Case Study in Inter-Arab Politics." Ph.D. dissertation, American University, 1986.

Al-Suwaidi, Jamal S., ed. *Iran and the Gulf: A Search for Stability.* The Emirates Center for Strategic Studies and Research, Abu Dhabi. London: I.B. Tauris, 1996.

Amirie, Abbas. *The Persian Gulf and Indian Ocean in International Politics.* Tehran: Institute for International Political and Economic Studies, 1975.

Anani, Ahmad and Ken Whittingham. *The Early History of the Gulf Arabs.* London: Longman, 1986.

Anscombe, Frederick F. *The Ottoman Gulf: The Creation of Kuwait, Saudi Arabia and Qatar.* New York, NY: Columbia University Press, 1997.

Anthony, John Duke. *The United Arab Emirates: Dynamics of State Formation.* Emirates Lecture Series No. 35. Abu Dhabi: The Emirates Center for Strategic Studies and Research, 2002.

— "The Gulf Cooperation Council." *Journal of South Asian and Middle Eastern Studies* 5 (1982): 3–18.

— "United Arab Emirates: Socio-political developments." *AEI Foreign Policy and Defense Review* 2 (1980): 56–60.

— *Arab States of the Lower Gulf: People, Politics, Petroleum*. Washington, DC: The Middle East Institute, 1975.

— "The Union of Arab Amirates," *Middle East Journal* 26 (1972): 271–287.

Balfour-Paul, Glen. *The End of Empire in the Middle East: Britain's Relinquishment of Power in her last three Arab Dependencies*. Cambridge: Cambridge University Press, 1991.

— "Recent Developments in the Persian Gulf." *Royal Central Asian Journal* 56 (1969): 12–19.

Barrault, Michele. *The United Arab Emirates*. N.p.: Editions Michel Hetier, 1993.

Beblawi, Hazem and Giacomo Luciani, eds. *The Rentier State*. London: Croom Helm, 1987.

Beck, Nelson R. "Britain's withdrawal from the Persian Gulf and the Formation of the United Arab Emirates, 1968–1971." *Towson State Journal of International Affairs* 12 (1978).

Belgrave, Sir Charles. *The Pirate Coast*. Beirut: Librairie du Liban, 1972.

Berlin, Isaiah. *The Hedgehog and the Fox: An essay on Tolstoy's view of history*. London: Phoenix, 1999 reprint.

Berreby, Jean-Jacques. "Progrès et Évolution des Principautés Arabes du Golfe Persique." *Orient* 4 (1963): 25–34.

— "La Situation Politique des Émirats du Golfe Persique." *Politique Etrangère* 27 (1962): 567–580.

Bhutani, Surendra, ed. *Contemporary Gulf*. New Delhi: Academic Press, 1980.

Bidwell, Robin, ed. *Arabian Personalities of the Early Twentieth Century*. Cambridge: The Oleander Press, 1986.

Black-Michaud, Jacob. *Cohesive Force: Feud in the Mediterranean and Middle East*. New York, NY: St. Martin's Press, 1975.

Blunt, Lady Anne. *Bedouin Tribes of the Euphrates*. Volumes I and II. London: John Murray, 1879.

Boustead, Hugh. *The Wind of Morning: The Autobiography of Hugh Boustead*. London: Chatto and Windus, 1971.

— "Abu Dhabi 1761–1963." *Royal Central Asian Journal* 50 (1963): 273–277.

Brown, L. Carl, ed. *Imperial Legacy: The Ottoman Imprint on the Balkans and the Middle East*. New York, NY: Columbia University Press, 1996.

Bruiton, J.Y. "The Arabian Peninsula: The Protectorates and Sheikhdoms." *Rev. Égyptienne de Droit International* 3 (1947): 25–38.

Brummett, Palmira. *Ottoman Seapower and Levantine Diplomacy in the Age of Discovery*. Albany, NY: State University of New York Press, 1994.

The Buraimi Memorials 1955: United Kingdom and Saudi Arabia. 3 Volumes. Gerrards Cross: Archive Editions, 1987.

Burdett, A.L.P., ed. *Records of the Emirates 1966–1971*. 6 Volumes. Gerrards Cross: Archive Editions, 2002.

Burrows, Bernard. *Footnotes in the Sand: The Gulf in Transition 1953–1958*. Wilton, Salisbury: Michael Russell, 1990.

Butt, Gerald. *The Lion in the Sand: The British in the Middle East*. London: Bloomsbury, 1995.

Butti, Obaid A. "Imperialism, Tribal Structure, and the Development of Ruling Elites: A Socioeconomic History of the Trucial States between 1892 and 1939." Ph.D. dissertation, Georgetown University, 1992.

Caroe, Olaf. *Wells of Power*. London: Macmillan & Co., 1951.

Caton, Steven. "Power, Persuasion, and Language: A Critique of the Segmentary Model in the Middle East." *International Journal of Middle East Studies* 19, 1 (February 1987): 77–102.

Chaudhuri, K.N. *Trade and Civilisation in the Indian Ocean: An Economic History from the Rise of Islam to 1750*. London: Cambridge University Press, 1985.

Chubin, Shahram. *Security in the Gulf 4: The Role of Outside Powers*. London: International Institute for Strategic Studies, 1982.

— ed. *Security in the Persian Gulf 1: Domestic Political Factors*. London: International Institute for Strategic Studies, 1981.

Clayton, Peter. *Two Alpha Lima*. London: Janus Publishing Company, 1994.

Clements, Frank A. *United Arab Emirates: World Bibliographical Series*, Vol. 43. Oxford: The Clio Press, 1983.

Cleveland, William L. *A History of the Modern Middle East*. Boulder, CO: Westview Press, 1994.

Codrai, Ronald. *The Seven Shaikhdoms: Life in the Trucial States before the Federation of the United Arab Emirates*. London: Stacey International, 1990.

— "Desert Sheikhdoms of Arabia's Pirate Coast." *National Geographic* 110 (July 1956): 65–104.

Cole, Donald P. and Soraya Al-Torki. "Was Arabia Tribal? A Re-interpretation of the pre-oil Society." *Journal of South Asian and Middle Eastern Studies* 15 (1992): 71–87.

Cooperation Council for the Arab States of the Gulf. Secretariat General. *Closing Statements of the Sessions of the Supreme Council, Sessions 1–18*. Riyadh: Secretariat General, 1998.

Cordes, Rainer and Fred Scholz. *Bedouins, Wealth, and Change: A Study of Rural Development in the United Arab Emirates and the Sultanate of Oman*. Tokyo: The United Nations University, 1980.

Cordesman, Anthony H. *Bahrain, Oman, Qatar, and the UAE: Challenges of Security*. Boulder, CO: Westview Press, 1997.

— *The Gulf and the Search for Strategic Stability*. Boulder, CO: Westview Press, 1984.

Cottrell, Alvin J., ed. *The Persian Gulf States: A General Survey*. Baltimore: Johns Hopkins University Press, 1980.

Cox, Percy. "Some Gulf memories." *Times of India Annual* (1928).

— "Some excursions in Oman." *Geographical Journal* LXVI (September 1925).

Crystal, Jill. "Sources of Power: Social Stratification and Political Influence in the Arabian Gulf." Unpublished paper presented at the Annual Meeting of the Middle East Studies Association, Portland, Oregon, October 1992.

— *Oil and Politics in the Gulf: Rulers and Merchants in Kuwait and Qatar.* New York, NY: Cambridge University Press, 1990.

Curzon, George N., *Persia and the Persian Question.* 2 Volumes. London: Frank Cass & Co. Ltd., 1966.

Daa'ir, Samira Ali Said bin. *Educational Change in the United Arab Emirates (1977–1987).* Abu Dhabi: The Cultural Foundation, n.d.

Daniels, John. *Abu Dhabi: A Portrait.* London: Longman, 1974.

Dawood, Salman Hassan. "Technology Planning for the Post-Oil Era in the United Arab Emirates (UAE)." Ph.D. dissertation, University of Bradford, 1988.

Delacroix, Jacques. "The Distributive State in the World System." *Studies in Comparative International Development* 15 (Fall 1980): 5–21.

Development Plans of the GCC States 1962–1995: United Arab Emirates 1 and 2. Gerrards Cross: Archive Editions, 1994.

Dresch, Paul. *Tribes, Government, and History in Yemen.* Oxford: Clarendon Press, 1993.

— "The Significance of the Course Events take in Segmentary Systems." *American Ethnologist* 13, 2 (May 1986): 309–324.

— "The Position of Shaykhs among the Northern Tribes of Yemen," *Man* 19 (March 1984): 31–49.

Eickelman, Dale F. *The Middle East: An Anthropological Approach.* Second edition. Englewood Cliffs, NJ: Prentice Hall, 1989.

— "Kings and People: Oman's State Consultative Council." *Middle East Journal* 38 (Winter 1984): 51–71.

— "The Art of Memory: Islamic Education and its Social Reproduction." *Comparative Studies in Society and History* 20 (October 1978): 485–516.

El Taib, Mohammed Suleiman. *Mawsu'at al-qaba'il al-arabiyya* (*Encyclopaedia of Arab Tribes*). Cairo: Dar al-Fakr al-Arabi, 1996.

Esfandari, Haleh and A.L. Udovitch, eds. *The Economic Dimensions of Middle Eastern History: Essays in Honor of Charles Issawi.* Princeton, NJ: The Darwin Press, 1990.

Farago, Ladislas. *The Riddle of Arabia.* London: Robert Hale Ltd., 1939.

Farès, Bichr. *L'honneur chez les Arabes avant l'Islam.* Paris: Librairie d'Amérique et d'Orient, 1932.

Fenelon, K.G. *The United Arab Emirates: An Economic and Social Survey.* Second edition. London: Longman, 1976.

Findlow, Sally. *The United Arab Emirates: Nationalism and Arab-Islamic Identity.* The Emirates Occasional Papers No. 39. Abu Dhabi: The Emirates Center for Strategic Studies and Research, 2000.

Fischer, John. "The Safety of our Indian Empire: Lord Curzon and the British Predominance in the Arabian Peninsula, 1919." *Middle Eastern Studies* 33 (July 1997): 494–520.

Food and Agriculture Organization of the United Nations. *Agricultural Development in the United Arab Emirates: Report on the Present Position, Prospects and Priorities.* FAO Technical Advisory Service, Near East Regional Office, Cairo, 1973.

Fromkin, David. *A Peace to End all Peace: The Fall of the Ottoman Empire and the Creation of the Modern Middle East.* New York, NY: Henry Holt, 1989.

Geertz, Clifford. *Local Knowledge: Further Essays in Interpretative Anthropology.* New York, NY: Basic Books, 1983.

Gerber, Haim. *The Social Origins of the Modern Middle East.* Boulder, CO: Lynne Rienner Publishers, 1987.

Ghareeb, Edmund and Ibrahim Al Abed, eds. *Perspectives on the United Arab Emirates.* London: Trident Press, 1997.

Gibbons, Stanley. *Stamp Catalogue: Part 19, The Middle East.* Fifth edition. London: Stanley Gibbons Ltd., 1996.

Goody, Jack. *The East in the West.* Cambridge: Cambridge University Press, 1996.

Harrison, Paul W., M.D. *The Arab at Home.* New York, NY: Thomas Y. Crowell Company, 1924.

Hawley, Donald. *The Trucial States.* London: George Allen & Unwin Ltd., 1970.

Hay, Sir Rupert. "The Impact of the Oil Industry on the Persian Gulf Sheikhdoms." *Middle East Journal* 9 (1955): 361–372.

Healey, Dennis. *The Time of My Life.* London: Michael Joseph, 1989.

Heard-Bey, Frauke. *From Trucial States to United Arab Emirates: A Society in Transition.* Second enlarged edition. London and New York, NY: Longman, 1996.

— "Der Prozess der Staatswerdung in arabischen Ölexportländern." *Vierteljahreshefte für Zeitgeschichte* 23 (April 1975): 155–209.

— "Development Anomalies in the Bedouin Oases of al-Liwa." *Asian Affairs* 61 (October 1974): 272–286.

— "The Gulf States and Oman in Transition." *Asian Affairs* 59 (1972): 14–22.

Henderson, Edward. *Arabian Destiny: The Complete Autobiography.* London: Motivate Publishing, 1999.

— *This Strange Eventful History: Memoirs of Earlier Days in the UAE and Oman.* London: Quartet Books, 1988. Reprint Dubai: Motivate Publishing, 1993.

Holden, David. *Farewell to Arabia.* New York, NY: Walker and Company, 1966.

Hollis, Rosemary, ed. *Oil and Regional Development in the Gulf.* London: Royal Institute of International Affairs, 1998.

Hopwood, Derek, ed. *The Arabian Peninsula: Society and Politics.* London: Allen & Unwin, 1972.

Hottinger, Arnold. "Das Projekt einer Föderation am Persischen Golf: Die Golf-Emirate im Spannungsfeld widerstreitender Interessen." *Europa Archiv* 24 (February 25, 1969): 122–130.

Hourani, Albert H. *A History of the Arab Peoples*. London: Faber and Faber, 1991.

— Philip S. Khoury and Mary C. Wilson, eds. *The Modern Middle East: A Reader*. Berkeley and Los Angeles, CA: University of California Press, 1993.

Hudson, Michael C. *Arab Politics: The Search for Legitimacy*. New Haven, CT: Yale University Press, 1977.

Huntington, Samuel P. *Political Order in Changing Societies*. New Haven, CT: Yale University Press, 1968.

Ibn Khaldun. *The Muqaddimah: An Introduction to History*. 3 Volumes. Translated by Franz Rosenthal. London and Henley: Routledge and Kegan Paul, 1958.

Izzard, Molly. *The Gulf: Arabia's Western Approaches*. London: John Murray, 1979.

Jabbur, Jibrail S. *The Bedouins and the Desert: Aspects of Nomadic Life in the Arab East*. Translated by Lawrence I. Conrad. Edited by Suhayl J. Jabbur and Lawrence I. Conrad. Albany, NY: State University of New York Press, 1995.

Johns, Richard. "The Emergence of the United Arab Emirates." *Middle East International* (March 1973): 8–10.

Joyce, Miriam. "On the Road to Unity: The Trucial States from a British Perspective, 1960–1966." *Middle Eastern Studies* 23 (April 1999): 45–60.

Kanafani, Aida Sami. "Aesthetics and Ritual in the United Arab Emirates." Ph.D. dissertation, University of Texas at Austin, 1979.

Kazim, Aqil. *The United Arab Emirates A.D. 600 to the Present: A Socio-Discursive Transformation in the Arabian Gulf*. Dubai: Gulf Book Centre, 2000.

Kechichian, Joseph A., ed. *A Century in Thirty Years: Shaikh Zayed and the United Arab Emirates*. Washington, DC: Middle East Policy Council, 2000.

— "The Gulf Cooperation Council: Search for Security in the Persian Gulf." Ph.D. dissertation, University of Virginia, 1985.

Kedourie, Elie and Sylvia G. Haim, eds. *Essays on the Economic History of the Middle East*. London: Frank Cass, 1988.

Kelly, J.B. *Arabia, the Gulf and the West*. London: Basic Books, 1980.

— *Britain and the Persian Gulf 1795–1880*. Oxford: The Clarendon Press, 1968.

— "The Future in Arabia." *International Affairs* 42 (October 1966): 619–640.

— *Eastern Arabian Frontiers*. London and New York, NY: Frederick Praeger, 1964.

Khalifa, Ali Mohammed. "The United Arab Emirates: Unity in Fragmentation – A Study in Ministate Integration in a Complex Setting, 1968–1976." Ph.D. dissertation, University of California, Santa Barbara, 1978.

Khoury, Enver M. *The United Arab Emirates: Its Political System and Politics*. Hyattsville, MD: Institute of Middle Eastern and North African Affairs, 1980.

Khoury, Philip S. and Joseph Kostiner, eds. *Tribes and State Formation in the Middle East*. Berkeley, CA: University of California Press, 1990.

Kumar, Ravinder. *India and the Persian Gulf Region 1858–1907: A Study in British Imperial Policy*. Bombay, India: Asian Publishing House, 1965.

Lancaster, William. *The Rwala Bedouin Today*. London: Cambridge University Press, 1981.

Lapidus, Ira M. *A History of Islamic Societies*. Cambridge: Cambridge University Press, 1988.

Laqueur, Walter Z. *The Middle East in Transition*. London: Routledge and Kegan Paul, 1958.

Lienhardt, Peter. *Shaikhdoms of Eastern Arabia*. Edited by Ahmed Al-Shahi. Oxford: Palgrave Macmillan, 2001.

— "The Authority of Shaykhs in the Gulf: An Essay in Nineteenth-Century History." *Arabian Studies* II (1975): 61–75.

Lindholm, Charles. "Kinship Structures and Political Authority: The Middle East and Central Asia." *Comparative Studies in Society and History* 28 (April 1986): 334–355.

Lindt, A.R. "Politics in the Persian Gulf." *Journal of the Royal Central Asian Society* 36 (1939): 619–633.

Litwak, Robert. *Security in the Persian Gulf 2: Sources of Inter-State Conflict*. London: International Institute for Strategic Studies, 1981.

Long, David and Christian Koch, eds. *Gulf Security in the Twenty-First Century*. Abu Dhabi: The Emirates Center for Strategic Studies and Research, 1998.

Lorimer, J.G. *Gazetteer of the Persian Gulf, Oman and Central Arabia*. Volumes 1–9. Gerrards Cross: Archive Editions, 1986.

Luce, William. "Britain in the Persian Gulf." *Round Table* 227 (July 1967): 277–283.

Mahdi, Muhsin. *Ibn Khaldoun's Philosophy of History*. London: George Allen & Unwin, 1957.

Mallakh, Ragaei El. *The Economic Development of the United Arab Emirates*. London: Croom Helm, 1981.

— "The Challenge of Affluence: Abu Dhabi." *Middle East Journal* 24 (1970): 135–146.

Mann, Clarence C. *Abu Dhabi: Birth of an Oil Shaikhdom*. Beirut: Khayats, 1969.

Marlowe, John. *The Persian Gulf in the Twentieth Century*. New York, NY: Praeger, 1962.

Matejka, J.C. "Political Participation in the Arab World: The Majlis Mechanism." Ph.D. dissertation, University of Texas at Austin, 1983.

McKay, Margaret. *Timeless Arabia*. Cairo: Dar Al-Mareef, n.d.

Melamid, Alexander. "The Buraimi Oasis Dispute." *Middle Eastern Affairs* 7 (February 1956): 56–63.

Miles, Col. S.B. *The Countries and Tribes of the Persian Gulf*. 2 Volumes. London: Harrisons and Sons, 1919.

Morris, Claud. *The Desert Falcon: The story of H.H. Sheikh Zayed Bin Sultan Al Nahiyan, President of the United Arab Emirates*. London: Outline Series of Books, 1976.

Morris, James. *Sultan in Oman*. London: Faber and Faber, n.d.

Moyse-Bartlett, H. *The Pirates of Trucial Oman*. London: MacDonald, 1966.

Murden, Simon. *Emergent Regional Powers and International Relations in the Gulf 1988–1991*. Reading: Ithaca Press, 1995.

Musil, Alois. *The Manners and Customs of the Rwala Bedouins*. New York, NY: American Geographical Society, 1928.

Nakhleh, Emile A. *The Gulf Cooperation Council: Politics, Petroleum and Prospects*. New York, NY: Praeger, 1986.

Niblock, Tim, ed. *Social and Economic Development in the Arab Gulf*. London: Croom Helm, 1980.

Owen, Roderic. *The Golden Bubble: Arabian Gulf Documentary*. London: Collins, 1957.

Palmer, Michael A. *Guardians of the Gulf*. New York, NY: The Free Press, 1992.

Peck, Malcolm C. *Historical Dictionary of the Gulf Arab States*. Asian Historical Dictionaries No. 21. Lanham, MD: The Scarecrow Press, Inc., 1997.

— *The United Arab Emirates: A Venture in Unity*. London: Croom Helm, 1986.

Peristany, J.G. *Honour and Shame: The Values of Mediterranean Society*. Chicago, IL: University of Chicago Press, 1966.

Persian Gulf Administration Reports: 1873–1957. 11 Volumes. Gerrards Cross: Archive Editions, 1986.

Peterson, Erik R. *The Gulf Cooperation Council: Search for Unity in a Dynamic Region*. Boulder, CO: Westview Press, 1988.

Peterson, J.E. *The Arab Gulf States: Steps Towards Political Participation*. New York, NY: Praeger Publishers, 1988.

— *Defending Arabia*. New York, NY: St. Martin's Press, 1986.

— "Tribes and Politics in Eastern Arabia," *Middle East Journal* 31 (Summer 1977): 297–312.

— ed. *American Interests in the Middle East*. Washington, DC: The Middle East Institute, 1969.

Philby, H. St. J.B. *The Empty Quarter*. New York, NY: Henry Holt and Company, 1933.

Phillips, Wendall. *Unknown Oman*. London: Longman, 1966.

Pivka, Otto von. *Armies of the Middle East*. Cambridge: Patrick Stephens Ltd., 1979.

Plascov, Avi. *Security in the Persian Gulf 3: Modernization, Political Development and Stability*. London: International Institute for Strategic Studies, 1982.

Political Diaries of the Persian Gulf. Volumes 17–20. Gerrards Cross: Archive Editions, 1990.

Price, David Lynn. "Abu Dhabi: Prospects for Federation." *Washington Quarterly* 2 (1979): 102–106.

Priestland, Jane, ed. *The Buraimi Dispute: Contemporary Documents 1950–1961*. 10 Volumes. Gerrards Cross: Archive Editions, 1992.

Ramahi, Seif A. El-Wady. *Economics and Political Evolution in the Arabian Gulf States*. New York, NY: Carlton Press, 1973.

Ramazani, R.K. *The Gulf Cooperation Council: Record and Analysis*. Charlottesville, VA: University of Virginia Press, 1988.

Rashid, A. "Government and Administration in the United Arab Amirates." *Bulletin of Arab Research and Studies* 6 (July 1975): 71–85.

Rashid, Noor Ali. *The UAE: Visions of Change.* Dubai: Motivate Publishing, 1997.

— *Abu Dhabi: Life and Times.* Dubai: Motivate Publishing, 1996.

Reich, Bernard, ed. *Political Leaders of the Contemporary Middle East and North Africa: A Biographical Dictionary.* New York, NY: Greenwood Press, 1990.

Rice, Michael. *The Archaeology of the Arabian Gulf.* London: Routledge, 1994.

Rizvi, S.N. Asad. "From Tents to High Rise: Economic Development of the United Arab Emirates." *Middle Eastern Studies* 29 (October 1993): 664–678.

Rosenfeld, Henry. "The Social Composition of the Military in the Process of State Formation in the Arabian Desert." *Journal of the Royal Anthropological Society* 95 (1965): 75–86, 174–194.

Rugh, William A. *Diplomacy and Defense Policy of the United Arab Emirates.* Emirates Lecture Series No. 38. Abu Dhabi: The Emirates Center for Strategic Studies and Research, 2002.

— "The United Arab Emirates: What Are the Sources of Its Stability." *Middle East Policy* 5 (September 1997): 14–24.

— "The Foreign Policy of the United Arab Emirates." *Middle East Journal* 50 (Winter 1996): 56–70.

Rush, Alan de Lacy. *Ruling Families of Arabia: United Arab Emirates.* Volumes 1 and 2. Gerrards Cross: Archive Editions, 1991.

Sadik, Mohammad and William P. Snavely, eds. *Bahrain, Qatar and the United Arab Emirates: Colonial Past, Present Problems, Future Prospects.* Lexington, MA: Lexington Books, 1972.

Salibi, Kamal. *A History of Arabia.* Beirut: Caravan Books, 1980.

Salzman, Philip Carl. "Tribal Organization and Subsistence: A Response to Emmanuel Marx." *American Anthropologist* 81 (March 1979): 121–125.

Sanger, Richard. *The Arabian Peninsula.* Ithaca, NY: Cornell University Press, 1954.

Schofield, Richard, ed. *Territorial Foundations of the Gulf States.* London: UCL Press, 1994.

— ed. *Arabian Boundary Disputes.* Volumes 16–18. Gerrards Cross: Archive Editions, 1992.

Sheikh Zayed. *Hopes and Deeds.* Beirut: Book and Publishing Establishment, 1990.

Shephard, Anthony. *Arabian Adventure.* London: Collins, 1961.

Shukla, Ramesh. *The UAE: Formative Years 1965–75. A Collection of historical photographs.* Dubai: Motivate Publishing, 1995.

Sindelar, H. Richard III and J.E. Peterson, eds. *Crosscurrents in the Gulf: Arab, Regional and Global Interests.* New York, NY: Routledge, 1988.

Slot, B.J. *The Arabs of the Gulf 1602–1784.* Second edition. Leidschendam: Slot, 1995.

Smith, M.G. "Segmentary Lineage Systems." *Journal of the Royal Anthropological Institute* 86 (July–December 1956): 39–80.

Smith, W. Robertson. *Kinship and Marriage in Early Arabia*. Beirut: United Publishers, 1973.

Stewart, Frank Henderson. *Honor*. Chicago, IL: University of Chicago Press, 1994.

Sweet, Louise E., ed. *Peoples and Cultures of the Middle East: An Anthropological Reader*. 2 Volumes. Garden City, NY: The Natural History Press, 1970.

— "Pirates or Politics? Arab Societies of the Persian or Arabian Gulf." *Ethnohistory* 11 (1964): 32–54.

Tally, Robert E.L. "Dubai: Past, Present and Future." 2 Volumes. Master's Thesis: American University of Beirut, 1967.

Tammam, Hamdi. *Zayed bin Sultan Al-Nahayyan: The Leader and the March*. Second revised edition. Tokyo: Dai Nippon Printing Company, 1983.

Taryam, Abdullah Omran. *The Establishment of the United Arab Emirates, 1950–85*. London: Croom Helm, 1987.

Taylor, Andrew. *Travelling the Sands: Sagas of Exploration in the Arabian Peninsula*. Dubai: Motivate Publishing, 1995.

Thesiger, Wilfred. *Visions of a Nomad*. Dubai: Motivate Publishing, 1994.

— *Arabian Sands*. London: Longmans, Green, 1959; reprint London: Penguin Books, 1991.

— "Travel on the Trucial Coast." *Geographical Magazine* 21 (1949): 110–118.

— "Hawking in Arabia." *Listener* 42 (November 10, 1949): 803–804.

Thomas, Bertram. *Arabia Felix: Across the 'Empty Quarter' of Arabia*. New York, NY: Charles Scribner's Sons, 1932.

Toy, Barbara. *The Highway of the Three Kings*. London: John Murray, 1968.

Trench, Richard, ed. *Gazetteer of Arabian Tribes*. Appendices 1–3. Gerrards Cross: Archive Editions, 1996.

Tuson, Penelope, ed. *Records of the Emirates: Primary Documents 1820–1958*. 12 Volumes. Gerrards Cross: Archive Editions, 1990.

United Arab Emirates. Association of Popular Heritage Revival. *Zayed: the Glorious*. Dubai: Association of Popular Heritage Revival, n.d.

— The Federal National Council. *The United Arab Emirates Constitution*. 1997.

— Ministry of Oil and Mineral Wealth. *UAE Oil Statistical Review* 1977–. Abu Dhabi: Ministry of Oil and Mineral Wealth, Statistics Department, n.d.

— Ministry of Oil and Mineral Wealth. *Petroleum in the United Arab Emirates*. Abu Dhabi: Ministry of Oil and Mineral Wealth, Public Relations Department, 1974.

— Ministry of Information and Culture. *GCC: Arab Gulf Cooperation Council. The 19th GCC Summit, December 1998*. London: Trident Press, 1998.

— Ministry of Information and Culture. *The United Arab Emirates*. Abu Dhabi: UAE Ministry of Information and Culture, 1995.

— Ministry of Information and Culture. *United Arab Emirates Yearbook 1995–*. London: Trident Press.

— Ministry of Information and Culture. *United Arab Emirates: A Record of Achievement 1979–1981*. Abu Dhabi: Department of Press and Publications, n.d.

— *Partners for Progress: A Report on the United Arab Emirates 1971–1976*. Abu Dhabi: Department of Press and Publications, n.d.

— *The Petroleum Concession Agreements of the United Arab Emirates 1939–1981*. Compiled by Mana Saeed Al-Otaiba. London: Croom Helm, 1982.

United Kingdom
   Foreign Office to 1968, FO 371, General Correspondence (cited as Unpublished FO)
   Foreign and Commonwealth Office after 1968, FCO 8 (cited as Unpublished FCO)

United States
   National Archives and Records Administration, College Park, Maryland
      Department of State
         Record Group 250 to 1963 (Listed as Unpublished NARA)
         Record Group 59 after 1963 (Listed as Unpublished NARA)

Van der Meulen, D. *The Wells of Ibn Saud*. London: John Murray, 1957.

Van der Meulen, Hendrik. "The Role of Tribal and Kinship Ties in the Politics of the United Arab Emirates." Ph.D. dissertation, Fletcher School of Law and Diplomacy, 1997.

Vine, Peter J., ed. *Natural Emirates: Wildlife and Environment of the United Arab Emirates*. London: Trident Press, 1996.

Walker, Julian. *Tyro on the Trucial Coast*. Durham: The Memoir Club, 1999.

Waves of Time: The Maritime History of the United Arab Emirates. London: Trident Press, 1998.

Whitelock, H.H. "An Account of the Arabs who inhabited the Coast between Ras al-Khaimah and Abu Thabee in the Gulf of Persia, generally called the Pirate Coast." *Transaction of the Bombay Geographical Society 1836–1838*: 32–54.

Wilkinson, J.C. *Arabia's Frontiers: The Story of Britain's Boundary Drawing in the Desert*. London: I.B. Tauris, 1991.

— *The Imamate tradition in Oman*. Cambridge: Cambridge University Press, 1987.

— "Traditional Concepts of Territory in South East Arabia." *The Geographical Journal* 146 (November 1983): 301–315.

— *Water and Tribal Settlement in South-East Arabia: A Study of the Aflāj of Oman*. Oxford: Oxford University Press, 1977.

Wilson, Sir Arnold T. *The Persian Gulf*. London: George Allen & Unwin, 1928.

Wilson, Harold. *A Personal Record: The Labour Government, 1964–1970*. Boston, MA: Little, Brown and Company, 1971.

Women in the UAE. Abu Dhabi: The UAE Women's Federation, 1995.

Yapp, M.E. *The Near East Since the First World War: A History to 1995*. Second edition. London: Longman, 1996.

Zahedi, Mahbub Jamal. *Gulf Post: Story of Post in the Gulf*. Karachi, Pakistan: Sanaa Publications, 1994.

Zahlan, Rosemarie Said. *The Making of the Modern Gulf States: Kuwait, Bahrain, Qatar, the United Arab Emirates and Oman.* Updated edition. Reading: Ithaca Press, 1998.

— *The Origins of the United Arab Emirates: A Political and Social History of the Trucial States.* London: Macmillan Press, 1978.

Ziyad, Abdul Rahman. *Zayed bin Sultan Al Nahyan: A Life of Achievement.* London: The Main Event Limited, 1982.

Trucial Oman Scouts 90, 91, 130,
134, 138, 139, 207, 220, 221,
222, 292n83
Trucial States 6, 39, 48–49, 147, 160,
263–264n5
Trucial States Council 111, 114–116,
132–133, 134, 141, 173, 175,
179–180, 182, 184, 185, 197,
291–292n73, 299n42
Trucial States Development Office
(TSDO) 103, 133–134, 146, 184,
312n3
Truman, Harry, US President
286n17
Tunb, Greater and Lesser 232–233,
329n4
Turkey/Turks 134, 330n13; *see also*
Ottoman Empire
Turki Bin 'Utaishan 89, 90, 93

U
UAE *see* United Arab Emirates
UDF *see* Union Defence Force
Umm al Qaiwain 186, 194, 276n41
research stations 332n27
Rulers 177, 281n80, 299n43,
333n38
Union Defence Force (UDF) 207,
208–209, 211, 222–223, 225,
226, 333n34
United Arab Emirates 1, 2, 3–4, 6, 7,
148, 165–167, 171ff
administrative structure 189–191,
194, 195, 198, 199–201, 210,
213–214, 245–246, 258

afforestation 205, 206
agricultural policies 204, 205, 241,
256–257
armed forces 207, 208–209, 211,
217–218, 219–227
building of infrastructure 194,
202–204, 249
commerce and industry 250, 252,
254
communications network 212, 218,
252
desalination plants 255–256
Economic Directorate 348n80
education/educational facilities
156, 186, 187, 203, 218,
250–252, 253
Environment and Human
Resources Directorate 348n80
environmentalism 254–257; *see also*
afforestation; agricultural
policies
flag 188, 192, 193, 214
foreign aid 240–241
foreign policies 219, 227–234, 239,
240
GDP 250
health care and hospitals 249, 250
life expectancy 250
National Day 192, 193
and national identity 196, 199, 200,
212, 214, 253–254
oil industry 217, 249–250
postage stamps 214, 335–336n54
Provisional Constitution 185–188,
190, 208, 209, 212, 213, 222

THE EMIRATES CENTER FOR STRATEGIC STUDIES AND RESEARCH

The Emirates Center for Strategic Studies and Research (ECSSR) is an independent research institution dedicated to the promotion of professional studies and educational excellence in the UAE, the Gulf and the Arab world. Since its establishment in Abu Dhabi in 1994, ECSSR has served as a focal point for scholarship on political, economic and social matters. Indeed, ECSSR is at the forefront of analysis and commentary on Arab affairs.

The Center provides a forum for the scholarly exchange of ideas by hosting conferences and symposia, organizing workshops, sponsoring a lecture series and publishing original and translated books and research papers. ECSSR also has an active fellowship and grant program for the writing of scholarly books and for the translation into Arabic of works relevant to the Center's mission. Moreover, ECSSR has a large library including rare and specialized holdings and a state-of-the-art technology center, which has developed an award-winning website that is a unique and comprehensive source of information on the Gulf.

Through these and other activities, ECSSR aspires to engage in mutually beneficial professional endeavors with comparable institutions worldwide, and to contribute to the general educational and scientific development of the UAE.